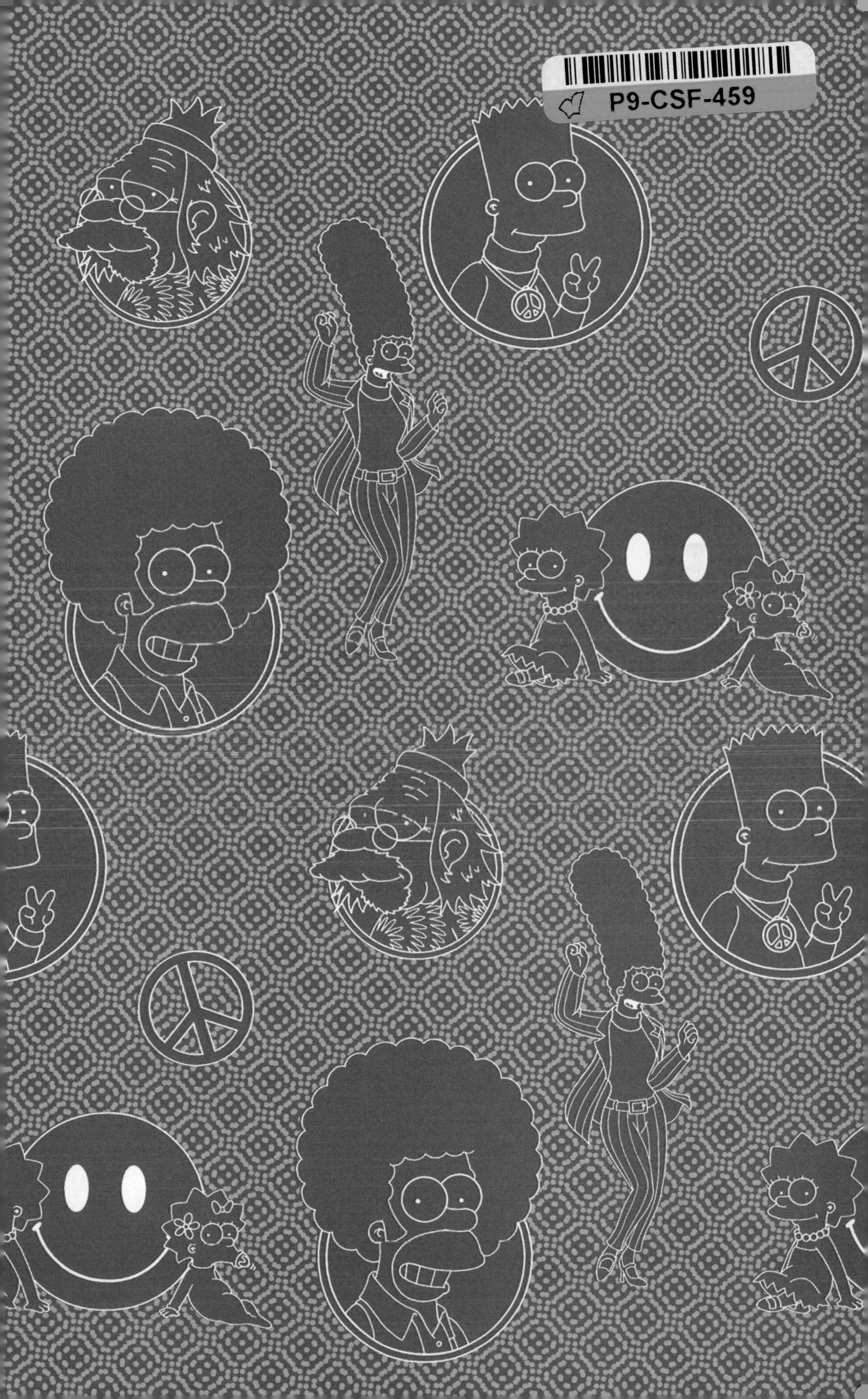

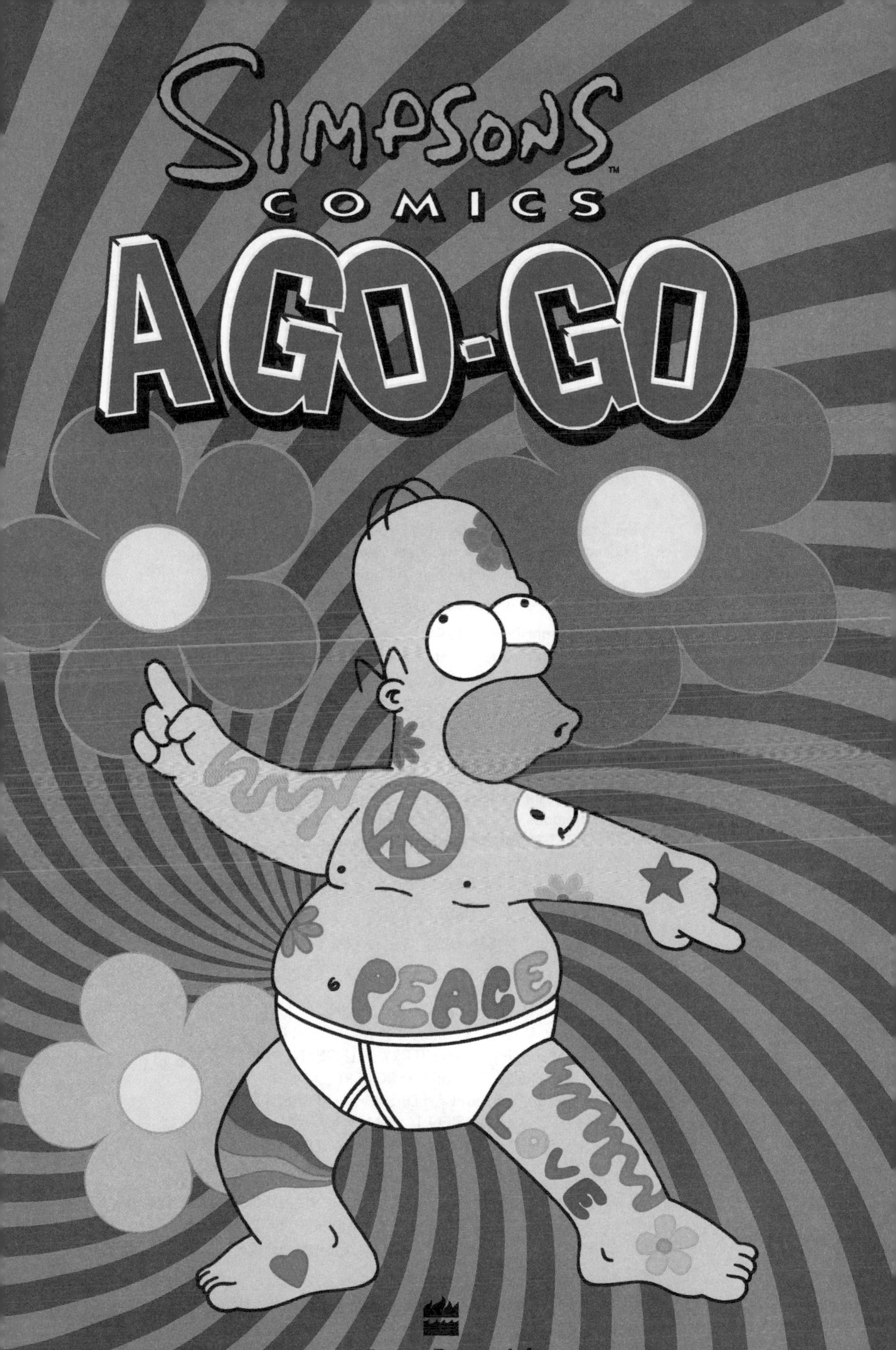
Simpsons™
COMICS
A-GO-GO
PEACE
LOVE

HarperPerennial
A Division of HarperCollinsPublishers

To the loving memory
of Snowball I:
Marge's abstract
art isn't the same
without you.

SIMPSONS COMICS A GO-GO

Copyright ©1992,1995,1997, 1998, & 1999 by
Bongo Entertainment, Inc. All rights reserved.

HarperCollins books may be purchased for educational, business,or sales
promotional use. For information, please write:
Special Markets Department
HarperCollins Publishers, Inc.
10 East 53rd Street, New York, NY 10022

FIRST EDITION

ISBN 0-06-095566-X

99 00 01 02 03 RRD 10 9 8 7 6 5 4 3 2 1

Publisher: MATT GROENING
Art Director / Editor: BILL MORRISON
Managing Editor: TERRY DELEGEANE
Director of Operations: ROBERT ZAUGH
Book Design/Assistant Art Director: NATHAN KANE
Production: KAREN BATES, CHIA-HSIEN JASON HO, MIKE ROTE, CHRIS UNGAR
Legal Guardian: SUSAN GRODE

Contributing Artists:
TIM BAVINGTON, JEANNINE BLACK, LUIS ESCOBAR, STEPHANIE GLADDEN, TIM
HARKINS, NATHAN KANE, ROBERT KRAMER, BILL MORRISON, DAVID MOWRY, PHIL
ORTIZ, MIKE ROTE, ERICK TRAN, CHRIS UNGAR, CINDY VANCE, STEVE VANCE

Contributing Writers:
IAN BOOTHBY, SCOTT M. GIMPLE, ROB HAMMERSLEY, JIM LINCOLN, BILL
MORRISON, JEFF ROSENTHAL, BILLY RUBENSTEIN, DAN STUDNEY

PRINTED IN CANADA

CONTENTS

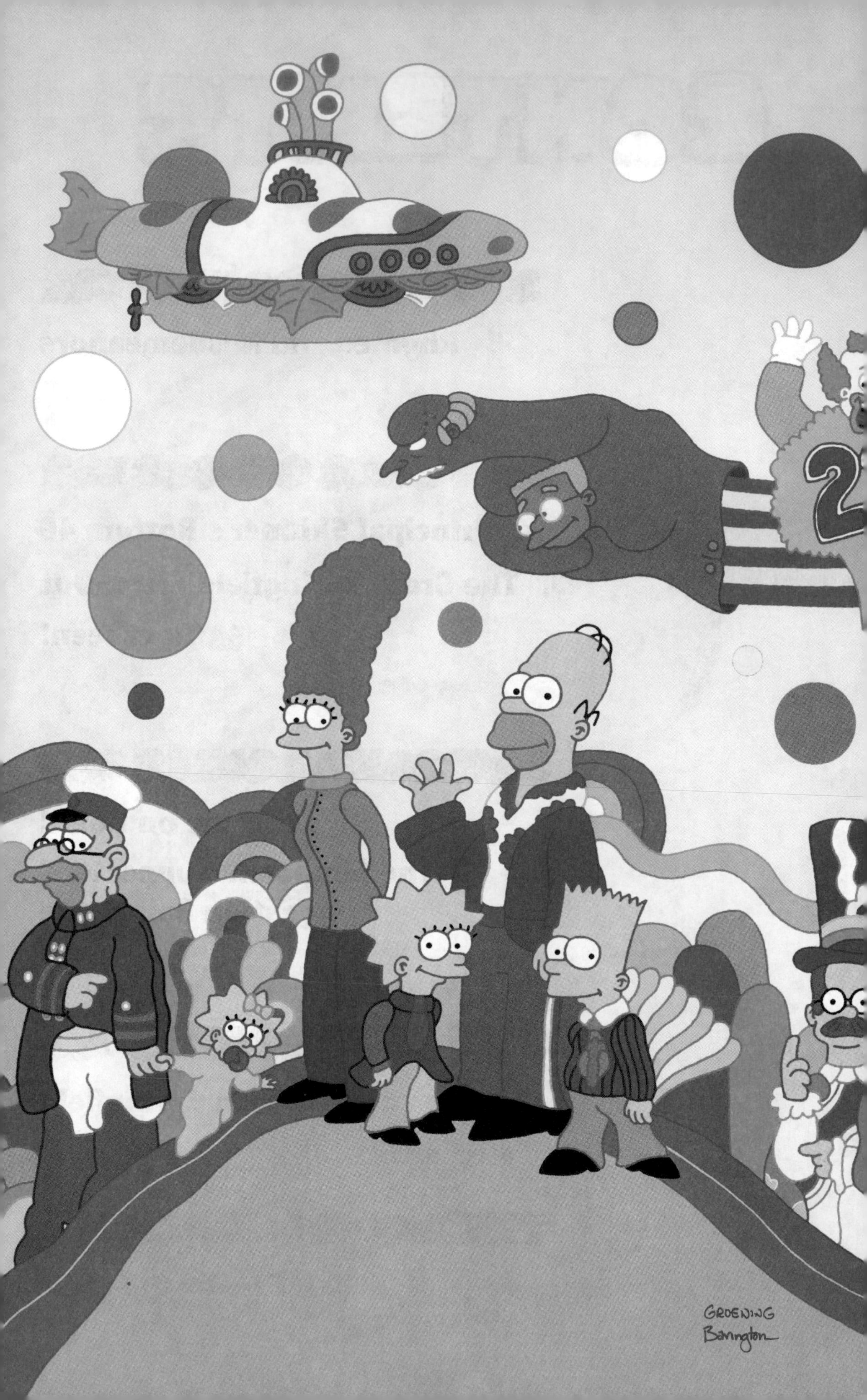
GROENING
Barrington

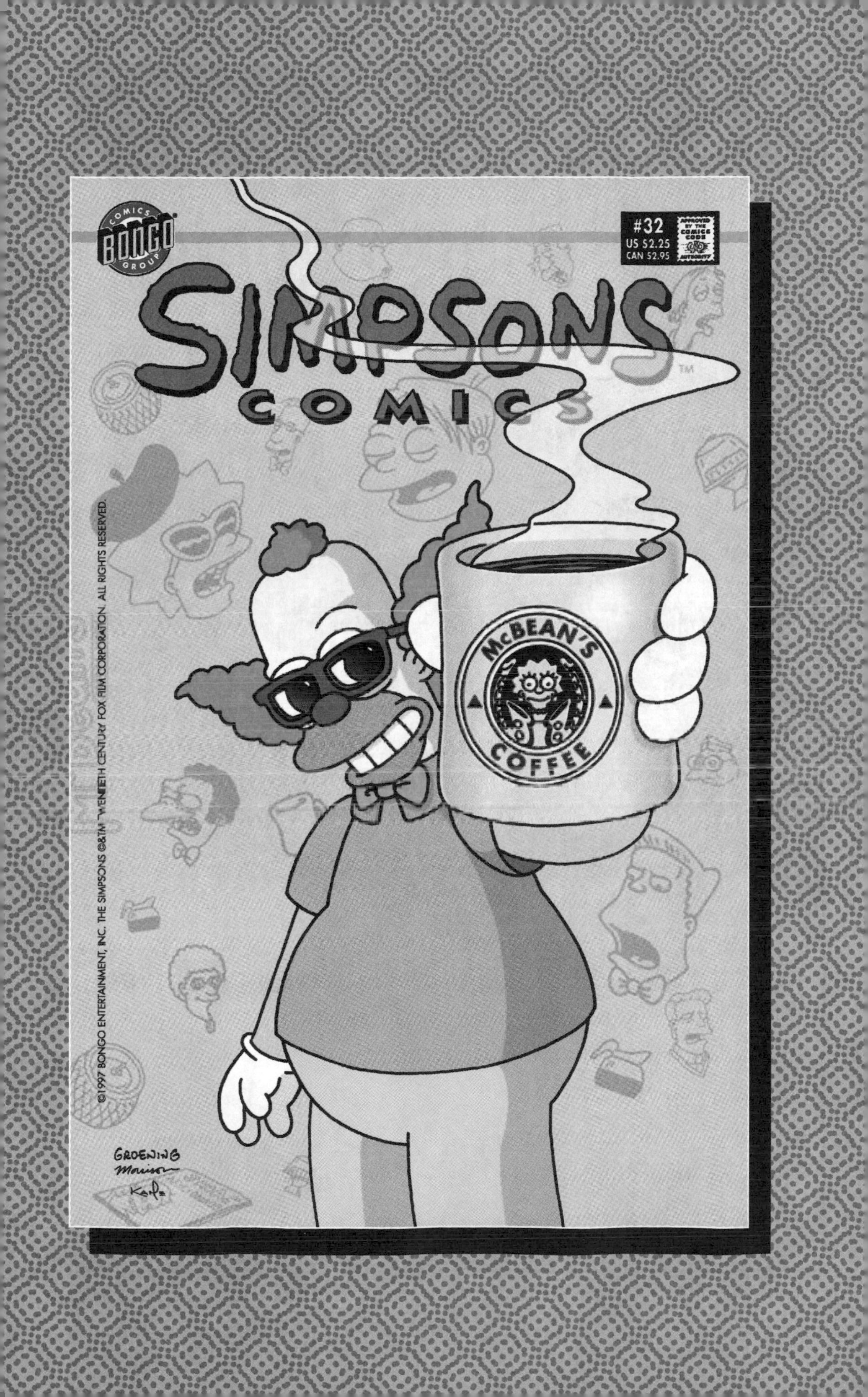
BONGO COMICS GROUP
#32
US $2.25
CAN $2.95
APPROVED BY THE COMICS CODE AUTHORITY
SIMPSONS™
COMICS
McBEAN'S
COFFEE
©1997 BONGO ENTERTAINMENT, INC. THE SIMPSONS ©&TM TWENTIETH CENTURY FOX FILM CORPORATION. ALL RIGHTS RESERVED.
GROENING

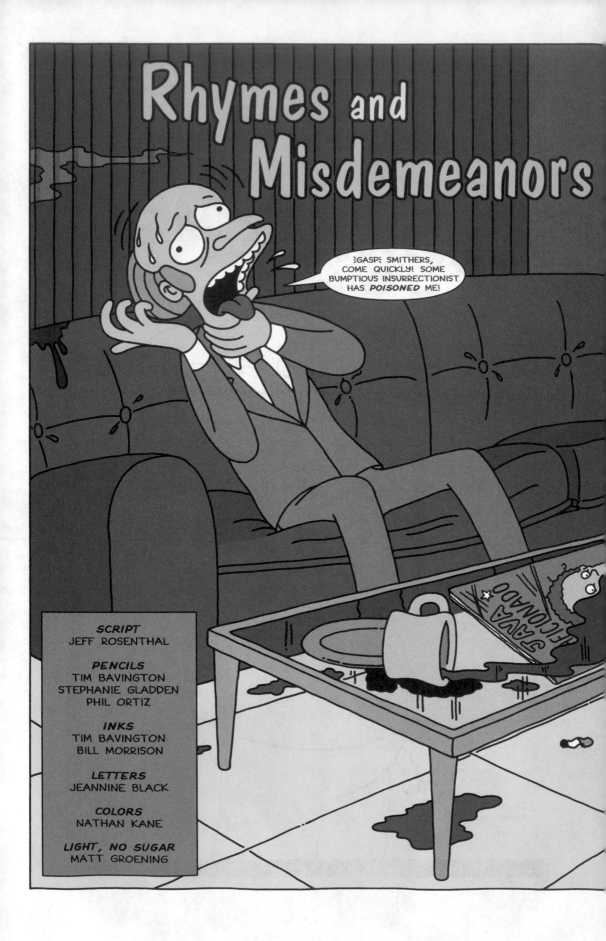

Rhymes and Misdemeanors

GASP! SMITHERS, COME QUICKLY! SOME BUMPTIOUS INSURRECTIONIST HAS *POISONED* ME!

SCRIPT
JEFF ROSENTHAL

PENCILS
TIM BAVINGTON
STEPHANIE GLADDEN
PHIL ORTIZ

INKS
TIM BAVINGTON
BILL MORRISON

LETTERS
JEANNINE BLACK

COLORS
NATHAN KANE

LIGHT, NO SUGAR
MATT GROENING

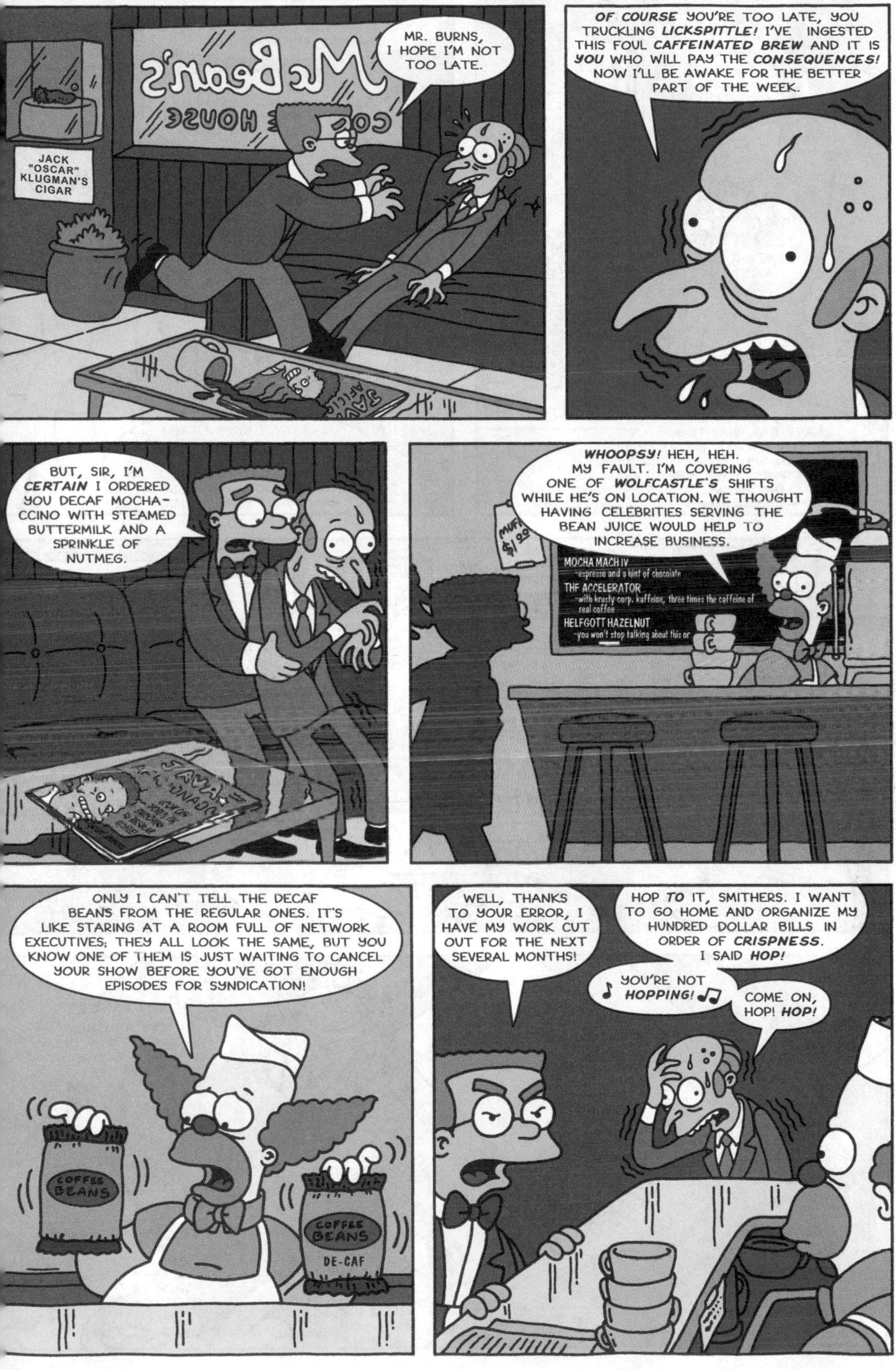
JACK "OSCAR" KLUGMAN'S CIGAR
MR. BURNS, I HOPE I'M NOT TOO LATE.
OF COURSE YOU'RE TOO LATE, YOU TRUCKLING LICKSPITTLE! I'VE INGESTED THIS FOUL CAFFEINATED BREW AND IT IS YOU WHO WILL PAY THE CONSEQUENCES! NOW I'LL BE AWAKE FOR THE BETTER PART OF THE WEEK.
BUT, SIR, I'M CERTAIN I ORDERED YOU DECAF MOCHACCINO WITH STEAMED BUTTERMILK AND A SPRINKLE OF NUTMEG.
WHOOPSY! HEH, HEH. MY FAULT. I'M COVERING ONE OF WOLFCASTLE'S SHIFTS WHILE HE'S ON LOCATION. WE THOUGHT HAVING CELEBRITIES SERVING THE BEAN JUICE WOULD HELP TO INCREASE BUSINESS.
MOCHA MACH IV
-espresso and a hint of chocolate
THE ACCELERATOR
-with krusty corp. kaffeine, three times the caffeine of real coffee
HELFGOTT HAZELNUT
-you won't stop talking about this or
ONLY I CAN'T TELL THE DECAF BEANS FROM THE REGULAR ONES. IT'S LIKE STARING AT A ROOM FULL OF NETWORK EXECUTIVES; THEY ALL LOOK THE SAME, BUT YOU KNOW ONE OF THEM IS JUST WAITING TO CANCEL YOUR SHOW BEFORE YOU'VE GOT ENOUGH EPISODES FOR SYNDICATION!
COFFEE BEANS
COFFEE BEANS DE-CAF
WELL, THANKS TO YOUR ERROR, I HAVE MY WORK CUT OUT FOR THE NEXT SEVERAL MONTHS!
HOP TO IT, SMITHERS. I WANT TO GO HOME AND ORGANIZE MY HUNDRED DOLLAR BILLS IN ORDER OF CRISPNESS. I SAID HOP!
YOU'RE NOT HOPPING!
COME ON, HOP! HOP!

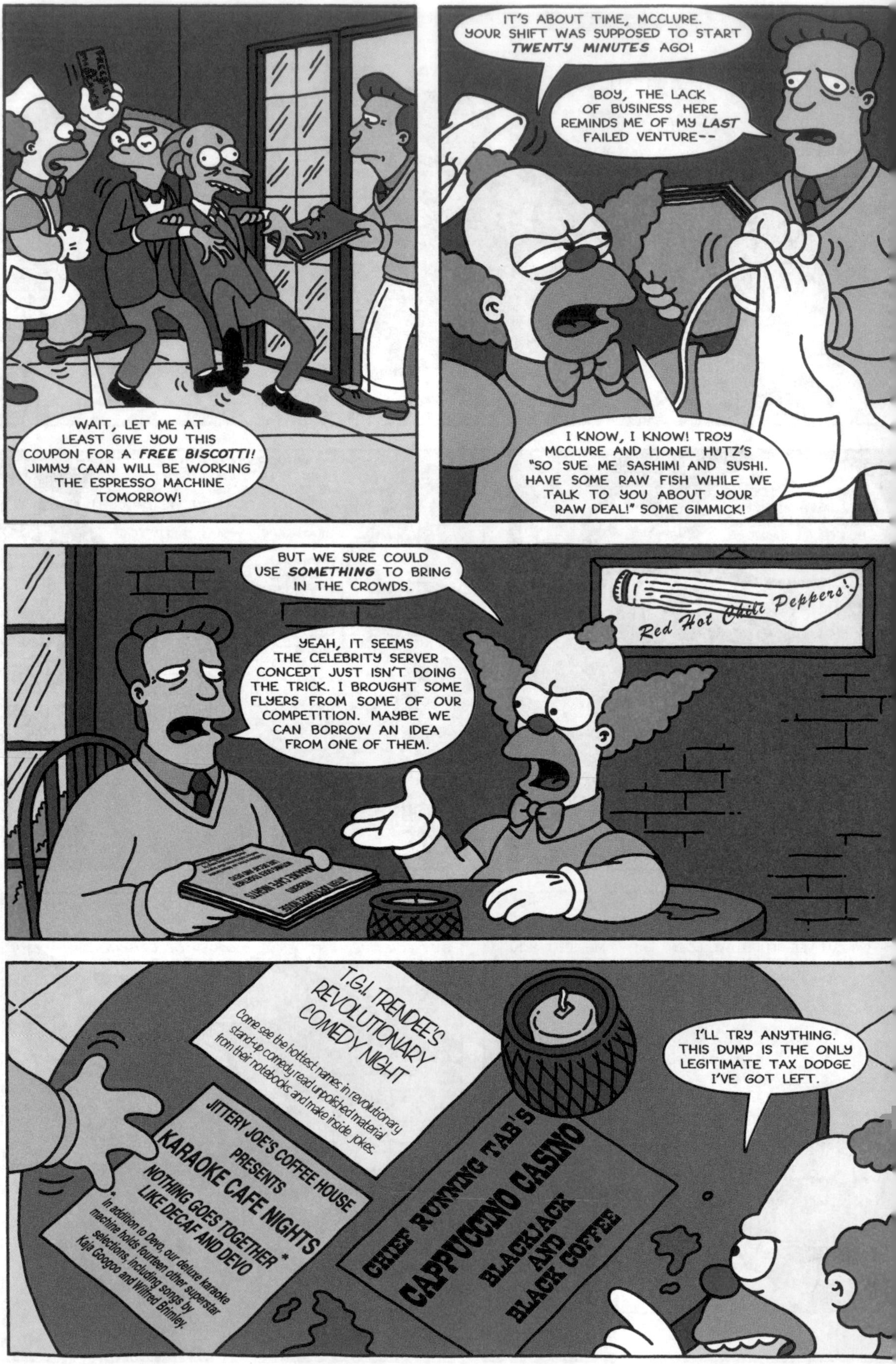

WAIT, LET ME AT LEAST GIVE YOU THIS COUPON FOR A **FREE BISCOTTI**! JIMMY CAAN WILL BE WORKING THE ESPRESSO MACHINE TOMORROW!
IT'S ABOUT TIME, MCCLURE. YOUR SHIFT WAS SUPPOSED TO START **TWENTY MINUTES** AGO!
BOY, THE LACK OF BUSINESS HERE REMINDS ME OF MY *LAST* FAILED VENTURE--
I KNOW, I KNOW! TROY MCCLURE AND LIONEL HUTZ'S "SO SUE ME SASHIMI AND SUSHI. HAVE SOME RAW FISH WHILE WE TALK TO YOU ABOUT YOUR RAW DEAL!" SOME GIMMICK!
BUT WE SURE COULD USE **SOMETHING** TO BRING IN THE CROWDS.
Red Hot Chili Peppers
YEAH, IT SEEMS THE CELEBRITY SERVER CONCEPT JUST ISN'T DOING THE TRICK. I BROUGHT SOME FLYERS FROM SOME OF OUR COMPETITION. MAYBE WE CAN BORROW AN IDEA FROM ONE OF THEM.
T.G.I. TRENDEE'S REVOLUTIONARY COMEDY NIGHT
Come see the hottest names in revolutionary stand-up comedy read unpolished material from their notebooks and make inside jokes.
JITTERY JOE'S COFFEE HOUSE PRESENTS
KARAOKE CAFE NIGHTS
NOTHING GOES TOGETHER LIKE DECAF AND DEVO*
* In addition to Devo, our deluxe karaoke machine holds fourteen other superstar selections, including songs by Kaja Googoo and Wilfred Brimley.
CHIEF RUNNING TAB'S
CAPPUCCINO CASINO
BLACKJACK AND BLACK COFFEE
I'LL TRY ANYTHING. THIS DUMP IS THE ONLY LEGITIMATE TAX DODGE I'VE GOT LEFT.

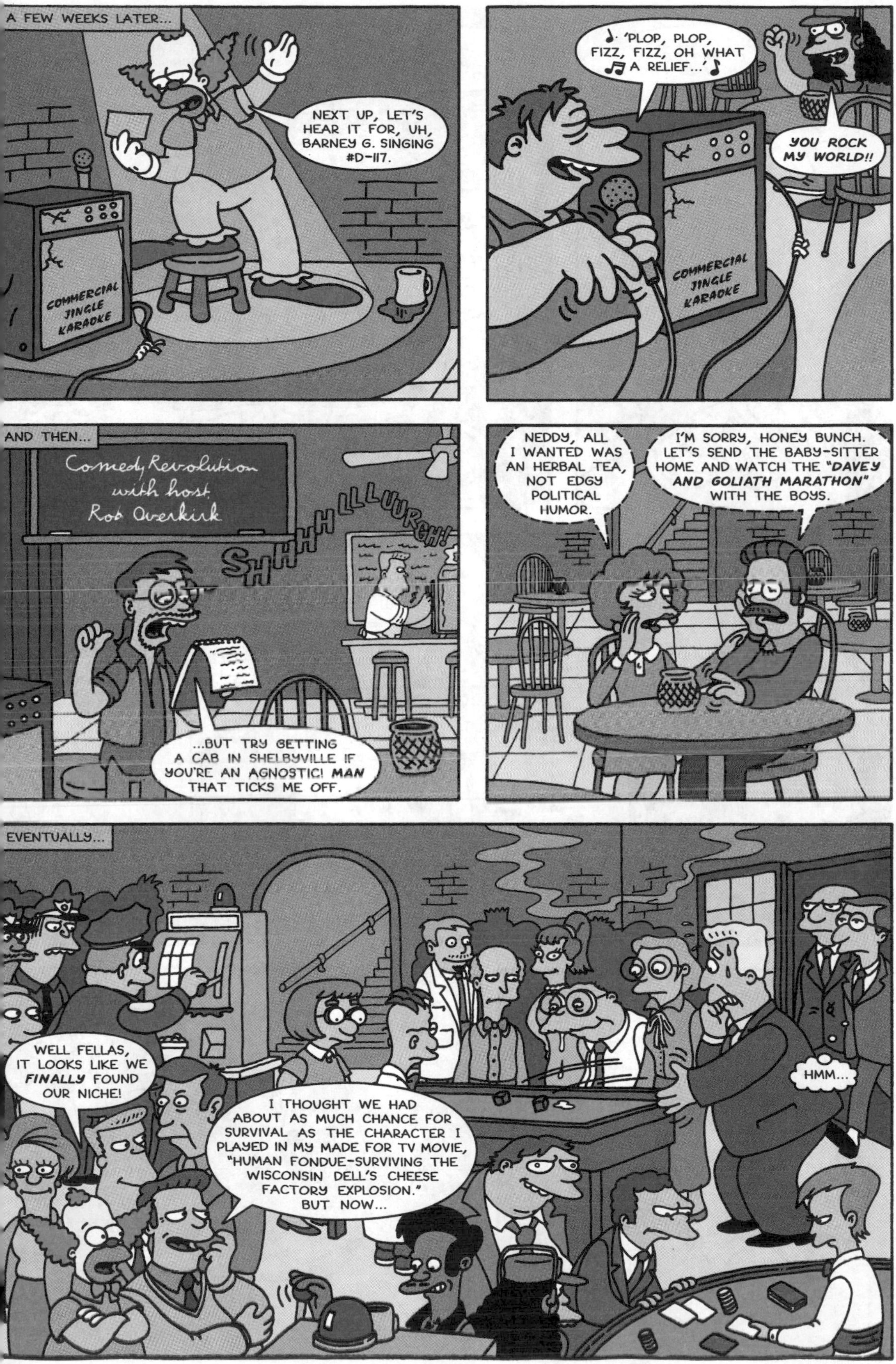

A FEW WEEKS LATER...
NEXT UP, LET'S HEAR IT FOR, UH, BARNEY G. SINGING #D-117.
COMMERCIAL JINGLE KARAOKE
'PLOP, PLOP, FIZZ, FIZZ, OH WHAT A RELIEF...'
YOU ROCK MY WORLD!!
COMMERCIAL JINGLE KARAOKE
AND THEN...
Comedy Revolution with host Rob Overkirk
SHHHHLLLUURGH!
...BUT TRY GETTING A CAB IN SHELBYVILLE IF YOU'RE AN AGNOSTIC! MAN THAT TICKS ME OFF.
NEDDY, ALL I WANTED WAS AN HERBAL TEA, NOT EDGY POLITICAL HUMOR.
I'M SORRY, HONEY BUNCH. LET'S SEND THE BABY-SITTER HOME AND WATCH THE "DAVEY AND GOLIATH MARATHON" WITH THE BOYS.
EVENTUALLY...
WELL FELLAS, IT LOOKS LIKE WE FINALLY FOUND OUR NICHE!
I THOUGHT WE HAD ABOUT AS MUCH CHANCE FOR SURVIVAL AS THE CHARACTER I PLAYED IN MY MADE FOR TV MOVIE, "HUMAN FONDUE-SURVIVING THE WISCONSIN DELL'S CHEESE FACTORY EXPLOSION." BUT NOW...
HMM...

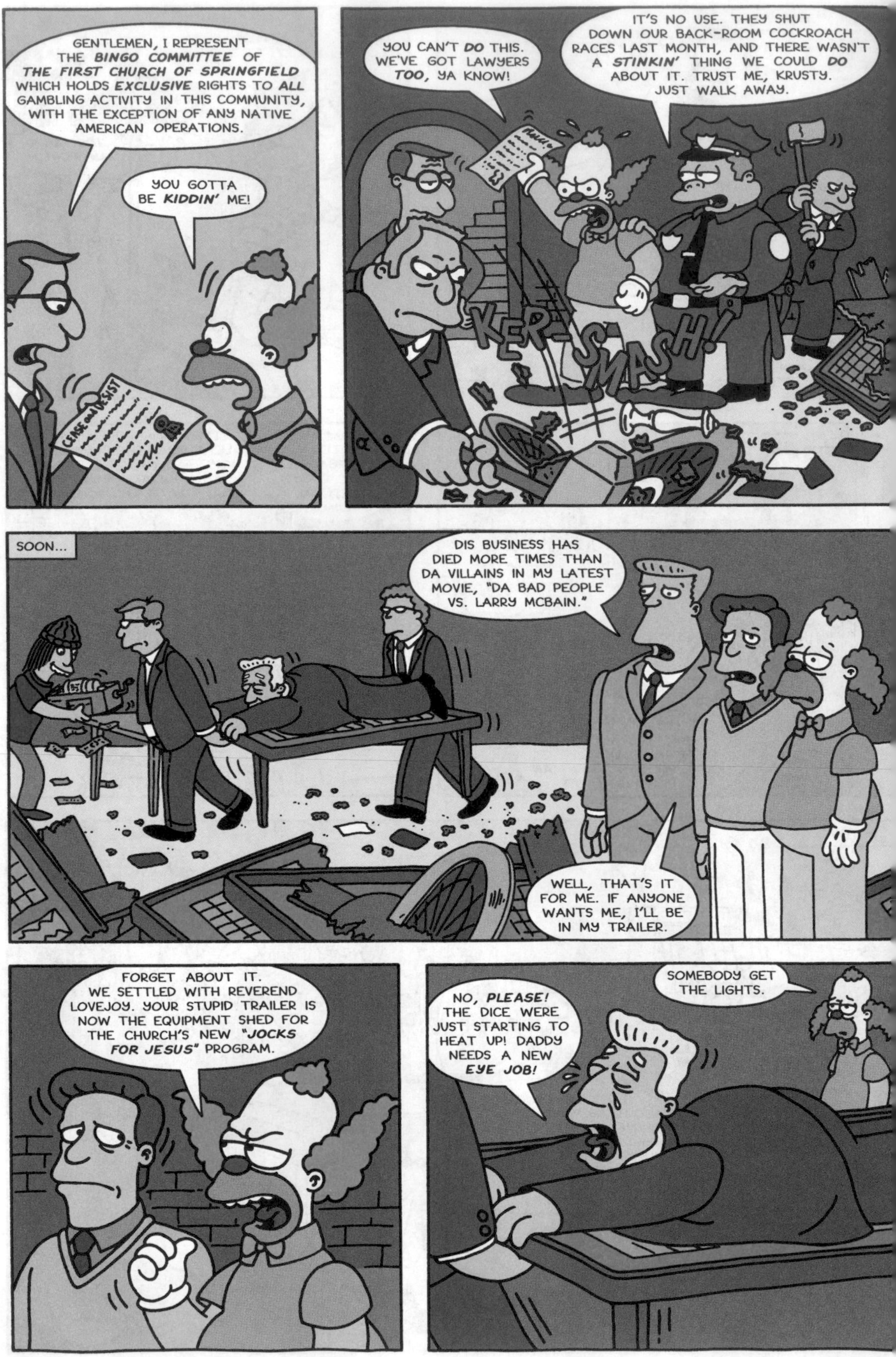
GENTLEMEN, I REPRESENT THE BINGO COMMITTEE OF THE FIRST CHURCH OF SPRINGFIELD WHICH HOLDS EXCLUSIVE RIGHTS TO ALL GAMBLING ACTIVITY IN THIS COMMUNITY, WITH THE EXCEPTION OF ANY NATIVE AMERICAN OPERATIONS.
YOU GOTTA BE KIDDIN' ME!
CEASE and DESIST
YOU CAN'T DO THIS. WE'VE GOT LAWYERS TOO, YA KNOW!
IT'S NO USE. THEY SHUT DOWN OUR BACK-ROOM COCKROACH RACES LAST MONTH, AND THERE WASN'T A STINKIN' THING WE COULD DO ABOUT IT. TRUST ME, KRUSTY. JUST WALK AWAY.
KER-SMASH!
SOON...
DIS BUSINESS HAS DIED MORE TIMES THAN DA VILLAINS IN MY LATEST MOVIE, "DA BAD PEOPLE VS. LARRY MCBAIN."
WELL, THAT'S IT FOR ME. IF ANYONE WANTS ME, I'LL BE IN MY TRAILER.
FORGET ABOUT IT. WE SETTLED WITH REVEREND LOVEJOY. YOUR STUPID TRAILER IS NOW THE EQUIPMENT SHED FOR THE CHURCH'S NEW "JOCKS FOR JESUS" PROGRAM.
SOMEBODY GET THE LIGHTS.
NO, PLEASE! THE DICE WERE JUST STARTING TO HEAT UP! DADDY NEEDS A NEW EYE JOB!

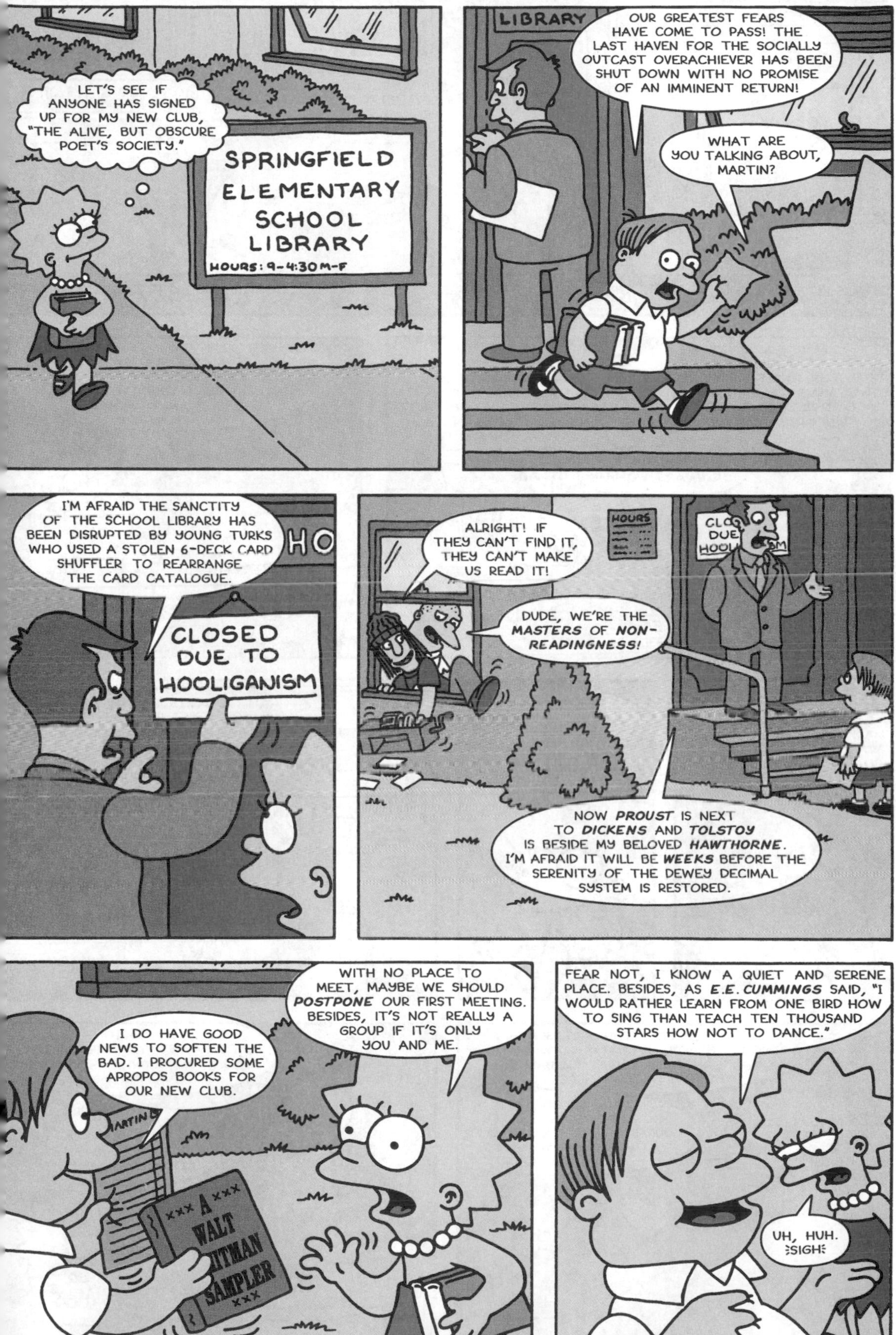
LET'S SEE IF ANYONE HAS SIGNED UP FOR MY NEW CLUB, "THE ALIVE, BUT OBSCURE POET'S SOCIETY."
SPRINGFIELD ELEMENTARY SCHOOL LIBRARY
HOURS: 9-4:30 M-F
LIBRARY
OUR GREATEST FEARS HAVE COME TO PASS! THE LAST HAVEN FOR THE SOCIALLY OUTCAST OVERACHIEVER HAS BEEN SHUT DOWN WITH NO PROMISE OF AN IMMINENT RETURN!
WHAT ARE YOU TALKING ABOUT, MARTIN?
I'M AFRAID THE SANCTITY OF THE SCHOOL LIBRARY HAS BEEN DISRUPTED BY YOUNG TURKS WHO USED A STOLEN 6-DECK CARD SHUFFLER TO REARRANGE THE CARD CATALOGUE.
CLOSED DUE TO HOOLIGANISM
ALRIGHT! IF THEY CAN'T FIND IT, THEY CAN'T MAKE US READ IT!
DUDE, WE'RE THE MASTERS OF NON-READINGNESS!
HOURS
NOW PROUST IS NEXT TO DICKENS AND TOLSTOY IS BESIDE MY BELOVED HAWTHORNE. I'M AFRAID IT WILL BE WEEKS BEFORE THE SERENITY OF THE DEWEY DECIMAL SYSTEM IS RESTORED.
I DO HAVE GOOD NEWS TO SOFTEN THE BAD. I PROCURED SOME APROPOS BOOKS FOR OUR NEW CLUB.
WITH NO PLACE TO MEET, MAYBE WE SHOULD POSTPONE OUR FIRST MEETING. BESIDES, IT'S NOT REALLY A GROUP IF IT'S ONLY YOU AND ME.
A WALT WHITMAN SAMPLER
FEAR NOT, I KNOW A QUIET AND SERENE PLACE. BESIDES, AS E.E. CUMMINGS SAID, "I WOULD RATHER LEARN FROM ONE BIRD HOW TO SING THAN TEACH TEN THOUSAND STARS HOW NOT TO DANCE."
UH, HUH. SIGH

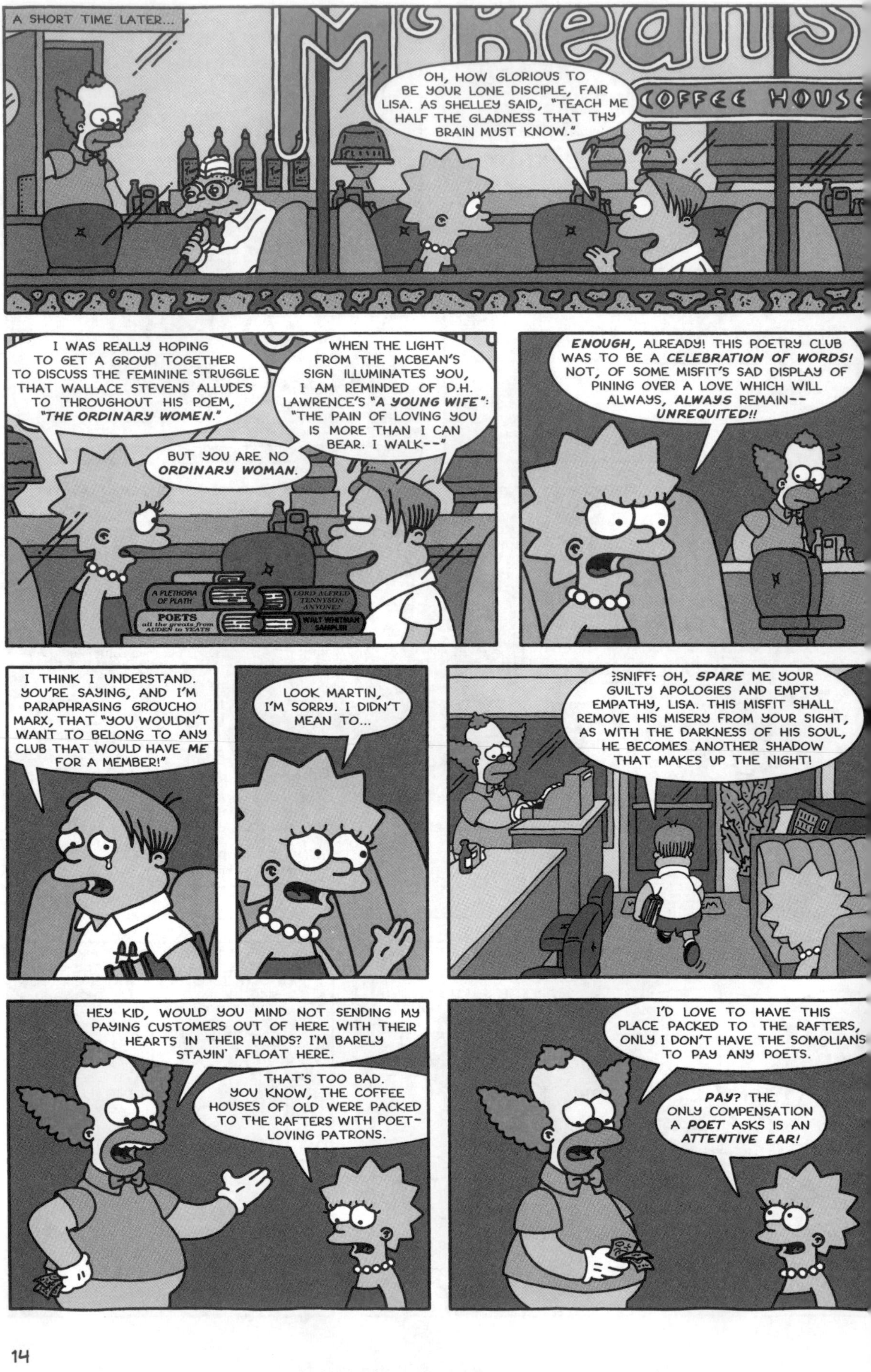
A SHORT TIME LATER...
McBEAN'S COFFEE HOUSE
OH, HOW GLORIOUS TO BE YOUR LONE DISCIPLE, FAIR LISA. AS SHELLEY SAID, "TEACH ME HALF THE GLADNESS THAT THY BRAIN MUST KNOW."
I WAS REALLY HOPING TO GET A GROUP TOGETHER TO DISCUSS THE FEMININE STRUGGLE THAT WALLACE STEVENS ALLUDES TO THROUGHOUT HIS POEM, "THE ORDINARY WOMEN."
BUT YOU ARE NO ORDINARY WOMAN.
WHEN THE LIGHT FROM THE MCBEAN'S SIGN ILLUMINATES YOU, I AM REMINDED OF D.H. LAWRENCE'S "A YOUNG WIFE": "THE PAIN OF LOVING YOU IS MORE THAN I CAN BEAR. I WALK--"
A PLETHORA OF PLATH
LORD ALFRED TENNYSON ANYONE?
POETS all the greats from AUDEN to YEATS
WALT WHITMAN SAMPLER
ENOUGH, ALREADY! THIS POETRY CLUB WAS TO BE A CELEBRATION OF WORDS! NOT, OF SOME MISFIT'S SAD DISPLAY OF PINING OVER A LOVE WHICH WILL ALWAYS, ALWAYS REMAIN-- UNREQUITED!!
I THINK I UNDERSTAND. YOU'RE SAYING, AND I'M PARAPHRASING GROUCHO MARX, THAT "YOU WOULDN'T WANT TO BELONG TO ANY CLUB THAT WOULD HAVE ME FOR A MEMBER!"
LOOK MARTIN, I'M SORRY. I DIDN'T MEAN TO...
SNIFF OH, SPARE ME YOUR GUILTY APOLOGIES AND EMPTY EMPATHY, LISA. THIS MISFIT SHALL REMOVE HIS MISERY FROM YOUR SIGHT, AS WITH THE DARKNESS OF HIS SOUL, HE BECOMES ANOTHER SHADOW THAT MAKES UP THE NIGHT!
HEY KID, WOULD YOU MIND NOT SENDING MY PAYING CUSTOMERS OUT OF HERE WITH THEIR HEARTS IN THEIR HANDS? I'M BARELY STAYIN' AFLOAT HERE.
THAT'S TOO BAD. YOU KNOW, THE COFFEE HOUSES OF OLD WERE PACKED TO THE RAFTERS WITH POET-LOVING PATRONS.
I'D LOVE TO HAVE THIS PLACE PACKED TO THE RAFTERS, ONLY I DON'T HAVE THE SOMOLIANS TO PAY ANY POETS.
PAY? THE ONLY COMPENSATION A POET ASKS IS AN ATTENTIVE EAR!

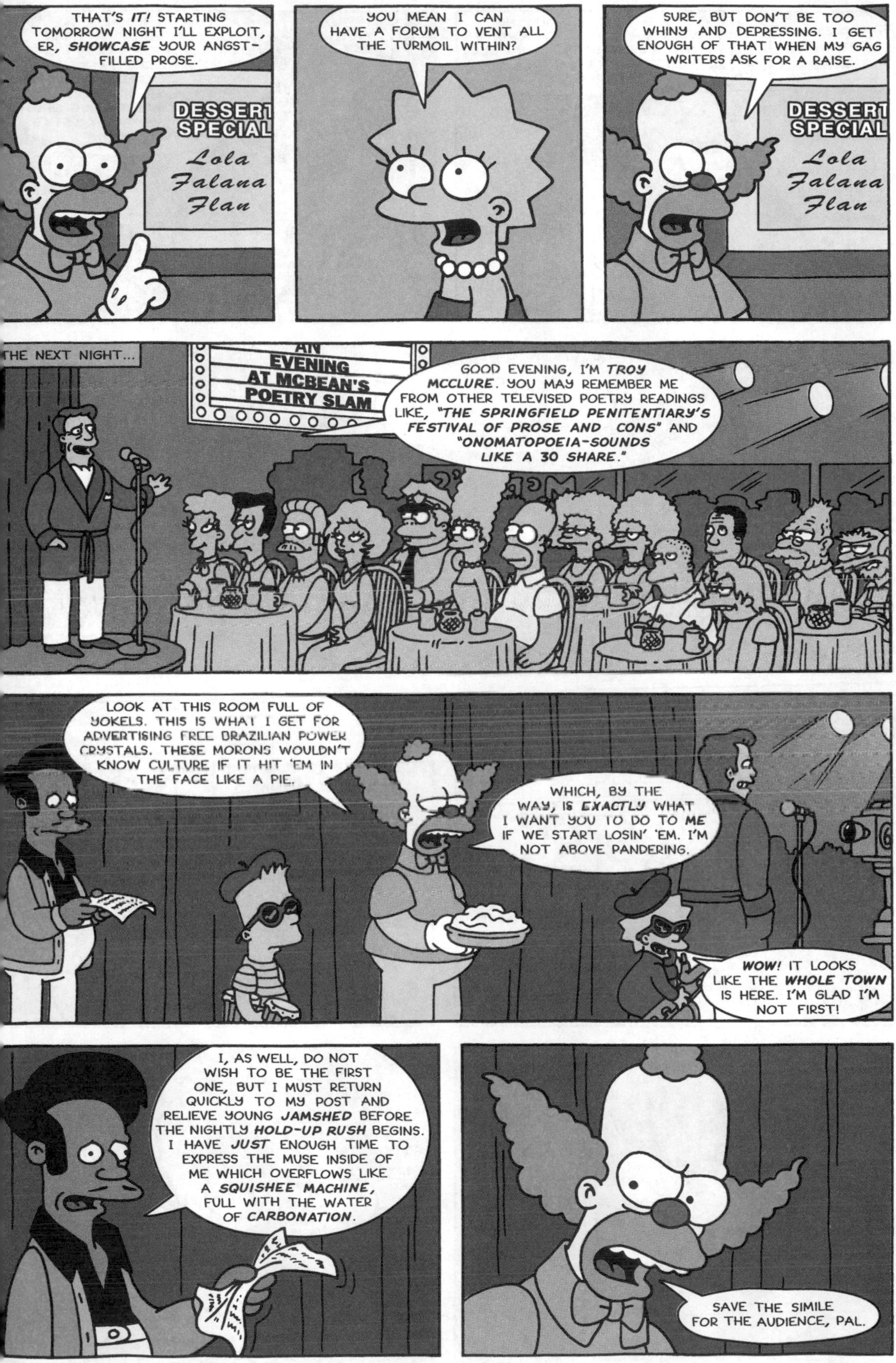
THAT'S IT! STARTING TOMORROW NIGHT I'LL EXPLOIT, ER, SHOWCASE YOUR ANGST-FILLED PROSE.
DESSERT SPECIAL Lola Falana Flan
YOU MEAN I CAN HAVE A FORUM TO VENT ALL THE TURMOIL WITHIN?
SURE, BUT DON'T BE TOO WHINY AND DEPRESSING. I GET ENOUGH OF THAT WHEN MY GAG WRITERS ASK FOR A RAISE.
DESSERT SPECIAL Lola Falana Flan
THE NEXT NIGHT...
AN EVENING AT MCBEAN'S POETRY SLAM
GOOD EVENING, I'M TROY MCCLURE. YOU MAY REMEMBER ME FROM OTHER TELEVISED POETRY READINGS LIKE, "THE SPRINGFIELD PENITENTIARY'S FESTIVAL OF PROSE AND CONS" AND "ONOMATOPOEIA-SOUNDS LIKE A 30 SHARE."
LOOK AT THIS ROOM FULL OF YOKELS. THIS IS WHAT I GET FOR ADVERTISING FREE BRAZILIAN POWER CRYSTALS. THESE MORONS WOULDN'T KNOW CULTURE IF IT HIT 'EM IN THE FACE LIKE A PIE.
WHICH, BY THE WAY, IS EXACTLY WHAT I WANT YOU TO DO TO ME IF WE START LOSIN' 'EM. I'M NOT ABOVE PANDERING.
WOW! IT LOOKS LIKE THE WHOLE TOWN IS HERE. I'M GLAD I'M NOT FIRST!
I, AS WELL, DO NOT WISH TO BE THE FIRST ONE, BUT I MUST RETURN QUICKLY TO MY POST AND RELIEVE YOUNG JAMSHED BEFORE THE NIGHTLY HOLD-UP RUSH BEGINS. I HAVE JUST ENOUGH TIME TO EXPRESS THE MUSE INSIDE OF ME WHICH OVERFLOWS LIKE A SQUISHEE MACHINE, FULL WITH THE WATER OF CARBONATION.
SAVE THE SIMILE FOR THE AUDIENCE, PAL.

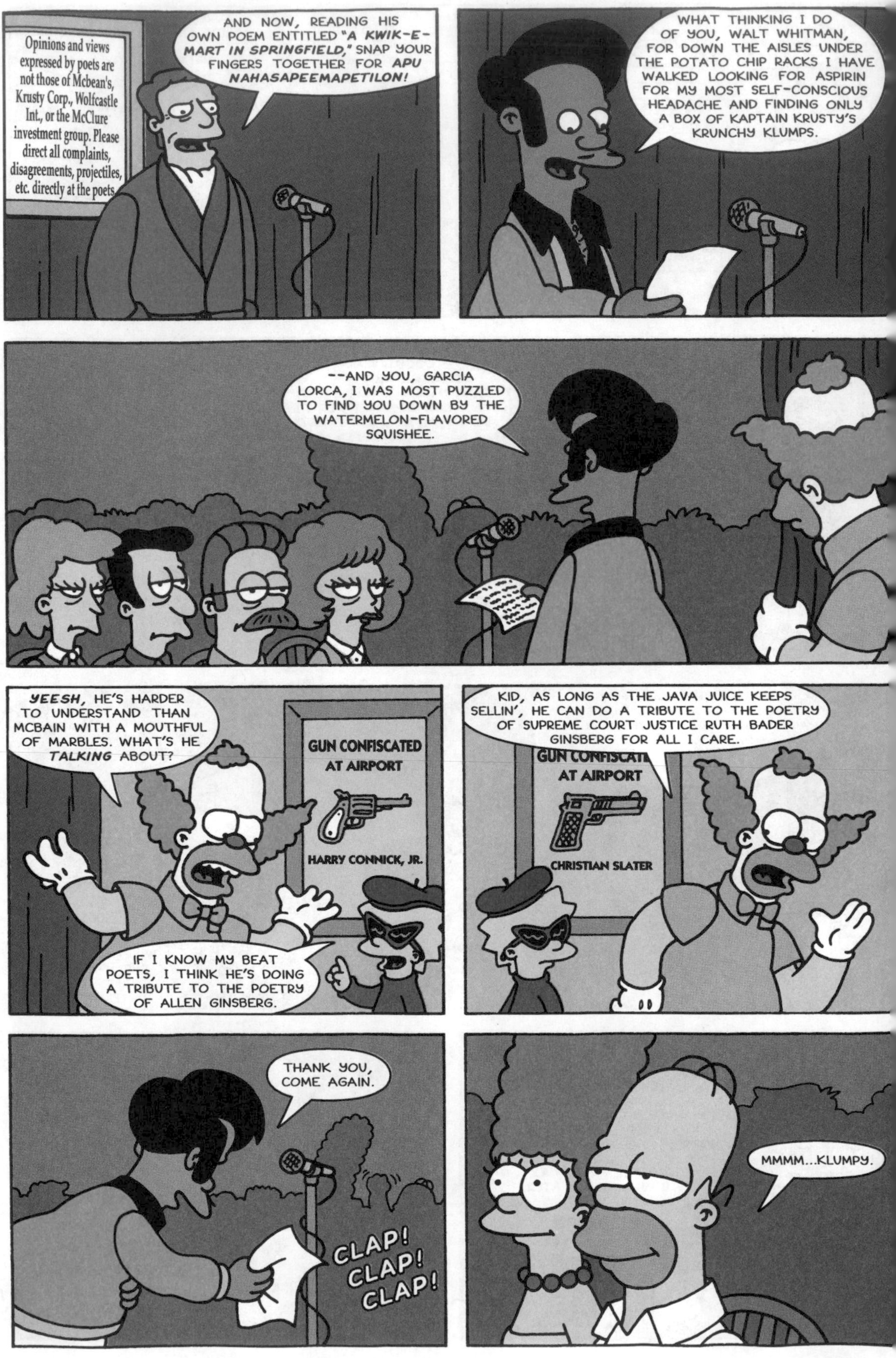
Opinions and views expressed by poets are not those of Mcbean's, Krusty Corp., Wolfcastle Int., or the McClure investment group. Please direct all complaints, disagreements, projectiles, etc. directly at the poets.
AND NOW, READING HIS OWN POEM ENTITLED "A KWIK-E-MART IN SPRINGFIELD," SNAP YOUR FINGERS TOGETHER FOR APU NAHASAPEEMAPETILON!
WHAT THINKING I DO OF YOU, WALT WHITMAN, FOR DOWN THE AISLES UNDER THE POTATO CHIP RACKS I HAVE WALKED LOOKING FOR ASPIRIN FOR MY MOST SELF-CONSCIOUS HEADACHE AND FINDING ONLY A BOX OF KAPTAIN KRUSTY'S KRUNCHY KLUMPS.
--AND YOU, GARCIA LORCA, I WAS MOST PUZZLED TO FIND YOU DOWN BY THE WATERMELON-FLAVORED SQUISHEE.
YEESH, HE'S HARDER TO UNDERSTAND THAN MCBAIN WITH A MOUTHFUL OF MARBLES. WHAT'S HE TALKING ABOUT?
GUN CONFISCATED AT AIRPORT
HARRY CONNICK, JR.
IF I KNOW MY BEAT POETS, I THINK HE'S DOING A TRIBUTE TO THE POETRY OF ALLEN GINSBERG.
KID, AS LONG AS THE JAVA JUICE KEEPS SELLIN', HE CAN DO A TRIBUTE TO THE POETRY OF SUPREME COURT JUSTICE RUTH BADER GINSBERG FOR ALL I CARE.
GUN CONFISCATED AT AIRPORT
CHRISTIAN SLATER
THANK YOU, COME AGAIN.
CLAP! CLAP! CLAP!
MMMM...KLUMPY.

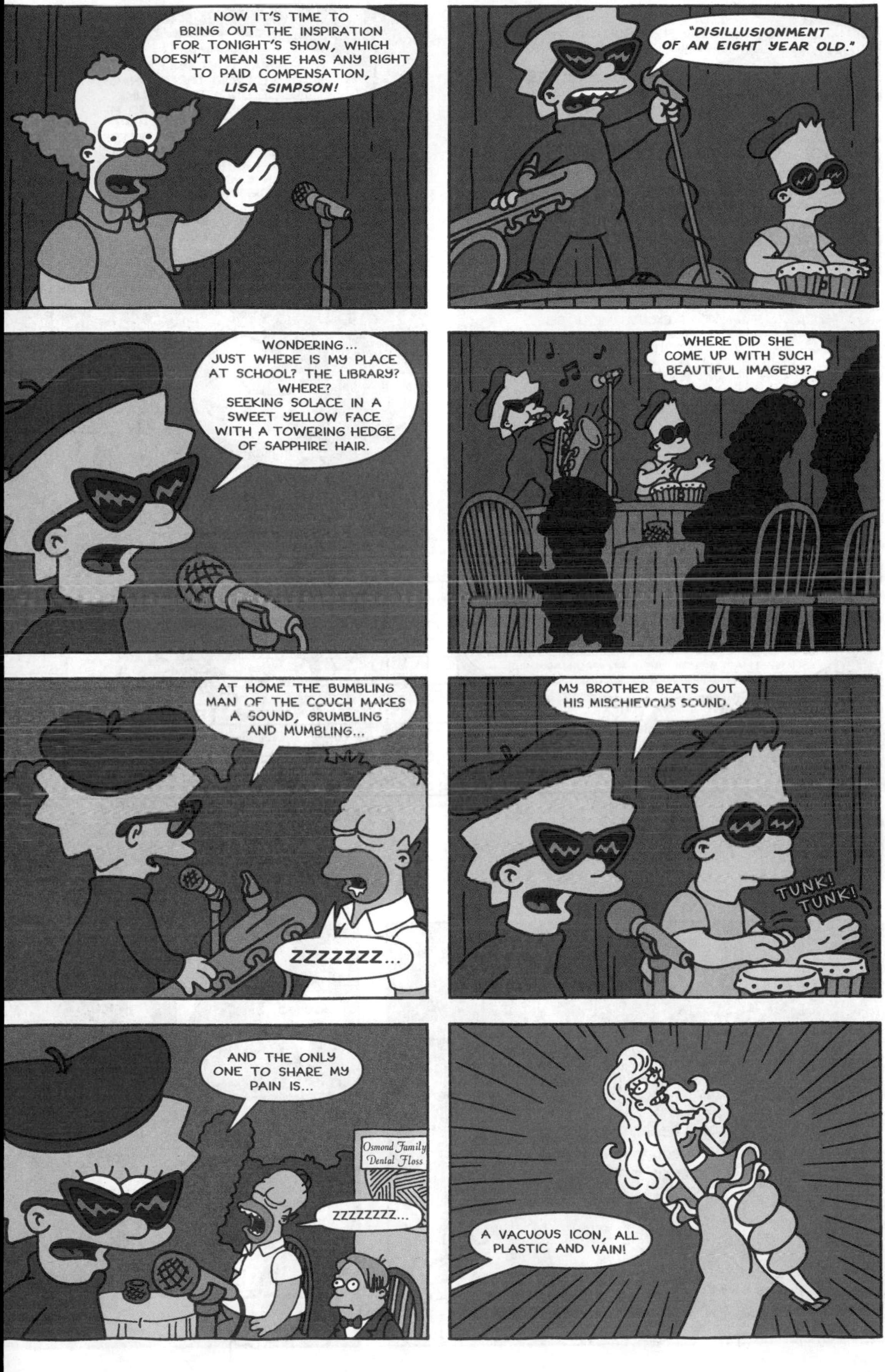
NOW IT'S TIME TO BRING OUT THE INSPIRATION FOR TONIGHT'S SHOW, WHICH DOESN'T MEAN SHE HAS ANY RIGHT TO PAID COMPENSATION, LISA SIMPSON!
"DISILLUSIONMENT OF AN EIGHT YEAR OLD."
WONDERING... JUST WHERE IS MY PLACE AT SCHOOL? THE LIBRARY? WHERE? SEEKING SOLACE IN A SWEET YELLOW FACE WITH A TOWERING HEDGE OF SAPPHIRE HAIR.
WHERE DID SHE COME UP WITH SUCH BEAUTIFUL IMAGERY?
AT HOME THE BUMBLING MAN OF THE COUCH MAKES A SOUND, GRUMBLING AND MUMBLING...
ZZZZZZZ...
MY BROTHER BEATS OUT HIS MISCHIEVOUS SOUND.
TUNK! TUNK!
AND THE ONLY ONE TO SHARE MY PAIN IS...
Osmond Family Dental Floss
ZZZZZZZZ...
A VACUOUS ICON, ALL PLASTIC AND VAIN!

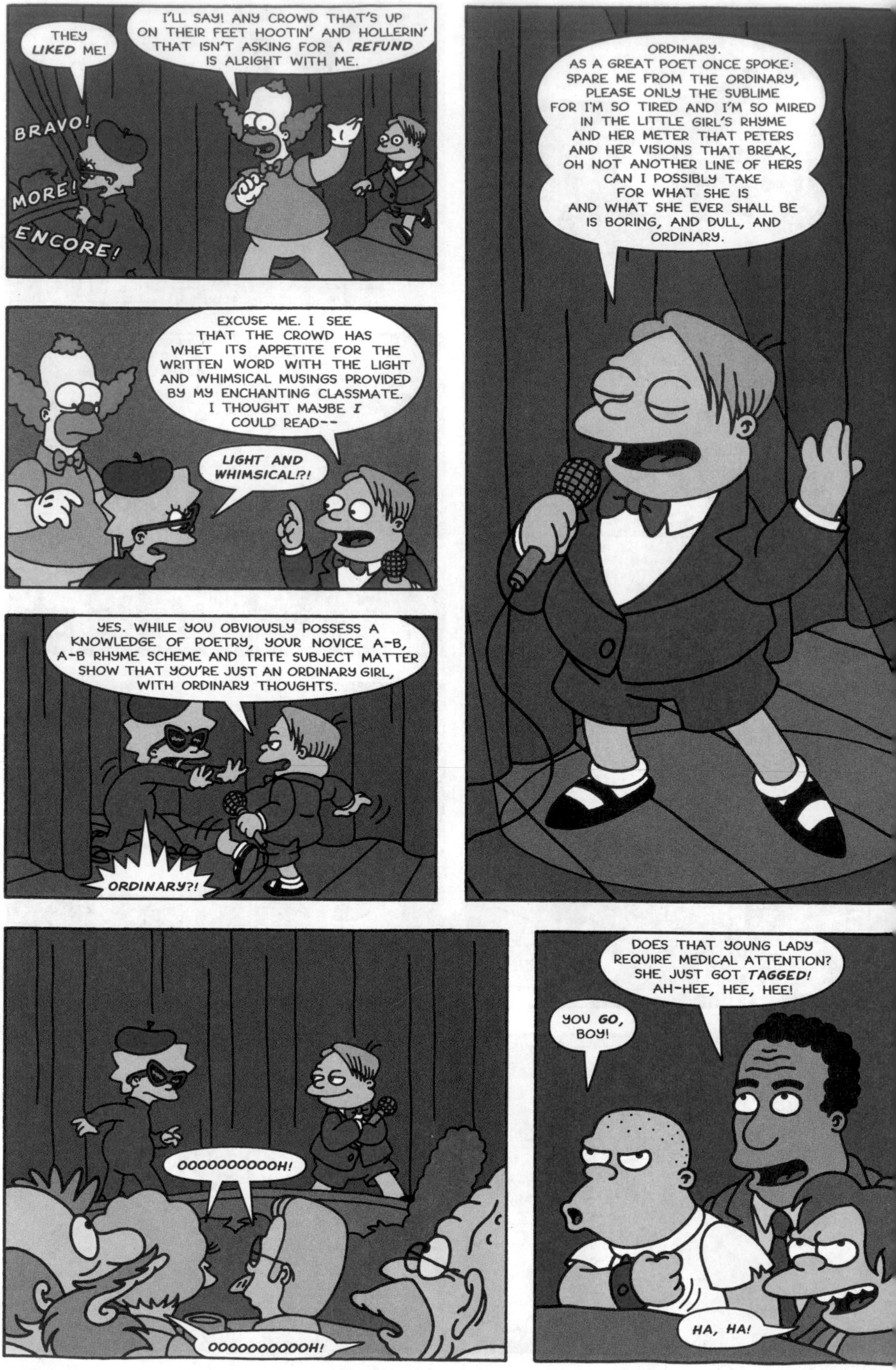

THEY LIKED ME!
I'LL SAY! ANY CROWD THAT'S UP ON THEIR FEET HOOTIN' AND HOLLERIN' THAT ISN'T ASKING FOR A REFUND IS ALRIGHT WITH ME.
BRAVO!
MORE!
ENCORE!
EXCUSE ME. I SEE THAT THE CROWD HAS WHET ITS APPETITE FOR THE WRITTEN WORD WITH THE LIGHT AND WHIMSICAL MUSINGS PROVIDED BY MY ENCHANTING CLASSMATE. I THOUGHT MAYBE I COULD READ--
LIGHT AND WHIMSICAL!?!
YES. WHILE YOU OBVIOUSLY POSSESS A KNOWLEDGE OF POETRY, YOUR NOVICE A-B, A-B RHYME SCHEME AND TRITE SUBJECT MATTER SHOW THAT YOU'RE JUST AN ORDINARY GIRL, WITH ORDINARY THOUGHTS.
ORDINARY?!
ORDINARY.
AS A GREAT POET ONCE SPOKE:
SPARE ME FROM THE ORDINARY,
PLEASE ONLY THE SUBLIME
FOR I'M SO TIRED AND I'M SO MIRED
IN THE LITTLE GIRL'S RHYME
AND HER METER THAT PETERS
AND HER VISIONS THAT BREAK,
OH NOT ANOTHER LINE OF HERS
CAN I POSSIBLY TAKE
FOR WHAT SHE IS
AND WHAT SHE EVER SHALL BE
IS BORING, AND DULL, AND
ORDINARY.
OOOOOOOOOOH!
OOOOOOOOOOH!
YOU GO, BOY!
DOES THAT YOUNG LADY REQUIRE MEDICAL ATTENTION? SHE JUST GOT TAGGED! AH-HEE, HEE, HEE!
HA, HA!

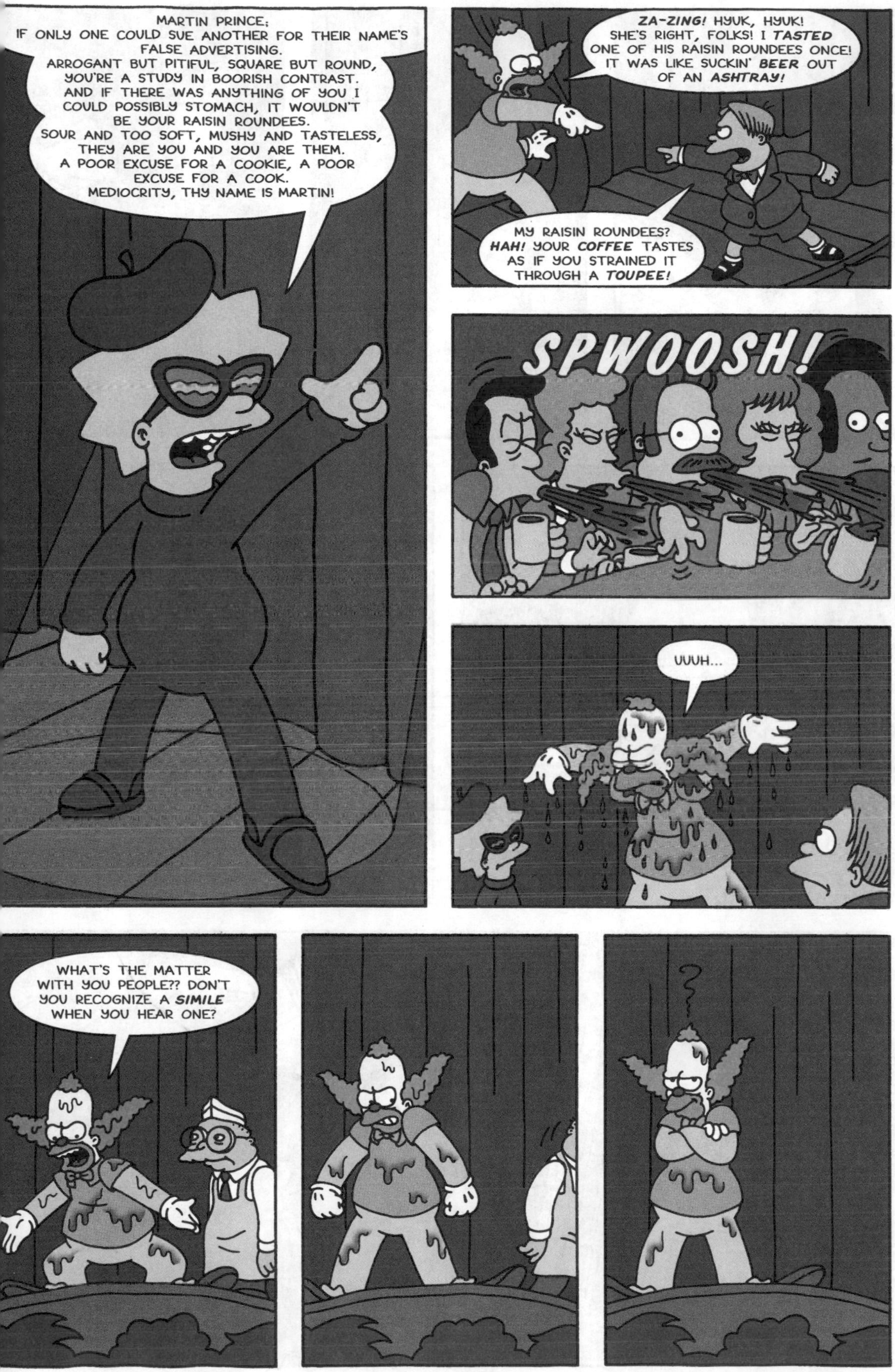
MARTIN PRINCE; IF ONLY ONE COULD SUE ANOTHER FOR THEIR NAME'S FALSE ADVERTISING. ARROGANT BUT PITIFUL, SQUARE BUT ROUND, YOU'RE A STUDY IN BOORISH CONTRAST. AND IF THERE WAS ANYTHING OF YOU I COULD POSSIBLY STOMACH, IT WOULDN'T BE YOUR RAISIN ROUNDEES. SOUR AND TOO SOFT, MUSHY AND TASTELESS, THEY ARE YOU AND YOU ARE THEM. A POOR EXCUSE FOR A COOKIE, A POOR EXCUSE FOR A COOK. MEDIOCRITY, THY NAME IS MARTIN!
MY RAISIN ROUNDEES? HAH! YOUR COFFEE TASTES AS IF YOU STRAINED IT THROUGH A TOUPEE!
ZA-ZING! HYUK, HYUK! SHE'S RIGHT, FOLKS! I TASTED ONE OF HIS RAISIN ROUNDEES ONCE! IT WAS LIKE SUCKIN' BEER OUT OF AN ASHTRAY!
SPWOOSH!
UUUH...
WHAT'S THE MATTER WITH YOU PEOPLE?? DON'T YOU RECOGNIZE A SIMILE WHEN YOU HEAR ONE?
?

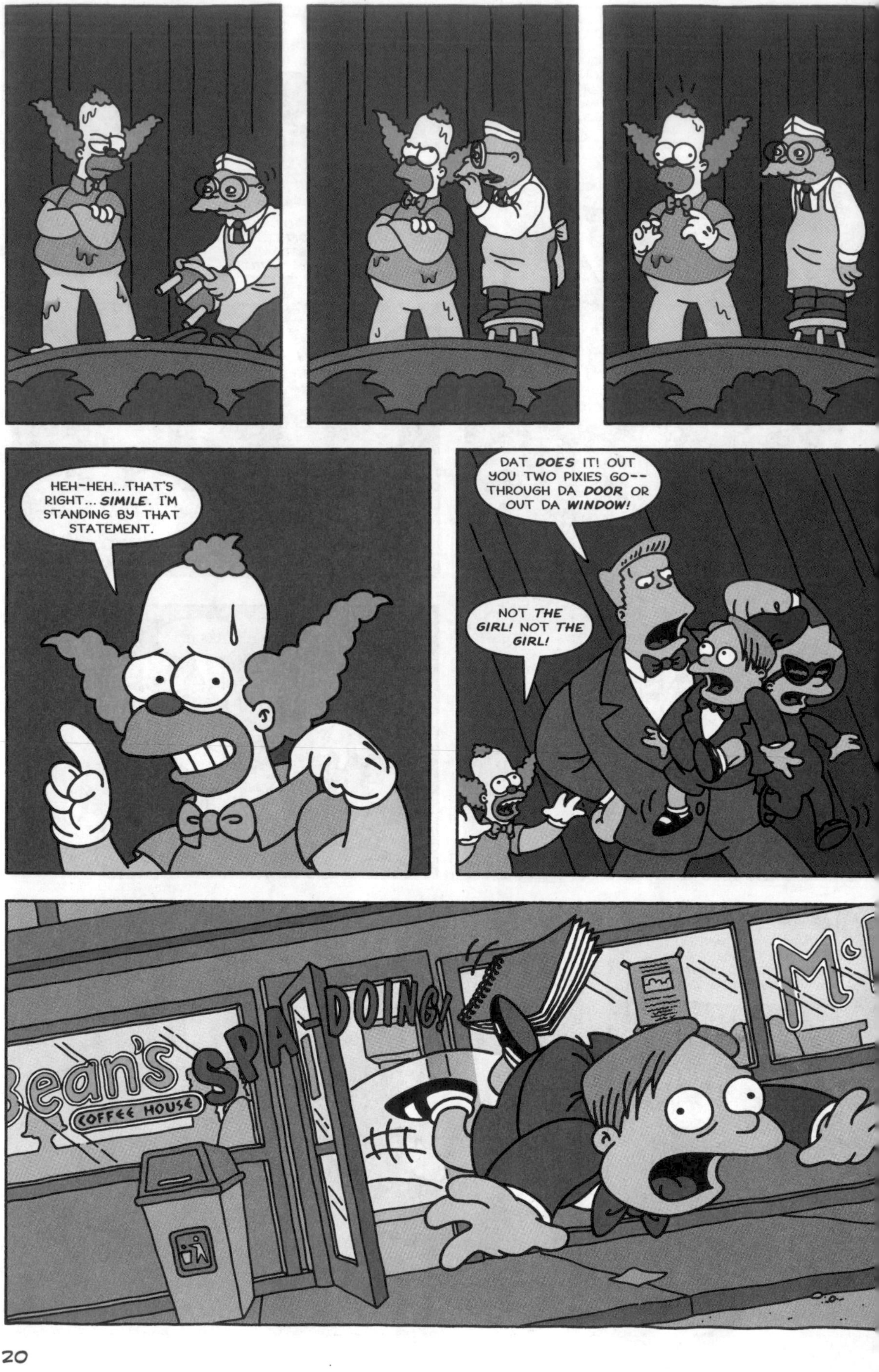
HEH-HEH...THAT'S RIGHT... SIMILE. I'M STANDING BY THAT STATEMENT.
DAT DOES IT! OUT YOU TWO PIXIES GO-- THROUGH DA DOOR OR OUT DA WINDOW!
NOT THE GIRL! NOT THE GIRL!
SPA-DOING!
Bean's
COFFEE HOUSE

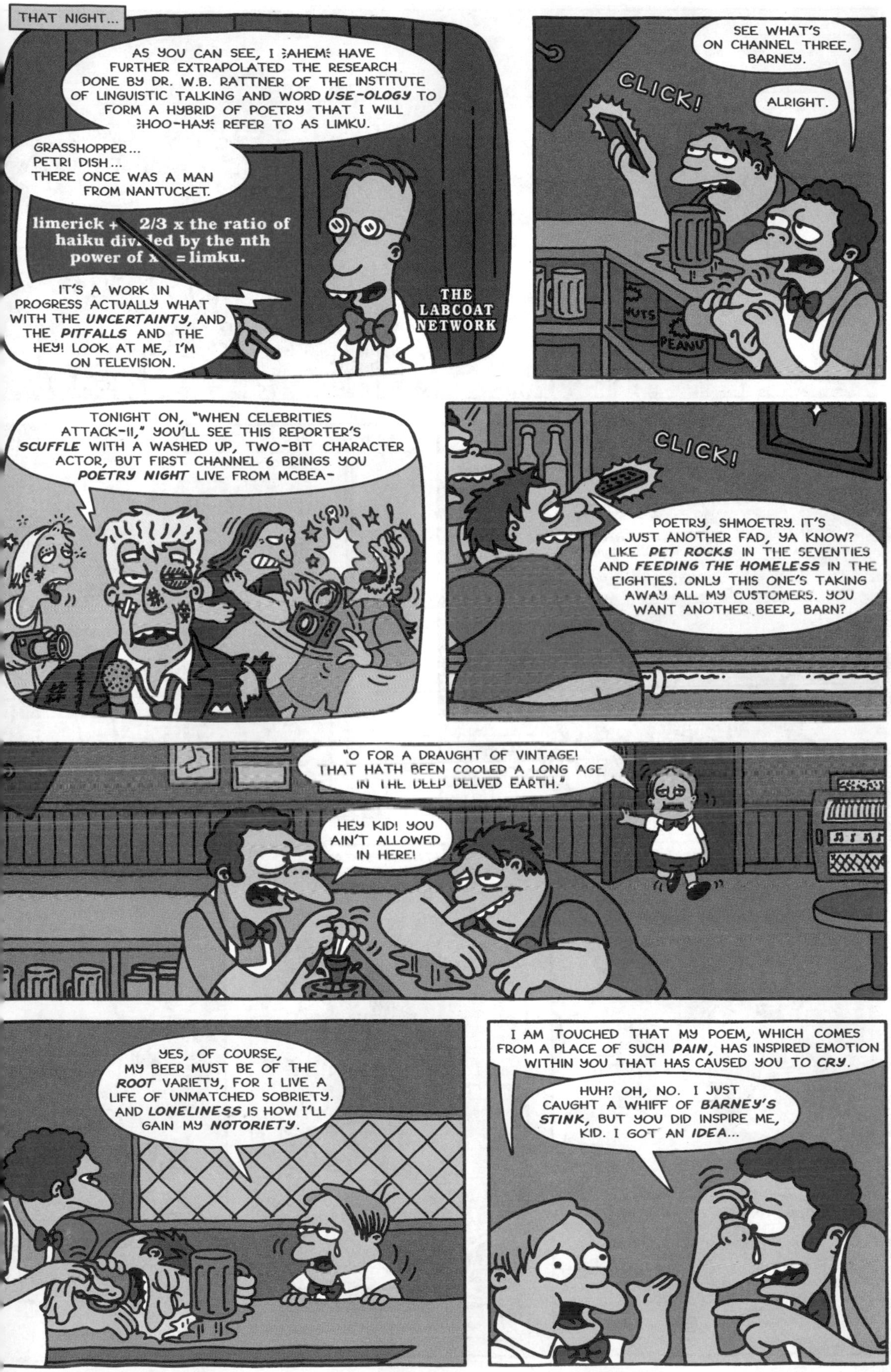

THAT NIGHT...
AS YOU CAN SEE, I ;AHEM; HAVE FURTHER EXTRAPOLATED THE RESEARCH DONE BY DR. W.B. RATTNER OF THE INSTITUTE OF LINGUISTIC TALKING AND WORD USE-OLOGY TO FORM A HYBRID OF POETRY THAT I WILL ;HOO-HAY; REFER TO AS LIMKU.
GRASSHOPPER... PETRI DISH... THERE ONCE WAS A MAN FROM NANTUCKET.
limerick + 2/3 x the ratio of haiku divided by the nth power of x = limku.
IT'S A WORK IN PROGRESS ACTUALLY WHAT WITH THE UNCERTAINTY, AND THE PITFALLS AND THE HEY! LOOK AT ME, I'M ON TELEVISION.
THE LABCOAT NETWORK
SEE WHAT'S ON CHANNEL THREE, BARNEY.
CLICK!
ALRIGHT.
NUTS
PEANU
TONIGHT ON, "WHEN CELEBRITIES ATTACK-II," YOU'LL SEE THIS REPORTER'S SCUFFLE WITH A WASHED UP, TWO-BIT CHARACTER ACTOR, BUT FIRST CHANNEL 6 BRINGS YOU POETRY NIGHT LIVE FROM MCBEA-
CLICK!
POETRY, SHMOETRY. IT'S JUST ANOTHER FAD, YA KNOW? LIKE PET ROCKS IN THE SEVENTIES AND FEEDING THE HOMELESS IN THE EIGHTIES. ONLY THIS ONE'S TAKING AWAY ALL MY CUSTOMERS. YOU WANT ANOTHER BEER, BARN?
"O FOR A DRAUGHT OF VINTAGE! THAT HATH BEEN COOLED A LONG AGE IN THE DEEP DELVED EARTH."
HEY KID! YOU AIN'T ALLOWED IN HERE!
YES, OF COURSE, MY BEER MUST BE OF THE ROOT VARIETY, FOR I LIVE A LIFE OF UNMATCHED SOBRIETY. AND LONELINESS IS HOW I'LL GAIN MY NOTORIETY.
I AM TOUCHED THAT MY POEM, WHICH COMES FROM A PLACE OF SUCH PAIN, HAS INSPIRED EMOTION WITHIN YOU THAT HAS CAUSED YOU TO CRY.
HUH? OH, NO. I JUST CAUGHT A WHIFF OF BARNEY'S STINK, BUT YOU DID INSPIRE ME, KID. I GOT AN IDEA...

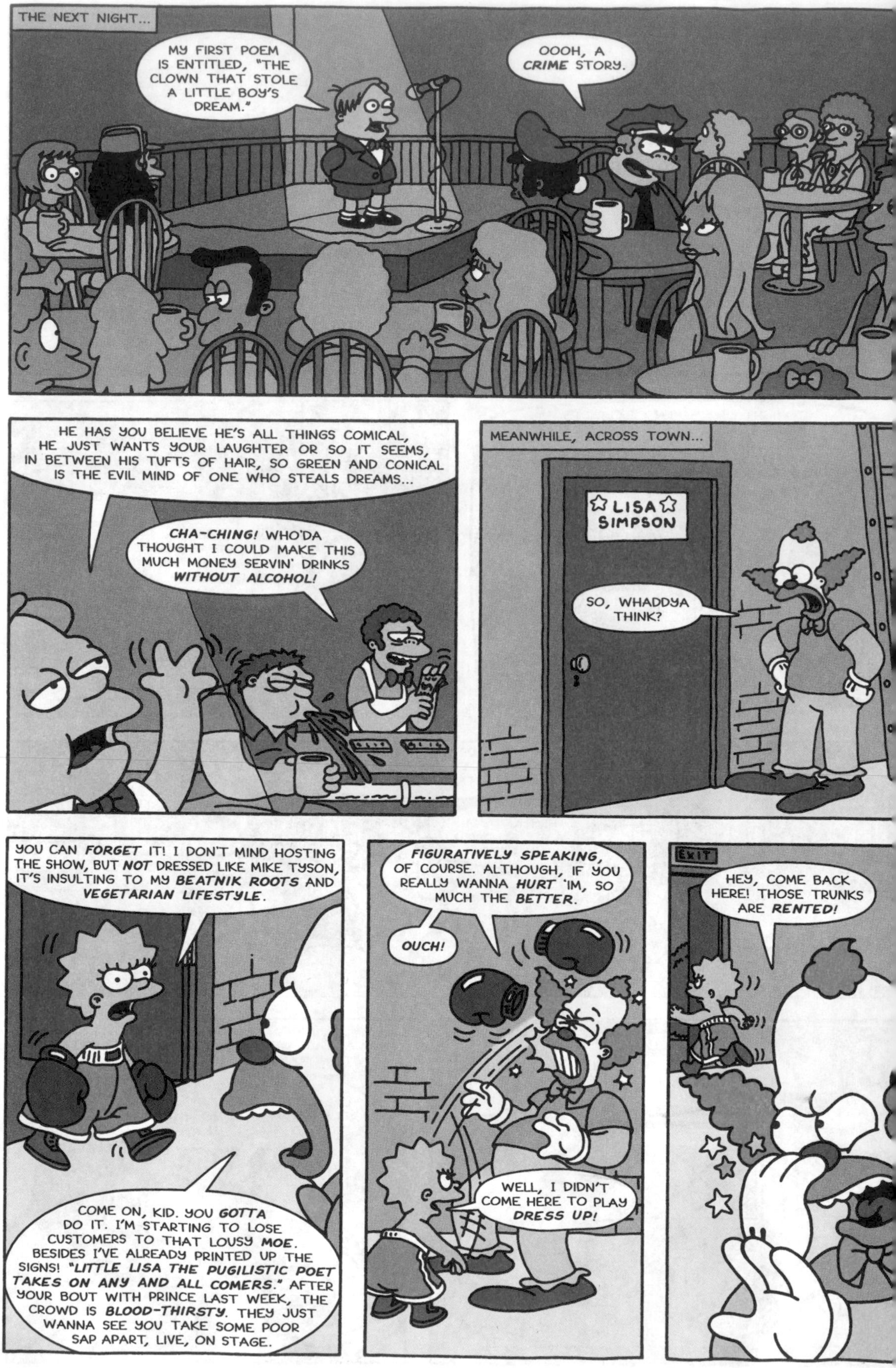
THE NEXT NIGHT...
MY FIRST POEM IS ENTITLED, "THE CLOWN THAT STOLE A LITTLE BOY'S DREAM."
OOOH, A CRIME STORY.
HE HAS YOU BELIEVE HE'S ALL THINGS COMICAL, HE JUST WANTS YOUR LAUGHTER OR SO IT SEEMS, IN BETWEEN HIS TUFTS OF HAIR, SO GREEN AND CONICAL IS THE EVIL MIND OF ONE WHO STEALS DREAMS...
CHA-CHING! WHO'DA THOUGHT I COULD MAKE THIS MUCH MONEY SERVIN' DRINKS WITHOUT ALCOHOL!
MEANWHILE, ACROSS TOWN...
LISA SIMPSON
SO, WHADDYA THINK?
YOU CAN FORGET IT! I DON'T MIND HOSTING THE SHOW, BUT NOT DRESSED LIKE MIKE TYSON, IT'S INSULTING TO MY BEATNIK ROOTS AND VEGETARIAN LIFESTYLE.
COME ON, KID. YOU GOTTA DO IT. I'M STARTING TO LOSE CUSTOMERS TO THAT LOUSY MOE. BESIDES I'VE ALREADY PRINTED UP THE SIGNS! "LITTLE LISA THE PUGILISTIC POET TAKES ON ANY AND ALL COMERS." AFTER YOUR BOUT WITH PRINCE LAST WEEK, THE CROWD IS BLOOD-THIRSTY. THEY JUST WANNA SEE YOU TAKE SOME POOR SAP APART, LIVE, ON STAGE.
FIGURATIVELY SPEAKING, OF COURSE. ALTHOUGH, IF YOU REALLY WANNA HURT 'IM, SO MUCH THE BETTER.
OUCH!
WELL, I DIDN'T COME HERE TO PLAY DRESS UP!
EXIT
HEY, COME BACK HERE! THOSE TRUNKS ARE RENTED!

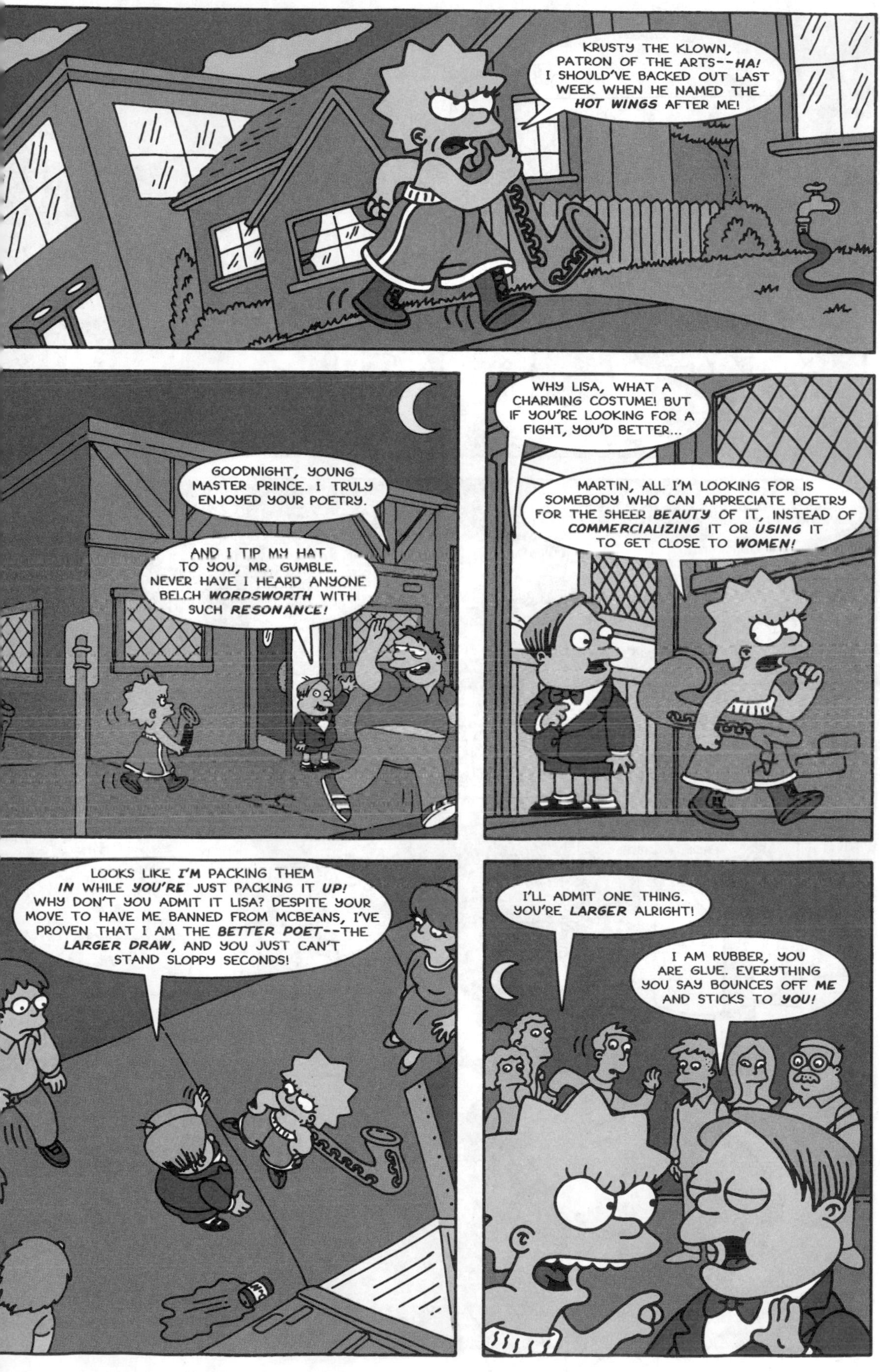
KRUSTY THE KLOWN, PATRON OF THE ARTS--HA! I SHOULD'VE BACKED OUT LAST WEEK WHEN HE NAMED THE HOT WINGS AFTER ME!
GOODNIGHT, YOUNG MASTER PRINCE. I TRULY ENJOYED YOUR POETRY.
AND I TIP MY HAT TO YOU, MR. GUMBLE. NEVER HAVE I HEARD ANYONE BELCH WORDSWORTH WITH SUCH RESONANCE!
WHY LISA, WHAT A CHARMING COSTUME! BUT IF YOU'RE LOOKING FOR A FIGHT, YOU'D BETTER...
MARTIN, ALL I'M LOOKING FOR IS SOMEBODY WHO CAN APPRECIATE POETRY FOR THE SHEER BEAUTY OF IT, INSTEAD OF COMMERCIALIZING IT OR USING IT TO GET CLOSE TO WOMEN!
LOOKS LIKE I'M PACKING THEM IN WHILE YOU'RE JUST PACKING IT UP! WHY DON'T YOU ADMIT IT LISA? DESPITE YOUR MOVE TO HAVE ME BANNED FROM MCBEANS, I'VE PROVEN THAT I AM THE BETTER POET--THE LARGER DRAW, AND YOU JUST CAN'T STAND SLOPPY SECONDS!
I'LL ADMIT ONE THING. YOU'RE LARGER ALRIGHT!
I AM RUBBER, YOU ARE GLUE. EVERYTHING YOU SAY BOUNCES OFF ME AND STICKS TO YOU!

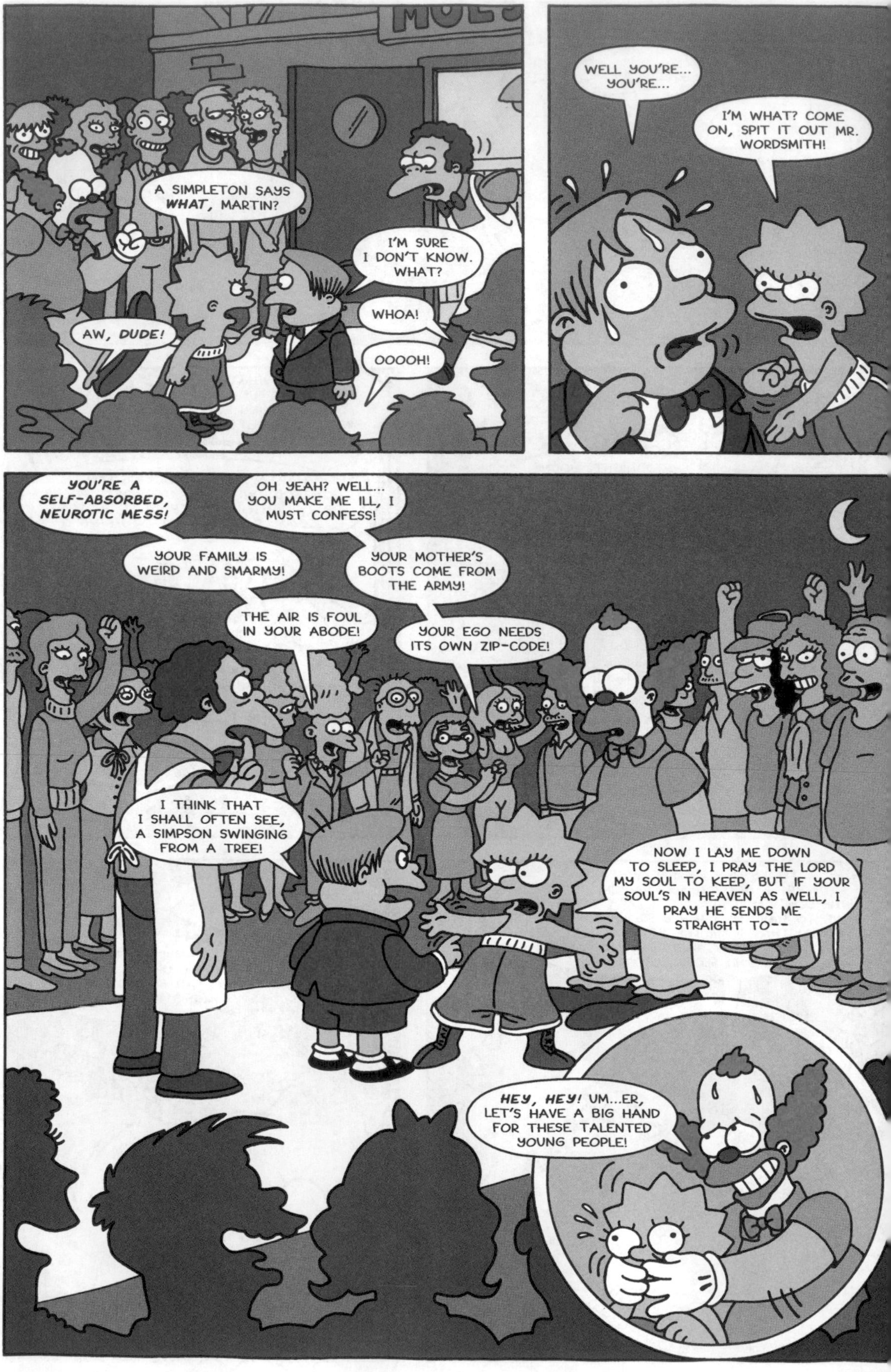
A SIMPLETON SAYS *WHAT*, MARTIN?
I'M SURE I DON'T KNOW. WHAT?
AW, *DUDE!*
WHOA!
OOOOH!
WELL YOU'RE... YOU'RE...
I'M WHAT? COME ON, SPIT IT OUT MR. WORDSMITH!
YOU'RE A SELF-ABSORBED, NEUROTIC MESS!
OH YEAH? WELL... YOU MAKE ME ILL, I MUST CONFESS!
YOUR FAMILY IS WEIRD AND SMARMY!
YOUR MOTHER'S BOOTS COME FROM THE ARMY!
THE AIR IS FOUL IN YOUR ABODE!
YOUR EGO NEEDS ITS OWN ZIP-CODE!
I THINK THAT I SHALL OFTEN SEE, A SIMPSON SWINGING FROM A TREE!
NOW I LAY ME DOWN TO SLEEP, I PRAY THE LORD MY SOUL TO KEEP, BUT IF YOUR SOUL'S IN HEAVEN AS WELL, I PRAY HE SENDS ME STRAIGHT TO--
HEY, HEY! UM...ER, LET'S HAVE A BIG HAND FOR THESE TALENTED YOUNG PEOPLE!

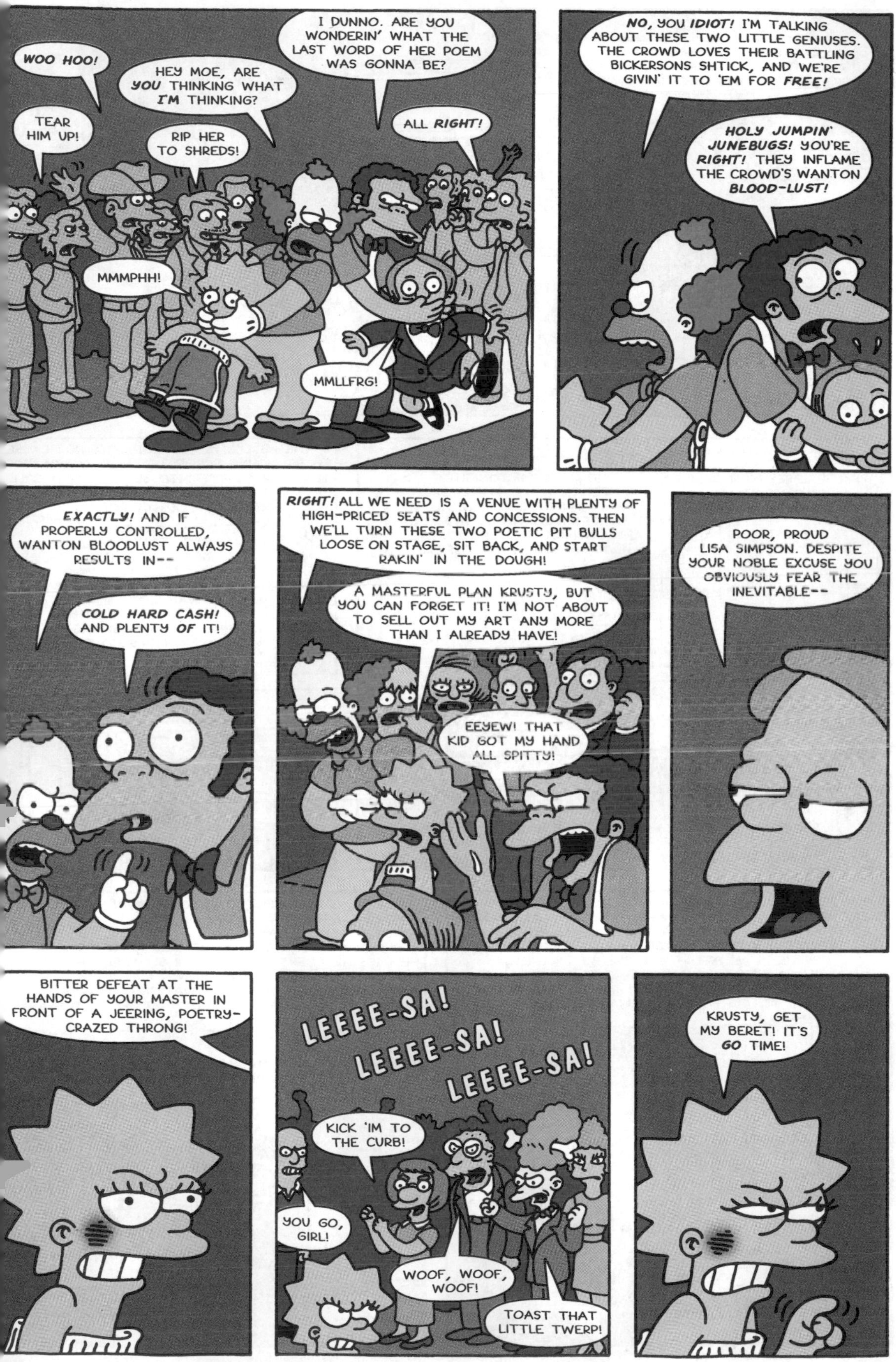
WOO HOO!
TEAR HIM UP!
HEY MOE, ARE YOU THINKING WHAT I'M THINKING?
RIP HER TO SHREDS!
I DUNNO. ARE YOU WONDERIN' WHAT THE LAST WORD OF HER POEM WAS GONNA BE?
ALL RIGHT!
MMMPHH!
MMLLFRG!
NO, YOU IDIOT! I'M TALKING ABOUT THESE TWO LITTLE GENIUSES. THE CROWD LOVES THEIR BATTLING BICKERSONS SHTICK, AND WE'RE GIVIN' IT TO 'EM FOR FREE!
HOLY JUMPIN' JUNEBUGS! YOU'RE RIGHT! THEY INFLAME THE CROWD'S WANTON BLOOD-LUST!
EXACTLY! AND IF PROPERLY CONTROLLED, WANTON BLOODLUST ALWAYS RESULTS IN--
COLD HARD CASH! AND PLENTY OF IT!
RIGHT! ALL WE NEED IS A VENUE WITH PLENTY OF HIGH-PRICED SEATS AND CONCESSIONS. THEN WE'LL TURN THESE TWO POETIC PIT BULLS LOOSE ON STAGE, SIT BACK, AND START RAKIN' IN THE DOUGH!
A MASTERFUL PLAN KRUSTY, BUT YOU CAN FORGET IT! I'M NOT ABOUT TO SELL OUT MY ART ANY MORE THAN I ALREADY HAVE!
EEYEW! THAT KID GOT MY HAND ALL SPITTY!
POOR, PROUD LISA SIMPSON. DESPITE YOUR NOBLE EXCUSE YOU OBVIOUSLY FEAR THE INEVITABLE--
BITTER DEFEAT AT THE HANDS OF YOUR MASTER IN FRONT OF A JEERING, POETRY-CRAZED THRONG!
LEEEE-SA! LEEEE-SA! LEEEE-SA!
KICK 'IM TO THE CURB!
YOU GO, GIRL!
WOOF, WOOF, WOOF!
TOAST THAT LITTLE TWERP!
KRUSTY, GET MY BERET! IT'S GO TIME!

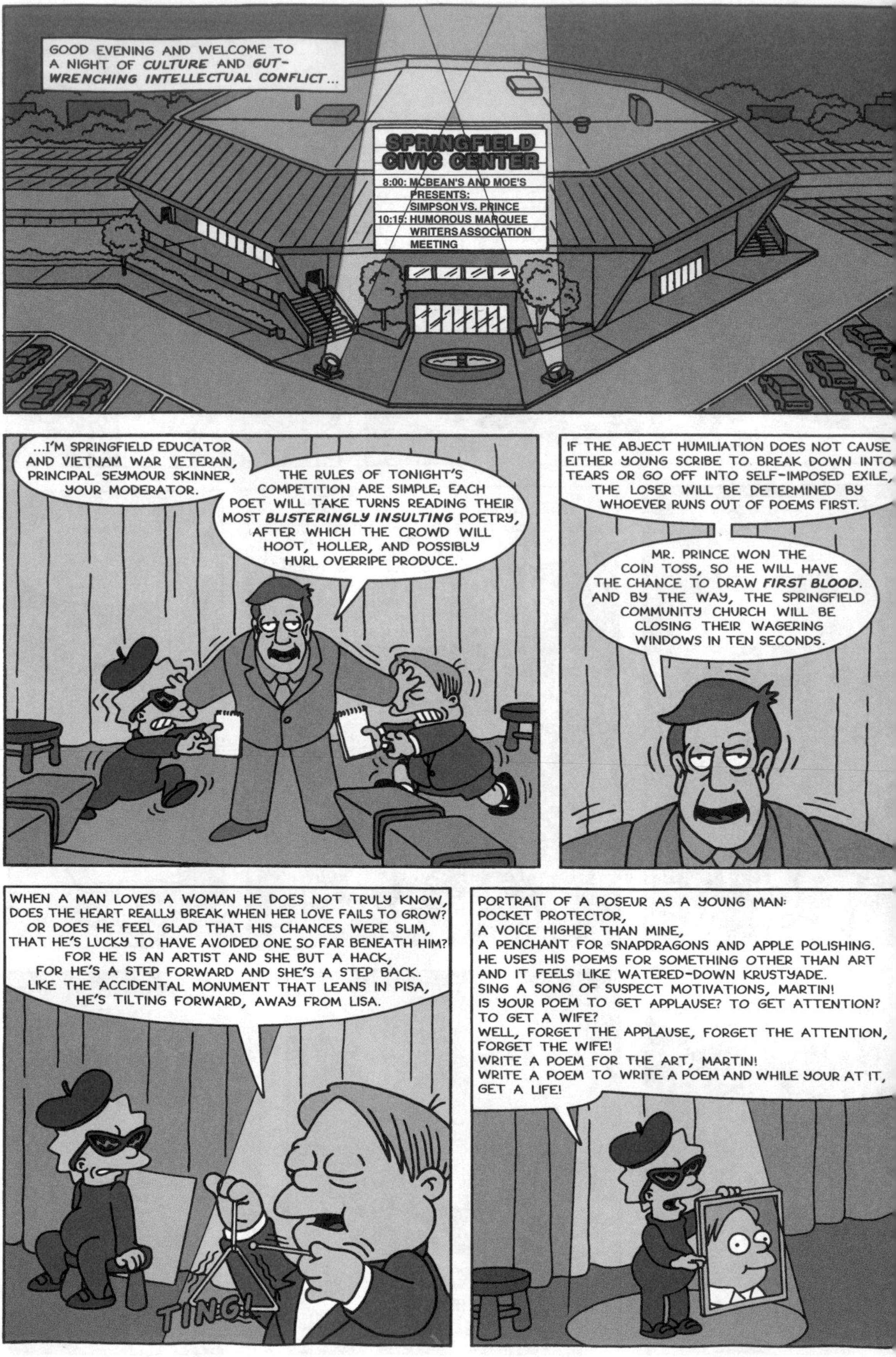

GOOD EVENING AND WELCOME TO A NIGHT OF CULTURE AND GUT-WRENCHING INTELLECTUAL CONFLICT...
SPRINGFIELD CIVIC CENTER
8:00: MCBEAN'S AND MOE'S PRESENTS: SIMPSON VS. PRINCE
10:15: HUMOROUS MARQUEE WRITERS ASSOCIATION MEETING
...I'M SPRINGFIELD EDUCATOR AND VIETNAM WAR VETERAN, PRINCIPAL SEYMOUR SKINNER, YOUR MODERATOR.
THE RULES OF TONIGHT'S COMPETITION ARE SIMPLE; EACH POET WILL TAKE TURNS READING THEIR MOST BLISTERINGLY INSULTING POETRY, AFTER WHICH THE CROWD WILL HOOT, HOLLER, AND POSSIBLY HURL OVERRIPE PRODUCE.
IF THE ABJECT HUMILIATION DOES NOT CAUSE EITHER YOUNG SCRIBE TO BREAK DOWN INTO TEARS OR GO OFF INTO SELF-IMPOSED EXILE, THE LOSER WILL BE DETERMINED BY WHOEVER RUNS OUT OF POEMS FIRST.
MR. PRINCE WON THE COIN TOSS, SO HE WILL HAVE THE CHANCE TO DRAW FIRST BLOOD. AND BY THE WAY, THE SPRINGFIELD COMMUNITY CHURCH WILL BE CLOSING THEIR WAGERING WINDOWS IN TEN SECONDS.
WHEN A MAN LOVES A WOMAN HE DOES NOT TRULY KNOW, DOES THE HEART REALLY BREAK WHEN HER LOVE FAILS TO GROW? OR DOES HE FEEL GLAD THAT HIS CHANCES WERE SLIM, THAT HE'S LUCKY TO HAVE AVOIDED ONE SO FAR BENEATH HIM? FOR HE IS AN ARTIST AND SHE BUT A HACK, FOR HE'S A STEP FORWARD AND SHE'S A STEP BACK. LIKE THE ACCIDENTAL MONUMENT THAT LEANS IN PISA, HE'S TILTING FORWARD, AWAY FROM LISA.
TING!
PORTRAIT OF A POSEUR AS A YOUNG MAN: POCKET PROTECTOR, A VOICE HIGHER THAN MINE, A PENCHANT FOR SNAPDRAGONS AND APPLE POLISHING. HE USES HIS POEMS FOR SOMETHING OTHER THAN ART AND IT FEELS LIKE WATERED-DOWN KRUSTYADE. SING A SONG OF SUSPECT MOTIVATIONS, MARTIN! IS YOUR POEM TO GET APPLAUSE? TO GET ATTENTION? TO GET A WIFE? WELL, FORGET THE APPLAUSE, FORGET THE ATTENTION, FORGET THE WIFE! WRITE A POEM FOR THE ART, MARTIN! WRITE A POEM TO WRITE A POEM AND WHILE YOUR AT IT, GET A LIFE!

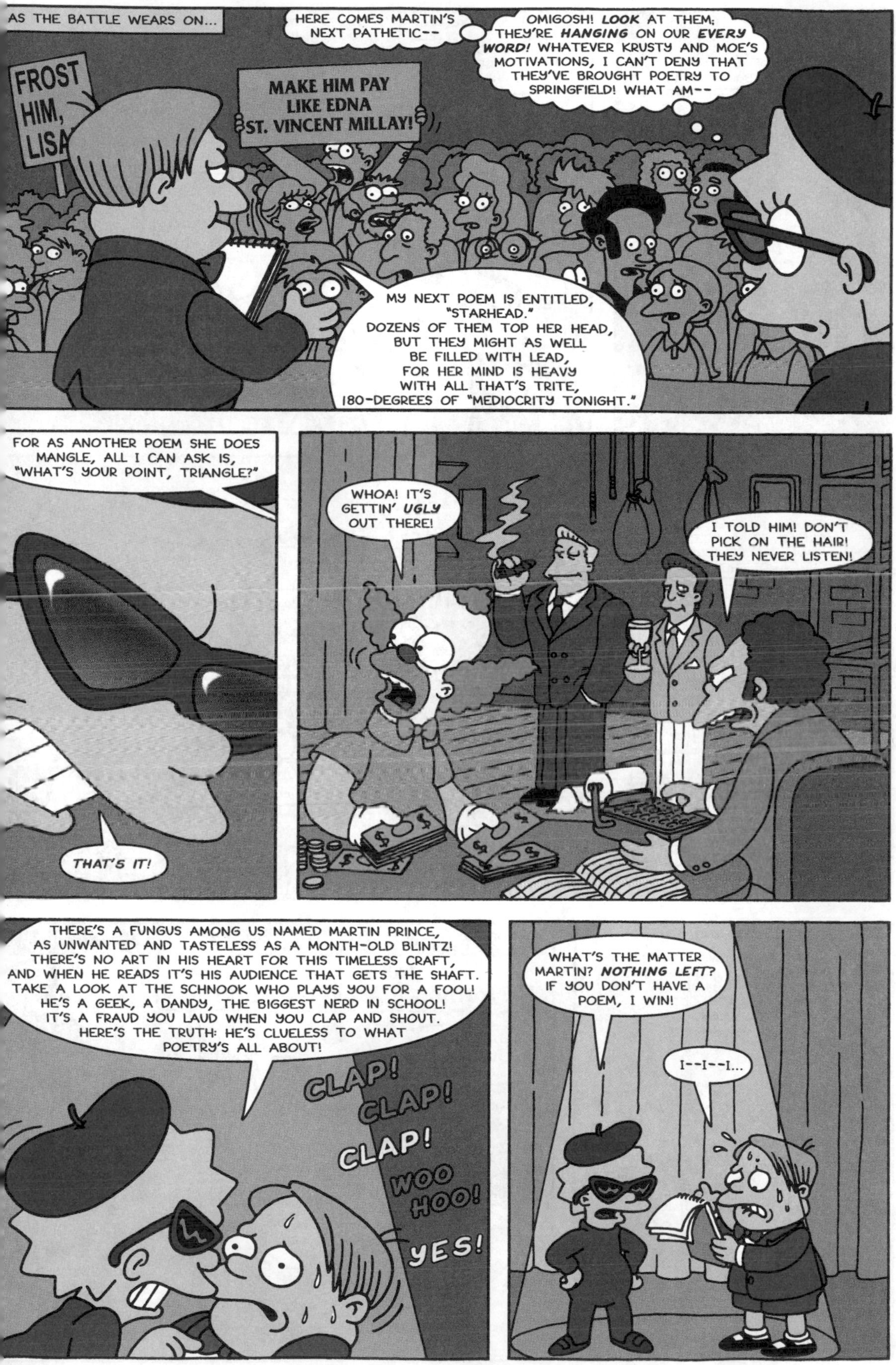
AS THE BATTLE WEARS ON...
HERE COMES MARTIN'S NEXT PATHETIC--
OMIGOSH! LOOK AT THEM; THEY'RE HANGING ON OUR EVERY WORD! WHATEVER KRUSTY AND MOE'S MOTIVATIONS, I CAN'T DENY THAT THEY'VE BROUGHT POETRY TO SPRINGFIELD! WHAT AM--
FROST HIM, LISA
MAKE HIM PAY LIKE EDNA ST. VINCENT MILLAY!
MY NEXT POEM IS ENTITLED, "STARHEAD." DOZENS OF THEM TOP HER HEAD, BUT THEY MIGHT AS WELL BE FILLED WITH LEAD, FOR HER MIND IS HEAVY WITH ALL THAT'S TRITE, 180-DEGREES OF "MEDIOCRITY TONIGHT."
FOR AS ANOTHER POEM SHE DOES MANGLE, ALL I CAN ASK IS, "WHAT'S YOUR POINT, TRIANGLE?"
THAT'S IT!
WHOA! IT'S GETTIN' UGLY OUT THERE!
I TOLD HIM! DON'T PICK ON THE HAIR! THEY NEVER LISTEN!
THERE'S A FUNGUS AMONG US NAMED MARTIN PRINCE, AS UNWANTED AND TASTELESS AS A MONTH-OLD BLINTZ! THERE'S NO ART IN HIS HEART FOR THIS TIMELESS CRAFT, AND WHEN HE READS IT'S HIS AUDIENCE THAT GETS THE SHAFT. TAKE A LOOK AT THE SCHNOOK WHO PLAYS YOU FOR A FOOL! HE'S A GEEK, A DANDY, THE BIGGEST NERD IN SCHOOL! IT'S A FRAUD YOU LAUD WHEN YOU CLAP AND SHOUT. HERE'S THE TRUTH: HE'S CLUELESS TO WHAT POETRY'S ALL ABOUT!
CLAP! CLAP! CLAP! WOO HOO! YES!
WHAT'S THE MATTER MARTIN? NOTHING LEFT? IF YOU DON'T HAVE A POEM, I WIN!
I--I--I...

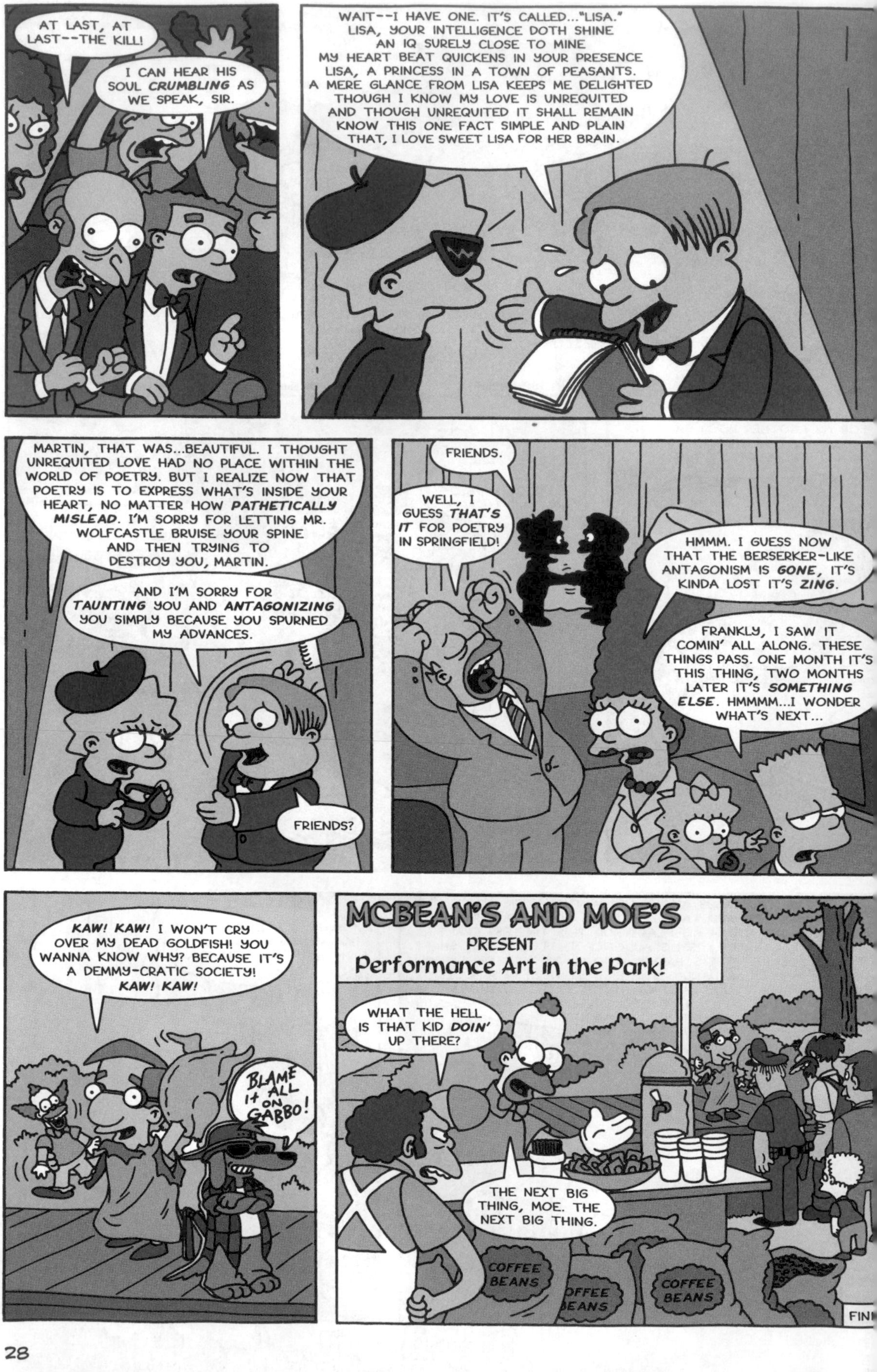
AT LAST, AT LAST--THE KILL!
I CAN HEAR HIS SOUL CRUMBLING AS WE SPEAK, SIR.
WAIT--I HAVE ONE. IT'S CALLED..."LISA." LISA, YOUR INTELLIGENCE DOTH SHINE AN IQ SURELY CLOSE TO MINE MY HEART BEAT QUICKENS IN YOUR PRESENCE LISA, A PRINCESS IN A TOWN OF PEASANTS. A MERE GLANCE FROM LISA KEEPS ME DELIGHTED THOUGH I KNOW MY LOVE IS UNREQUITED AND THOUGH UNREQUITED IT SHALL REMAIN KNOW THIS ONE FACT SIMPLE AND PLAIN THAT, I LOVE SWEET LISA FOR HER BRAIN.
MARTIN, THAT WAS...BEAUTIFUL. I THOUGHT UNREQUITED LOVE HAD NO PLACE WITHIN THE WORLD OF POETRY. BUT I REALIZE NOW THAT POETRY IS TO EXPRESS WHAT'S INSIDE YOUR HEART, NO MATTER HOW PATHETICALLY MISLEAD. I'M SORRY FOR LETTING MR. WOLFCASTLE BRUISE YOUR SPINE AND THEN TRYING TO DESTROY YOU, MARTIN.
AND I'M SORRY FOR TAUNTING YOU AND ANTAGONIZING YOU SIMPLY BECAUSE YOU SPURNED MY ADVANCES.
FRIENDS?
FRIENDS.
WELL, I GUESS THAT'S IT FOR POETRY IN SPRINGFIELD!
HMMM. I GUESS NOW THAT THE BERSERKER-LIKE ANTAGONISM IS GONE, IT'S KINDA LOST IT'S ZING.
FRANKLY, I SAW IT COMIN' ALL ALONG. THESE THINGS PASS. ONE MONTH IT'S THIS THING, TWO MONTHS LATER IT'S SOMETHING ELSE. HMMMM...I WONDER WHAT'S NEXT...
KAW! KAW! I WON'T CRY OVER MY DEAD GOLDFISH! YOU WANNA KNOW WHY? BECAUSE IT'S A DEMMY-CRATIC SOCIETY! KAW! KAW!
BLAME it ALL on GABBO!
MCBEAN'S AND MOE'S PRESENT Performance Art in the Park!
WHAT THE HELL IS THAT KID DOIN' UP THERE?
THE NEXT BIG THING, MOE. THE NEXT BIG THING.
COFFEE BEANS
OFFEE BEANS
COFFEE BEANS
FIN

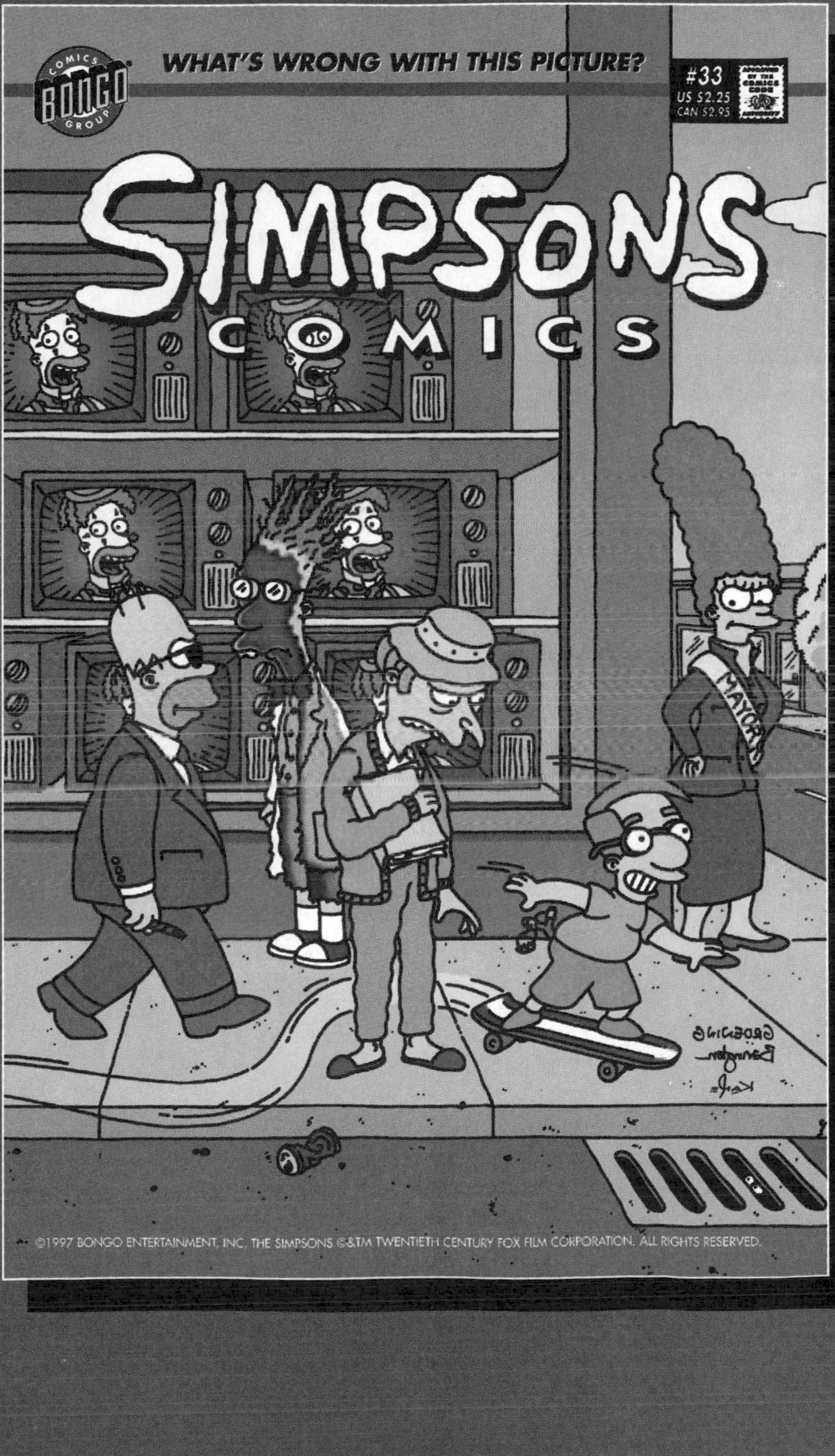
COMICS BONGO GROUP
WHAT'S WRONG WITH THIS PICTURE?
#33
US $2.25
CAN $2.95
SIMPSONS
COMICS
MAYOR
©1997 BONGO ENTERTAINMENT, INC. THE SIMPSONS ©&TM TWENTIETH CENTURY FOX FILM CORPORATION. ALL RIGHTS RESERVED.

Principal Skinner's Bottom 40

40. The first day of yet another school year
39. Wretched, ungrateful students who fail to appreciate the priceless gift we educators are trying to bestow upon them
38. Hooliganism
37. Having to actually eat in the cafeteria occasionally, to keep up appearances
36. Students who don't clean their plates
35. Recurrent screaming nightmares that I am a grade school principal
34. The way Groundskeeper Willie always fertilizes whichever section of the school grounds is upwind from my office window
33. "Talent" Night
32. The way the sound of a cherry-bombed toilet sets off my Vietnam flashbacks
31. Food fights
30. The smell of the teachers' lounge
29. When a trusted hall monitor goes bad
28. Whoever is drinking out of the flask I keep in my bottom drawer
27. Unflattering caricatures of me spraypainted on school walls
26. Namby-pamby school board members who won't allow kids to be spanked like in the good old days
25. The ongoing failure of the Springfield School Board to name me "Principal of the Year"
24. Teachers who lack the gumption to flunk their entire class
23. Water balloons
22. Comic books
21. Slingshots
20. Stink bombs
19. Mayhem
18. Kids who won't snitch on their friends

17. The embarrassment of yet another 0-14 season for our Junior Pumas soccer team
16. Having to change my unlisted home pho number 21 times in the last year—and still they call
15. Whoever started the vicious rumor tha wear a toupee
14. Disorder
13. Whoever keeps writing, "I AM A WIENER" in the dirt on my car's back window
12. Parent-teacher meetings
11. Faculty meetings
10. Uppity teachers who think they are more important to this institution than I am
9. The fact that the kids have learned my childhood nickname "Spanky"
8. Seeing former students go on to achieve great success in the outside world— fortunately, very few of them have
7. Boom boxes
6. T-shirts with slogans that encourage disrespect for authority
5. Snotty little punks who laugh at me beh my back
4. Knowing I have to endure another 17 years of this living hell before I can ta early retirement
3. Underachievers who are proud of it
2. Bart Simpson
1. El Barto—whoever you are, I vow that someday I will make you pay!

MATT GROENING

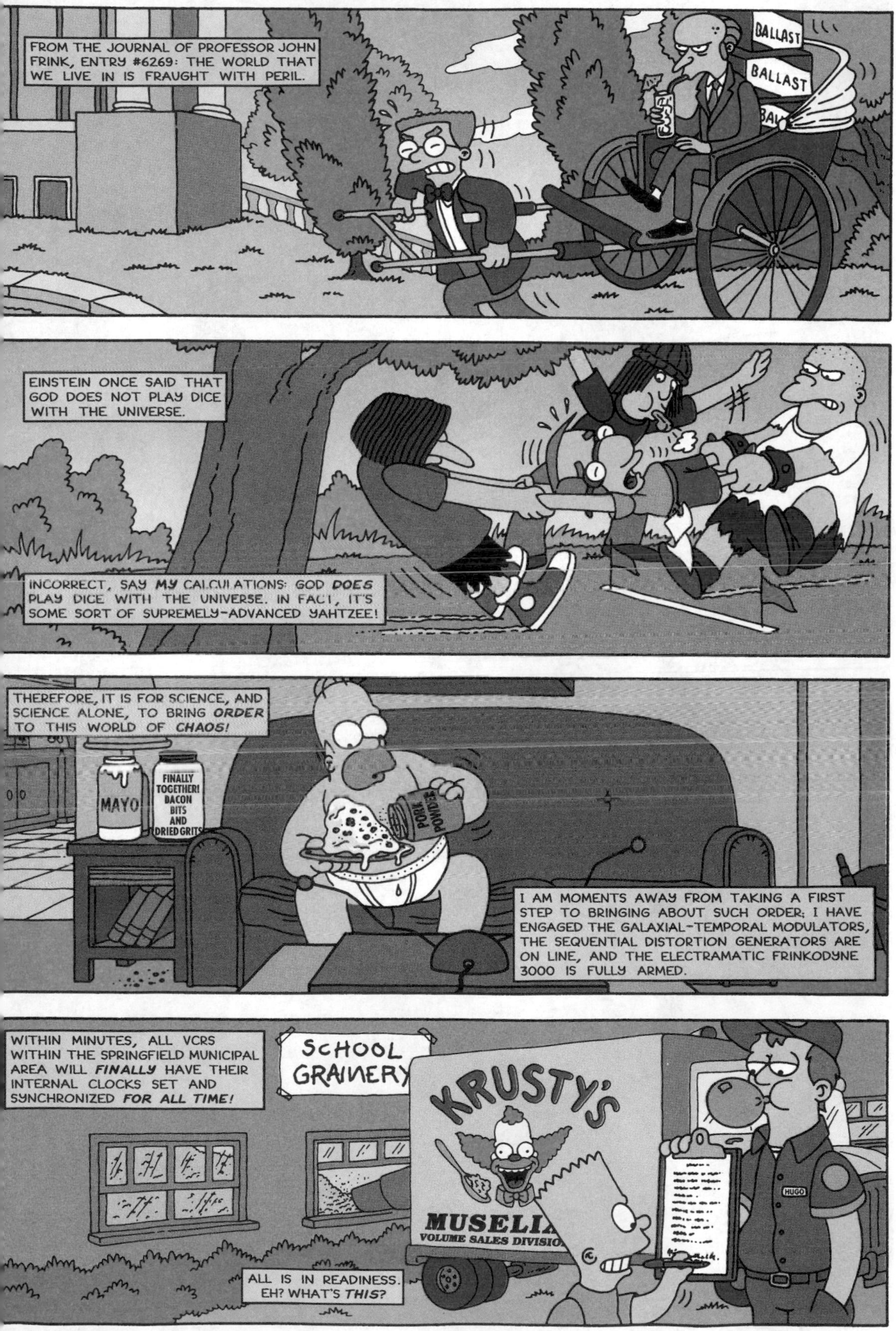
FROM THE JOURNAL OF PROFESSOR JOHN FRINK, ENTRY #6269: THE WORLD THAT WE LIVE IN IS FRAUGHT WITH PERIL.
BALLAST
BALLAST
EINSTEIN ONCE SAID THAT GOD DOES NOT PLAY DICE WITH THE UNIVERSE.
INCORRECT, SAY MY CALCULATIONS: GOD DOES PLAY DICE WITH THE UNIVERSE. IN FACT, IT'S SOME SORT OF SUPREMELY-ADVANCED YAHTZEE!
THEREFORE, IT IS FOR SCIENCE, AND SCIENCE ALONE, TO BRING ORDER TO THIS WORLD OF CHAOS!
MAYO
FINALLY TOGETHER! BACON BITS AND DRIED GRITS
PORK POWDER
I AM MOMENTS AWAY FROM TAKING A FIRST STEP TO BRINGING ABOUT SUCH ORDER: I HAVE ENGAGED THE GALAXIAL-TEMPORAL MODULATORS, THE SEQUENTIAL DISTORTION GENERATORS ARE ON LINE, AND THE ELECTRAMATIC FRINKODYNE 3000 IS FULLY ARMED.
WITHIN MINUTES, ALL VCRS WITHIN THE SPRINGFIELD MUNICIPAL AREA WILL FINALLY HAVE THEIR INTERNAL CLOCKS SET AND SYNCHRONIZED FOR ALL TIME!
SCHOOL GRAINERY
KRUSTY'S
MUSELI
VOLUME SALES DIVISIO
HUGO
ALL IS IN READINESS. EH? WHAT'S THIS?

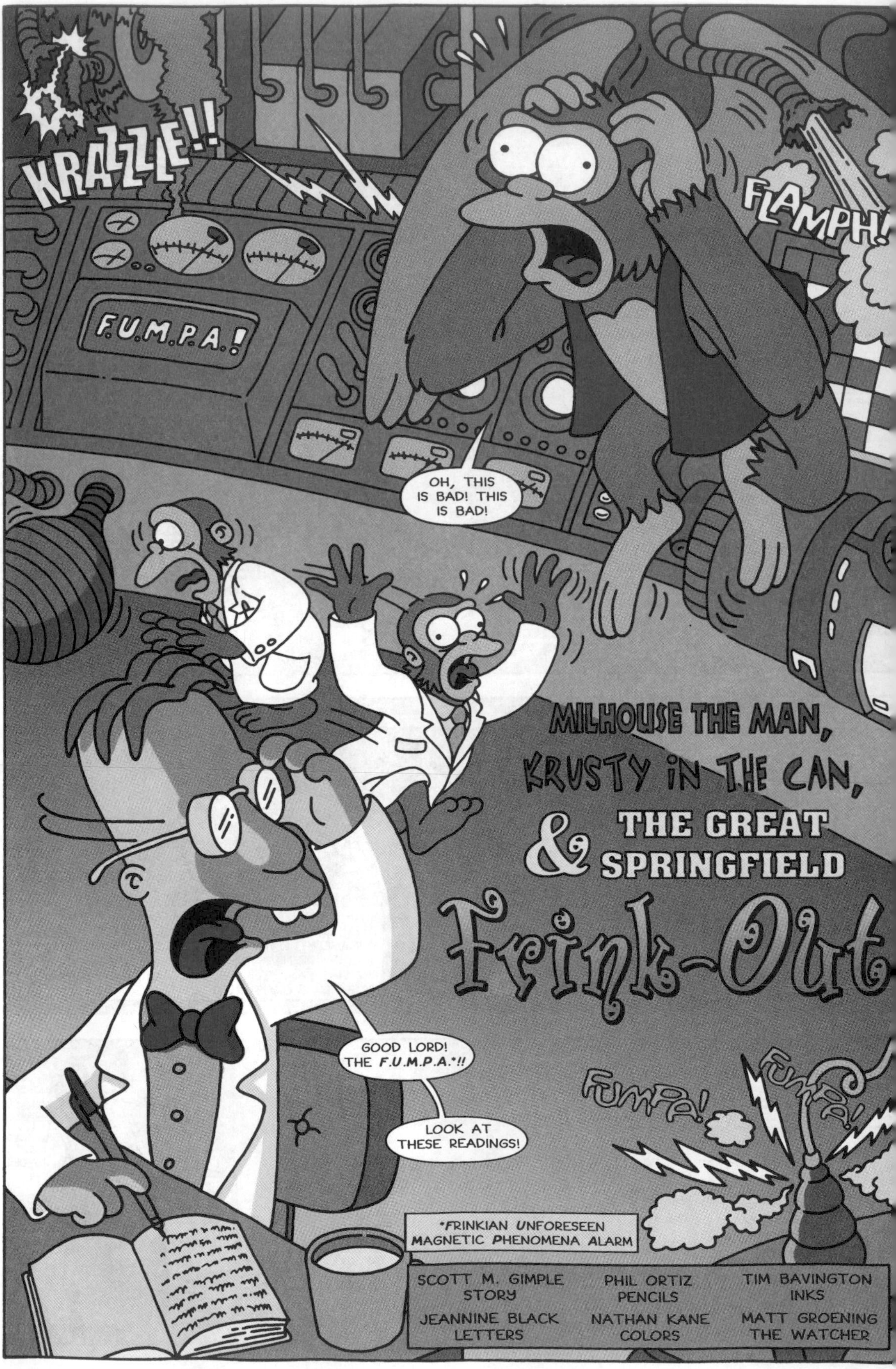
KRAZZLE!!
FLAMPH!
F.U.M.P.A.!
OH, THIS IS BAD! THIS IS BAD!
MILHOUSE THE MAN, KRUSTY IN THE CAN, & THE GREAT SPRINGFIELD Frink-Out
GOOD LORD! THE F.U.M.P.A.*!!
LOOK AT THESE READINGS!
FUMPA!
FUMPA!
*FRINKIAN UNFORESEEN MAGNETIC PHENOMENA ALARM
SCOTT M. GIMPLE STORY
PHIL ORTIZ PENCILS
TIM BAVINGTON INKS
JEANNINE BLACK LETTERS
NATHAN KANE COLORS
MATT GROENING THE WATCHER

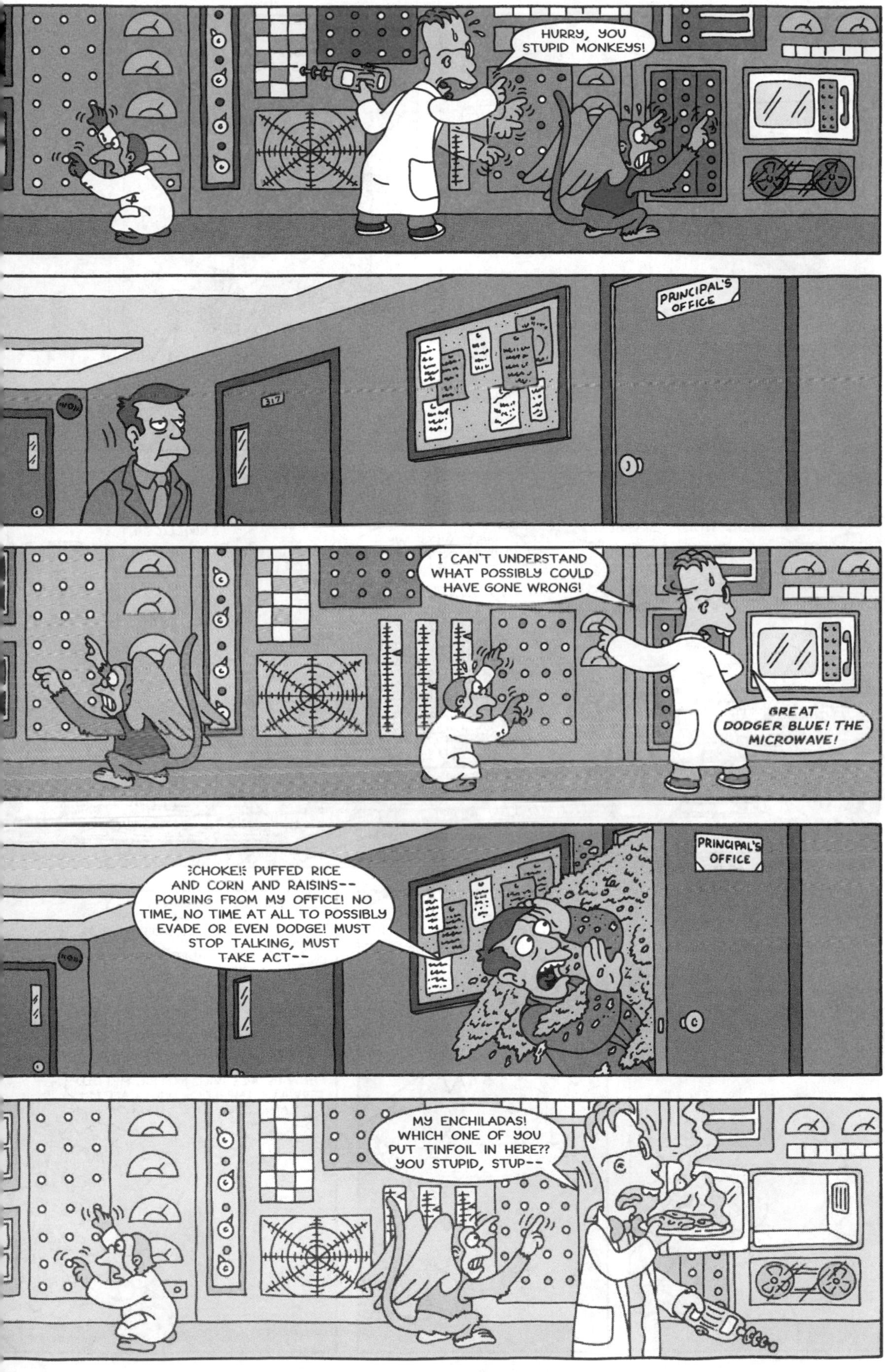
HURRY, YOU STUPID MONKEYS!
PRINCIPAL'S OFFICE
I CAN'T UNDERSTAND WHAT POSSIBLY COULD HAVE GONE WRONG!
GREAT DODGER BLUE! THE MICROWAVE!
PRINCIPAL'S OFFICE
CHOKE! PUFFED RICE AND CORN AND RAISINS-- POURING FROM MY OFFICE! NO TIME, NO TIME AT ALL TO POSSIBLY EVADE OR EVEN DODGE! MUST STOP TALKING, MUST TAKE ACT--
MY ENCHILADAS! WHICH ONE OF YOU PUT TINFOIL IN HERE?? YOU STUPID, STUP--

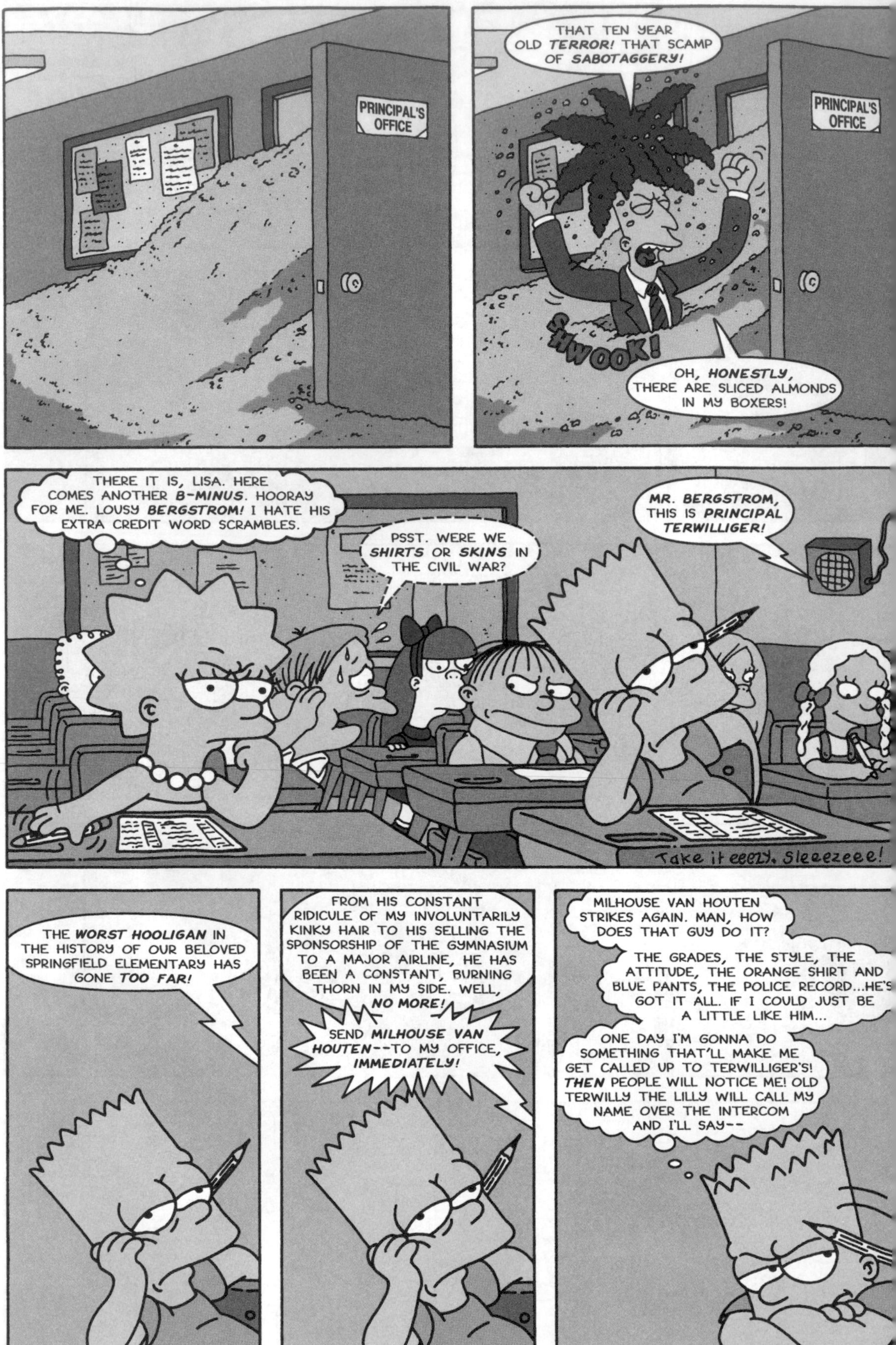
PRINCIPAL'S OFFICE
THAT TEN YEAR OLD TERROR! THAT SCAMP OF SABOTAGGERY!
PRINCIPAL'S OFFICE
SHWOOK!
OH, HONESTLY, THERE ARE SLICED ALMONDS IN MY BOXERS!
THERE IT IS, LISA. HERE COMES ANOTHER B-MINUS. HOORAY FOR ME. LOUSY BERGSTROM! I HATE HIS EXTRA CREDIT WORD SCRAMBLES.
PSST. WERE WE SHIRTS OR SKINS IN THE CIVIL WAR?
MR. BERGSTROM, THIS IS PRINCIPAL TERWILLIGER!
Take it eeezy. Sleeezeee!
THE WORST HOOLIGAN IN THE HISTORY OF OUR BELOVED SPRINGFIELD ELEMENTARY HAS GONE TOO FAR!
FROM HIS CONSTANT RIDICULE OF MY INVOLUNTARILY KINKY HAIR TO HIS SELLING THE SPONSORSHIP OF THE GYMNASIUM TO A MAJOR AIRLINE, HE HAS BEEN A CONSTANT, BURNING THORN IN MY SIDE. WELL, NO MORE!
SEND MILHOUSE VAN HOUTEN--TO MY OFFICE, IMMEDIATELY!
MILHOUSE VAN HOUTEN STRIKES AGAIN. MAN, HOW DOES THAT GUY DO IT?
THE GRADES, THE STYLE, THE ATTITUDE, THE ORANGE SHIRT AND BLUE PANTS, THE POLICE RECORD...HE'S GOT IT ALL. IF I COULD JUST BE A LITTLE LIKE HIM...
ONE DAY I'M GONNA DO SOMETHING THAT'LL MAKE ME GET CALLED UP TO TERWILLIGER'S! THEN PEOPLE WILL NOTICE ME! OLD TERWILLY THE LILLY WILL CALL MY NAME OVER THE INTERCOM AND I'LL SAY--

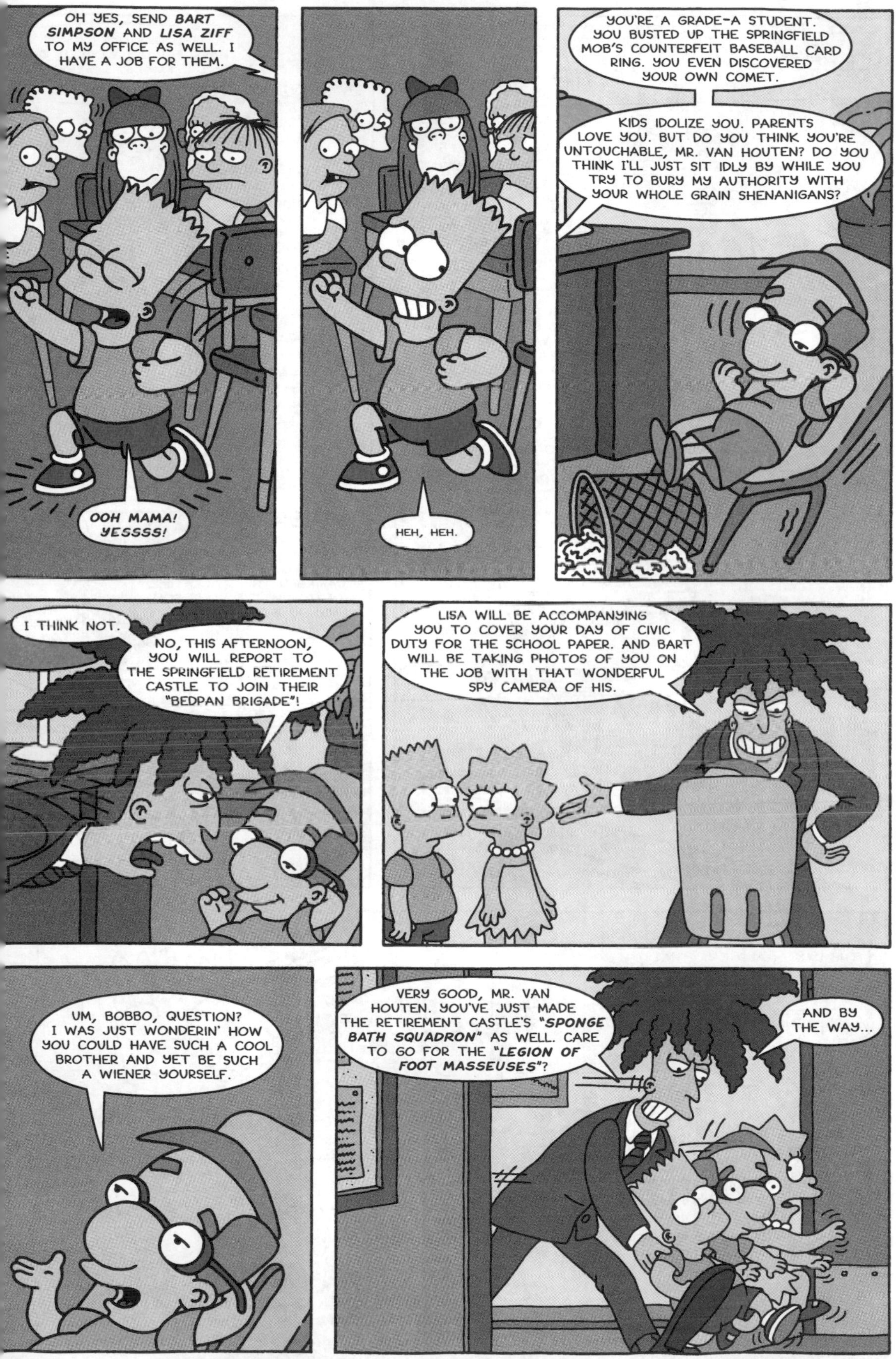
OH YES, SEND **BART SIMPSON** AND **LISA ZIFF** TO MY OFFICE AS WELL. I HAVE A JOB FOR THEM.
OOH MAMA! YESSSS!
HEH, HEH.
YOU'RE A GRADE-A STUDENT. YOU BUSTED UP THE SPRINGFIELD MOB'S COUNTERFEIT BASEBALL CARD RING. YOU EVEN DISCOVERED YOUR OWN COMET.
KIDS IDOLIZE YOU. PARENTS LOVE YOU. BUT DO YOU THINK YOU'RE UNTOUCHABLE, MR. VAN HOUTEN? DO YOU THINK I'LL JUST SIT IDLY BY WHILE YOU TRY TO BURY MY AUTHORITY WITH YOUR WHOLE GRAIN SHENANIGANS?
I THINK NOT.
NO, THIS AFTERNOON, YOU WILL REPORT TO THE SPRINGFIELD RETIREMENT CASTLE TO JOIN THEIR "BEDPAN BRIGADE"!
LISA WILL BE ACCOMPANYING YOU TO COVER YOUR DAY OF CIVIC DUTY FOR THE SCHOOL PAPER. AND BART WILL BE TAKING PHOTOS OF YOU ON THE JOB WITH THAT WONDERFUL SPY CAMERA OF HIS.
UM, BOBBO, QUESTION? I WAS JUST WONDERIN' HOW YOU COULD HAVE SUCH A COOL BROTHER AND YET BE SUCH A WIENER YOURSELF.
VERY GOOD, MR. VAN HOUTEN. YOU'VE JUST MADE THE RETIREMENT CASTLE'S ***"SPONGE BATH SQUADRON"*** AS WELL. CARE TO GO FOR THE ***"LEGION OF FOOT MASSEUSES"***?
AND BY THE WAY...

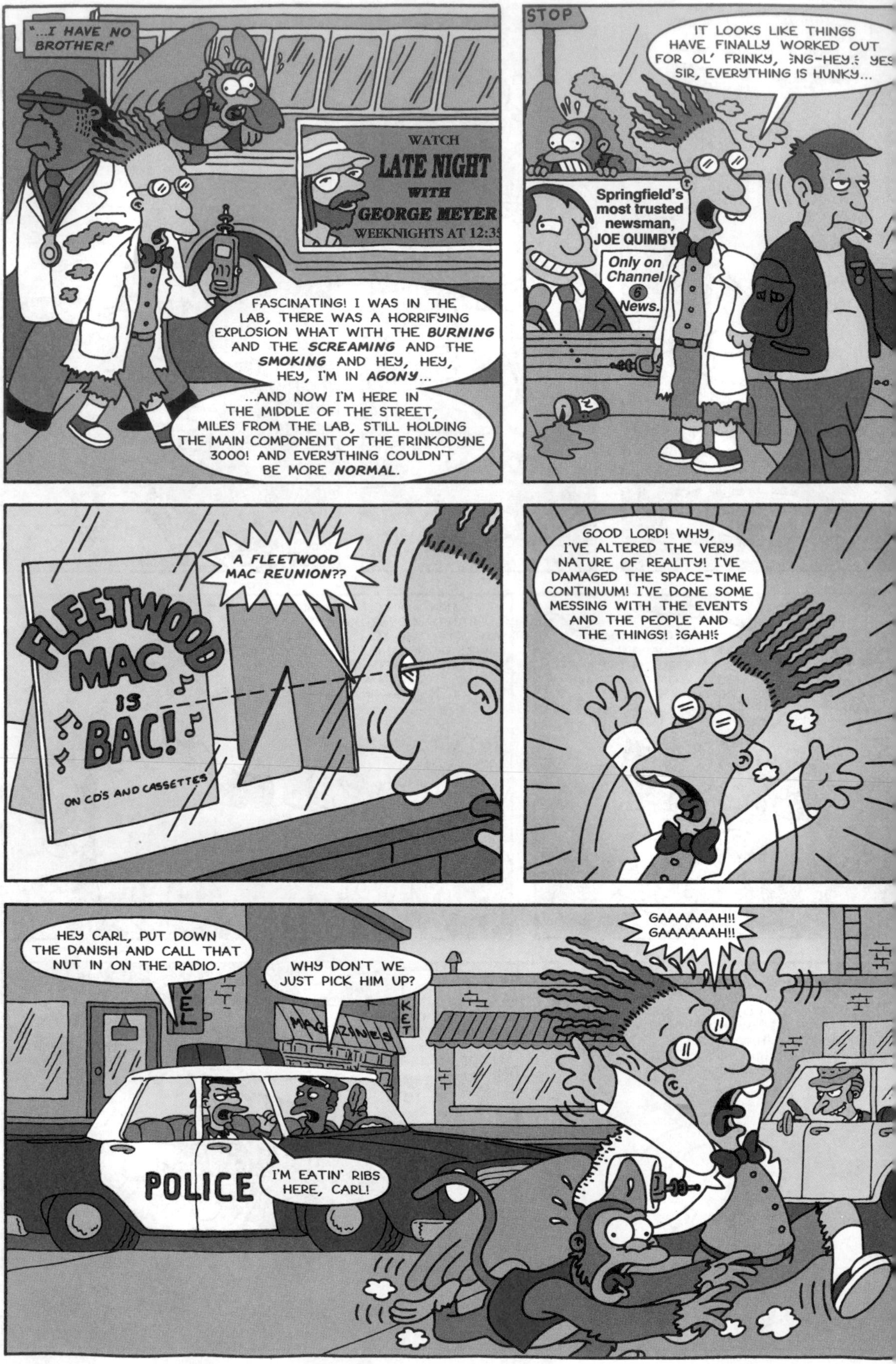
"...I HAVE NO BROTHER!"
WATCH LATE NIGHT WITH GEORGE MEYER WEEKNIGHTS AT 12:35
FASCINATING! I WAS IN THE LAB, THERE WAS A HORRIFYING EXPLOSION WHAT WITH THE BURNING AND THE SCREAMING AND THE SMOKING AND HEY, HEY, HEY, I'M IN AGONY...
...AND NOW I'M HERE IN THE MIDDLE OF THE STREET, MILES FROM THE LAB, STILL HOLDING THE MAIN COMPONENT OF THE FRINKODYNE 3000! AND EVERYTHING COULDN'T BE MORE NORMAL.
STOP
IT LOOKS LIKE THINGS HAVE FINALLY WORKED OUT FOR OL' FRINKY, ƎNG-HEY.Ǝ YES SIR, EVERYTHING IS HUNKY...
Springfield's most trusted newsman, JOE QUIMBY
Only on Channel 6 News.
A FLEETWOOD MAC REUNION??
FLEETWOOD MAC IS BAC!
ON CD'S AND CASSETTES
GOOD LORD! WHY, I'VE ALTERED THE VERY NATURE OF REALITY! I'VE DAMAGED THE SPACE-TIME CONTINUUM! I'VE DONE SOME MESSING WITH THE EVENTS AND THE PEOPLE AND THE THINGS! ƎGAH!Ǝ
HEY CARL, PUT DOWN THE DANISH AND CALL THAT NUT IN ON THE RADIO.
WHY DON'T WE JUST PICK HIM UP?
I'M EATIN' RIBS HERE, CARL!
GAAAAAAH!! GAAAAAAH!!
MAGAZINES
POLICE

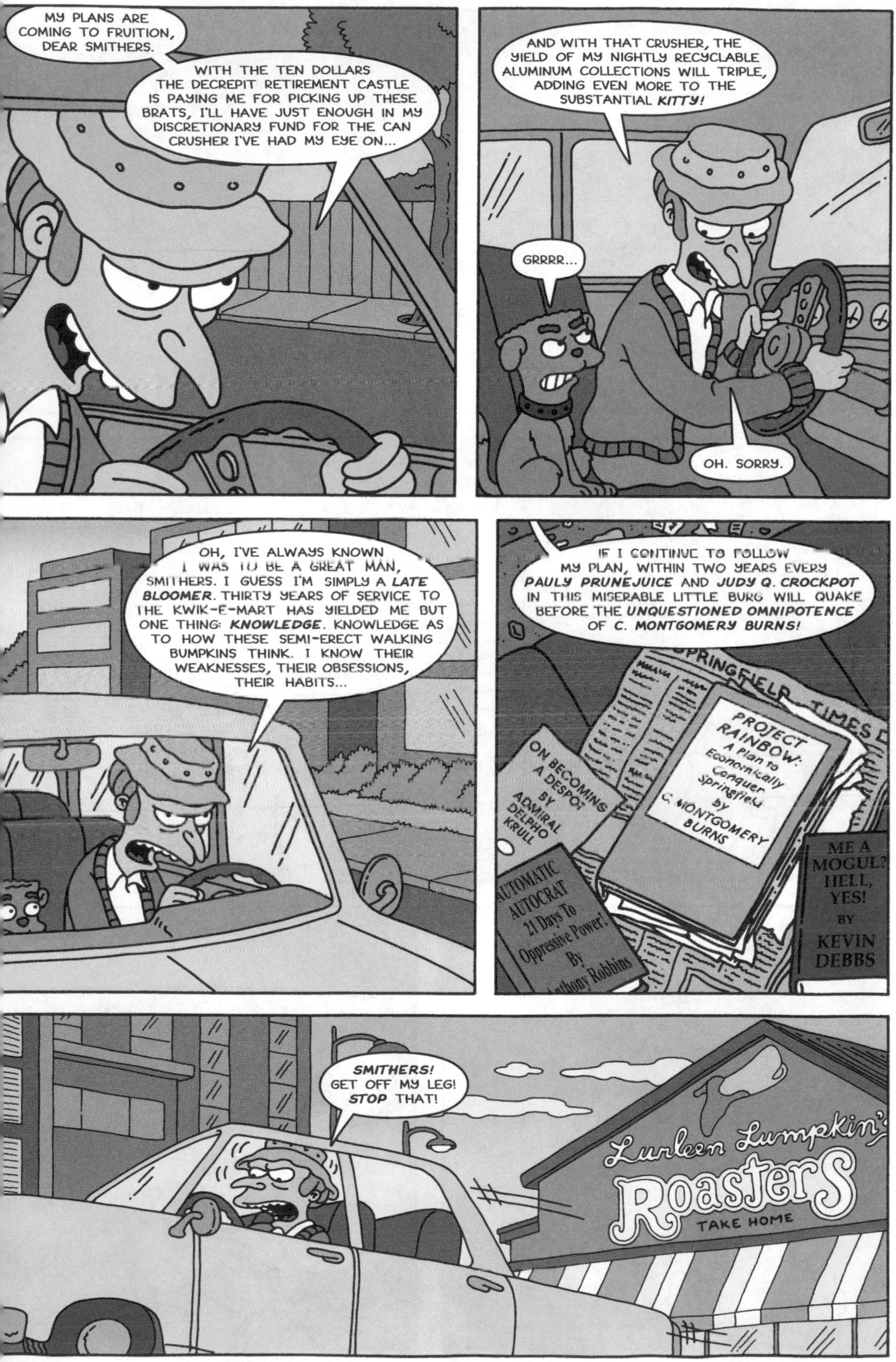
MY PLANS ARE COMING TO FRUITION, DEAR SMITHERS.
WITH THE TEN DOLLARS THE DECREPIT RETIREMENT CASTLE IS PAYING ME FOR PICKING UP THESE BRATS, I'LL HAVE JUST ENOUGH IN MY DISCRETIONARY FUND FOR THE CAN CRUSHER I'VE HAD MY EYE ON...
AND WITH THAT CRUSHER, THE YIELD OF MY NIGHTLY RECYCLABLE ALUMINUM COLLECTIONS WILL TRIPLE, ADDING EVEN MORE TO THE SUBSTANTIAL *KITTY!*
GRRRR...
OH. SORRY.
OH, I'VE ALWAYS KNOWN I WAS TO BE A GREAT MAN, SMITHERS. I GUESS I'M SIMPLY A *LATE BLOOMER*. THIRTY YEARS OF SERVICE TO THE KWIK-E-MART HAS YIELDED ME BUT ONE THING: *KNOWLEDGE*. KNOWLEDGE AS TO HOW THESE SEMI-ERECT WALKING BUMPKINS THINK. I KNOW THEIR WEAKNESSES, THEIR OBSESSIONS, THEIR HABITS...
IF I CONTINUE TO FOLLOW MY PLAN, WITHIN TWO YEARS EVERY *PAULY PRUNEJUICE* AND *JUDY Q. CROCKPOT* IN THIS MISERABLE LITTLE BURG WILL QUAKE BEFORE THE *UNQUESTIONED OMNIPOTENCE* OF *C. MONTGOMERY BURNS!*
SPRINGFIELD TIMES
PROJECT RAINBOW: A Plan to Economically Conquer Springfield by C. MONTGOMERY BURNS
ON BECOMING A DESPOT BY ADMIRAL DELPHO KRULL
AUTOMATIC AUTOCRAT 21 Days To Oppressive Power! By Anthony Robbins
ME A MOGUL? HELL, YES! BY KEVIN DEBBS
SMITHERS! GET OFF MY LEG! *STOP* THAT!
Lurleen Lumpkin's
Roasters
TAKE HOME

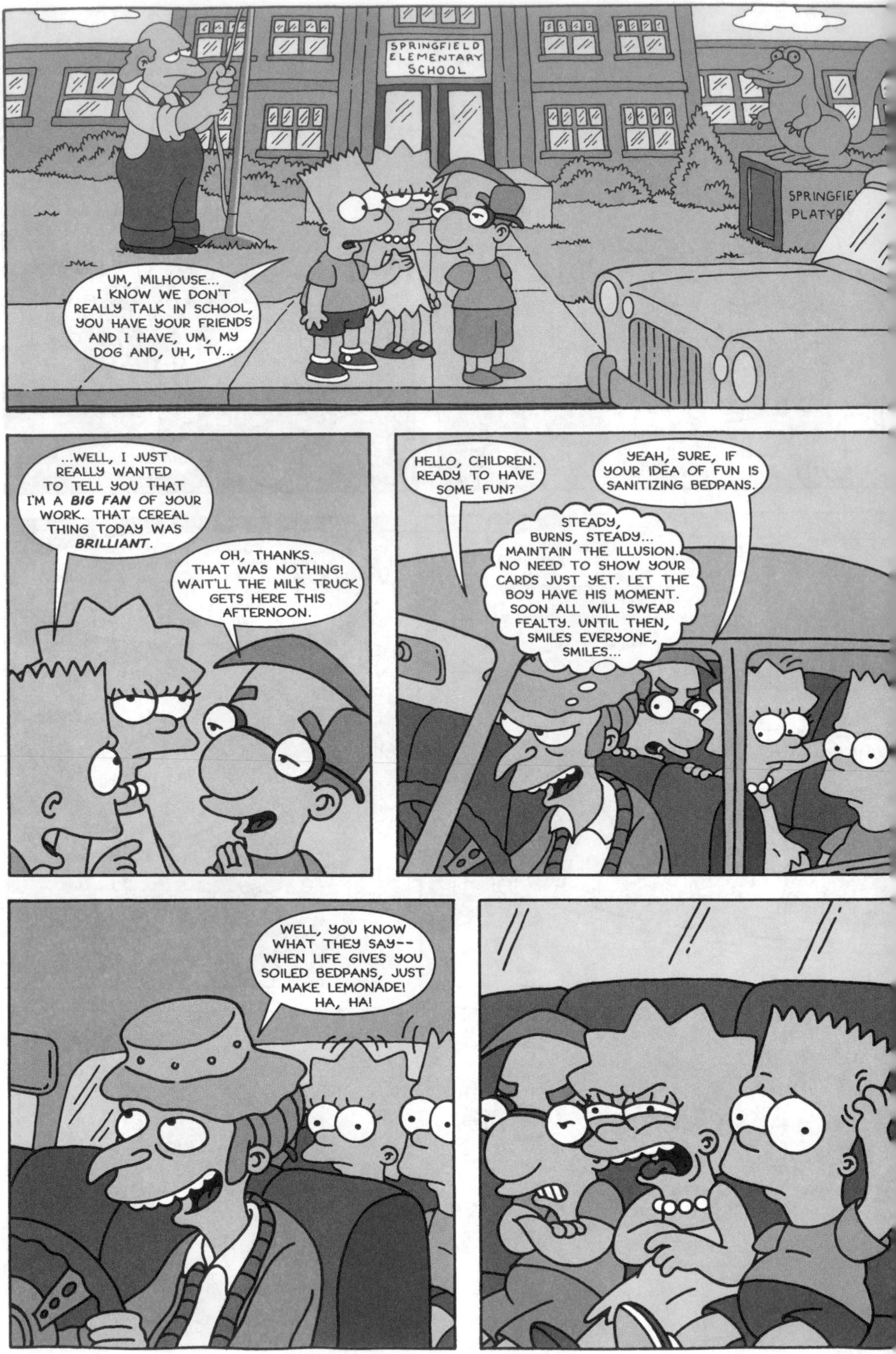
SPRINGFIELD ELEMENTARY SCHOOL
UM, MILHOUSE... I KNOW WE DON'T REALLY TALK IN SCHOOL, YOU HAVE YOUR FRIENDS AND I HAVE, UM, MY DOG AND, UH, TV...
...WELL, I JUST REALLY WANTED TO TELL YOU THAT I'M A BIG FAN OF YOUR WORK. THAT CEREAL THING TODAY WAS BRILLIANT.
OH, THANKS. THAT WAS NOTHING! WAIT'LL THE MILK TRUCK GETS HERE THIS AFTERNOON.
HELLO, CHILDREN. READY TO HAVE SOME FUN?
YEAH, SURE, IF YOUR IDEA OF FUN IS SANITIZING BEDPANS.
STEADY, BURNS, STEADY... MAINTAIN THE ILLUSION. NO NEED TO SHOW YOUR CARDS JUST YET. LET THE BOY HAVE HIS MOMENT. SOON ALL WILL SWEAR FEALTY. UNTIL THEN, SMILES EVERYONE, SMILES...
WELL, YOU KNOW WHAT THEY SAY-- WHEN LIFE GIVES YOU SOILED BEDPANS, JUST MAKE LEMONADE! HA, HA!

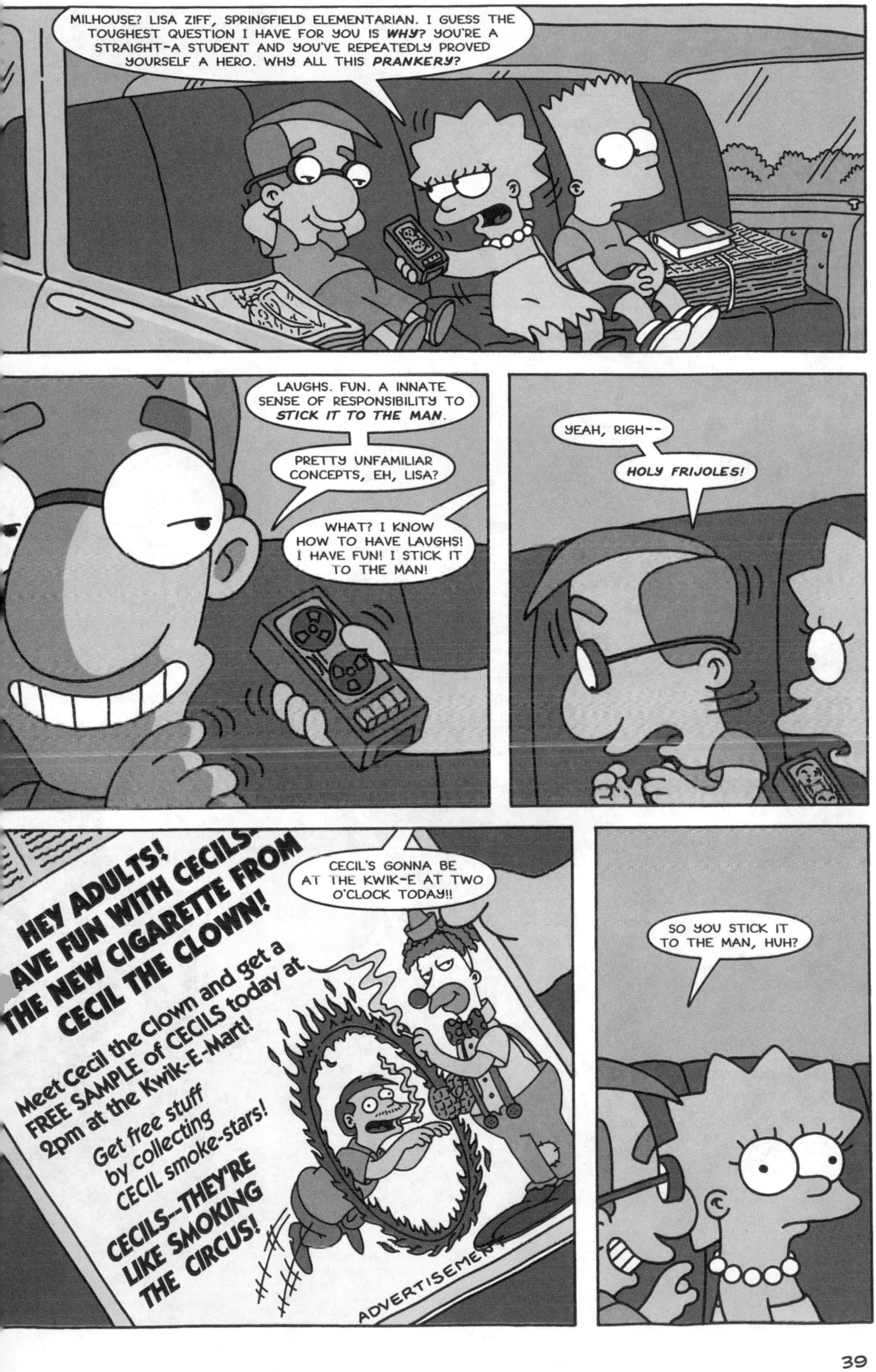
MILHOUSE? LISA ZIFF, SPRINGFIELD ELEMENTARIAN. I GUESS THE TOUGHEST QUESTION I HAVE FOR YOU IS WHY? YOU'RE A STRAIGHT-A STUDENT AND YOU'VE REPEATEDLY PROVED YOURSELF A HERO. WHY ALL THIS PRANKERY?
LAUGHS. FUN. A INNATE SENSE OF RESPONSIBILITY TO STICK IT TO THE MAN.
PRETTY UNFAMILIAR CONCEPTS, EH, LISA?
WHAT? I KNOW HOW TO HAVE LAUGHS! I HAVE FUN! I STICK IT TO THE MAN!
YEAH, RIGH--
HOLY FRIJOLES!
CECIL'S GONNA BE AT THE KWIK-E AT TWO O'CLOCK TODAY!!
HEY ADULTS!
AVE FUN WITH CECILS:
THE NEW CIGARETTE FROM
CECIL THE CLOWN!
Meet Cecil the Clown and get a
FREE SAMPLE of CECILS today at
2pm at the Kwik-E-Mart!
Get free stuff
by collecting
CECIL smoke-stars!
CECILS--THEY'RE
LIKE SMOKING
THE CIRCUS!
ADVERTISEMENT
SO YOU STICK IT TO THE MAN, HUH?

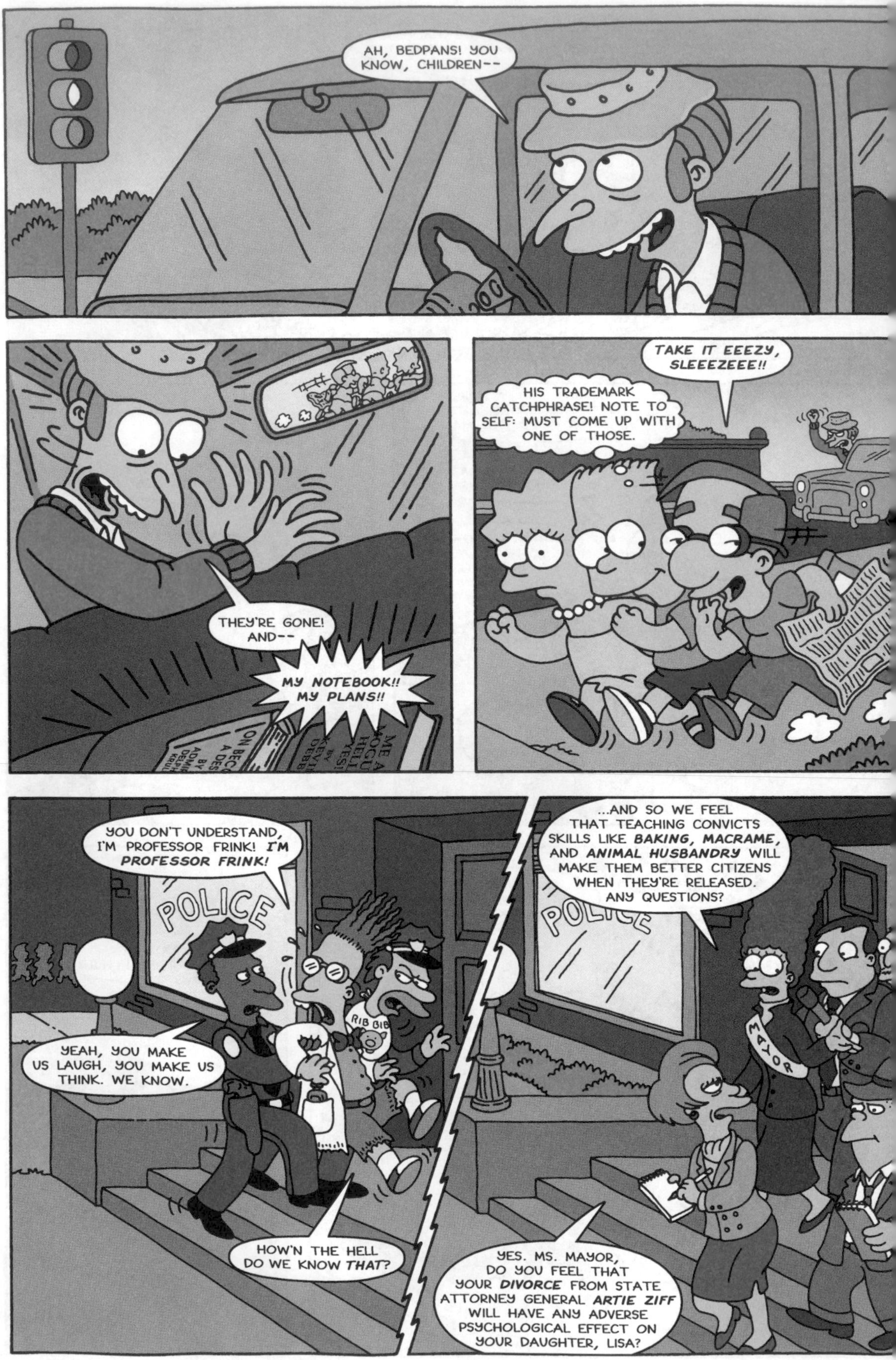
AH, BEDPANS! YOU KNOW, CHILDREN--
THEY'RE GONE! AND--
MY NOTEBOOK!! MY PLANS!!
TAKE IT EEEZY, SLEEEZEEE!!
HIS TRADEMARK CATCHPHRASE! NOTE TO SELF: MUST COME UP WITH ONE OF THOSE.
YOU DON'T UNDERSTAND, I'M PROFESSOR FRINK! I'M PROFESSOR FRINK!
POLICE
RIB BIB
YEAH, YOU MAKE US LAUGH, YOU MAKE US THINK. WE KNOW.
HOW'N THE HELL DO WE KNOW THAT?
...AND SO WE FEEL THAT TEACHING CONVICTS SKILLS LIKE BAKING, MACRAME, AND ANIMAL HUSBANDRY WILL MAKE THEM BETTER CITIZENS WHEN THEY'RE RELEASED. ANY QUESTIONS?
POLICE
MAYOR
YES. MS. MAYOR, DO YOU FEEL THAT YOUR DIVORCE FROM STATE ATTORNEY GENERAL ARTIE ZIFF WILL HAVE ANY ADVERSE PSYCHOLOGICAL EFFECT ON YOUR DAUGHTER, LISA?

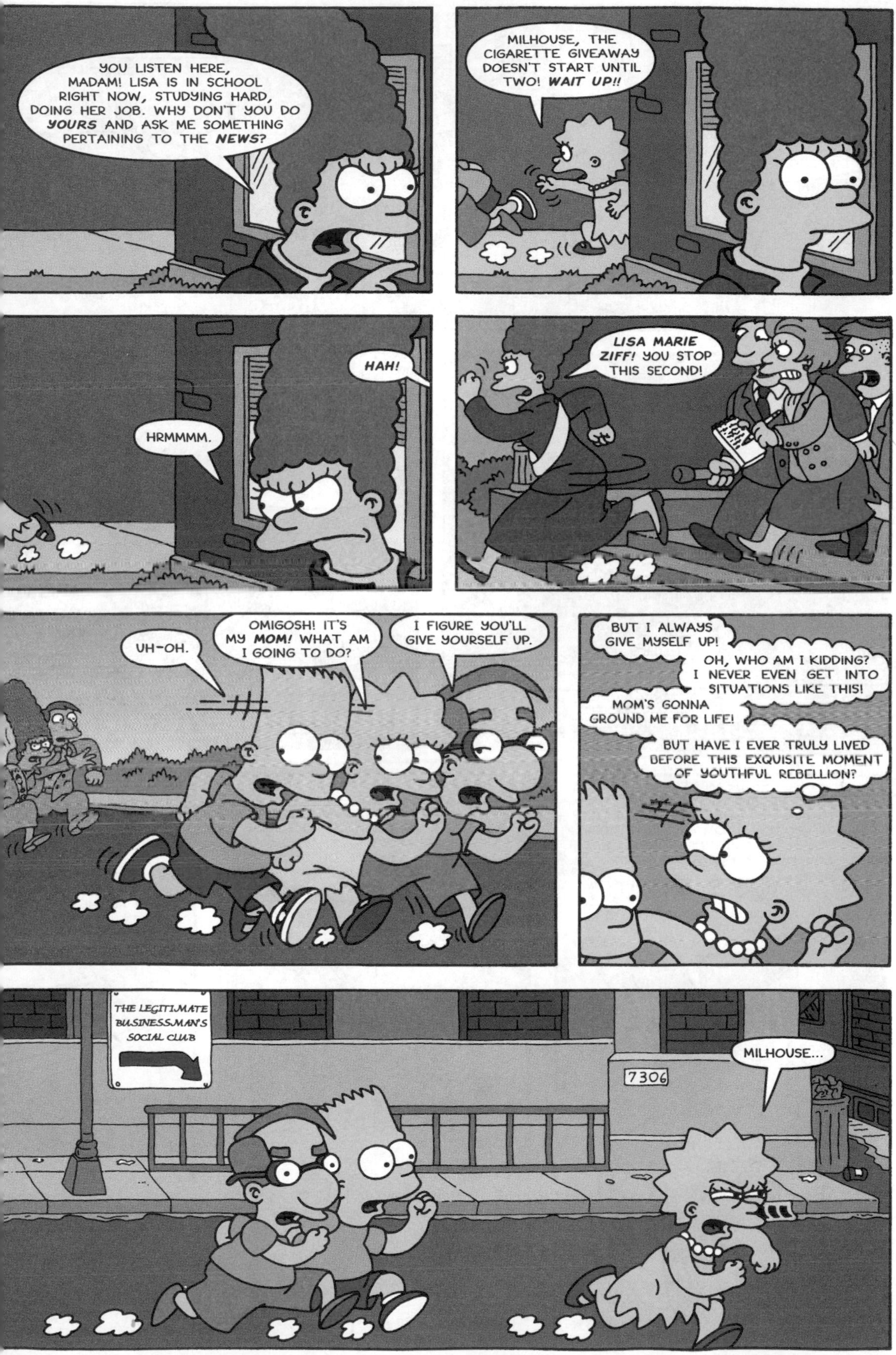
YOU LISTEN HERE, MADAM! LISA IS IN SCHOOL RIGHT NOW, STUDYING HARD, DOING HER JOB. WHY DON'T YOU DO *YOURS* AND ASK ME SOMETHING PERTAINING TO THE *NEWS*?
MILHOUSE, THE CIGARETTE GIVEAWAY DOESN'T START UNTIL TWO! *WAIT UP!!*
HRMMMM.
HAH!
LISA MARIE ZIFF! YOU STOP THIS SECOND!
UH-OH.
OMIGOSH! IT'S MY *MOM!* WHAT AM I GOING TO DO?
I FIGURE YOU'LL GIVE YOURSELF UP.
BUT I ALWAYS GIVE MYSELF UP!
OH, WHO AM I KIDDING? I NEVER EVEN GET INTO SITUATIONS LIKE THIS!
MOM'S GONNA GROUND ME FOR LIFE!
BUT HAVE I EVER TRULY LIVED BEFORE THIS EXQUISITE MOMENT OF YOUTHFUL REBELLION?
THE LEGITIMATE BUSINESSMAN'S SOCIAL CLUB
7306
MILHOUSE...

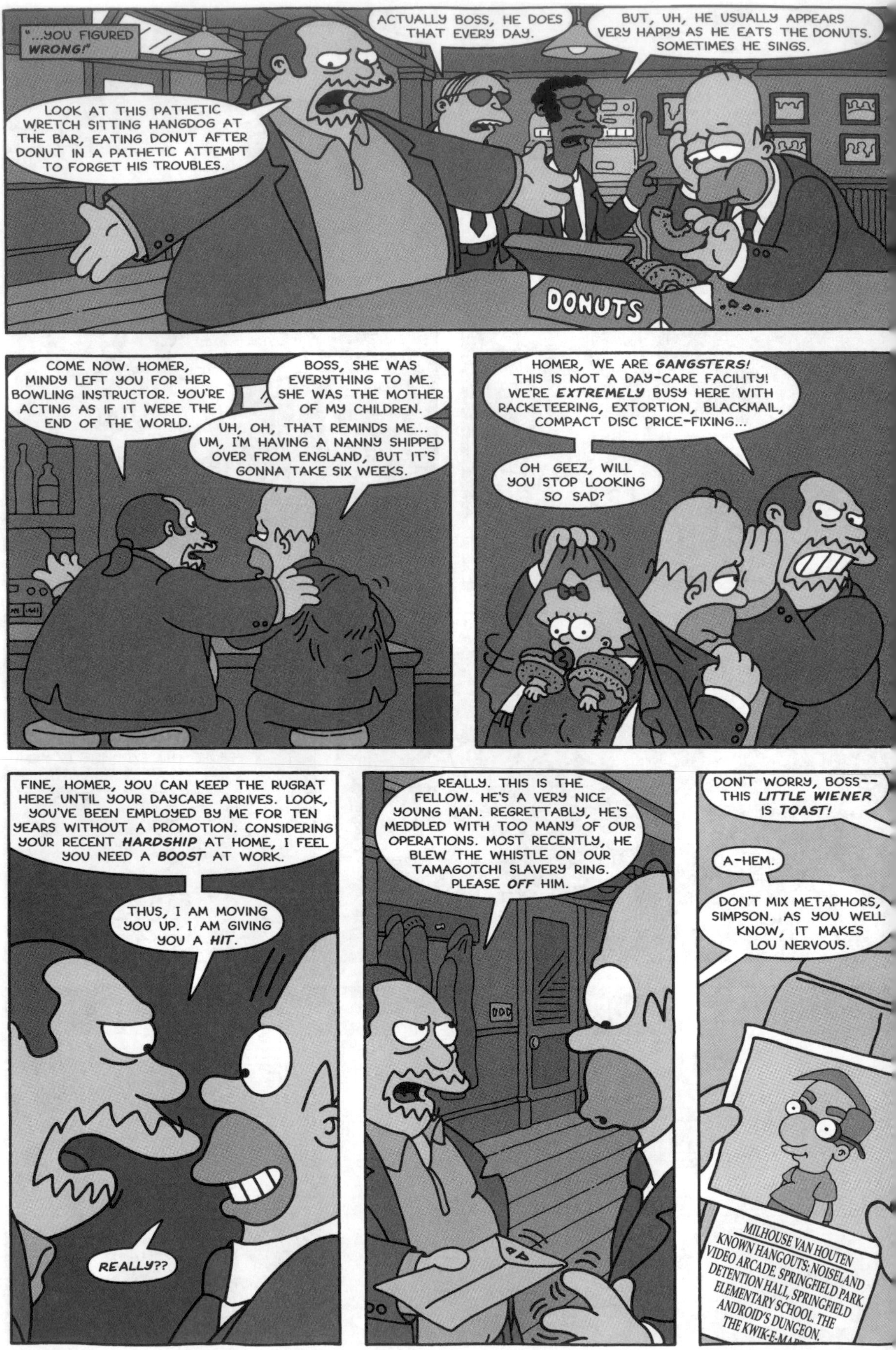

"...YOU FIGURED WRONG!"
LOOK AT THIS PATHETIC WRETCH SITTING HANGDOG AT THE BAR, EATING DONUT AFTER DONUT IN A PATHETIC ATTEMPT TO FORGET HIS TROUBLES.
ACTUALLY BOSS, HE DOES THAT EVERY DAY.
BUT, UH, HE USUALLY APPEARS VERY HAPPY AS HE EATS THE DONUTS. SOMETIMES HE SINGS.
DONUTS
COME NOW. HOMER, MINDY LEFT YOU FOR HER BOWLING INSTRUCTOR. YOU'RE ACTING AS IF IT WERE THE END OF THE WORLD.
BOSS, SHE WAS EVERYTHING TO ME. SHE WAS THE MOTHER OF MY CHILDREN.
UH, OH, THAT REMINDS ME... UM, I'M HAVING A NANNY SHIPPED OVER FROM ENGLAND, BUT IT'S GONNA TAKE SIX WEEKS.
HOMER, WE ARE GANGSTERS! THIS IS NOT A DAY-CARE FACILITY! WE'RE EXTREMELY BUSY HERE WITH RACKETEERING, EXTORTION, BLACKMAIL, COMPACT DISC PRICE-FIXING...
OH GEEZ, WILL YOU STOP LOOKING SO SAD?
FINE, HOMER, YOU CAN KEEP THE RUGRAT HERE UNTIL YOUR DAYCARE ARRIVES. LOOK, YOU'VE BEEN EMPLOYED BY ME FOR TEN YEARS WITHOUT A PROMOTION. CONSIDERING YOUR RECENT HARDSHIP AT HOME, I FEEL YOU NEED A BOOST AT WORK.
THUS, I AM MOVING YOU UP. I AM GIVING YOU A HIT.
REALLY??
REALLY. THIS IS THE FELLOW. HE'S A VERY NICE YOUNG MAN. REGRETTABLY, HE'S MEDDLED WITH TOO MANY OF OUR OPERATIONS. MOST RECENTLY, HE BLEW THE WHISTLE ON OUR TAMAGOTCHI SLAVERY RING. PLEASE OFF HIM.
DON'T WORRY, BOSS-- THIS LITTLE WIENER IS TOAST!
A-HEM.
DON'T MIX METAPHORS, SIMPSON. AS YOU WELL KNOW, IT MAKES LOU NERVOUS.
MILHOUSE VAN HOUTEN
KNOWN HANGOUTS: NOISELAND VIDEO ARCADE, SPRINGFIELD PARK, DETENTION HALL, SPRINGFIELD ELEMENTARY SCHOOL, THE ANDROID'S DUNGEON, THE KWIK-E-MA

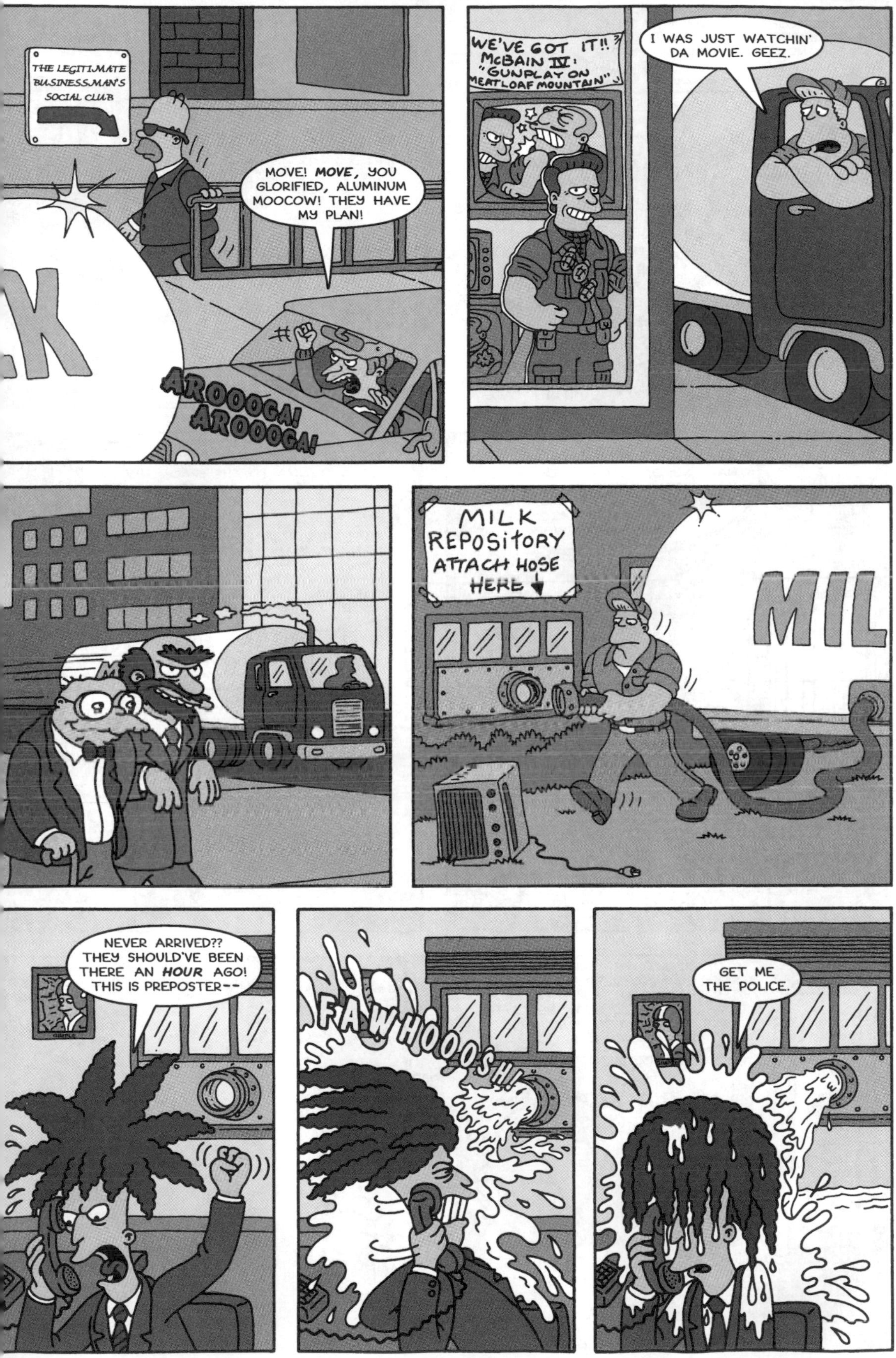
THE LEGITIMATE BUSINESSMAN'S SOCIAL CLUB
MOVE! MOVE, YOU GLORIFIED, ALUMINUM MOOCOW! THEY HAVE MY PLAN!
AROOOGA! AROOOGA!
WE'VE GOT IT!! McBAIN IV: "GUNPLAY ON MEATLOAF MOUNTAIN"
I WAS JUST WATCHIN' DA MOVIE. GEEZ.
MILK REPOSITORY ATTACH HOSE HERE
MIL
NEVER ARRIVED?? THEY SHOULD'VE BEEN THERE AN HOUR AGO! THIS IS PREPOSTER--
FAWHOOOOSH!
GET ME THE POLICE.

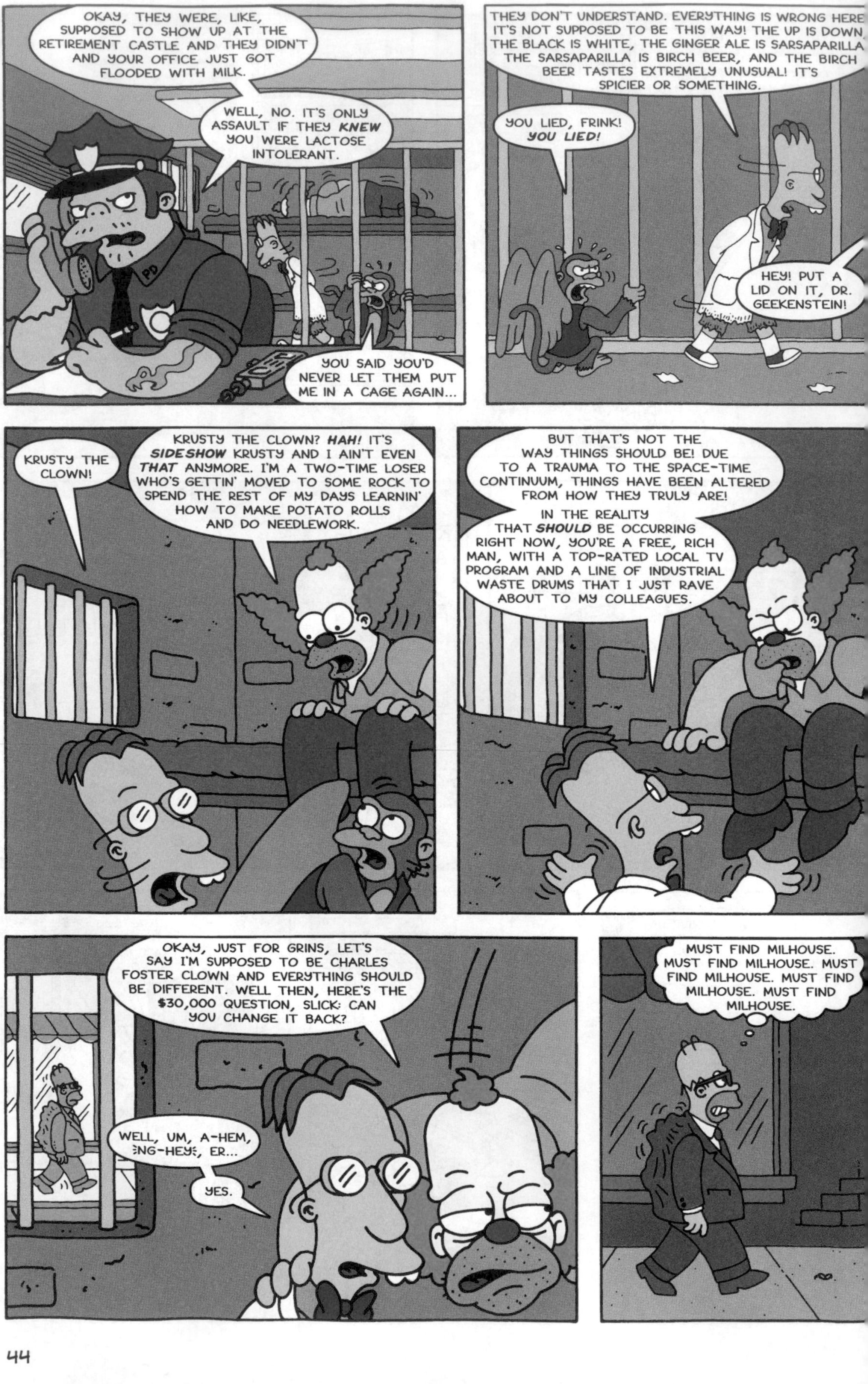
OKAY, THEY WERE, LIKE, SUPPOSED TO SHOW UP AT THE RETIREMENT CASTLE AND THEY DIDN'T AND YOUR OFFICE JUST GOT FLOODED WITH MILK.
WELL, NO. IT'S ONLY ASSAULT IF THEY KNEW YOU WERE LACTOSE INTOLERANT.
PD
YOU SAID YOU'D NEVER LET THEM PUT ME IN A CAGE AGAIN...
THEY DON'T UNDERSTAND. EVERYTHING IS WRONG HERE. IT'S NOT SUPPOSED TO BE THIS WAY! THE UP IS DOWN, THE BLACK IS WHITE, THE GINGER ALE IS SARSAPARILLA, THE SARSAPARILLA IS BIRCH BEER, AND THE BIRCH BEER TASTES EXTREMELY UNUSUAL! IT'S SPICIER OR SOMETHING.
YOU LIED, FRINK! YOU LIED!
HEY! PUT A LID ON IT, DR. GEEKENSTEIN!
KRUSTY THE CLOWN!
KRUSTY THE CLOWN? HAH! IT'S SIDESHOW KRUSTY AND I AIN'T EVEN THAT ANYMORE. I'M A TWO-TIME LOSER WHO'S GETTIN' MOVED TO SOME ROCK TO SPEND THE REST OF MY DAYS LEARNIN' HOW TO MAKE POTATO ROLLS AND DO NEEDLEWORK.
BUT THAT'S NOT THE WAY THINGS SHOULD BE! DUE TO A TRAUMA TO THE SPACE-TIME CONTINUUM, THINGS HAVE BEEN ALTERED FROM HOW THEY TRULY ARE!
IN THE REALITY THAT SHOULD BE OCCURRING RIGHT NOW, YOU'RE A FREE, RICH MAN, WITH A TOP-RATED LOCAL TV PROGRAM AND A LINE OF INDUSTRIAL WASTE DRUMS THAT I JUST RAVE ABOUT TO MY COLLEAGUES.
OKAY, JUST FOR GRINS, LET'S SAY I'M SUPPOSED TO BE CHARLES FOSTER CLOWN AND EVERYTHING SHOULD BE DIFFERENT. WELL THEN, HERE'S THE $30,000 QUESTION, SLICK: CAN YOU CHANGE IT BACK?
WELL, UM, A-HEM, ENG-HEY, ER...
YES.
MUST FIND MILHOUSE. MUST FIND MILHOUSE. MUST FIND MILHOUSE. MUST FIND MILHOUSE. MUST FIND MILHOUSE.

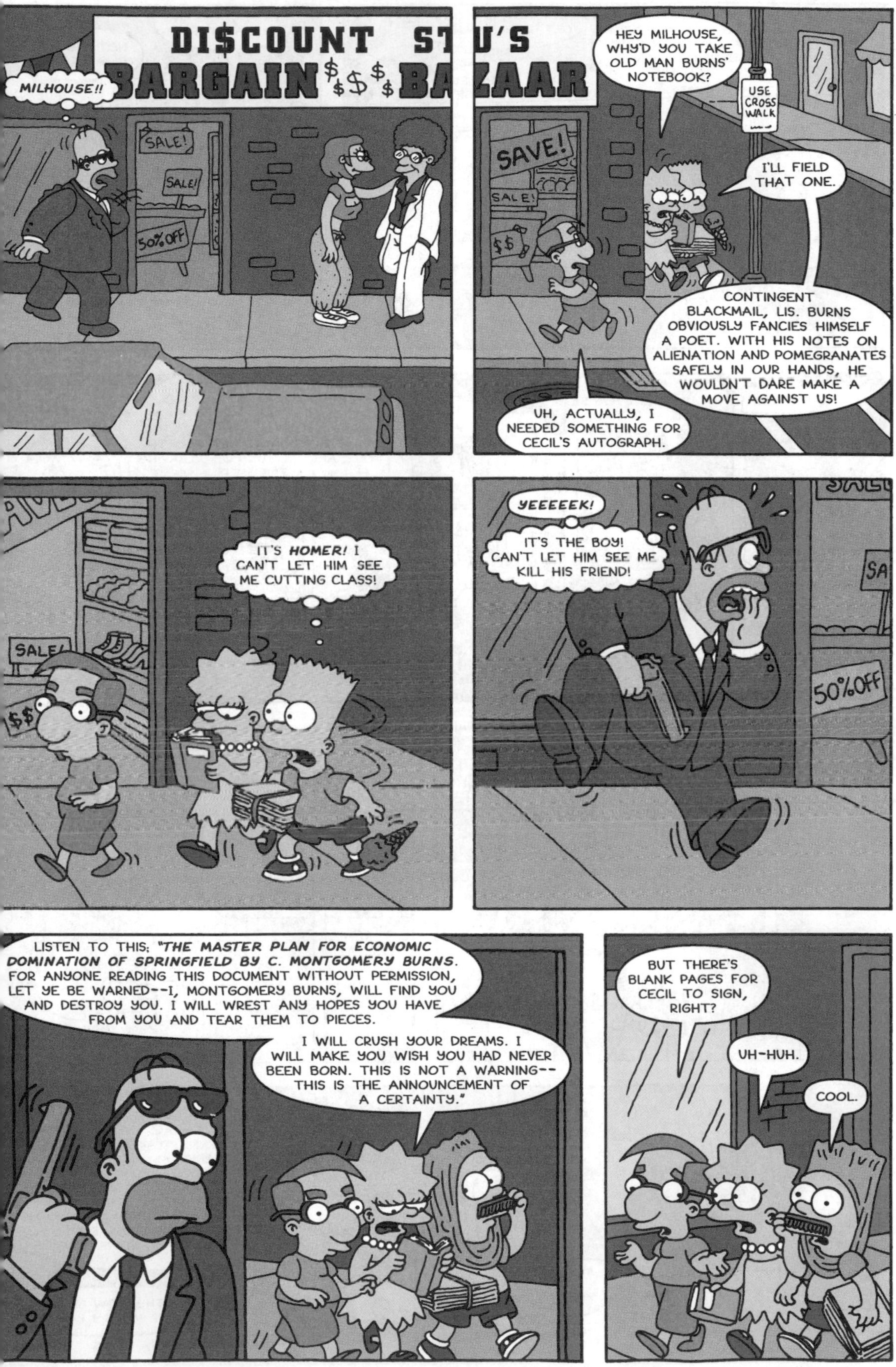
DI$COUNT STU'S
BARGAIN $ $ $ $ BAZAAR
MILHOUSE!!
SALE!
SALE!
50% OFF
HEY MILHOUSE, WHY'D YOU TAKE OLD MAN BURNS' NOTEBOOK?
USE CROSS WALK
SAVE!
SALE!
I'LL FIELD THAT ONE.
CONTINGENT BLACKMAIL, LIS. BURNS OBVIOUSLY FANCIES HIMSELF A POET. WITH HIS NOTES ON ALIENATION AND POMEGRANATES SAFELY IN OUR HANDS, HE WOULDN'T DARE MAKE A MOVE AGAINST US!
UH, ACTUALLY, I NEEDED SOMETHING FOR CECIL'S AUTOGRAPH.
IT'S *HOMER!* I CAN'T LET HIM SEE ME CUTTING CLASS!
SALE!
YEEEEEK!
IT'S THE BOY! CAN'T LET HIM SEE ME KILL HIS FRIEND!
50% OFF
LISTEN TO THIS: *"THE MASTER PLAN FOR ECONOMIC DOMINATION OF SPRINGFIELD BY C. MONTGOMERY BURNS.* FOR ANYONE READING THIS DOCUMENT WITHOUT PERMISSION, LET YE BE WARNED--I, MONTGOMERY BURNS, WILL FIND YOU AND DESTROY YOU. I WILL WREST ANY HOPES YOU HAVE FROM YOU AND TEAR THEM TO PIECES.
I WILL CRUSH YOUR DREAMS. I WILL MAKE YOU WISH YOU HAD NEVER BEEN BORN. THIS IS NOT A WARNING--THIS IS THE ANNOUNCEMENT OF A CERTAINTY."
BUT THERE'S BLANK PAGES FOR CECIL TO SIGN, RIGHT?
UH-HUH.
COOL.

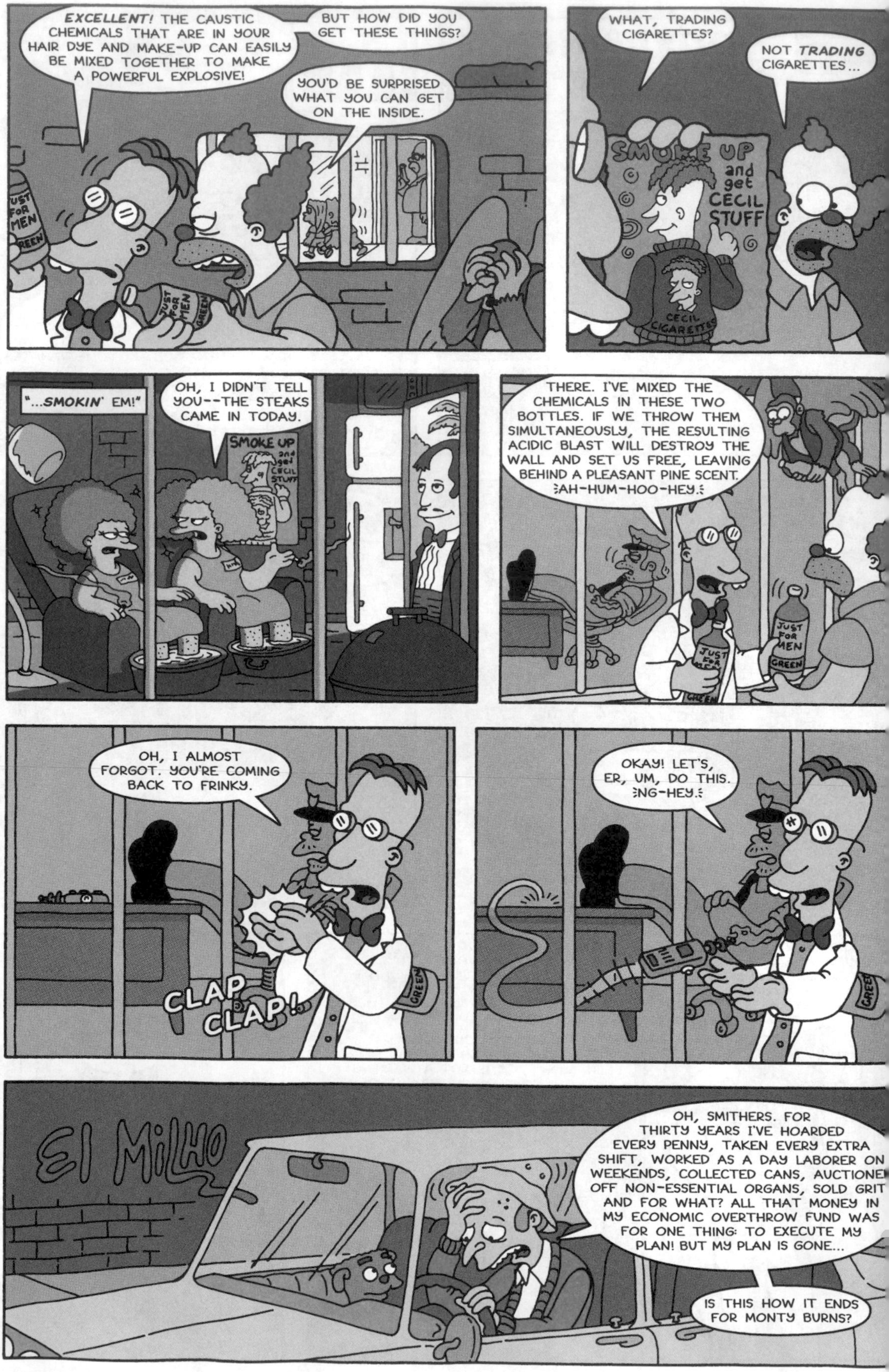
EXCELLENT! THE CAUSTIC CHEMICALS THAT ARE IN YOUR HAIR DYE AND MAKE-UP CAN EASILY BE MIXED TOGETHER TO MAKE A POWERFUL EXPLOSIVE!
BUT HOW DID YOU GET THESE THINGS?
YOU'D BE SURPRISED WHAT YOU CAN GET ON THE INSIDE.
JUST FOR MEN GREEN
WHAT, TRADING CIGARETTES?
NOT TRADING CIGARETTES...
SMOKE UP and get CECIL STUFF
CECIL CIGARETTES
"...SMOKIN' EM!"
OH, I DIDN'T TELL YOU--THE STEAKS CAME IN TODAY.
SMOKE UP
THERE. I'VE MIXED THE CHEMICALS IN THESE TWO BOTTLES. IF WE THROW THEM SIMULTANEOUSLY, THE RESULTING ACIDIC BLAST WILL DESTROY THE WALL AND SET US FREE, LEAVING BEHIND A PLEASANT PINE SCENT. AH-HUM-HOO-HEY.
JUST FOR MEN GREEN
OH, I ALMOST FORGOT. YOU'RE COMING BACK TO FRINKY.
CLAP CLAP!
OKAY! LET'S, ER, UM, DO THIS. NG-HEY.
El Milho
OH, SMITHERS. FOR THIRTY YEARS I'VE HOARDED EVERY PENNY, TAKEN EVERY EXTRA SHIFT, WORKED AS A DAY LABORER ON WEEKENDS, COLLECTED CANS, AUCTIONE OFF NON-ESSENTIAL ORGANS, SOLD GRIT AND FOR WHAT? ALL THAT MONEY IN MY ECONOMIC OVERTHROW FUND WAS FOR ONE THING: TO EXECUTE MY PLAN! BUT MY PLAN IS GONE...
IS THIS HOW IT ENDS FOR MONTY BURNS?

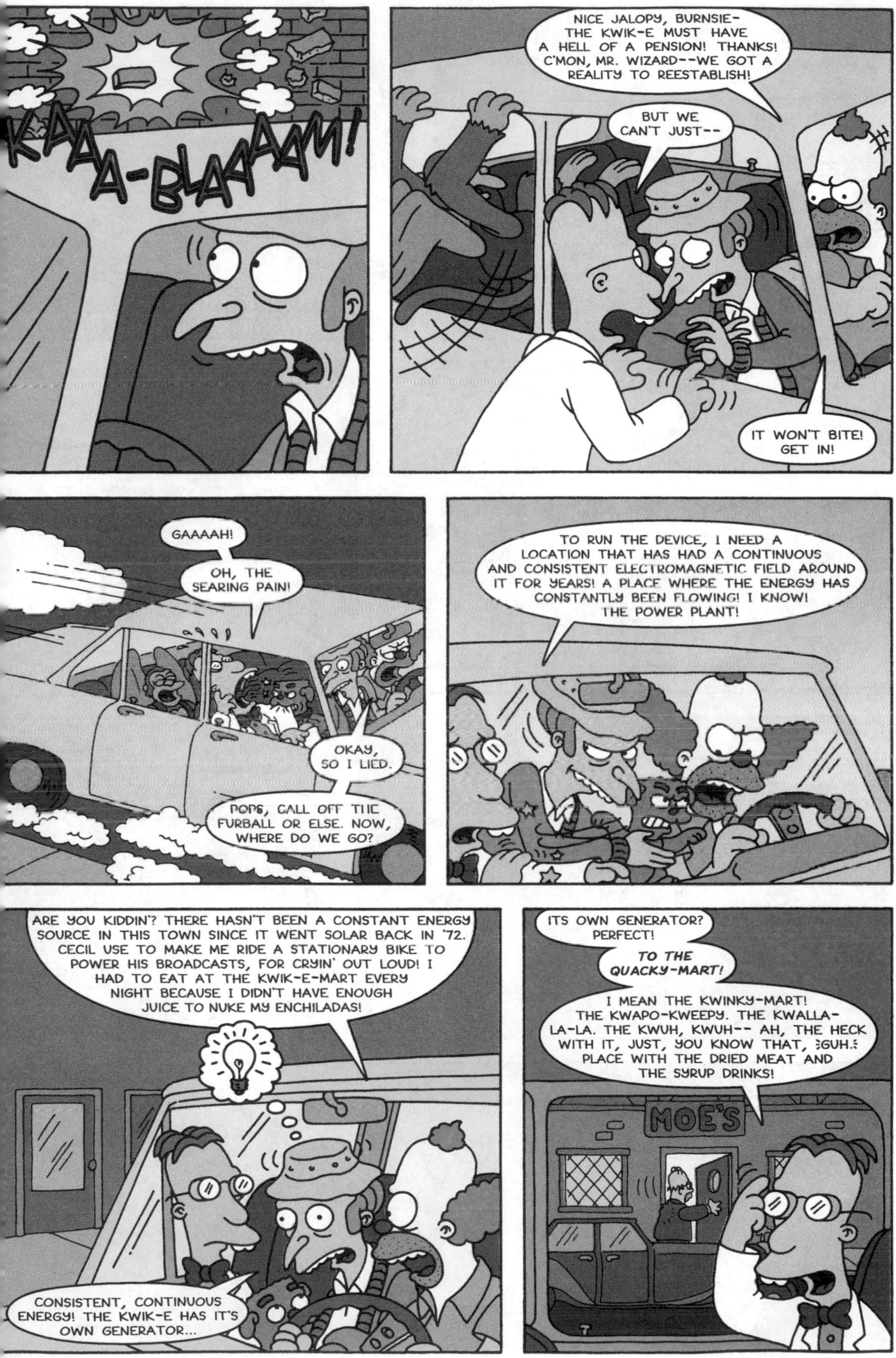
KAAAA-BLAAAAAM!
NICE JALOPY, BURNSIE- THE KWIK-E MUST HAVE A HELL OF A PENSION! THANKS! C'MON, MR. WIZARD--WE GOT A REALITY TO REESTABLISH!
BUT WE CAN'T JUST--
IT WON'T BITE! GET IN!
GAAAAH!
OH, THE SEARING PAIN!
OKAY, SO I LIED.
POPS, CALL OFF THE FURBALL OR ELSE. NOW, WHERE DO WE GO?
TO RUN THE DEVICE, I NEED A LOCATION THAT HAS HAD A CONTINUOUS AND CONSISTENT ELECTROMAGNETIC FIELD AROUND IT FOR YEARS! A PLACE WHERE THE ENERGY HAS CONSTANTLY BEEN FLOWING! I KNOW! THE POWER PLANT!
ARE YOU KIDDIN'? THERE HASN'T BEEN A CONSTANT ENERGY SOURCE IN THIS TOWN SINCE IT WENT SOLAR BACK IN '72. CECIL USE TO MAKE ME RIDE A STATIONARY BIKE TO POWER HIS BROADCASTS, FOR CRYIN' OUT LOUD! I HAD TO EAT AT THE KWIK-E-MART EVERY NIGHT BECAUSE I DIDN'T HAVE ENOUGH JUICE TO NUKE MY ENCHILADAS!
CONSISTENT, CONTINUOUS ENERGY! THE KWIK-E HAS IT'S OWN GENERATOR...
ITS OWN GENERATOR? PERFECT!
TO THE QUACKY-MART!
I MEAN THE KWINKY-MART! THE KWAPO-KWEEPY. THE KWALLA-LA-LA. THE KWUH, KWUH-- AH, THE HECK WITH IT, JUST, YOU KNOW THAT, ≷GUH.≷ PLACE WITH THE DRIED MEAT AND THE SYRUP DRINKS!
MOE'S

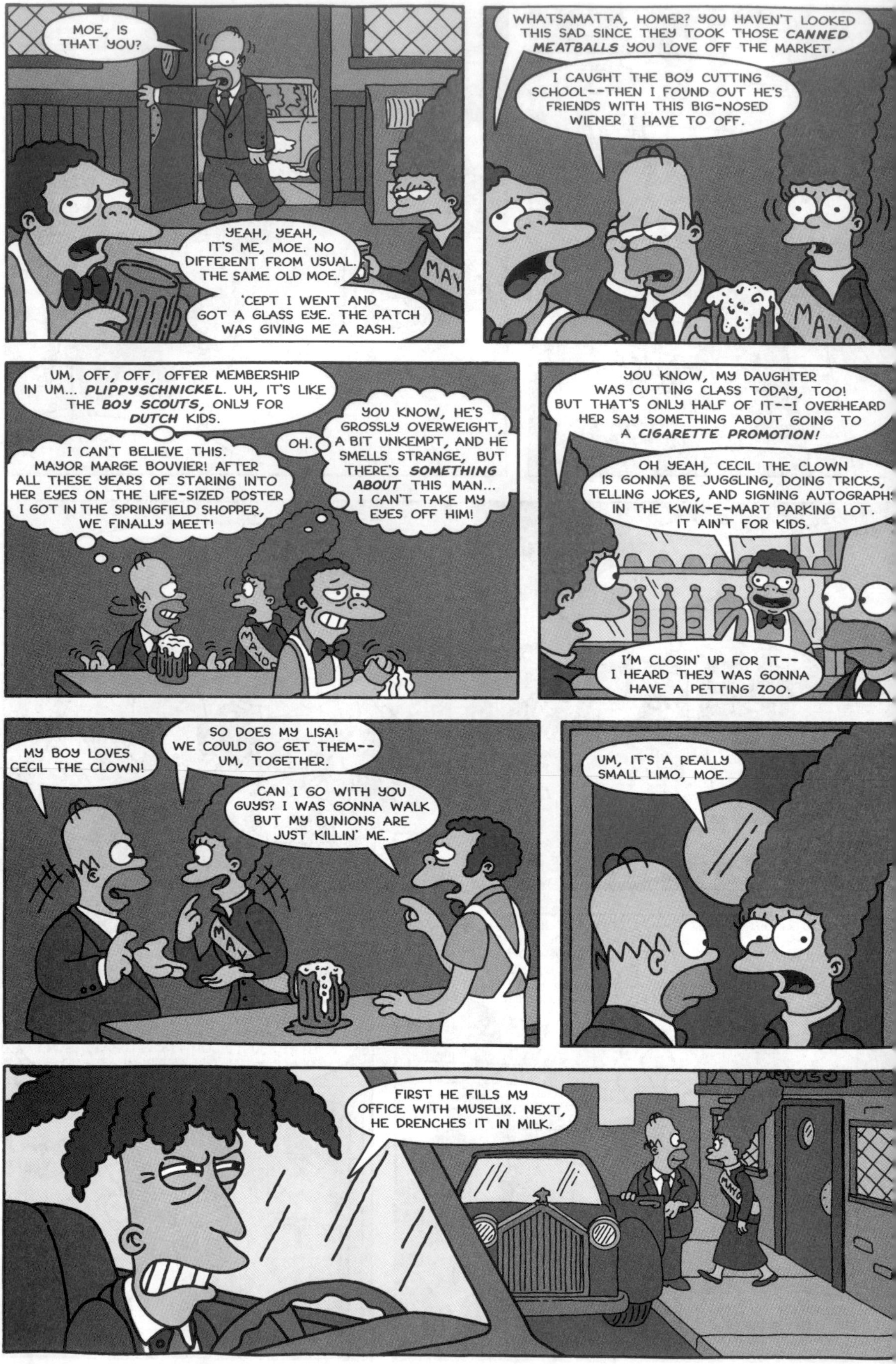
MOE, IS THAT YOU?
YEAH, YEAH, IT'S ME, MOE. NO DIFFERENT FROM USUAL. THE SAME OLD MOE.
'CEPT I WENT AND GOT A GLASS EYE. THE PATCH WAS GIVING ME A RASH.
MAY
WHATSAMATTA, HOMER? YOU HAVEN'T LOOKED THIS SAD SINCE THEY TOOK THOSE CANNED MEATBALLS YOU LOVE OFF THE MARKET.
I CAUGHT THE BOY CUTTING SCHOOL--THEN I FOUND OUT HE'S FRIENDS WITH THIS BIG-NOSED WIENER I HAVE TO OFF.
MAYO
UM, OFF, OFF, OFFER MEMBERSHIP IN UM... PLIPPYSCHNICKEL. UH, IT'S LIKE THE BOY SCOUTS, ONLY FOR DUTCH KIDS.
OH.
YOU KNOW, HE'S GROSSLY OVERWEIGHT, A BIT UNKEMPT, AND HE SMELLS STRANGE, BUT THERE'S SOMETHING ABOUT THIS MAN... I CAN'T TAKE MY EYES OFF HIM!
I CAN'T BELIEVE THIS. MAYOR MARGE BOUVIER! AFTER ALL THESE YEARS OF STARING INTO HER EYES ON THE LIFE-SIZED POSTER I GOT IN THE SPRINGFIELD SHOPPER, WE FINALLY MEET!
MAYOR
YOU KNOW, MY DAUGHTER WAS CUTTING CLASS TODAY, TOO! BUT THAT'S ONLY HALF OF IT--I OVERHEARD HER SAY SOMETHING ABOUT GOING TO A CIGARETTE PROMOTION!
OH YEAH, CECIL THE CLOWN IS GONNA BE JUGGLING, DOING TRICKS, TELLING JOKES, AND SIGNING AUTOGRAPHS IN THE KWIK-E-MART PARKING LOT. IT AIN'T FOR KIDS.
I'M CLOSIN' UP FOR IT-- I HEARD THEY WAS GONNA HAVE A PETTING ZOO.
MY BOY LOVES CECIL THE CLOWN!
SO DOES MY LISA! WE COULD GO GET THEM-- UM, TOGETHER.
CAN I GO WITH YOU GUYS? I WAS GONNA WALK BUT MY BUNIONS ARE JUST KILLIN' ME.
MAY
UM, IT'S A REALLY SMALL LIMO, MOE.
FIRST HE FILLS MY OFFICE WITH MUSELIX. NEXT, HE DRENCHES IT IN MILK.
MAYO

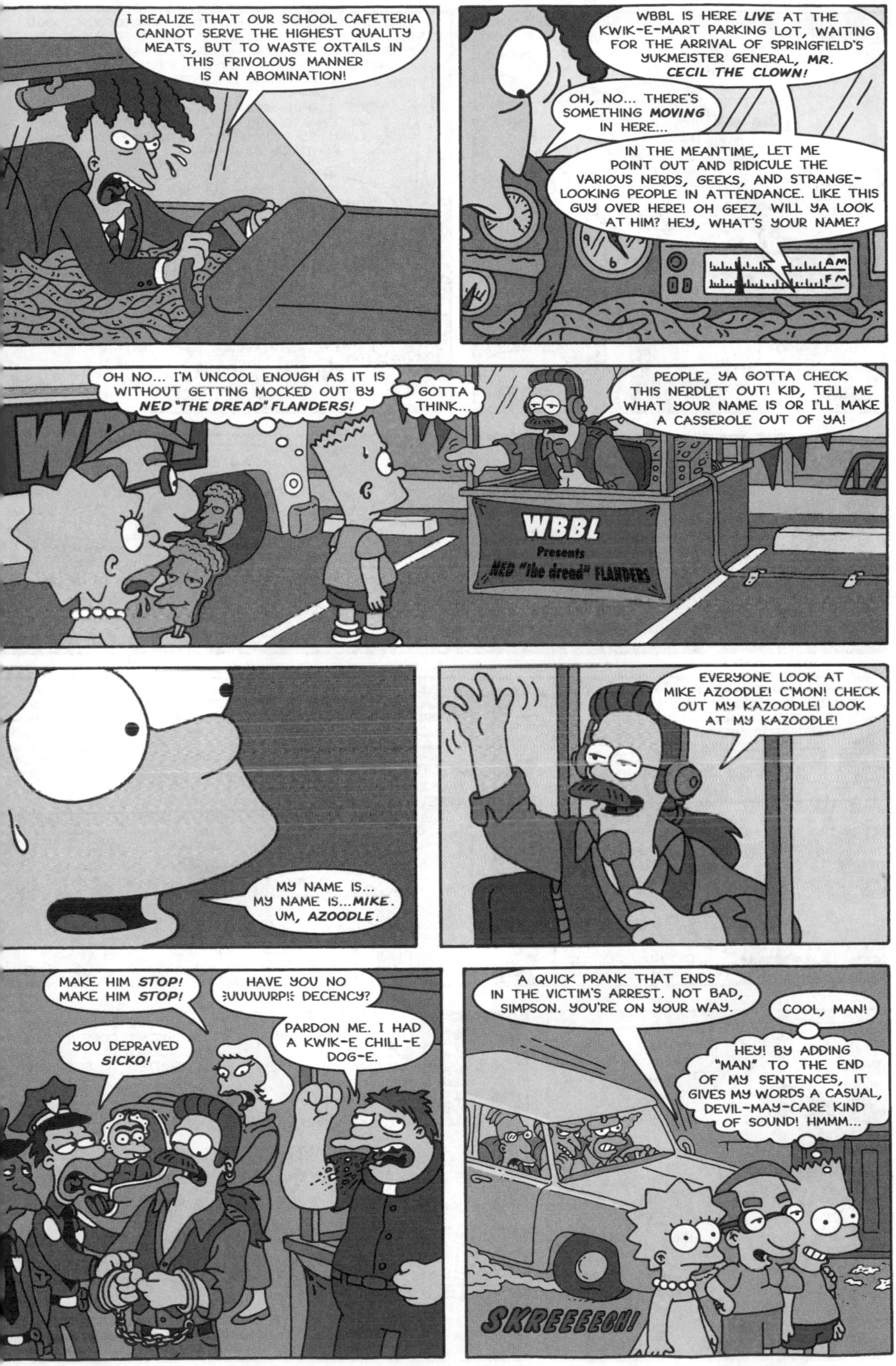

I REALIZE THAT OUR SCHOOL CAFETERIA CANNOT SERVE THE HIGHEST QUALITY MEATS, BUT TO WASTE OXTAILS IN THIS FRIVOLOUS MANNER IS AN ABOMINATION!
WBBL IS HERE **LIVE** AT THE KWIK-E-MART PARKING LOT, WAITING FOR THE ARRIVAL OF SPRINGFIELD'S YUKMEISTER GENERAL, **MR. CECIL THE CLOWN!**
OH, NO... THERE'S SOMETHING **MOVING** IN HERE...
IN THE MEANTIME, LET ME POINT OUT AND RIDICULE THE VARIOUS NERDS, GEEKS, AND STRANGE-LOOKING PEOPLE IN ATTENDANCE. LIKE THIS GUY OVER HERE! OH GEEZ, WILL YA LOOK AT HIM? HEY, WHAT'S YOUR NAME?
AM
FM
OH NO... I'M UNCOOL ENOUGH AS IT IS WITHOUT GETTING MOCKED OUT BY **NED "THE DREAD" FLANDERS!**
GOTTA THINK...
PEOPLE, YA GOTTA CHECK THIS NERDLET OUT! KID, TELL ME WHAT YOUR NAME IS OR I'LL MAKE A CASSEROLE OUT OF YA!
WBBL
WBBL Presents NED "the dread" FLANDERS
MY NAME IS... MY NAME IS...**MIKE**. UM, **AZOODLE**.
EVERYONE LOOK AT MIKE AZOODLE! C'MON! CHECK OUT MY KAZOODLE! LOOK AT MY KAZOODLE!
MAKE HIM **STOP!** MAKE HIM **STOP!**
HAVE YOU NO UUUUURP! DECENCY?
YOU DEPRAVED **SICKO!**
PARDON ME. I HAD A KWIK-E CHILL-E DOG-E.
A QUICK PRANK THAT ENDS IN THE VICTIM'S ARREST. NOT BAD, SIMPSON. YOU'RE ON YOUR WAY.
COOL, MAN!
HEY! BY ADDING "MAN" TO THE END OF MY SENTENCES, IT GIVES MY WORDS A CASUAL, DEVIL-MAY-CARE KIND OF SOUND! HMMM...
SKREEEEECH!

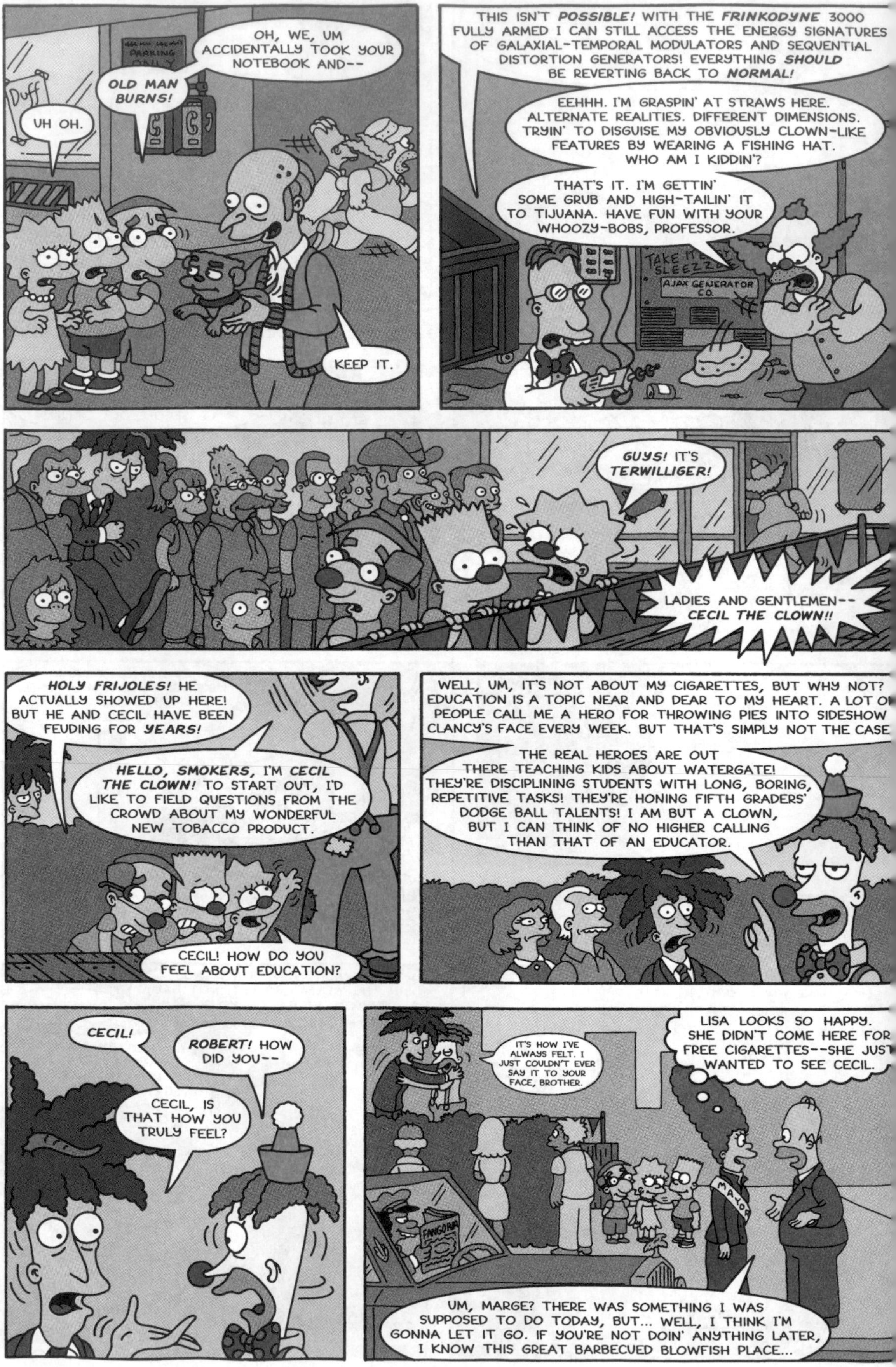

Duff
UH OH.
OLD MAN BURNS!
OH, WE, UM ACCIDENTALLY TOOK YOUR NOTEBOOK AND--
KEEP IT.
THIS ISN'T POSSIBLE! WITH THE FRINKODYNE 3000 FULLY ARMED I CAN STILL ACCESS THE ENERGY SIGNATURES OF GALAXIAL-TEMPORAL MODULATORS AND SEQUENTIAL DISTORTION GENERATORS! EVERYTHING SHOULD BE REVERTING BACK TO NORMAL!
EEHHH. I'M GRASPIN' AT STRAWS HERE. ALTERNATE REALITIES. DIFFERENT DIMENSIONS. TRYIN' TO DISGUISE MY OBVIOUSLY CLOWN-LIKE FEATURES BY WEARING A FISHING HAT. WHO AM I KIDDIN'?
THAT'S IT. I'M GETTIN' SOME GRUB AND HIGH-TAILIN' IT TO TIJUANA. HAVE FUN WITH YOUR WHOOZY-BOBS, PROFESSOR.
AJAX GENERATOR CO.
GUYS! IT'S TERWILLIGER!
LADIES AND GENTLEMEN-- CECIL THE CLOWN!!
HOLY FRIJOLES! HE ACTUALLY SHOWED UP HERE! BUT HE AND CECIL HAVE BEEN FEUDING FOR YEARS!
HELLO, SMOKERS, I'M CECIL THE CLOWN! TO START OUT, I'D LIKE TO FIELD QUESTIONS FROM THE CROWD ABOUT MY WONDERFUL NEW TOBACCO PRODUCT.
CECIL! HOW DO YOU FEEL ABOUT EDUCATION?
WELL, UM, IT'S NOT ABOUT MY CIGARETTES, BUT WHY NOT? EDUCATION IS A TOPIC NEAR AND DEAR TO MY HEART. A LOT O PEOPLE CALL ME A HERO FOR THROWING PIES INTO SIDESHOW CLANCY'S FACE EVERY WEEK. BUT THAT'S SIMPLY NOT THE CASE
THE REAL HEROES ARE OUT THERE TEACHING KIDS ABOUT WATERGATE! THEY'RE DISCIPLINING STUDENTS WITH LONG, BORING, REPETITIVE TASKS! THEY'RE HONING FIFTH GRADERS' DODGE BALL TALENTS! I AM BUT A CLOWN, BUT I CAN THINK OF NO HIGHER CALLING THAN THAT OF AN EDUCATOR.
CECIL!
ROBERT! HOW DID YOU--
CECIL, IS THAT HOW YOU TRULY FEEL?
IT'S HOW I'VE ALWAYS FELT. I JUST COULDN'T EVER SAY IT TO YOUR FACE, BROTHER.
LISA LOOKS SO HAPPY. SHE DIDN'T COME HERE FOR FREE CIGARETTES--SHE JUST WANTED TO SEE CECIL.
FANGORIA
MAYOR
UM, MARGE? THERE WAS SOMETHING I WAS SUPPOSED TO DO TODAY, BUT... WELL, I THINK I'M GONNA LET IT GO. IF YOU'RE NOT DOIN' ANYTHING LATER, I KNOW THIS GREAT BARBECUED BLOWFISH PLACE...

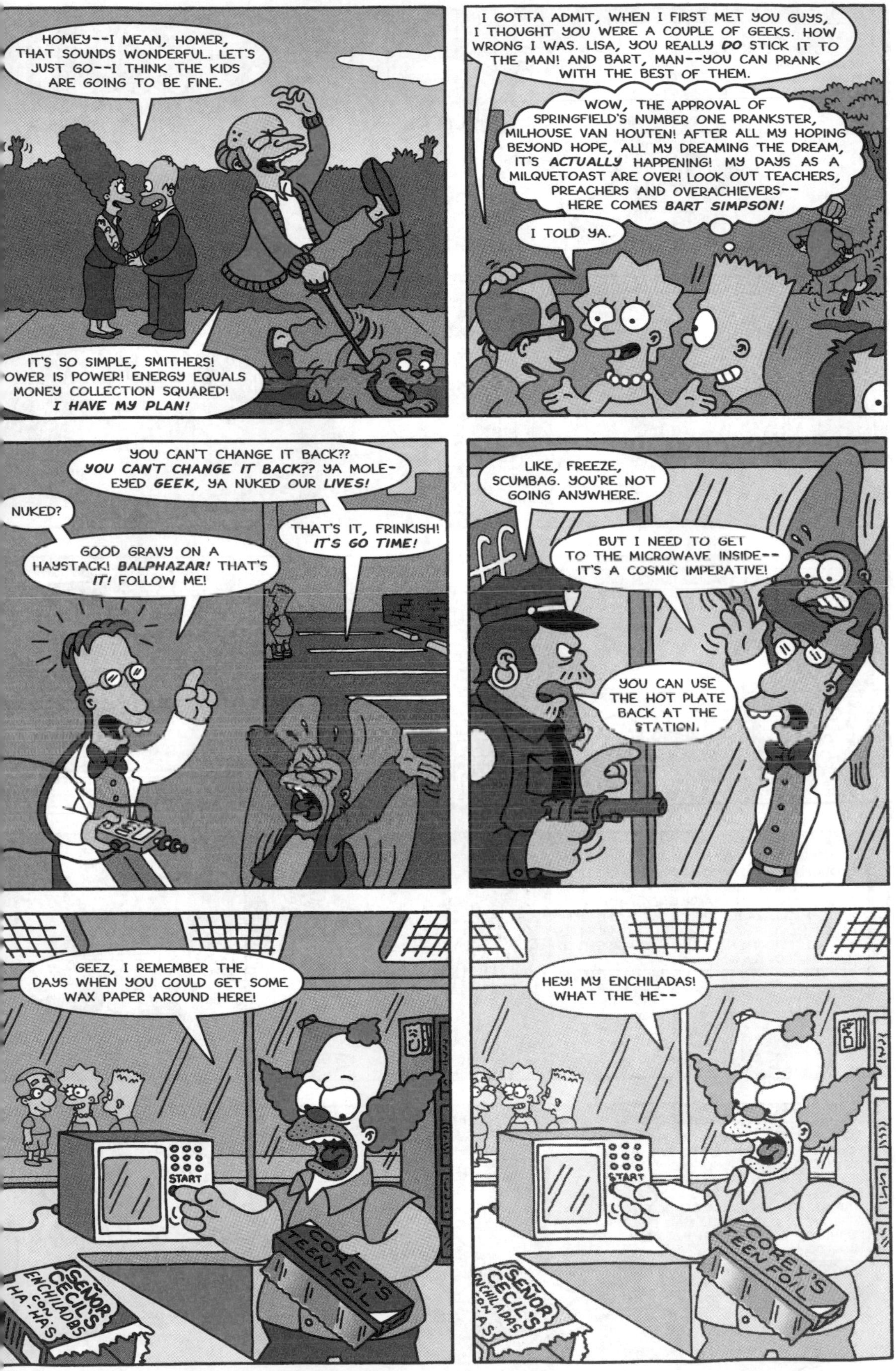
HOMEY--I MEAN, HOMER, THAT SOUNDS WONDERFUL. LET'S JUST GO--I THINK THE KIDS ARE GOING TO BE FINE.
IT'S SO SIMPLE, SMITHERS! OWER IS POWER! ENERGY EQUALS MONEY COLLECTION SQUARED! I HAVE MY PLAN!
I GOTTA ADMIT, WHEN I FIRST MET YOU GUYS, I THOUGHT YOU WERE A COUPLE OF GEEKS. HOW WRONG I WAS. LISA, YOU REALLY DO STICK IT TO THE MAN! AND BART, MAN--YOU CAN PRANK WITH THE BEST OF THEM.
WOW, THE APPROVAL OF SPRINGFIELD'S NUMBER ONE PRANKSTER, MILHOUSE VAN HOUTEN! AFTER ALL MY HOPING BEYOND HOPE, ALL MY DREAMING THE DREAM, IT'S ACTUALLY HAPPENING! MY DAYS AS A MILQUETOAST ARE OVER! LOOK OUT TEACHERS, PREACHERS AND OVERACHIEVERS--HERE COMES BART SIMPSON!
I TOLD YA.
YOU CAN'T CHANGE IT BACK?? YOU CAN'T CHANGE IT BACK?? YA MOLE-EYED GEEK, YA NUKED OUR LIVES!
NUKED?
GOOD GRAVY ON A HAYSTACK! BALPHAZAR! THAT'S IT! FOLLOW ME!
THAT'S IT, FRINKISH! IT'S GO TIME!
LIKE, FREEZE, SCUMBAG. YOU'RE NOT GOING ANYWHERE.
BUT I NEED TO GET TO THE MICROWAVE INSIDE--IT'S A COSMIC IMPERATIVE!
YOU CAN USE THE HOT PLATE BACK AT THE STATION.
GEEZ, I REMEMBER THE DAYS WHEN YOU COULD GET SOME WAX PAPER AROUND HERE!
START
COREY'S TEEN FOIL
SENOR CECIL'S ENCHILADAS CON HA-HA'S
HEY! MY ENCHILADAS! WHAT THE HE--
START
COREY'S TEEN FOIL
SENOR CECIL'S ENCHILADAS CON HA-HA'S

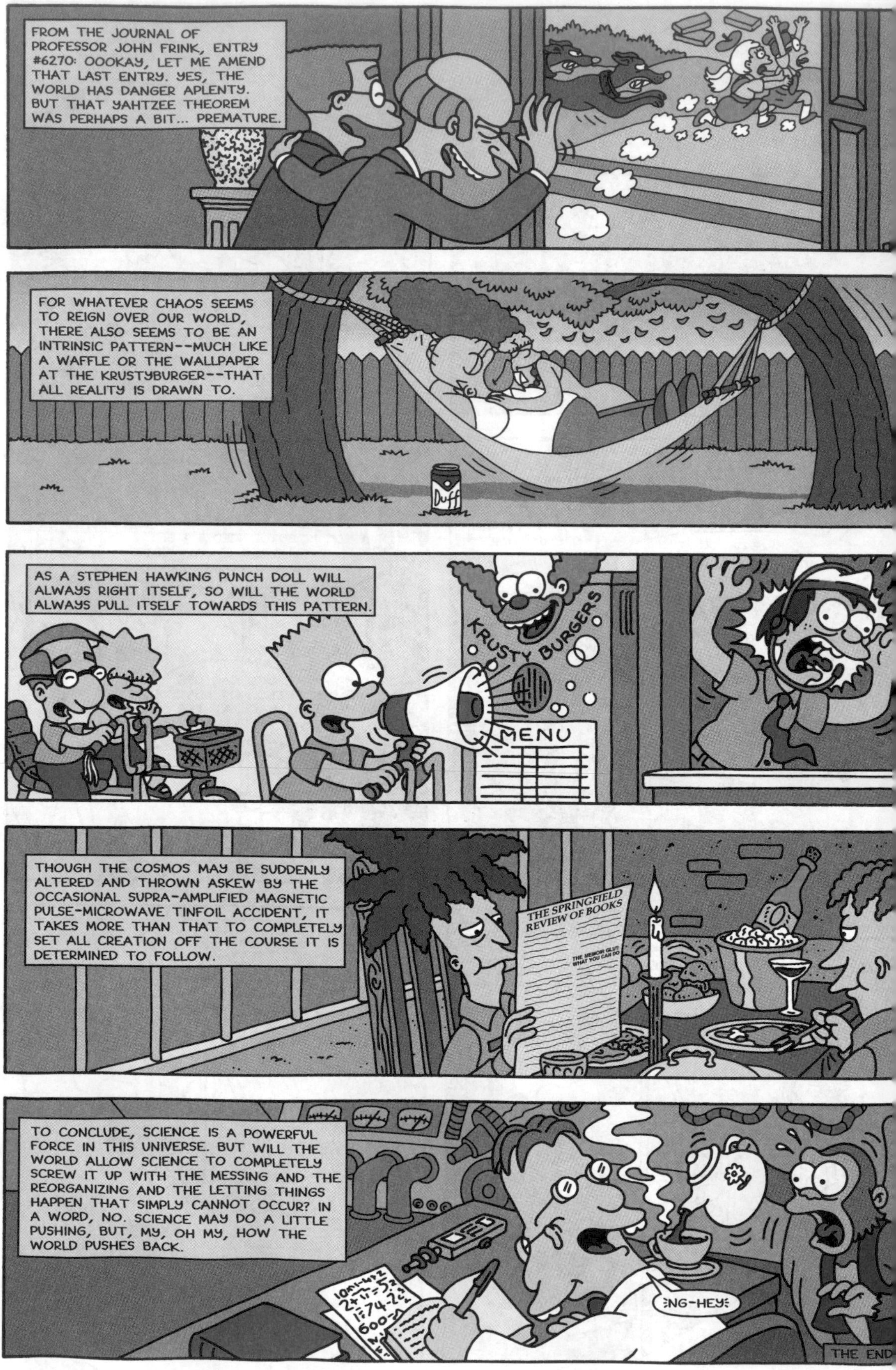
FROM THE JOURNAL OF PROFESSOR JOHN FRINK, ENTRY #6270: OOOKAY, LET ME AMEND THAT LAST ENTRY. YES, THE WORLD HAS DANGER APLENTY. BUT THAT YAHTZEE THEOREM WAS PERHAPS A BIT... PREMATURE.
FOR WHATEVER CHAOS SEEMS TO REIGN OVER OUR WORLD, THERE ALSO SEEMS TO BE AN INTRINSIC PATTERN--MUCH LIKE A WAFFLE OR THE WALLPAPER AT THE KRUSTYBURGER--THAT ALL REALITY IS DRAWN TO.
Duff
AS A STEPHEN HAWKING PUNCH DOLL WILL ALWAYS RIGHT ITSELF, SO WILL THE WORLD ALWAYS PULL ITSELF TOWARDS THIS PATTERN.
KRUSTY BURGERS
MENU
THOUGH THE COSMOS MAY BE SUDDENLY ALTERED AND THROWN ASKEW BY THE OCCASIONAL SUPRA-AMPLIFIED MAGNETIC PULSE-MICROWAVE TINFOIL ACCIDENT, IT TAKES MORE THAN THAT TO COMPLETELY SET ALL CREATION OFF THE COURSE IT IS DETERMINED TO FOLLOW.
THE SPRINGFIELD REVIEW OF BOOKS
TO CONCLUDE, SCIENCE IS A POWERFUL FORCE IN THIS UNIVERSE. BUT WILL THE WORLD ALLOW SCIENCE TO COMPLETELY SCREW IT UP WITH THE MESSING AND THE REORGANIZING AND THE LETTING THINGS HAPPEN THAT SIMPLY CANNOT OCCUR? IN A WORD, NO. SCIENCE MAY DO A LITTLE PUSHING, BUT, MY, OH MY, HOW THE WORLD PUSHES BACK.
NG-HEY
THE END

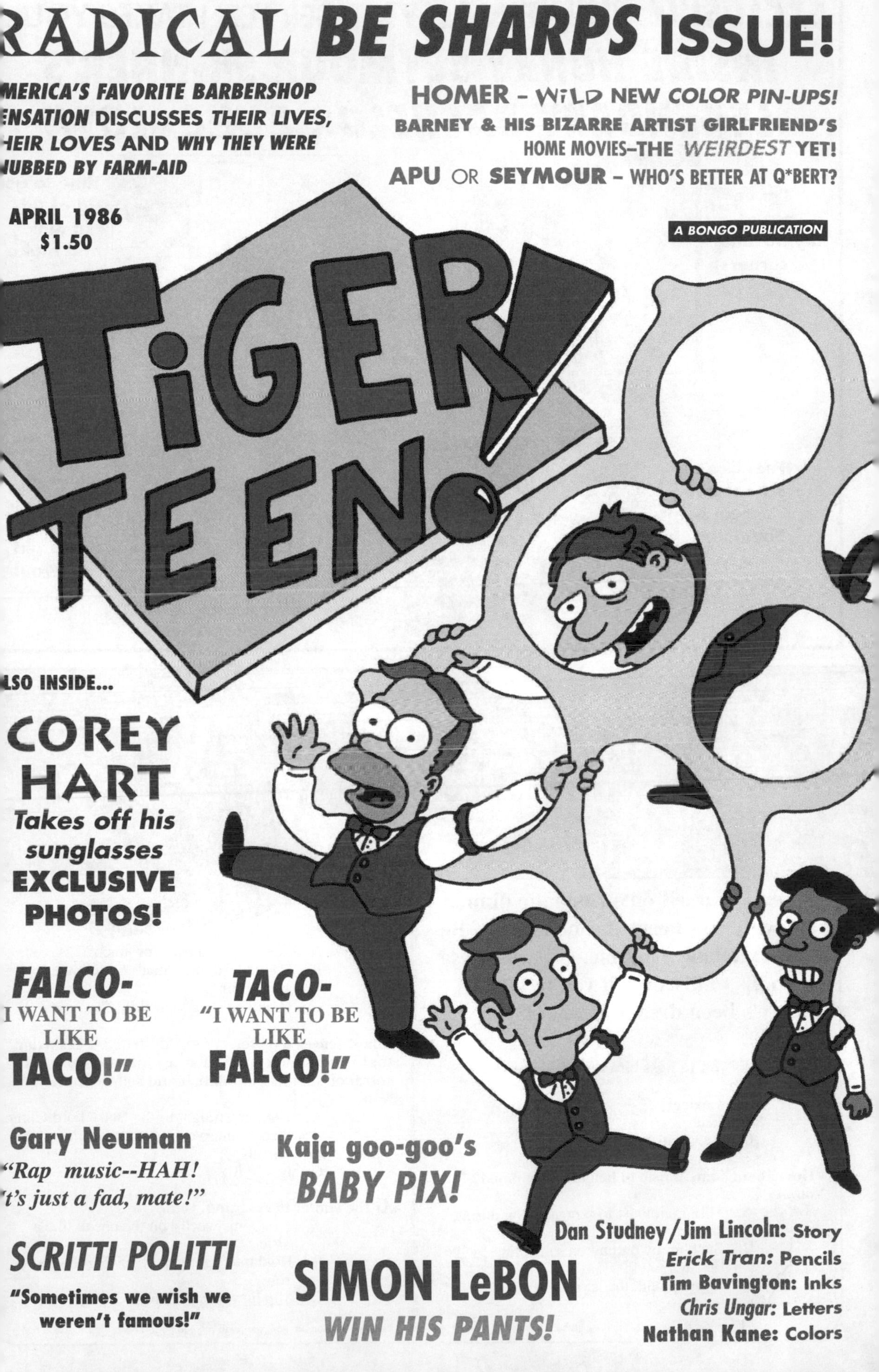

RADICAL BE SHARPS ISSUE!
MERICA'S FAVORITE BARBERSHOP
ENSATION DISCUSSES THEIR LIVES,
HEIR LOVES AND WHY THEY WERE
UBBED BY FARM-AID
HOMER - WILD NEW COLOR PIN-UPS!
BARNEY & HIS BIZARRE ARTIST GIRLFRIEND'S
HOME MOVIES–THE WEIRDEST YET!
APU OR SEYMOUR - WHO'S BETTER AT Q*BERT?
APRIL 1986
$1.50
A BONGO PUBLICATION
TIGER TEEN!
LSO INSIDE...
COREY HART
Takes off his sunglasses
EXCLUSIVE PHOTOS!
FALCO- I WANT TO BE LIKE TACO!"
TACO- "I WANT TO BE LIKE FALCO!"
Gary Neuman
"Rap music--HAH!
t's just a fad, mate!"
Kaja goo-goo's
BABY PIX!
SCRITTI POLITTI
"Sometimes we wish we weren't famous!"
SIMON LeBON
WIN HIS PANTS!
Dan Studney/Jim Lincoln: Story
Erick Tran: Pencils
Tim Bavington: Inks
Chris Ungar: Letters
Nathan Kane: Colors

EXCLUSIVE PIX! *FINALLY!* TIGER TEEN TAKES YOU..

INSIDE HUNKY SEYMOUR SKINNER'S LEGENDARY BACHELOR BUNGALOW!

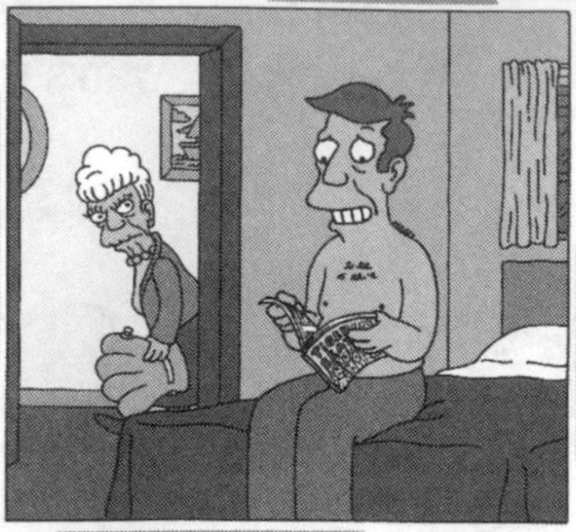

I'm very proud of my hospital corners!

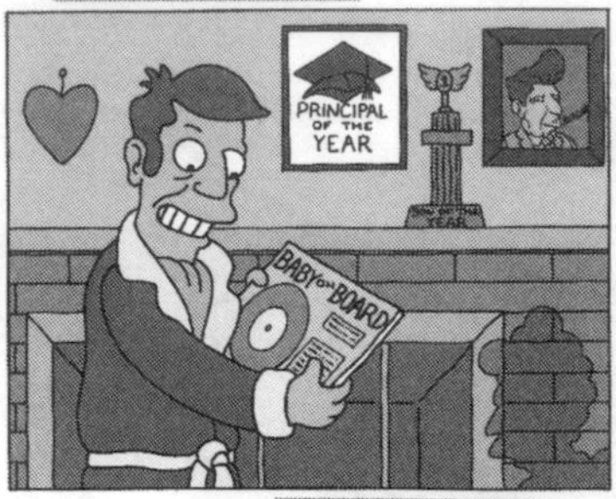
PRINCIPAL OF THE YEAR
BABY ON BOARD

Time to get rid of this old junk and make some room!

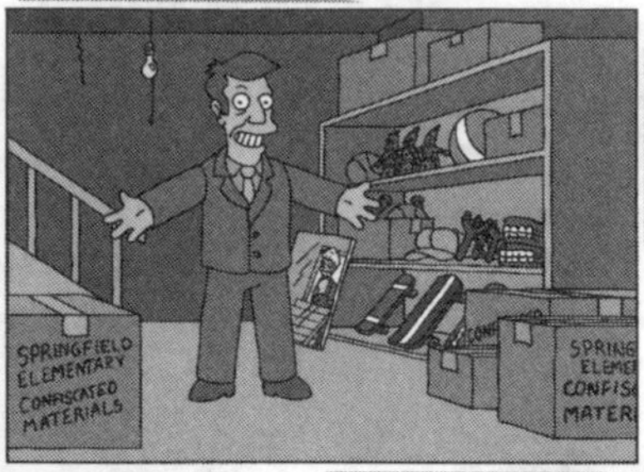
SPRINGFIELD ELEMENTARY CONFISCATED MATERIALS

Feel like a school girl again in Seymour's private playroom!

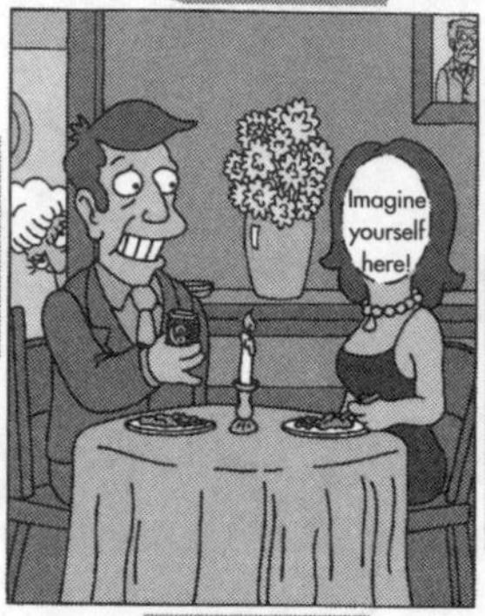
Imagine yourself here!

This empty chair is just waiting for a girl like you!

Barney's COMPATIBILITY QUIZ!

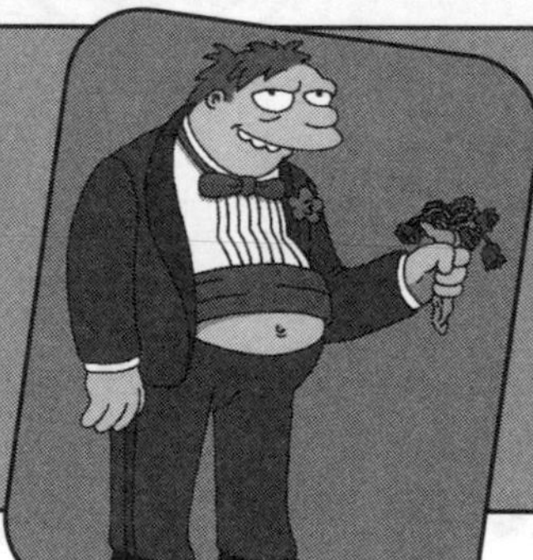

Imagine yourself on a romantic dinner date with that heart-throbbingest of Be Sharps, Barney Gumble. Answer these questions to discover if you're the girl Barney's been dreaming about!

Barney asks you to pass him the hors d'oeuvres. You reach for...

A. Caviar
B. Pate
C. Beer nuts

"How about some music to heighten the mood?" You...

A. Hire a violinist to serenade you during dessert
B. Suck up by putting on something by the Be-Sharps
C. Sign up with the karaoke guy

"Braaap!!"

A. "Oh. Corned beef for lunch?"
B. "Good lord of all that's holy, my eyes are burning!"
C. "Can I freshen your drink?"

You discover a pattern of self-destructive behavior that will ultimately lead Barney into a downward spiral of shame, humiliation and self-degradation. You...

A. Get him straight to the Betty Ford Clinic
B. Plan an intervention with his closest friends
C. Ignore it

At the end of the evening, you...

A. Kiss him sweetly on the cheek like a sister
B. Hold him tightly as if it were the last time
C. Slip him twenty bucks

If you answered 'C' to any or all of these questions, you are compatible with Barney. If 'A' or 'B' - you are compatible with the rest of the world.

HOMER SIMPSON
answers 40
intimate questions

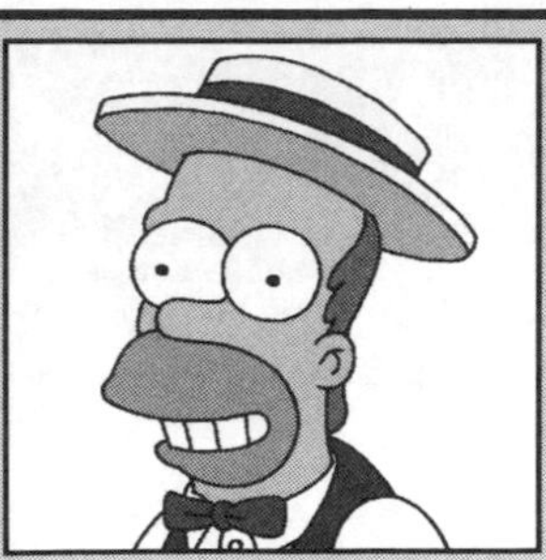

/hat are your hobbies?
enjoy poker with the boys, television, drinking beer, and safety ancing.

/hy do you prefer not to talk about your arriage?
arriage? I'm not married! Who told you I was married? at's ridiculous. I'm an eligible young bachelor with a swingin' ngle lifestyle. Just ask my wife, Marge. D'oh!!

it true that you don't care if you're called a quare?
ey, if loving barbershop is square, I don't want to be ound...man.

ou were a nuclear safety inspector before you became professional singer. How are the jobs different?
/ell, it's not too different. At the plant, I used to sneak into the room closet to wear funny hats and sing to myself. I guess the nly difference is that now I'm out of the closet. You can quote e on that!

/hat's the history of barbershop singing?
/ho do I look like, the freakin' Shell answer man? No, eriously...because people are always saying, "You look like that as guy!" What was the question again?

Word on the street is that you're a big donut fan. If you were a donut, what kind would you be?
Hmm... Well for one thing, I'd have sprinkles. And frosting. I'd be fashionably powdered and I would contain both jelly and cream. I would weigh over two hundred pounds and be chocolate rippled. There would be statues of me at baking schools and I would be served with fourteen gallons of milk! I would come with an extra bucket of sugar! People would compose songs about me! They'd make a tv movie about my life story! People would proclaim me Carby, King of the Donut Men. But I digress. I believe your original question had to do with some mythical donut street...?

Do you think the group will ever split up?
As long as they're putting music on vinyl, the Be Sharps will be there to record it.

Who are your favorite singers?
Ray Stevens has had a profound effect on me. The Doodletown Pipers are easily the world's greatest band. Of course, Grand Funk Railroad's music has been the soundtrack for my life and they opened up my mind to the possibility of time travel and inspired my lifelong dream--to build the world's biggest tom-tom.

Who is your favorite actor?
Oh, that guy...you know, the guy with the show. The one with the hair and the leg thingy.

What is your favorite food?
Pork chops, donuts, honey-roasted peanuts, my patented space-age moon waffles, ice cream cakes, Krusty burgers, Krusty burgers with cheese, Double Krusty burgers, frozen Salisbury steak dinners, corn dogs, Duff beer, beer nuts, pretzels, popcorn, cotton candy, vegimite sandwiches, anything with caramel coating, that stuff from France in the funny package, syrup, pudding roll-ups, chocolate, chocolate bars, chocolate kisses, chocolate milk, crumbled-up chocolatey things. Mmm...chocolate. This interview is over!

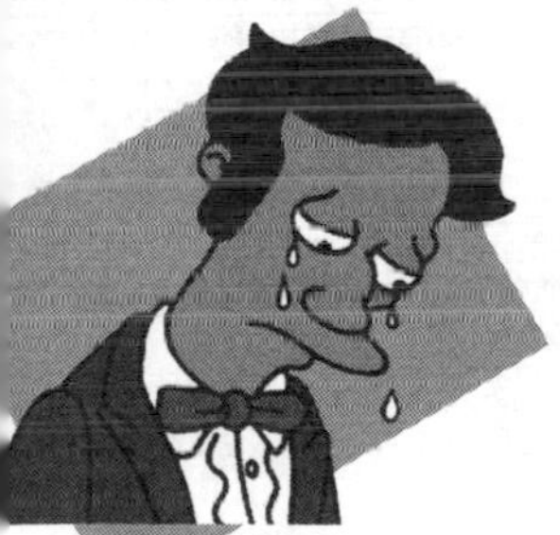

APU DE BEAUMARCHAIS
--LICK HIS TEARS AWAY

IN THE SECRET HEART of Apu de Beaumarchais, there is a corner with the word SORROW written on it. If you love Apu and would like to truly help lick his tears away (metaphorically, of course--tears have been proven to contain strains of certain viruses and Tiger Teen assumes no liability in the actual licking thereof), listen as he tells you about the things a girl can do to make him happy.

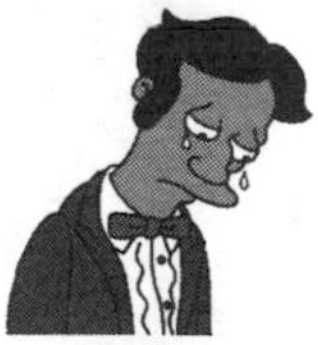

For a woman to give the awful, dark sadness in my soul the "rush of the bum", she will have to be a woman who concerns herself with the small, intimate details of life. A smile. A touch. The ever-so important freshness dating on dairy products.

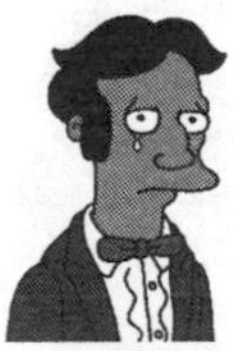

Much of my tormented misery comes from a lack of inner harmony and balance, along with an unnatural fear of large denominations of currency. If you were my friend and cared enough, when out shopping with me, you would always have exact change and use no bills larger than a twenty please.

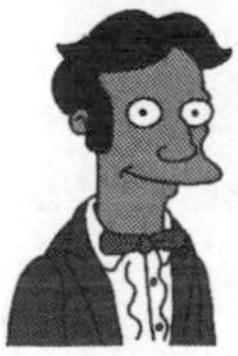

But the best way to shine a bright light into the ever-expanding blackness that eats away at my very being is a simple thing--always be open. Anyone who wishes to stop the flow of my salty tears will be conveniently available to me twenty-four hours a day. Including weekends and holidays. Thank you and come again.

EDNA KRABAPPEL grades *THE BE SHARPS*

Only one diehard dame in all of Springfield can lay claim to being a Be Sharps groupie from their earliest days back at Moe's Cavern--***Edna Krabappel.***

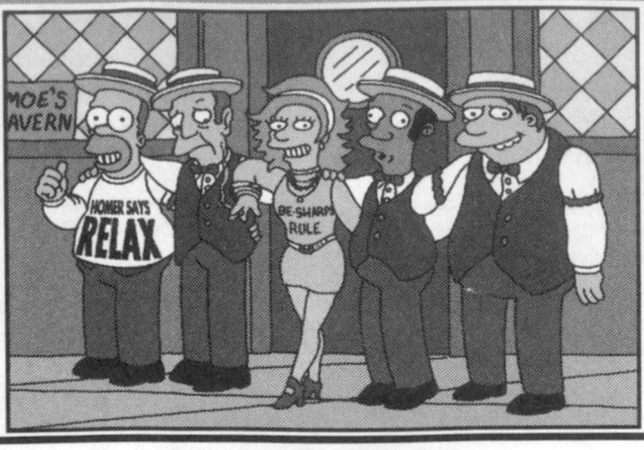
MOE'S CAVERN
HOMER SAYS RELAX
BE SHARPS RULE

Read on to find out which of the mega-popular barbershop quartet makes the 'cut'- and which Be Sharp comes up flat!"

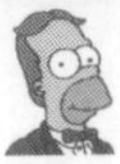

HOMER: B-minus. *"Nigel set up our date as a publicity stu Homer's the fun-loving one of the group. At the mall, we got kicked of Spencer's Gifts when he drank all the liquid out of the 'ever- flow beer tap!' Points off because for some reason, he refused to take back to his place for a nightcap. Maybe his house wasn't clean."*

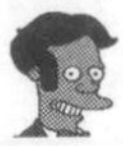

APU: B. *"He's got that whole eastern thing going. Once a girl has been held by the many arms of Vishnu, she's not likely to let go."*

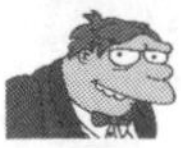

BARNEY: A-plus. *"With Barney there's no morning after. He can't even remember the night before."*

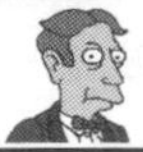

SEYMOUR: D-minus. *"The former principal has too many principles. What does a girl have to do anyway?"*

Photo Essay from the "WHERE ARE THEY NOW?" Files..

CLANCY WIGGUM: THE FIFTH BE SHARP

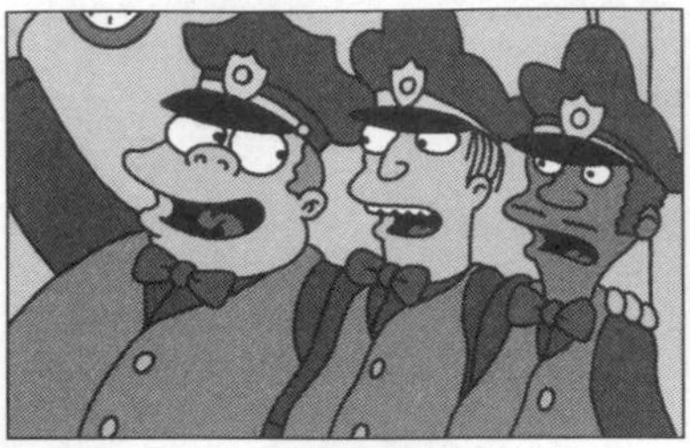

After being booted out of the Be Sharps, Wiggum started his own group: The Barber-Cop Quartet. The video from their single, 'Revolution No. 9-1-1' never achieved heavy rotation on the MTV chart.

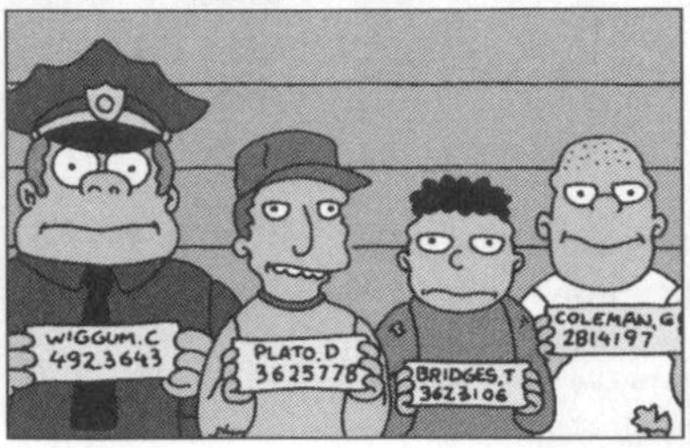
WIGGUM, C
4923643
PLATO, D
3625778
BRIDGES, T
3623106
COLEMAN, G
2814197

After the inevitable break-up, Clancy fell in with the wrong crowd, all desperately seeking to relive their former celebrity.

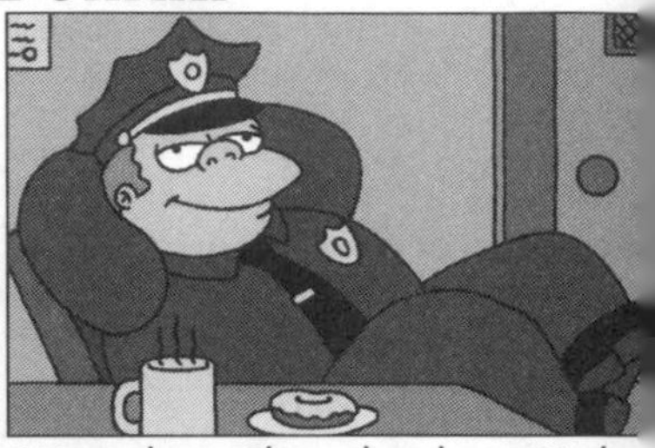

We spoke to Clancy by phone. He ha this to say: "No, I'm not bitter. I alway know deep in my heart that no matte what terrible things I've done, there always a place for me right here in the Springfield Police Department."

Even as we go to press, the ***Be Sharps*** are hard at work on their first-ever feature-length movie--

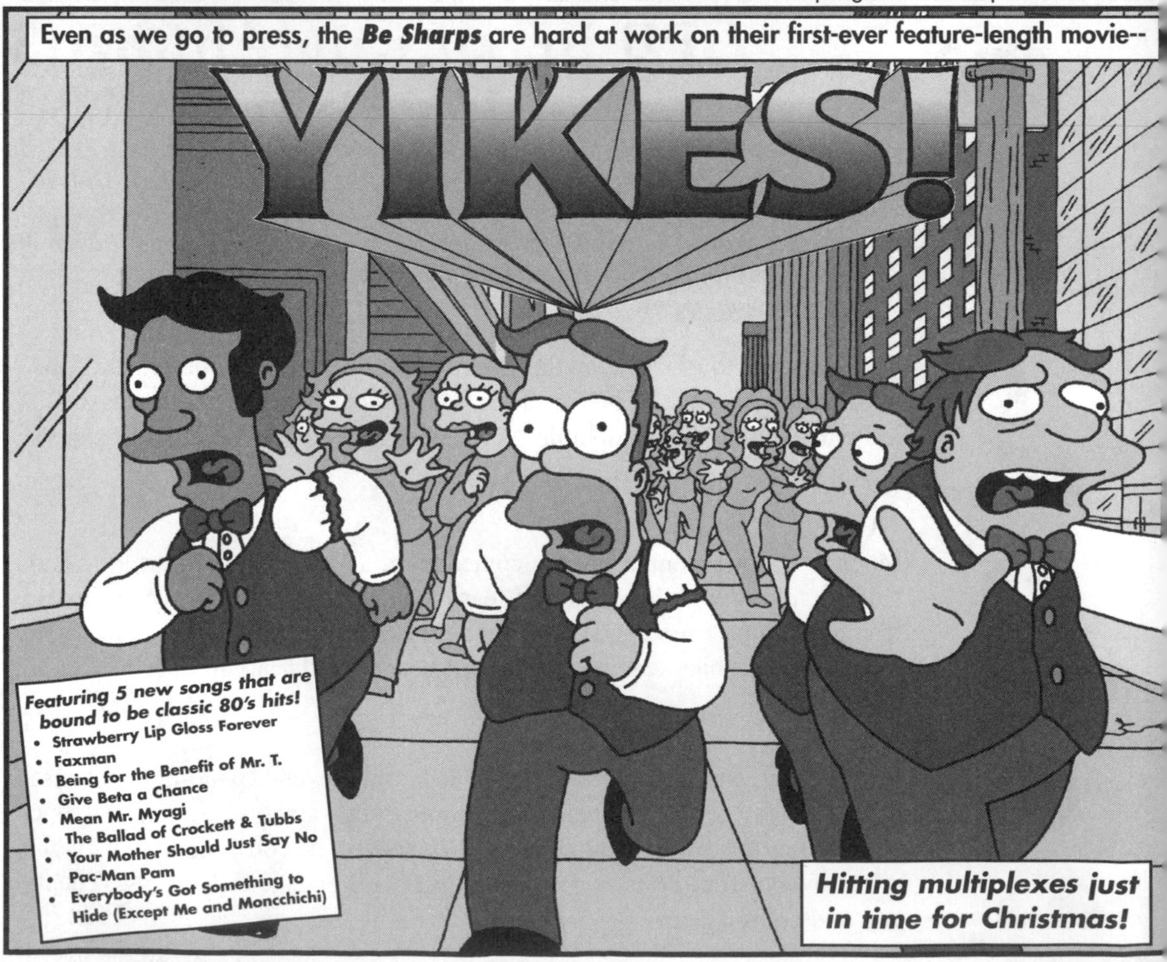
YIKES!

Featuring 5 new songs that are bound to be classic 80's hits!

- **Strawberry Lip Gloss Forever**
- **Faxman**
- **Being for the Benefit of Mr. T.**
- **Give Beta a Chance**
- **Mean Mr. Myagi**
- **The Ballad of Crockett & Tubbs**
- **Your Mother Should Just Say No**
- **Pac-Man Pam**
- **Everybody's Got Something to Hide (Except Me and Moncchichi)**

Hitting multiplexes just in time for Christmas!

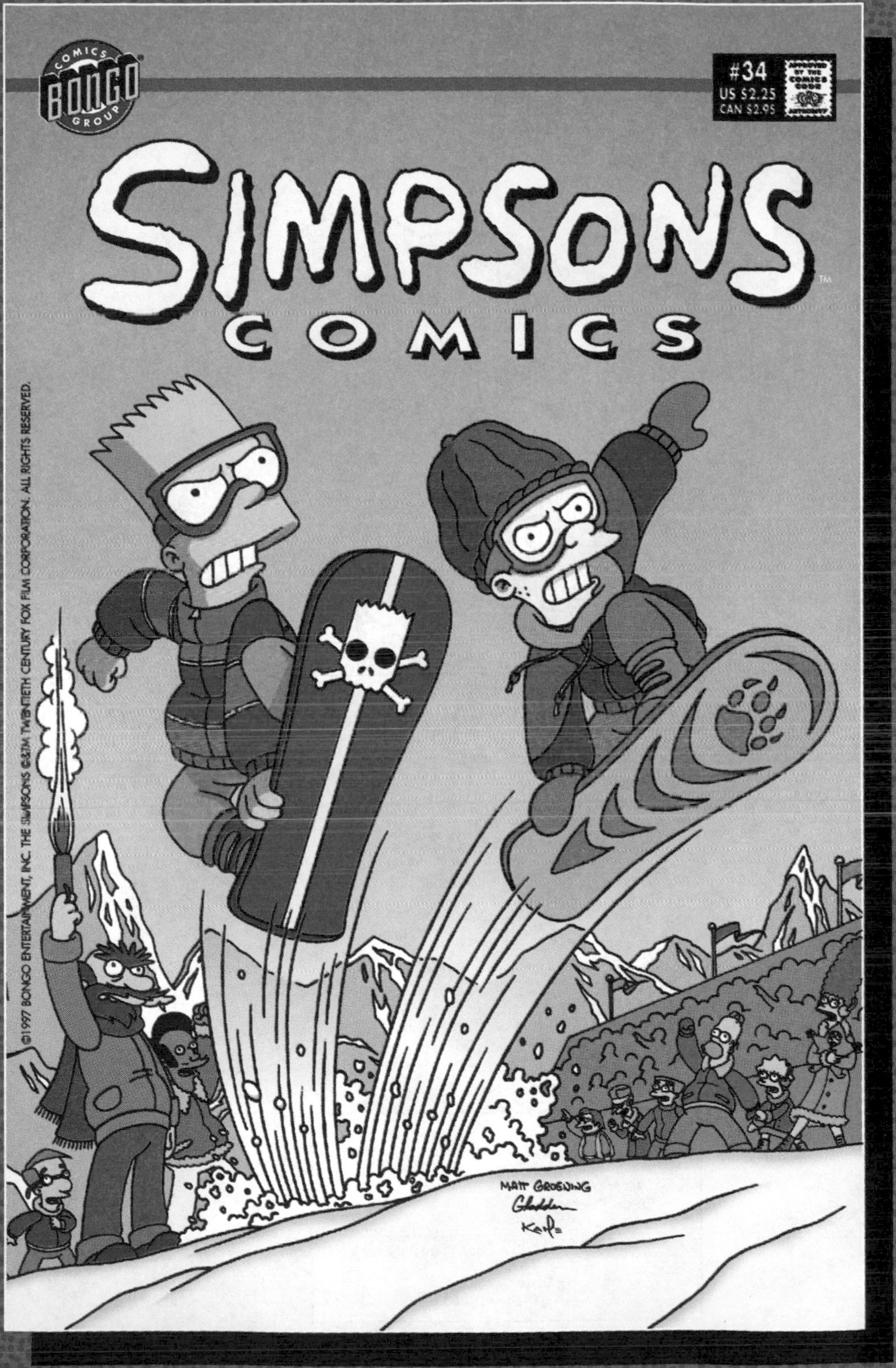
BONGO
COMICS GROUP
#34
US $2.25
CAN $2.95
SIMPSONS™
COMICS
©1997 BONGO ENTERTAINMENT, INC. THE SIMPSONS ©&TM TWENTIETH CENTURY FOX FILM CORPORATION. ALL RIGHTS RESERVED.
MATT GROENING

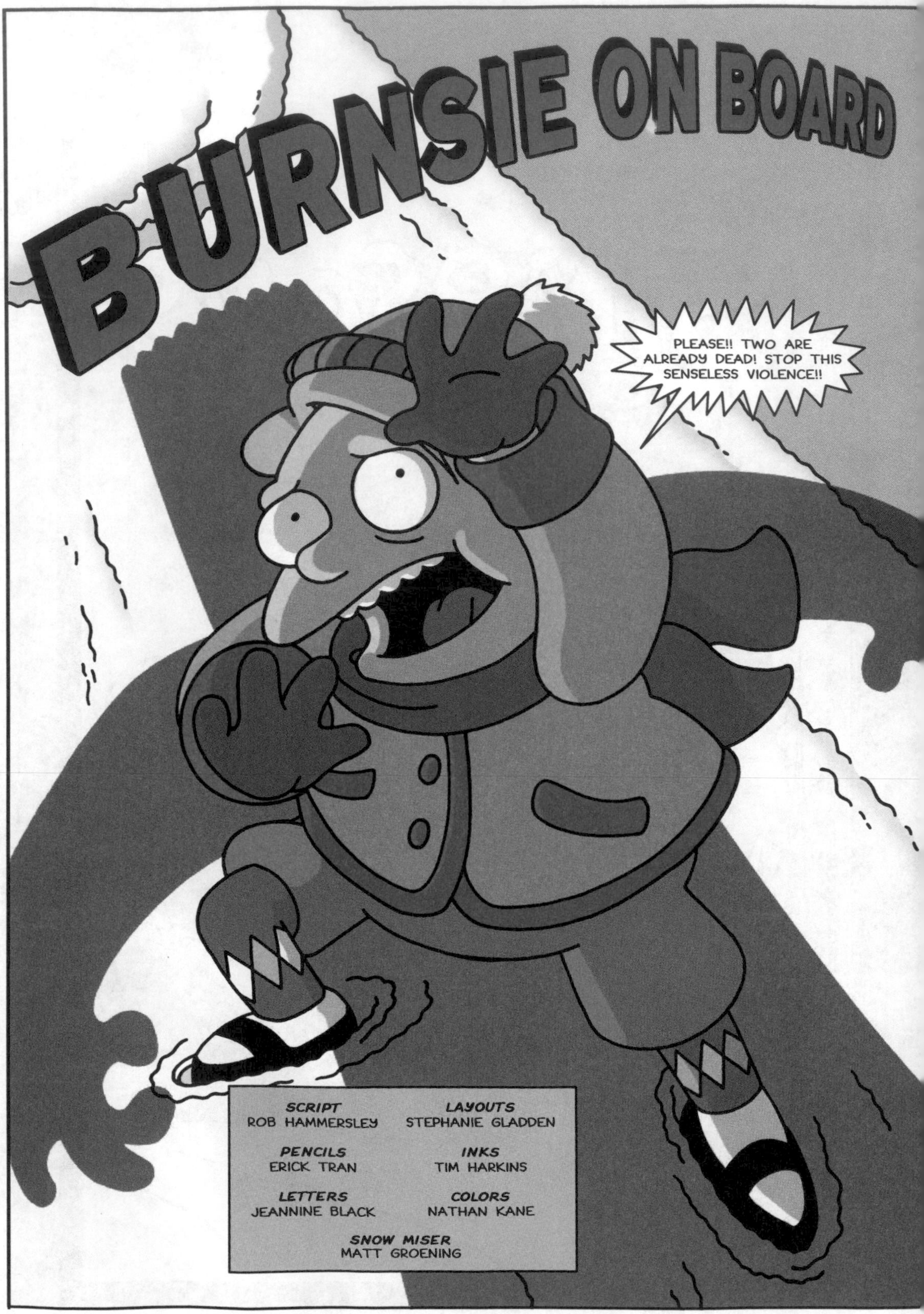
BURNSIE ON BOARD
PLEASE!! TWO ARE ALREADY DEAD! STOP THIS SENSELESS VIOLENCE!!
SCRIPT
ROB HAMMERSLEY
LAYOUTS
STEPHANIE GLADDEN
PENCILS
ERICK TRAN
INKS
TIM HARKINS
LETTERS
JEANNINE BLACK
COLORS
NATHAN KANE
SNOW MISER
MATT GROENING

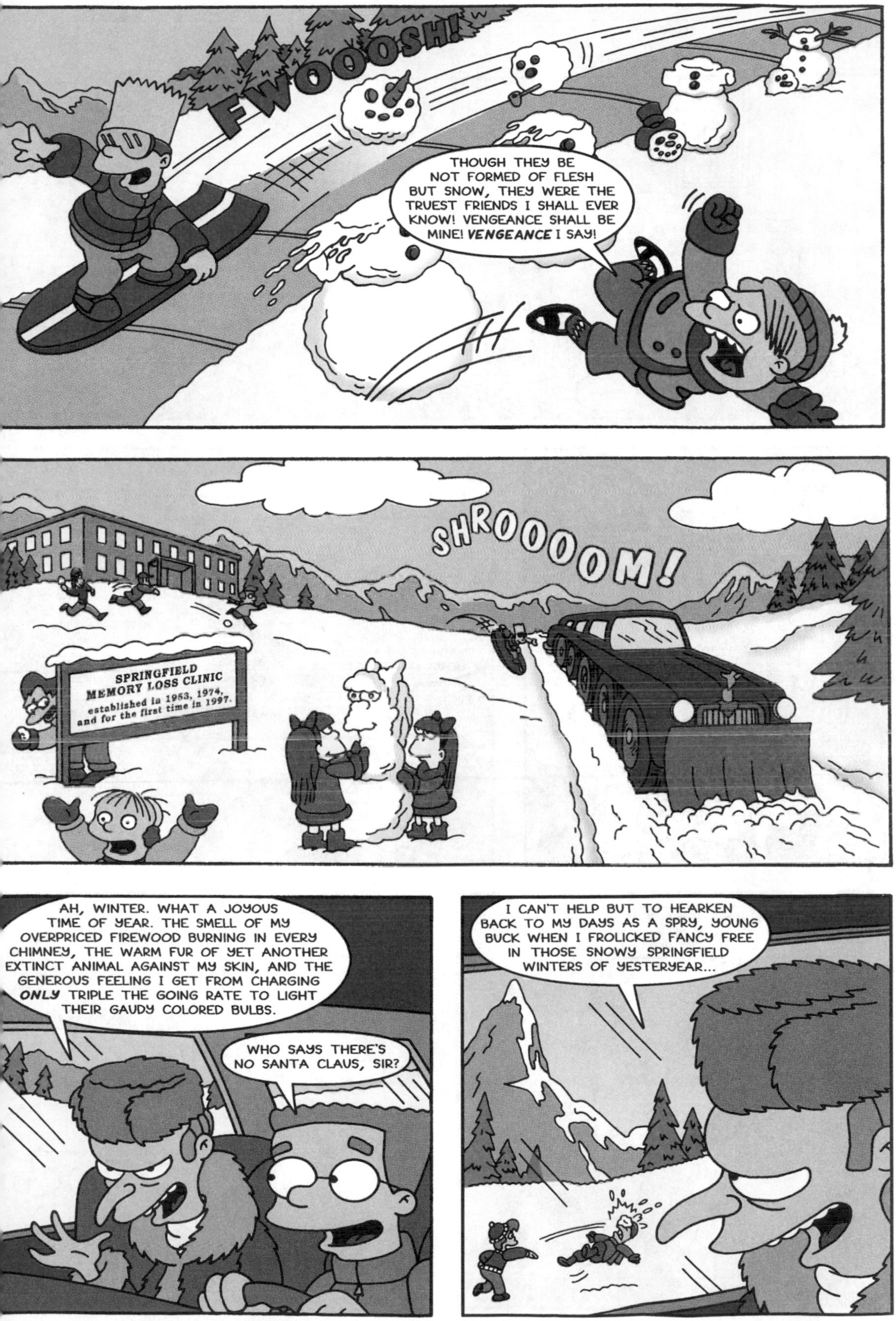
FWOOOSH!
THOUGH THEY BE NOT FORMED OF FLESH BUT SNOW, THEY WERE THE TRUEST FRIENDS I SHALL EVER KNOW! VENGEANCE SHALL BE MINE! *VENGEANCE* I SAY!
SHROOOOOM!
SPRINGFIELD MEMORY LOSS CLINIC established in 1953, 1974, and for the first time in 1997.
AH, WINTER. WHAT A JOYOUS TIME OF YEAR. THE SMELL OF MY OVERPRICED FIREWOOD BURNING IN EVERY CHIMNEY, THE WARM FUR OF YET ANOTHER EXTINCT ANIMAL AGAINST MY SKIN, AND THE GENEROUS FEELING I GET FROM CHARGING *ONLY* TRIPLE THE GOING RATE TO LIGHT THEIR GAUDY COLORED BULBS.
WHO SAYS THERE'S NO SANTA CLAUS, SIR?
I CAN'T HELP BUT TO HEARKEN BACK TO MY DAYS AS A SPRY, YOUNG BUCK WHEN I FROLICKED FANCY FREE IN THOSE SNOWY SPRINGFIELD WINTERS OF YESTERYEAR...

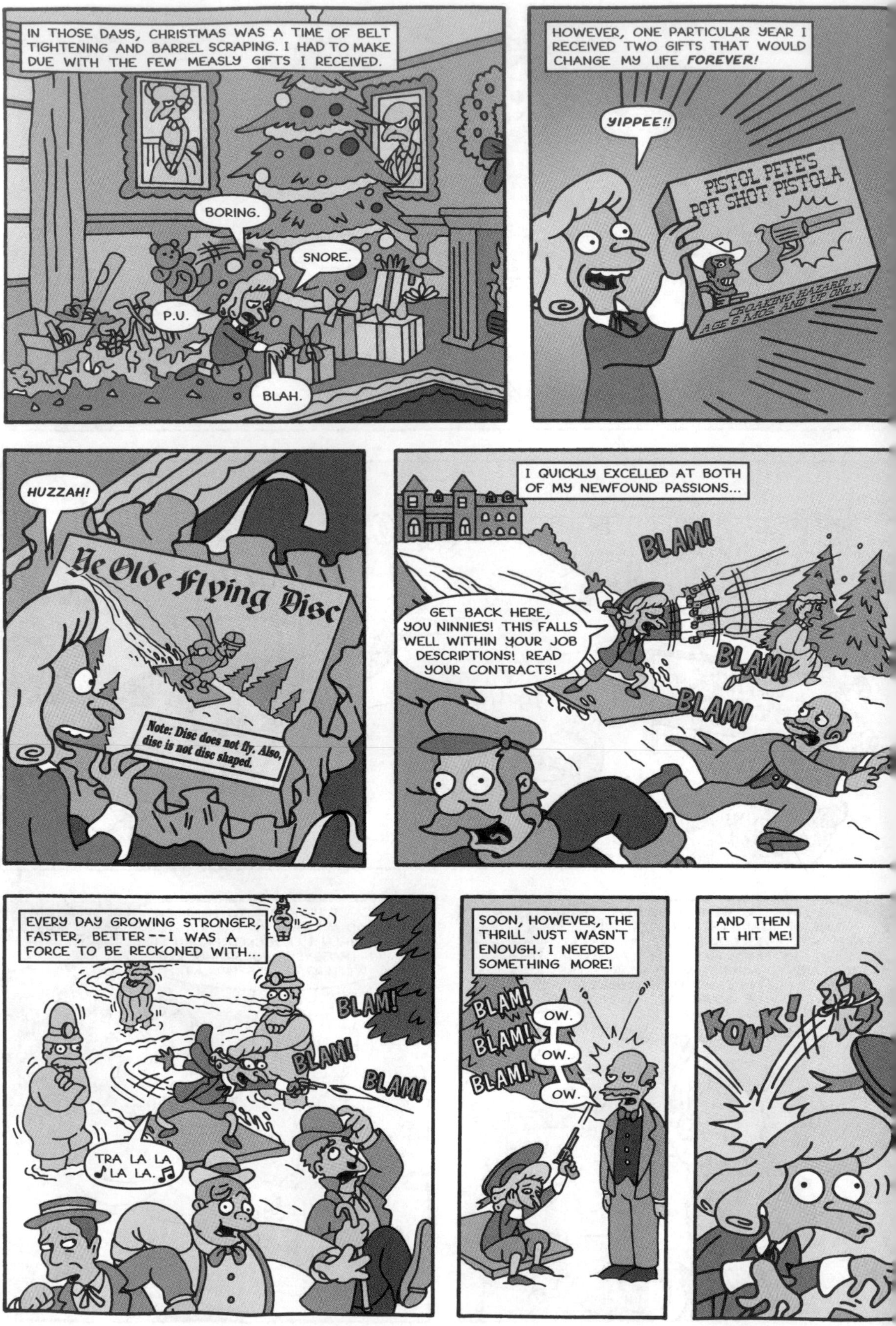
IN THOSE DAYS, CHRISTMAS WAS A TIME OF BELT TIGHTENING AND BARREL SCRAPING. I HAD TO MAKE DUE WITH THE FEW MEASLY GIFTS I RECEIVED.
BORING.
SNORE.
P.U.
BLAH.
HOWEVER, ONE PARTICULAR YEAR I RECEIVED TWO GIFTS THAT WOULD CHANGE MY LIFE FOREVER!
YIPPEE!!
PISTOL PETE'S POT SHOT PISTOLA
CROAKING HAZARD AGE 6 MOS. AND UP ONLY.
HUZZAH!
Ye Olde Flying Disc
Note: Disc does not fly. Also, disc is not disc shaped.
I QUICKLY EXCELLED AT BOTH OF MY NEWFOUND PASSIONS...
BLAM!
GET BACK HERE, YOU NINNIES! THIS FALLS WELL WITHIN YOUR JOB DESCRIPTIONS! READ YOUR CONTRACTS!
BLAM!
BLAM!
EVERY DAY GROWING STRONGER, FASTER, BETTER--I WAS A FORCE TO BE RECKONED WITH...
BLAM!
BLAM!
BLAM!
TRA LA LA LA LA.
SOON, HOWEVER, THE THRILL JUST WASN'T ENOUGH. I NEEDED SOMETHING MORE!
BLAM!
BLAM!
BLAM!
OW.
OW.
OW.
AND THEN IT HIT ME!
KONK!

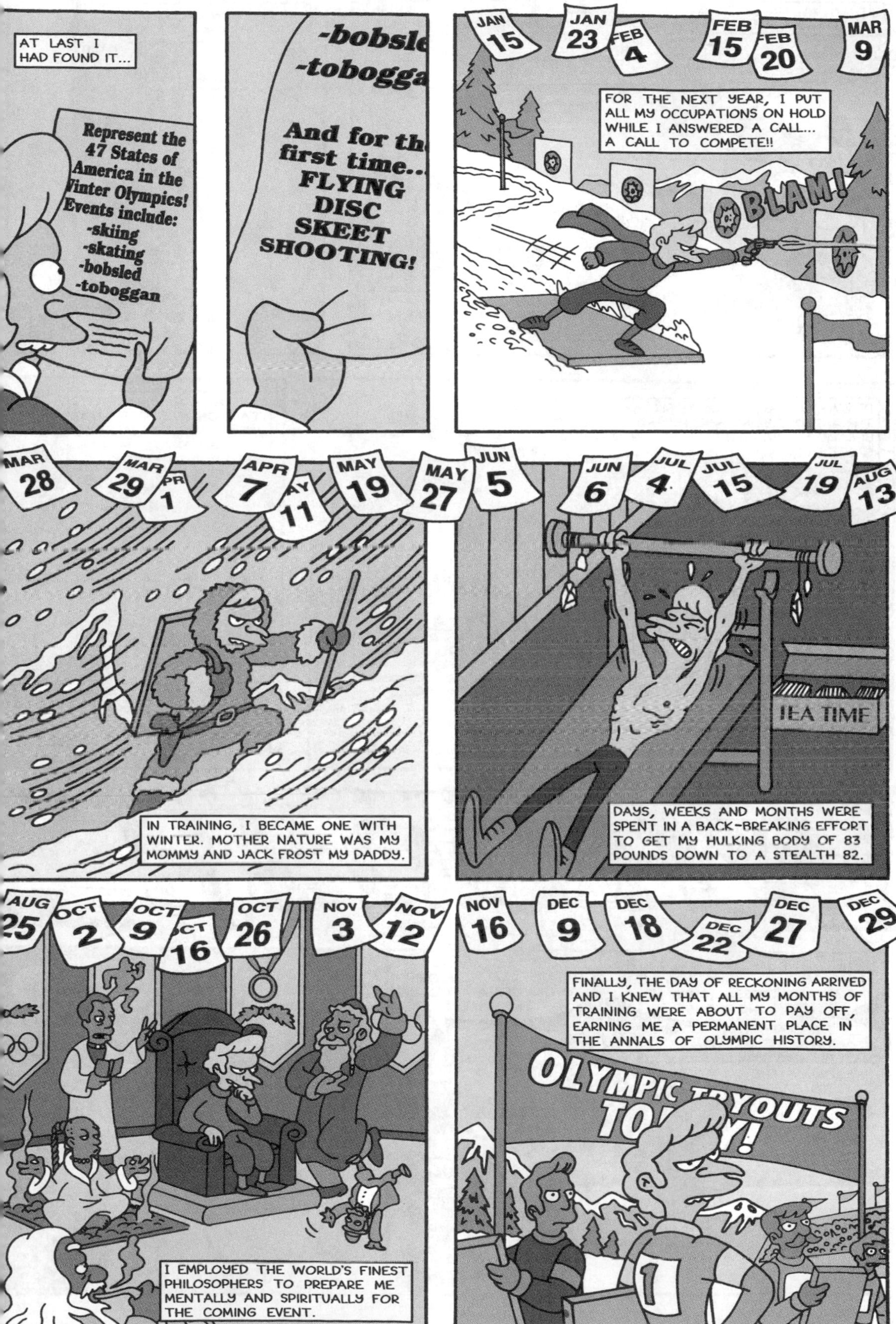
AT LAST I HAD FOUND IT...
Represent the 47 States of America in the Winter Olympics! Events include:
-skiing
-skating
-bobsled
-toboggan
And for the first time... FLYING DISC SKEET SHOOTING!
JAN 15
JAN 23
FEB 4
FEB 15
FEB 20
MAR 9
FOR THE NEXT YEAR, I PUT ALL MY OCCUPATIONS ON HOLD WHILE I ANSWERED A CALL... A CALL TO COMPETE!!
BLAM!
MAR 28
MAR 29
APR 7
MAY 19
MAY 27
JUN 5
JUN 6
JUL 4
JUL 15
JUL 19
AUG 13
IN TRAINING, I BECAME ONE WITH WINTER. MOTHER NATURE WAS MY MOMMY AND JACK FROST MY DADDY.
TEA TIME
DAYS, WEEKS AND MONTHS WERE SPENT IN A BACK-BREAKING EFFORT TO GET MY HULKING BODY OF 83 POUNDS DOWN TO A STEALTH 82.
OCT 2
OCT 9
OCT 26
NOV 3
NOV 12
NOV 16
DEC 9
DEC 18
DEC 22
DEC 27
DEC 29
I EMPLOYED THE WORLD'S FINEST PHILOSOPHERS TO PREPARE ME MENTALLY AND SPIRITUALLY FOR THE COMING EVENT.
FINALLY, THE DAY OF RECKONING ARRIVED AND I KNEW THAT ALL MY MONTHS OF TRAINING WERE ABOUT TO PAY OFF, EARNING ME A PERMANENT PLACE IN THE ANNALS OF OLYMPIC HISTORY.
1

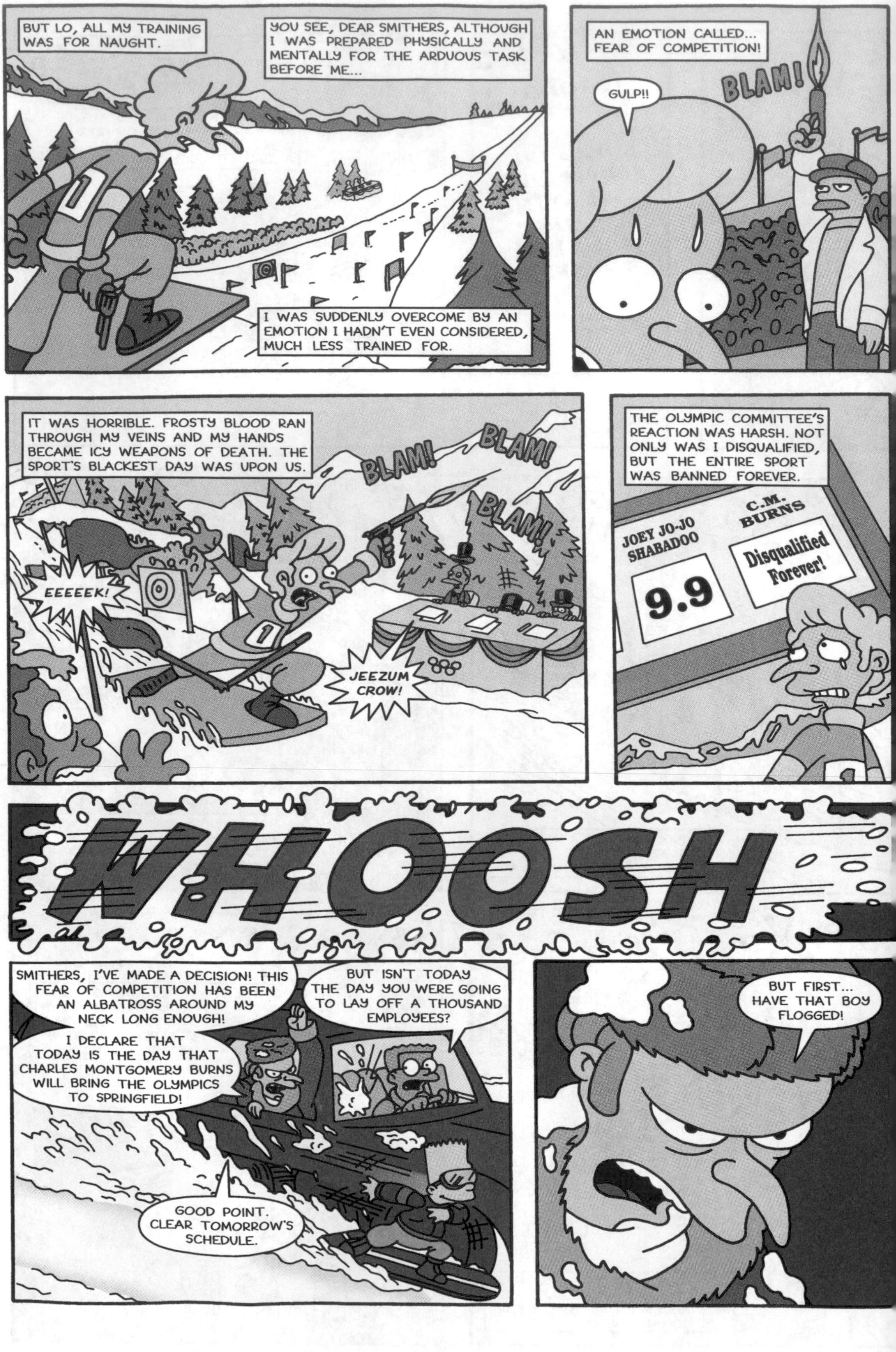
BUT LO, ALL MY TRAINING WAS FOR NAUGHT.
YOU SEE, DEAR SMITHERS, ALTHOUGH I WAS PREPARED PHYSICALLY AND MENTALLY FOR THE ARDUOUS TASK BEFORE ME...
I WAS SUDDENLY OVERCOME BY AN EMOTION I HADN'T EVEN CONSIDERED, MUCH LESS TRAINED FOR.
AN EMOTION CALLED... FEAR OF COMPETITION!
GULP!!
BLAM!
IT WAS HORRIBLE. FROSTY BLOOD RAN THROUGH MY VEINS AND MY HANDS BECAME ICY WEAPONS OF DEATH. THE SPORT'S BLACKEST DAY WAS UPON US.
BLAM!
BLAM!
BLAM!
EEEEEK!
JEEZUM CROW!
THE OLYMPIC COMMITTEE'S REACTION WAS HARSH. NOT ONLY WAS I DISQUALIFIED, BUT THE ENTIRE SPORT WAS BANNED FOREVER.
JOEY JO-JO SHABADOO
9.9
C.M. BURNS
Disqualified Forever!
WHOOSH
SMITHERS, I'VE MADE A DECISION! THIS FEAR OF COMPETITION HAS BEEN AN ALBATROSS AROUND MY NECK LONG ENOUGH!
I DECLARE THAT TODAY IS THE DAY THAT CHARLES MONTGOMERY BURNS WILL BRING THE OLYMPICS TO SPRINGFIELD!
BUT ISN'T TODAY THE DAY YOU WERE GOING TO LAY OFF A THOUSAND EMPLOYEES?
GOOD POINT. CLEAR TOMORROW'S SCHEDULE.
BUT FIRST... HAVE THAT BOY FLOGGED!

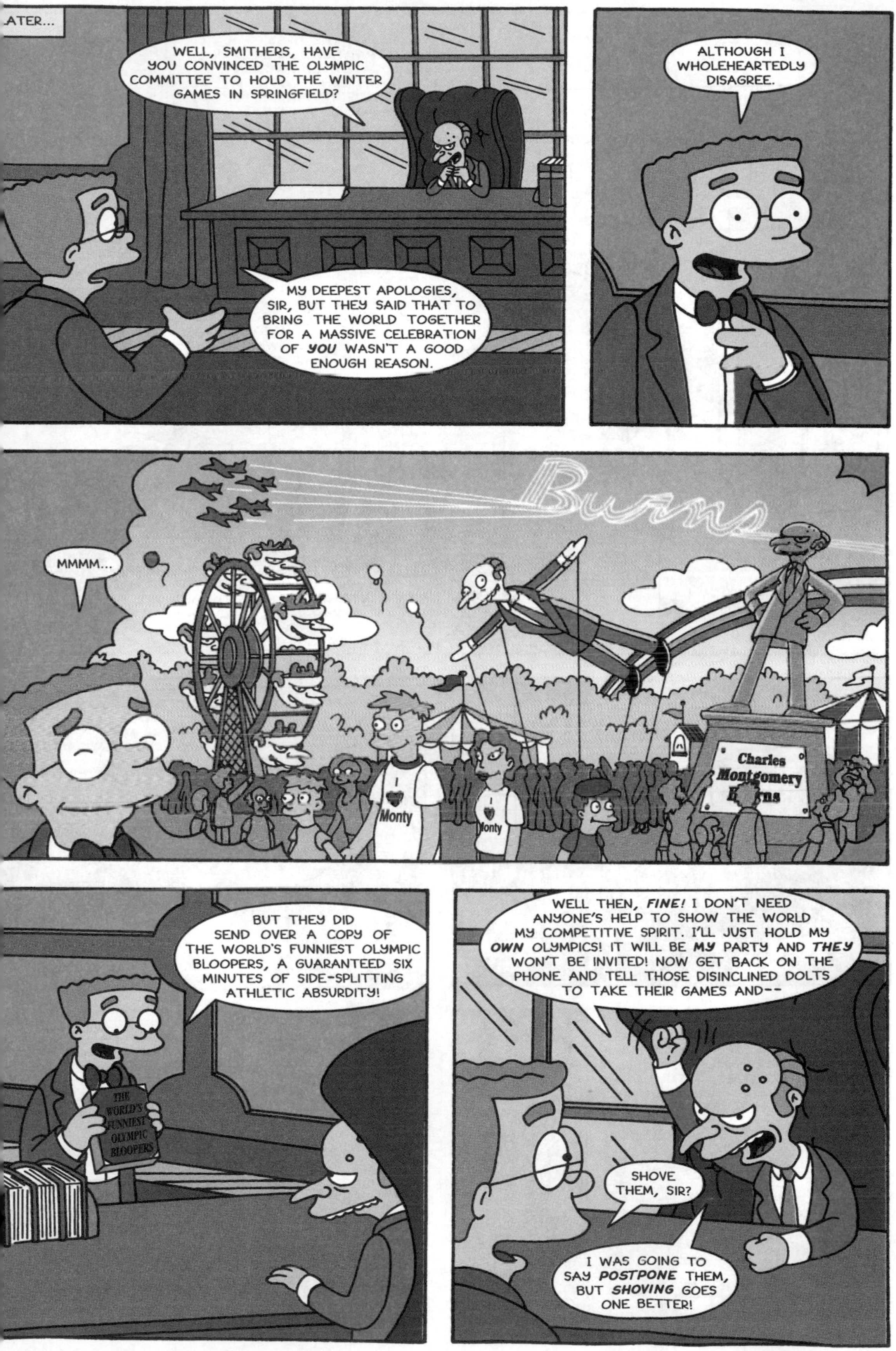
LATER...
WELL, SMITHERS, HAVE YOU CONVINCED THE OLYMPIC COMMITTEE TO HOLD THE WINTER GAMES IN SPRINGFIELD?
MY DEEPEST APOLOGIES, SIR, BUT THEY SAID THAT TO BRING THE WORLD TOGETHER FOR A MASSIVE CELEBRATION OF *YOU* WASN'T A GOOD ENOUGH REASON.
ALTHOUGH I WHOLEHEARTEDLY DISAGREE.
Burns
MMMM...
I Monty
I Monty
Charles Montgomery
BUT THEY DID SEND OVER A COPY OF THE WORLD'S FUNNIEST OLYMPIC BLOOPERS, A GUARANTEED SIX MINUTES OF SIDE-SPLITTING ATHLETIC ABSURDITY!
THE WORLD'S FUNNIEST OLYMPIC BLOOPERS
WELL THEN, *FINE!* I DON'T NEED ANYONE'S HELP TO SHOW THE WORLD MY COMPETITIVE SPIRIT. I'LL JUST HOLD MY *OWN* OLYMPICS! IT WILL BE *MY* PARTY AND *THEY* WON'T BE INVITED! NOW GET BACK ON THE PHONE AND TELL THOSE DISINCLINED DOLTS TO TAKE THEIR GAMES AND--
SHOVE THEM, SIR?
I WAS GOING TO SAY *POSTPONE* THEM, BUT *SHOVING* GOES ONE BETTER!

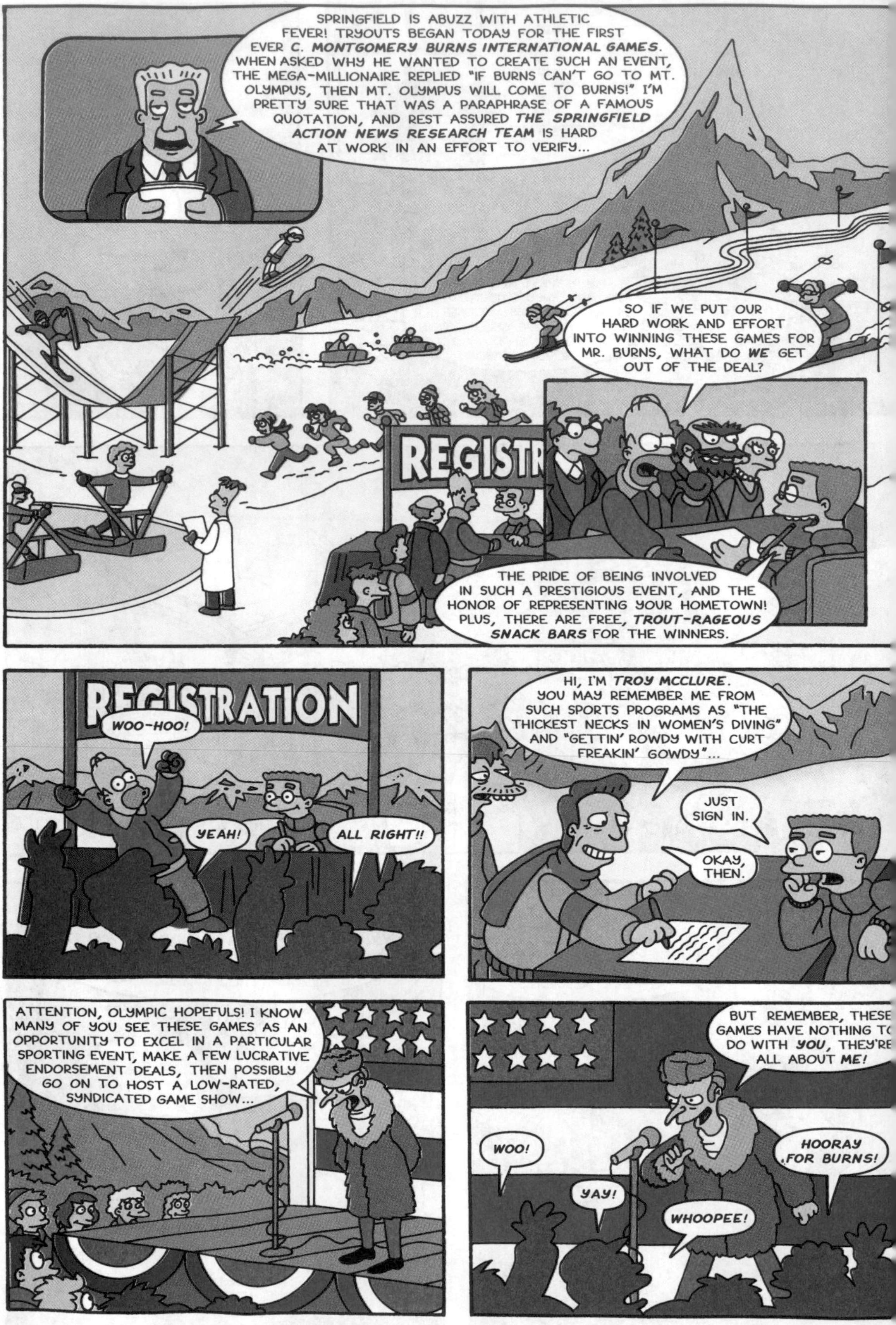
SPRINGFIELD IS ABUZZ WITH ATHLETIC FEVER! TRYOUTS BEGAN TODAY FOR THE FIRST EVER C. MONTGOMERY BURNS INTERNATIONAL GAMES. WHEN ASKED WHY HE WANTED TO CREATE SUCH AN EVENT, THE MEGA-MILLIONAIRE REPLIED "IF BURNS CAN'T GO TO MT. OLYMPUS, THEN MT. OLYMPUS WILL COME TO BURNS!" I'M PRETTY SURE THAT WAS A PARAPHRASE OF A FAMOUS QUOTATION, AND REST ASSURED THE SPRINGFIELD ACTION NEWS RESEARCH TEAM IS HARD AT WORK IN AN EFFORT TO VERIFY...
SO IF WE PUT OUR HARD WORK AND EFFORT INTO WINNING THESE GAMES FOR MR. BURNS, WHAT DO WE GET OUT OF THE DEAL?
REGISTR
THE PRIDE OF BEING INVOLVED IN SUCH A PRESTIGIOUS EVENT, AND THE HONOR OF REPRESENTING YOUR HOMETOWN! PLUS, THERE ARE FREE, TROUT-RAGEOUS SNACK BARS FOR THE WINNERS.
REGISTRATION
WOO-HOO!
YEAH!
ALL RIGHT!!
HI, I'M TROY MCCLURE. YOU MAY REMEMBER ME FROM SUCH SPORTS PROGRAMS AS "THE THICKEST NECKS IN WOMEN'S DIVING" AND "GETTIN' ROWDY WITH CURT FREAKIN' GOWDY"...
JUST SIGN IN.
OKAY, THEN.
ATTENTION, OLYMPIC HOPEFULS! I KNOW MANY OF YOU SEE THESE GAMES AS AN OPPORTUNITY TO EXCEL IN A PARTICULAR SPORTING EVENT, MAKE A FEW LUCRATIVE ENDORSEMENT DEALS, THEN POSSIBLY GO ON TO HOST A LOW-RATED, SYNDICATED GAME SHOW...
BUT REMEMBER, THESE GAMES HAVE NOTHING TO DO WITH YOU, THEY'RE ALL ABOUT ME!
WOO!
YAY!
WHOOPEE!
HOORAY FOR BURNS!

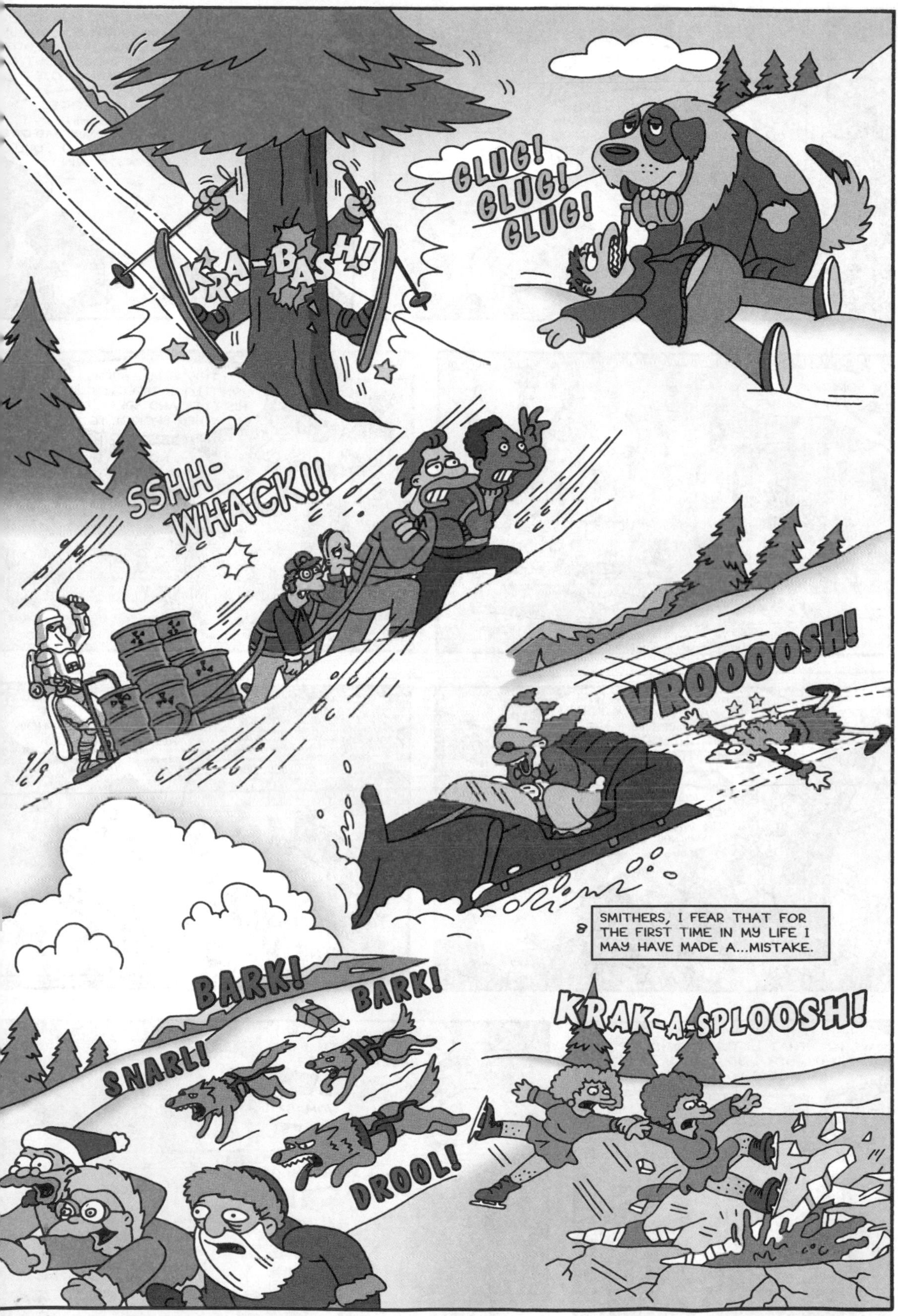
GLUG! GLUG! GLUG!
KRA-BASH!
SSHH-WHACK!!
VROOOOOSH!
SMITHERS, I FEAR THAT FOR THE FIRST TIME IN MY LIFE I MAY HAVE MADE A...MISTAKE.
BARK!
BARK!
SNARL!
DROOL!
KRAK-A-SPLOOSH!

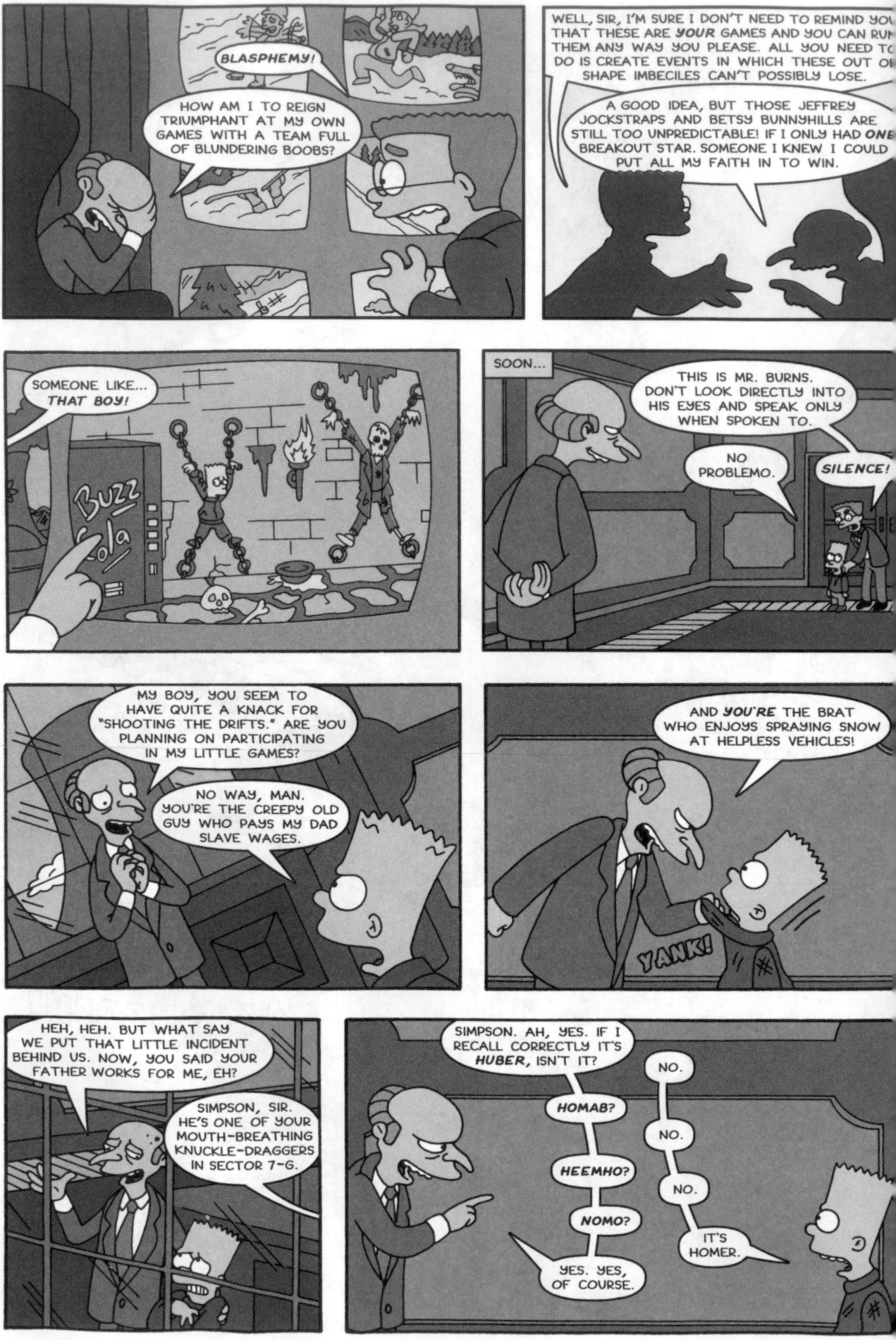
BLASPHEMY!
HOW AM I TO REIGN TRIUMPHANT AT MY OWN GAMES WITH A TEAM FULL OF BLUNDERING BOOBS?
WELL, SIR, I'M SURE I DON'T NEED TO REMIND YO THAT THESE ARE YOUR GAMES AND YOU CAN RU THEM ANY WAY YOU PLEASE. ALL YOU NEED T DO IS CREATE EVENTS IN WHICH THESE OUT O SHAPE IMBECILES CAN'T POSSIBLY LOSE.
A GOOD IDEA, BUT THOSE JEFFREY JOCKSTRAPS AND BETSY BUNNYHILLS ARE STILL TOO UNPREDICTABLE! IF I ONLY HAD ON BREAKOUT STAR. SOMEONE I KNEW I COULD PUT ALL MY FAITH IN TO WIN.
SOMEONE LIKE... THAT BOY!
Buzz Cola
SOON...
THIS IS MR. BURNS. DON'T LOOK DIRECTLY INTO HIS EYES AND SPEAK ONLY WHEN SPOKEN TO.
NO PROBLEMO.
SILENCE!
MY BOY, YOU SEEM TO HAVE QUITE A KNACK FOR "SHOOTING THE DRIFTS." ARE YOU PLANNING ON PARTICIPATING IN MY LITTLE GAMES?
NO WAY, MAN. YOU'RE THE CREEPY OLD GUY WHO PAYS MY DAD SLAVE WAGES.
AND YOU'RE THE BRAT WHO ENJOYS SPRAYING SNOW AT HELPLESS VEHICLES!
YANK!
HEH, HEH. BUT WHAT SAY WE PUT THAT LITTLE INCIDENT BEHIND US. NOW, YOU SAID YOUR FATHER WORKS FOR ME, EH?
SIMPSON, SIR. HE'S ONE OF YOUR MOUTH-BREATHING KNUCKLE-DRAGGERS IN SECTOR 7-G.
SIMPSON. AH, YES. IF I RECALL CORRECTLY IT'S HUBER, ISN'T IT?
NO.
HOMAB?
NO.
HEEMHO?
NO.
NOMO?
IT'S HOMER.
YES. YES, OF COURSE.

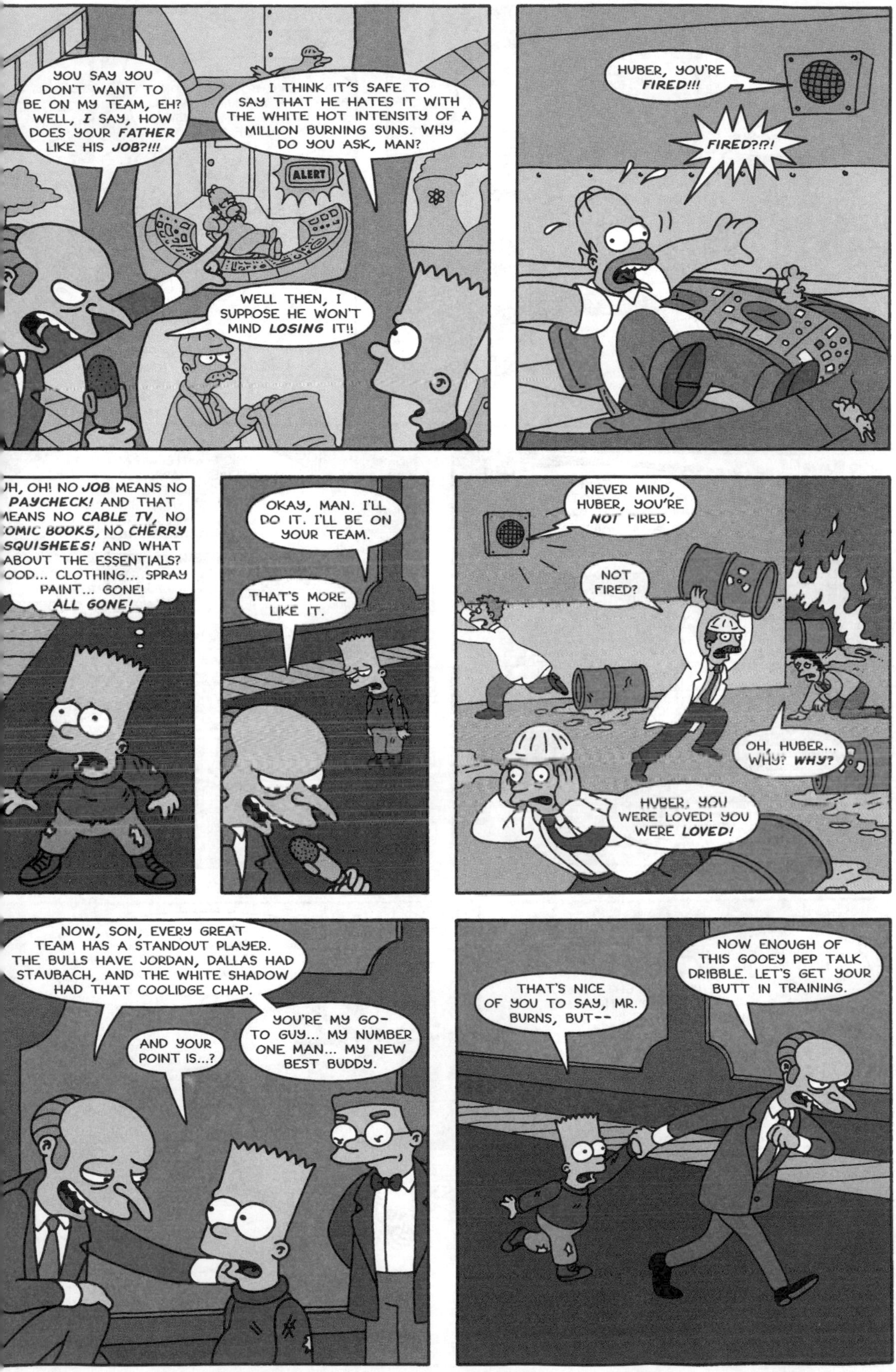
YOU SAY YOU DON'T WANT TO BE ON MY TEAM, EH? WELL, *I* SAY, HOW DOES YOUR *FATHER* LIKE HIS *JOB*?!!!
I THINK IT'S SAFE TO SAY THAT HE HATES IT WITH THE WHITE HOT INTENSITY OF A MILLION BURNING SUNS. WHY DO YOU ASK, MAN?
ALERT
WELL THEN, I SUPPOSE HE WON'T MIND *LOSING* IT!!
HUBER, YOU'RE *FIRED!!!*
FIRED?!?!
UH, OH! NO *JOB* MEANS NO *PAYCHECK!* AND THAT MEANS NO *CABLE TV,* NO *COMIC BOOKS,* NO *CHERRY SQUISHEES!* AND WHAT ABOUT THE ESSENTIALS? FOOD... CLOTHING... SPRAY PAINT... GONE! *ALL GONE!*
OKAY, MAN. I'LL DO IT. I'LL BE ON YOUR TEAM.
THAT'S MORE LIKE IT.
NEVER MIND, HUBER, YOU'RE *NOT* FIRED.
NOT FIRED?
OH, HUBER... WHY? *WHY?*
HUBER, YOU WERE LOVED! YOU WERE *LOVED!*
NOW, SON, EVERY GREAT TEAM HAS A STANDOUT PLAYER. THE BULLS HAVE JORDAN, DALLAS HAD STAUBACH, AND THE WHITE SHADOW HAD THAT COOLIDGE CHAP.
AND YOUR POINT IS...?
YOU'RE MY GO-TO GUY... MY NUMBER ONE MAN... MY NEW BEST BUDDY.
THAT'S NICE OF YOU TO SAY, MR. BURNS, BUT--
NOW ENOUGH OF THIS GOOEY PEP TALK DRIBBLE. LET'S GET YOUR BUTT IN TRAINING.

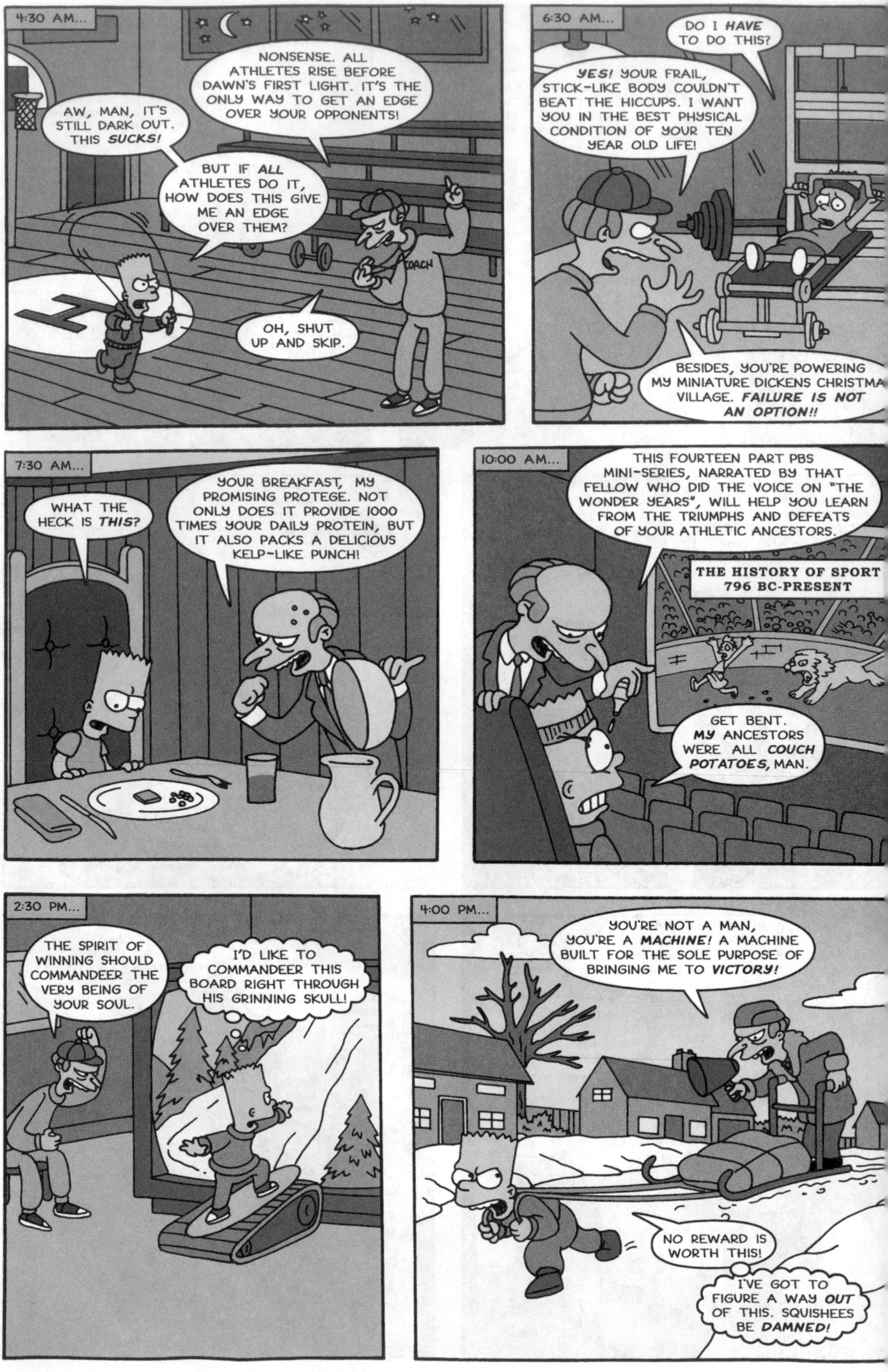
4:30 AM...
AW, MAN, IT'S STILL DARK OUT. THIS SUCKS!
NONSENSE. ALL ATHLETES RISE BEFORE DAWN'S FIRST LIGHT. IT'S THE ONLY WAY TO GET AN EDGE OVER YOUR OPPONENTS!
BUT IF ALL ATHLETES DO IT, HOW DOES THIS GIVE ME AN EDGE OVER THEM?
OH, SHUT UP AND SKIP.
COACH
6:30 AM...
DO I HAVE TO DO THIS?
YES! YOUR FRAIL, STICK-LIKE BODY COULDN'T BEAT THE HICCUPS. I WANT YOU IN THE BEST PHYSICAL CONDITION OF YOUR TEN YEAR OLD LIFE!
BESIDES, YOU'RE POWERING MY MINIATURE DICKENS CHRISTMA VILLAGE. FAILURE IS NOT AN OPTION!!
7:30 AM...
WHAT THE HECK IS THIS?
YOUR BREAKFAST, MY PROMISING PROTEGE. NOT ONLY DOES IT PROVIDE 1000 TIMES YOUR DAILY PROTEIN, BUT IT ALSO PACKS A DELICIOUS KELP-LIKE PUNCH!
10:00 AM...
THIS FOURTEEN PART PBS MINI-SERIES, NARRATED BY THAT FELLOW WHO DID THE VOICE ON "THE WONDER YEARS", WILL HELP YOU LEARN FROM THE TRIUMPHS AND DEFEATS OF YOUR ATHLETIC ANCESTORS.
THE HISTORY OF SPORT 796 BC-PRESENT
GET BENT. MY ANCESTORS WERE ALL COUCH POTATOES, MAN.
2:30 PM...
THE SPIRIT OF WINNING SHOULD COMMANDEER THE VERY BEING OF YOUR SOUL.
I'D LIKE TO COMMANDEER THIS BOARD RIGHT THROUGH HIS GRINNING SKULL!
4:00 PM...
YOU'RE NOT A MAN, YOU'RE A MACHINE! A MACHINE BUILT FOR THE SOLE PURPOSE OF BRINGING ME TO VICTORY!
NO REWARD IS WORTH THIS!
I'VE GOT TO FIGURE A WAY OUT OF THIS. SQUISHEES BE DAMNED!

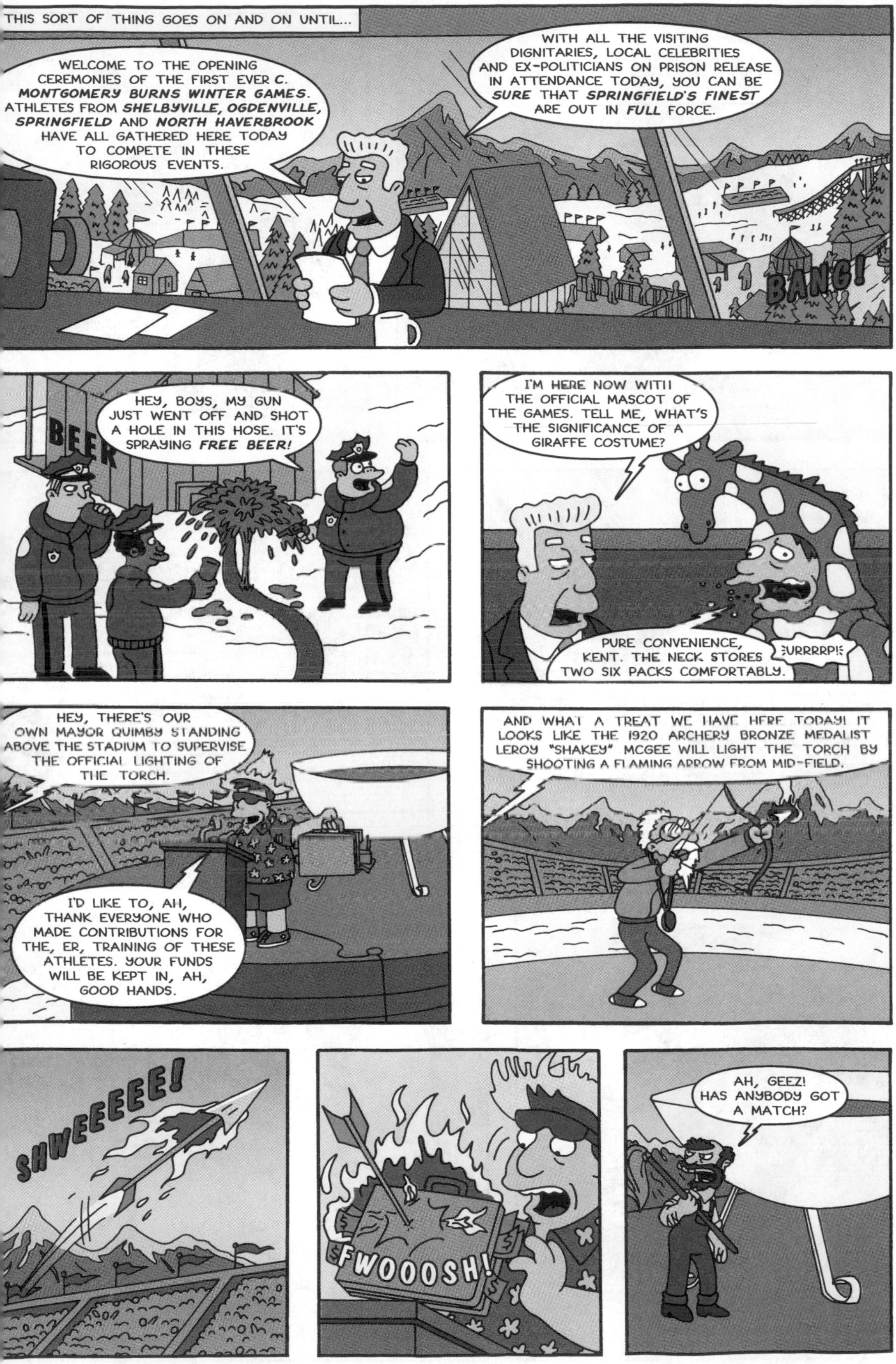

THIS SORT OF THING GOES ON AND ON UNTIL...
WELCOME TO THE OPENING CEREMONIES OF THE FIRST EVER C. MONTGOMERY BURNS WINTER GAMES. ATHLETES FROM SHELBYVILLE, OGDENVILLE, SPRINGFIELD AND NORTH HAVERBROOK HAVE ALL GATHERED HERE TODAY TO COMPETE IN THESE RIGOROUS EVENTS.
WITH ALL THE VISITING DIGNITARIES, LOCAL CELEBRITIES AND EX-POLITICIANS ON PRISON RELEASE IN ATTENDANCE TODAY, YOU CAN BE SURE THAT SPRINGFIELD'S FINEST ARE OUT IN FULL FORCE.
BANG!
BEER
HEY, BOYS, MY GUN JUST WENT OFF AND SHOT A HOLE IN THIS HOSE. IT'S SPRAYING FREE BEER!
I'M HERE NOW WITH THE OFFICIAL MASCOT OF THE GAMES. TELL ME, WHAT'S THE SIGNIFICANCE OF A GIRAFFE COSTUME?
PURE CONVENIENCE, KENT. THE NECK STORES TWO SIX PACKS COMFORTABLY.
URRRRP!
HEY, THERE'S OUR OWN MAYOR QUIMBY STANDING ABOVE THE STADIUM TO SUPERVISE THE OFFICIAL LIGHTING OF THE TORCH.
I'D LIKE TO, AH, THANK EVERYONE WHO MADE CONTRIBUTIONS FOR THE, ER, TRAINING OF THESE ATHLETES. YOUR FUNDS WILL BE KEPT IN, AH, GOOD HANDS.
AND WHAT A TREAT WE HAVE HERE TODAY! IT LOOKS LIKE THE 1920 ARCHERY BRONZE MEDALIST LEROY "SHAKEY" MCGEE WILL LIGHT THE TORCH BY SHOOTING A FLAMING ARROW FROM MID-FIELD.
SHWEEEEEE!
FWOOOSH!
AH, GEEZ! HAS ANYBODY GOT A MATCH?

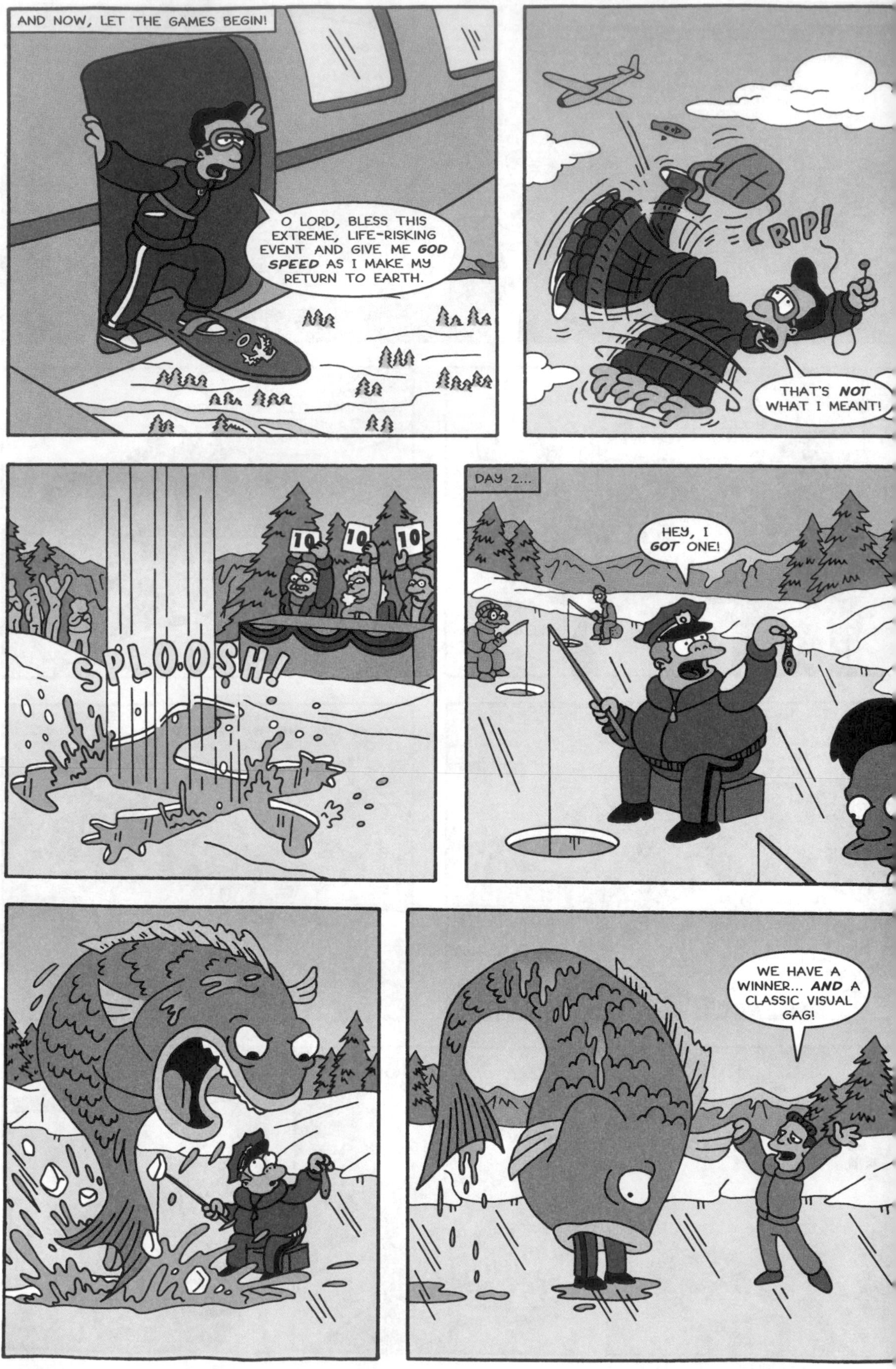
AND NOW, LET THE GAMES BEGIN!
O LORD, BLESS THIS EXTREME, LIFE-RISKING EVENT AND GIVE ME GOD SPEED AS I MAKE MY RETURN TO EARTH.
RIP!
THAT'S NOT WHAT I MEANT!
10
10
10
SPLOOSH!
DAY 2...
HEY, I GOT ONE!
WE HAVE A WINNER... AND A CLASSIC VISUAL GAG!

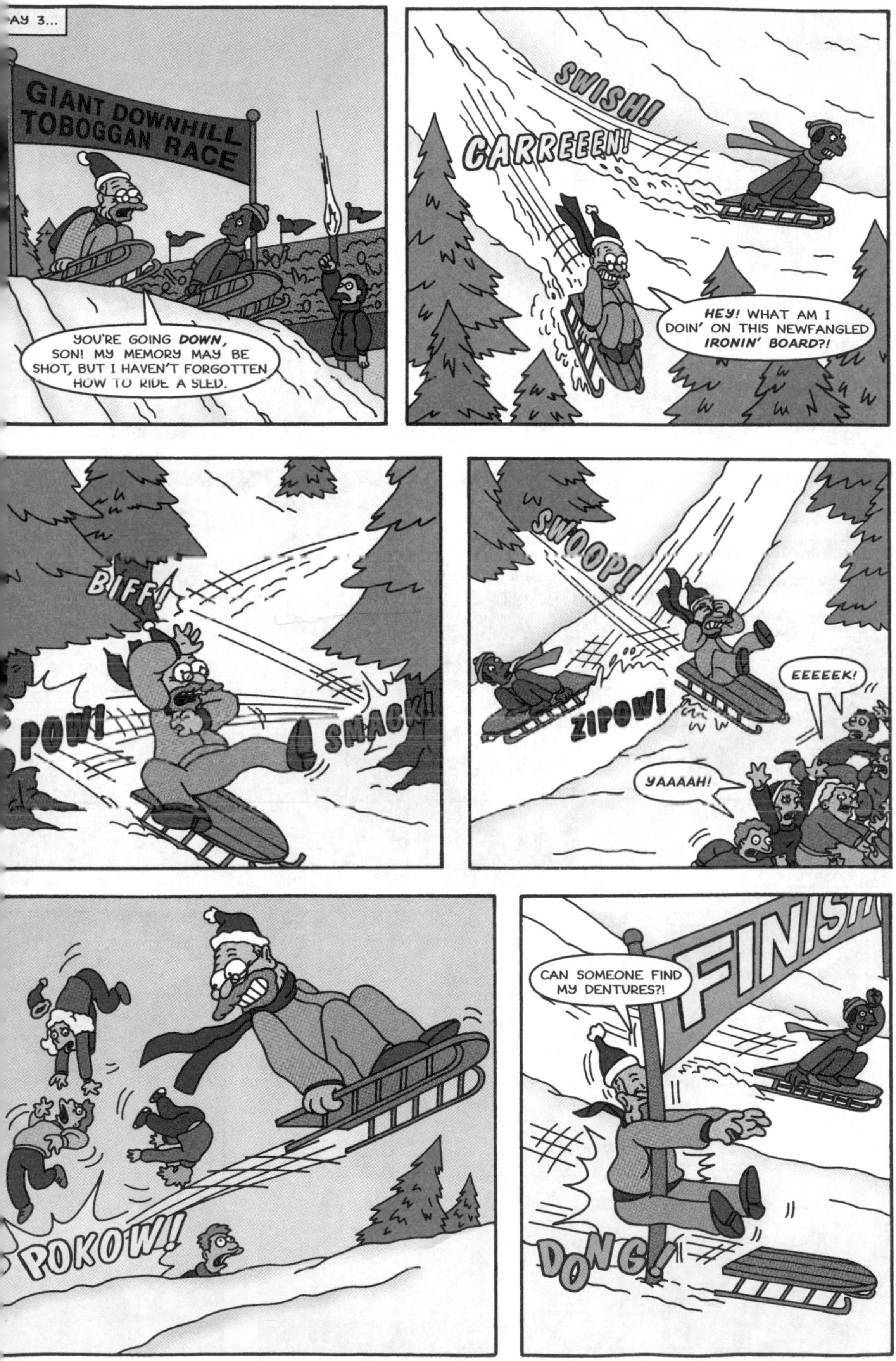
DAY 3...
GIANT DOWNHILL TOBOGGAN RACE
YOU'RE GOING DOWN, SON! MY MEMORY MAY BE SHOT, BUT I HAVEN'T FORGOTTEN HOW TO RIDE A SLED.
SWISH!
CARREEEN!
HEY! WHAT AM I DOIN' ON THIS NEWFANGLED IRONIN' BOARD?!
BIFF!
POW!
SMACK!
SWOOP!
ZIPOW!
EEEEEK!
YAAAAH!
POKOW!!
FINISH
CAN SOMEONE FIND MY DENTURES?!
DONG!!

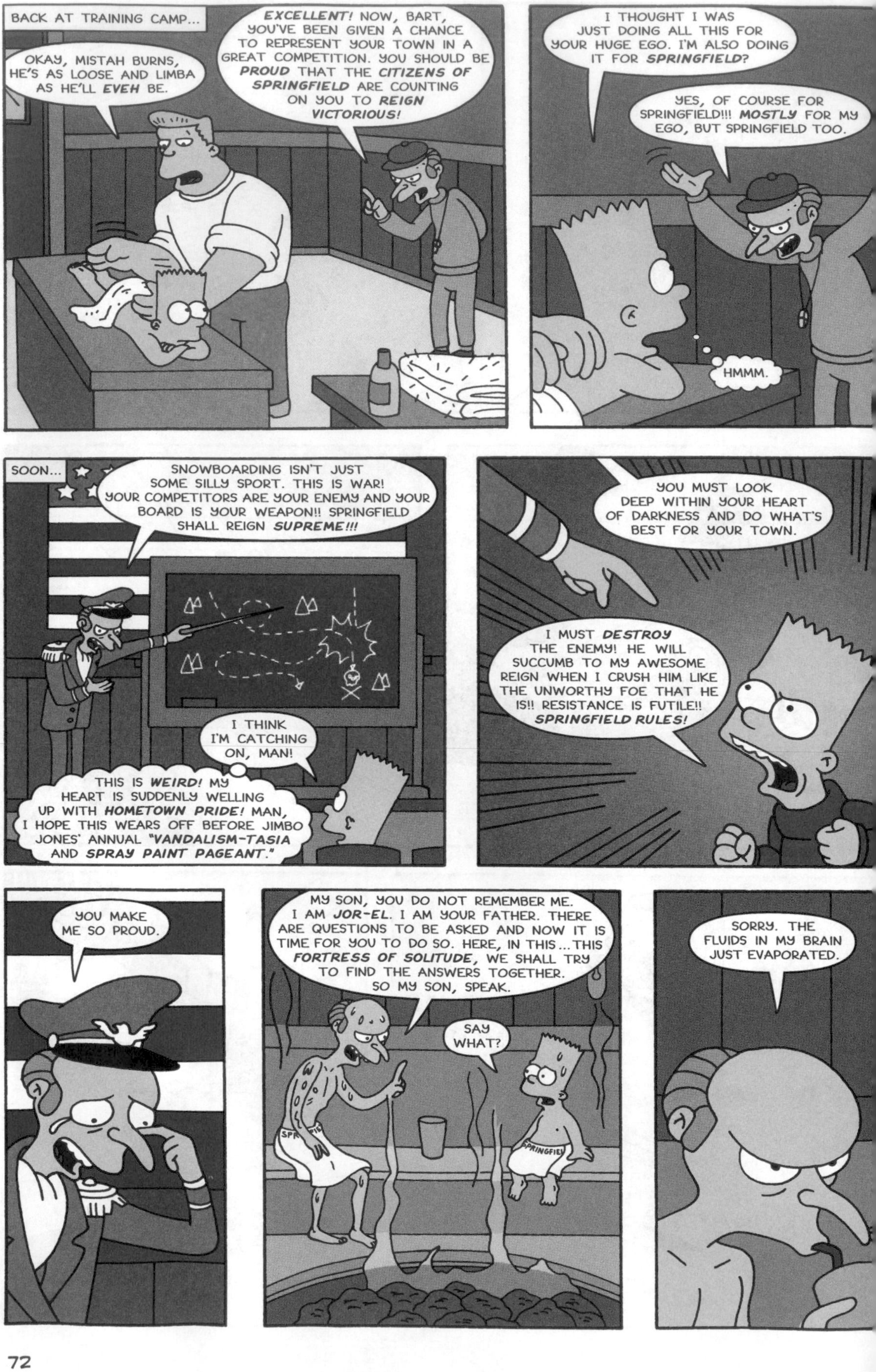
BACK AT TRAINING CAMP...
OKAY, MISTAH BURNS, HE'S AS LOOSE AND LIMBA AS HE'LL EVEH BE.
EXCELLENT! NOW, BART, YOU'VE BEEN GIVEN A CHANCE TO REPRESENT YOUR TOWN IN A GREAT COMPETITION. YOU SHOULD BE PROUD THAT THE CITIZENS OF SPRINGFIELD ARE COUNTING ON YOU TO REIGN VICTORIOUS!
I THOUGHT I WAS JUST DOING ALL THIS FOR YOUR HUGE EGO. I'M ALSO DOING IT FOR SPRINGFIELD?
YES, OF COURSE FOR SPRINGFIELD!!! MOSTLY FOR MY EGO, BUT SPRINGFIELD TOO.
HMMM.
SOON...
SNOWBOARDING ISN'T JUST SOME SILLY SPORT. THIS IS WAR! YOUR COMPETITORS ARE YOUR ENEMY AND YOUR BOARD IS YOUR WEAPON!! SPRINGFIELD SHALL REIGN SUPREME!!!
I THINK I'M CATCHING ON, MAN!
THIS IS WEIRD! MY HEART IS SUDDENLY WELLING UP WITH HOMETOWN PRIDE! MAN, I HOPE THIS WEARS OFF BEFORE JIMBO JONES' ANNUAL "VANDALISM-TASIA AND SPRAY PAINT PAGEANT."
YOU MUST LOOK DEEP WITHIN YOUR HEART OF DARKNESS AND DO WHAT'S BEST FOR YOUR TOWN.
I MUST DESTROY THE ENEMY! HE WILL SUCCUMB TO MY AWESOME REIGN WHEN I CRUSH HIM LIKE THE UNWORTHY FOE THAT HE IS!! RESISTANCE IS FUTILE!! SPRINGFIELD RULES!
YOU MAKE ME SO PROUD.
MY SON, YOU DO NOT REMEMBER ME. I AM JOR-EL. I AM YOUR FATHER. THERE ARE QUESTIONS TO BE ASKED AND NOW IT IS TIME FOR YOU TO DO SO. HERE, IN THIS...THIS FORTRESS OF SOLITUDE, WE SHALL TRY TO FIND THE ANSWERS TOGETHER. SO MY SON, SPEAK.
SAY WHAT?
SORRY. THE FLUIDS IN MY BRAIN JUST EVAPORATED.

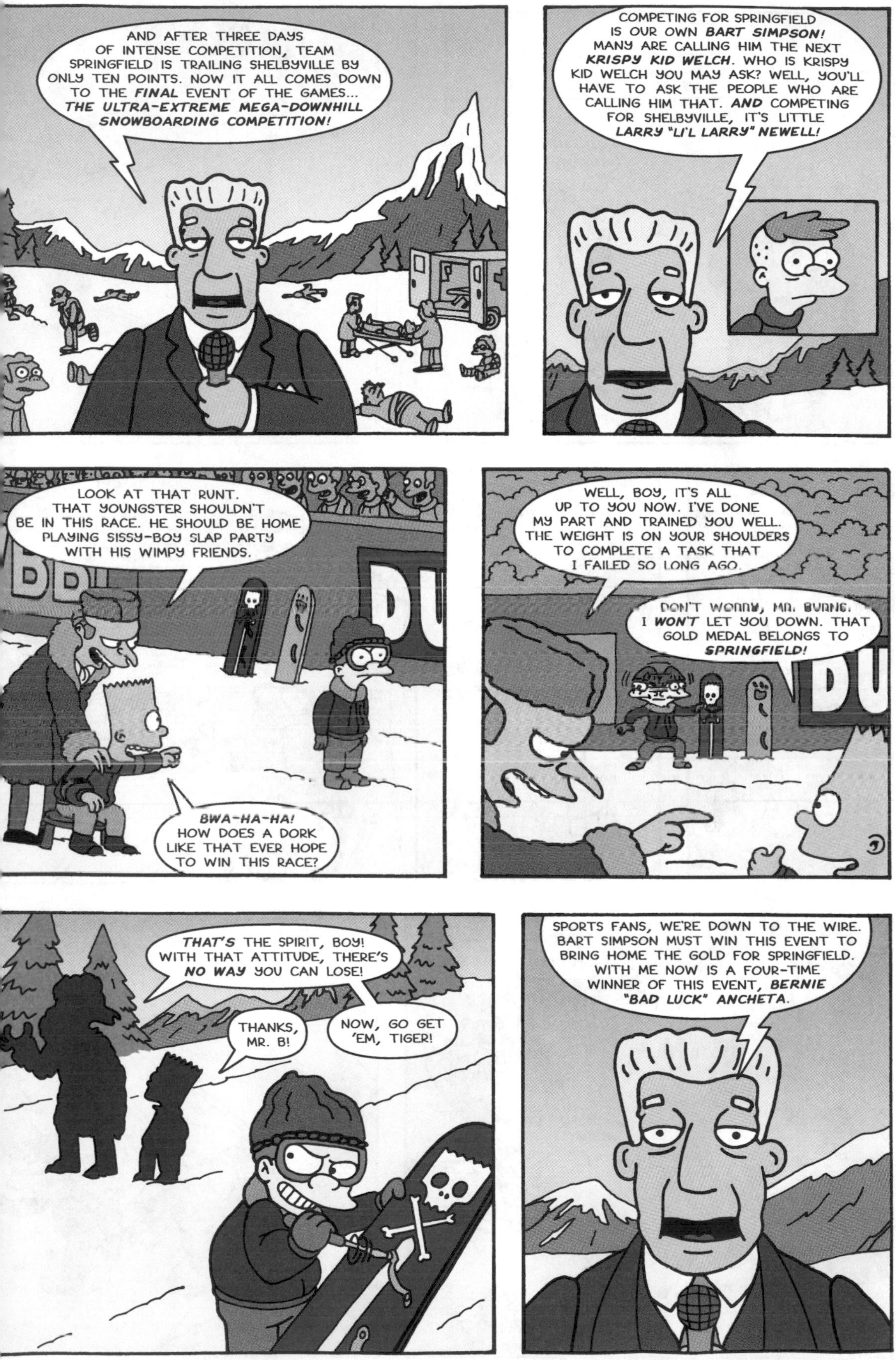
AND AFTER THREE DAYS OF INTENSE COMPETITION, TEAM SPRINGFIELD IS TRAILING SHELBYVILLE BY ONLY TEN POINTS. NOW IT ALL COMES DOWN TO THE *FINAL* EVENT OF THE GAMES... ***THE ULTRA-EXTREME MEGA-DOWNHILL SNOWBOARDING COMPETITION!***
COMPETING FOR SPRINGFIELD IS OUR OWN ***BART SIMPSON!*** MANY ARE CALLING HIM THE NEXT ***KRISPY KID WELCH***. WHO IS KRISPY KID WELCH YOU MAY ASK? WELL, YOU'LL HAVE TO ASK THE PEOPLE WHO ARE CALLING HIM THAT. ***AND*** COMPETING FOR SHELBYVILLE, IT'S LITTLE ***LARRY "LI'L LARRY" NEWELL!***
LOOK AT THAT RUNT. THAT YOUNGSTER SHOULDN'T BE IN THIS RACE. HE SHOULD BE HOME PLAYING SISSY-BOY SLAP PARTY WITH HIS WIMPY FRIENDS.
BWA-HA-HA! HOW DOES A DORK LIKE THAT EVER HOPE TO WIN THIS RACE?
WELL, BOY, IT'S ALL UP TO YOU NOW. I'VE DONE MY PART AND TRAINED YOU WELL. THE WEIGHT IS ON YOUR SHOULDERS TO COMPLETE A TASK THAT I FAILED SO LONG AGO.
DON'T WORRY, MR. BURNS. I ***WON'T*** LET YOU DOWN. THAT GOLD MEDAL BELONGS TO ***SPRINGFIELD!***
THAT'S THE SPIRIT, BOY! WITH THAT ATTITUDE, THERE'S ***NO WAY*** YOU CAN LOSE!
THANKS, MR. B!
NOW, GO GET 'EM, TIGER!
SPORTS FANS, WE'RE DOWN TO THE WIRE. BART SIMPSON MUST WIN THIS EVENT TO BRING HOME THE GOLD FOR SPRINGFIELD. WITH ME NOW IS A FOUR-TIME WINNER OF THIS EVENT, ***BERNIE "BAD LUCK" ANCHETA***.

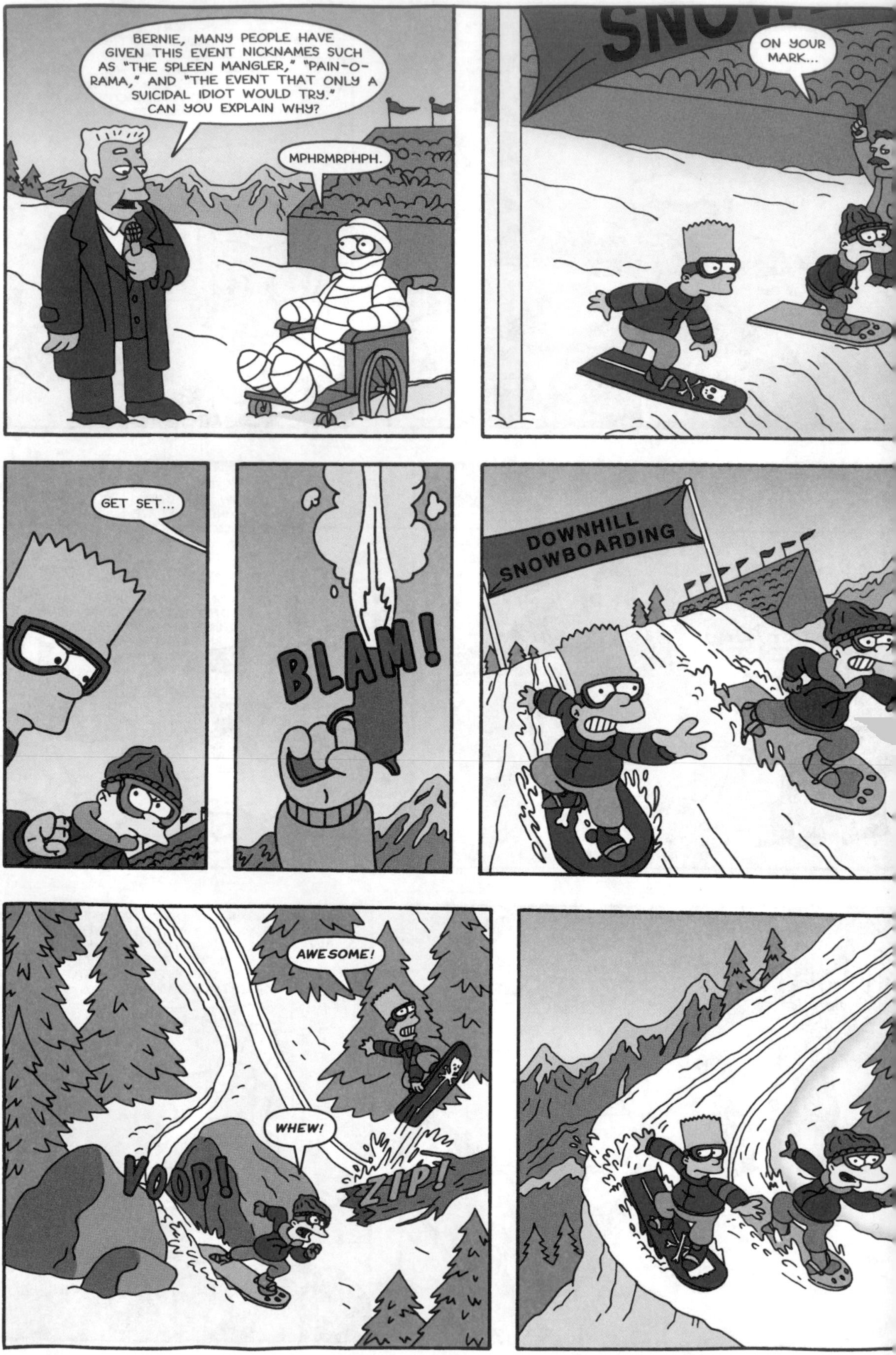
BERNIE, MANY PEOPLE HAVE GIVEN THIS EVENT NICKNAMES SUCH AS "THE SPLEEN MANGLER," "PAIN-O-RAMA," AND "THE EVENT THAT ONLY A SUICIDAL IDIOT WOULD TRY." CAN YOU EXPLAIN WHY?
MPHRMRPHPH.
ON YOUR MARK...
GET SET...
BLAM!
DOWNHILL SNOWBOARDING
AWESOME!
WHEW!
VOOP!
ZIP!

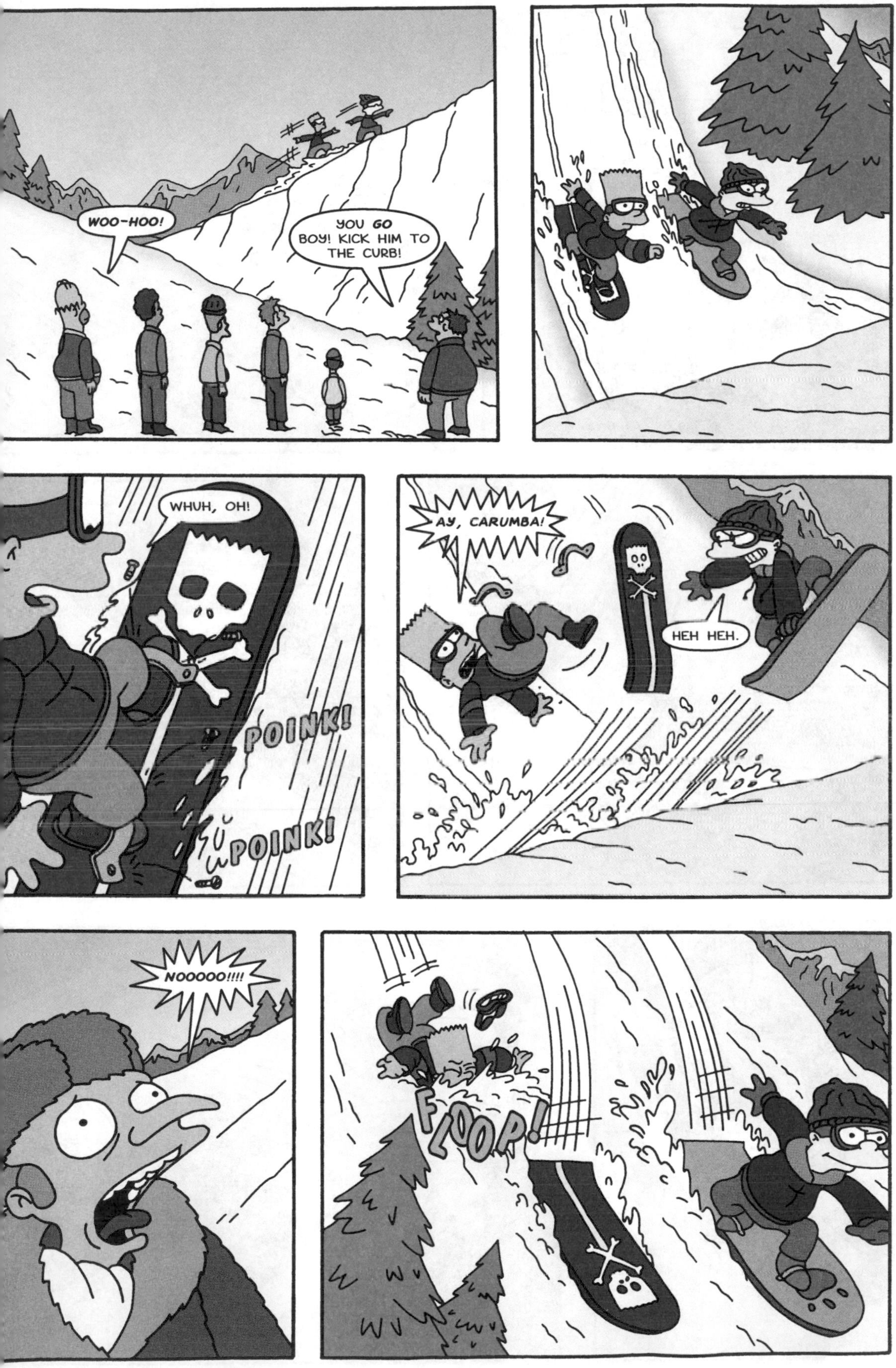
WOO-HOO!
YOU GO BOY! KICK HIM TO THE CURB!
WHUH, OH!
POINK!
POINK!
AY, CARUMBA!
HEH HEH.
NOOOOO!!!!
FLOOP!

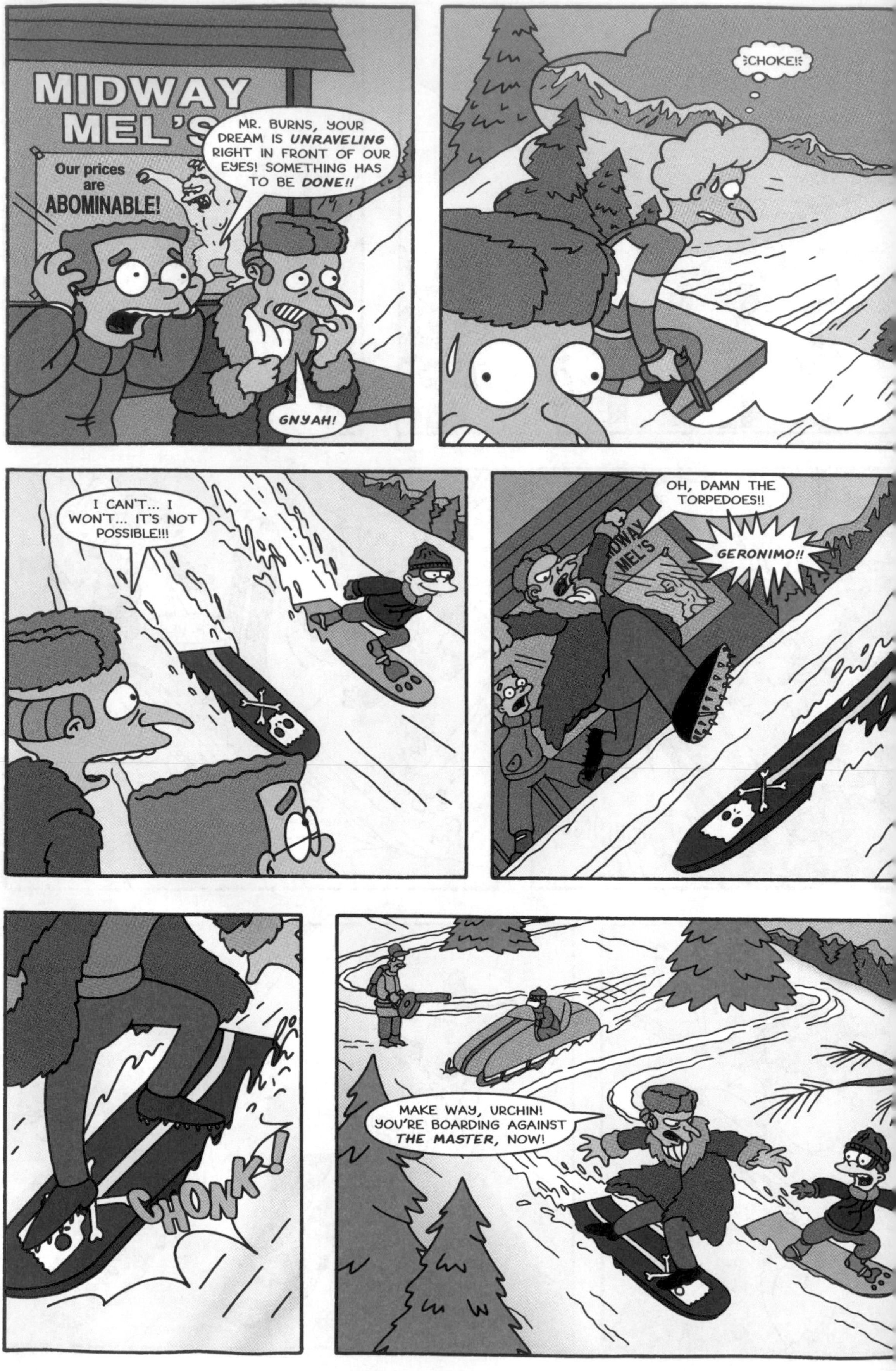
MIDWAY MEL'S
Our prices are ABOMINABLE!
MR. BURNS, YOUR DREAM IS UNRAVELING RIGHT IN FRONT OF OUR EYES! SOMETHING HAS TO BE DONE!!
GNYAH!
CHOKE!
I CAN'T... I WON'T... IT'S NOT POSSIBLE!!!
OH, DAMN THE TORPEDOES!!
GERONIMO!!
MIDWAY MEL'S
CHONK!
MAKE WAY, URCHIN! YOU'RE BOARDING AGAINST THE MASTER, NOW!

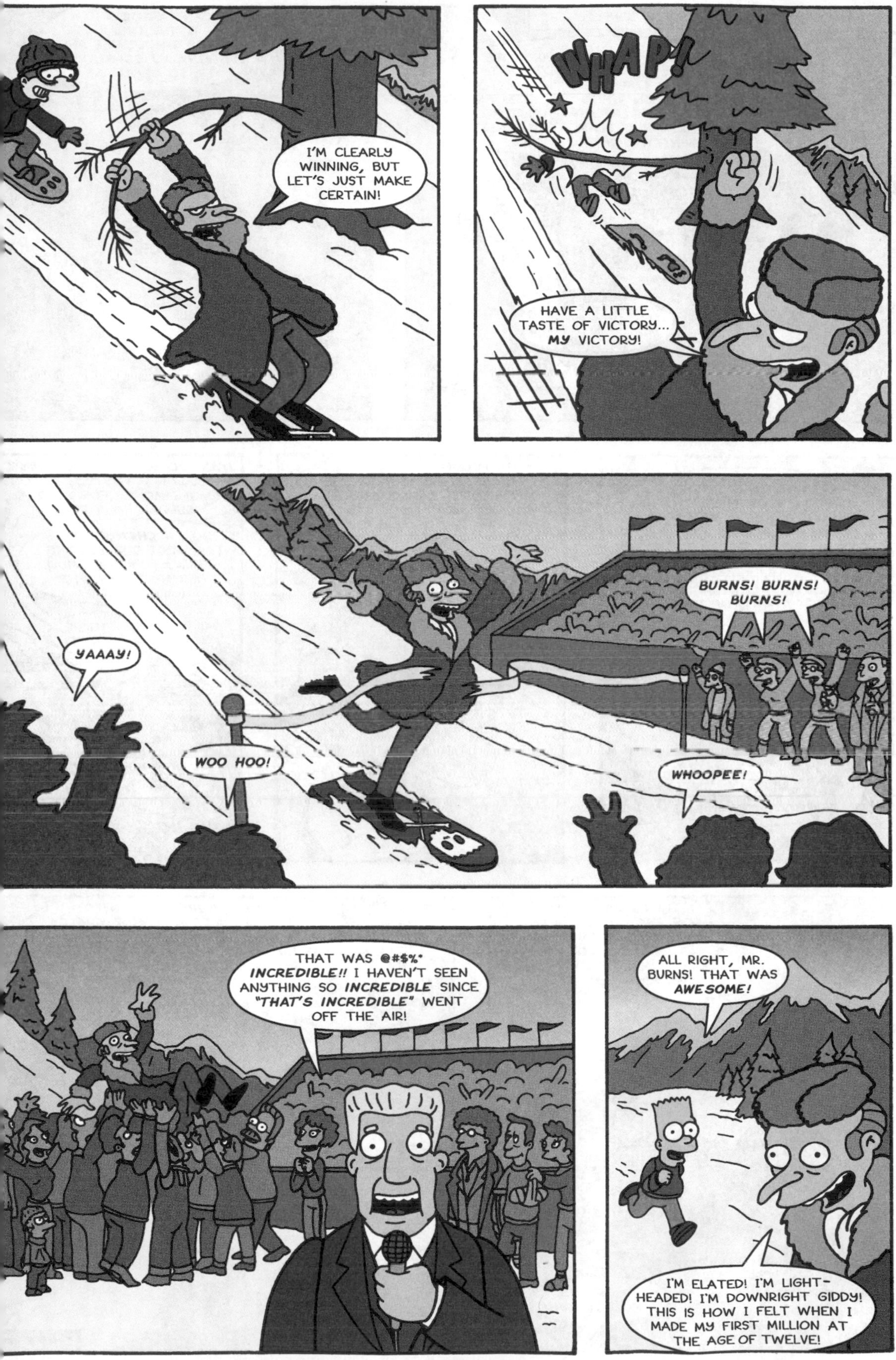
I'M CLEARLY WINNING, BUT LET'S JUST MAKE CERTAIN!
WHAP!
HAVE A LITTLE TASTE OF VICTORY... MY VICTORY!
YAAAY!
BURNS! BURNS! BURNS!
WOO HOO!
WHOOPEE!
THAT WAS @#$%* INCREDIBLE!! I HAVEN'T SEEN ANYTHING SO INCREDIBLE SINCE "THAT'S INCREDIBLE" WENT OFF THE AIR!
ALL RIGHT, MR. BURNS! THAT WAS AWESOME!
I'M ELATED! I'M LIGHT-HEADED! I'M DOWNRIGHT GIDDY! THIS IS HOW I FELT WHEN I MADE MY FIRST MILLION AT THE AGE OF TWELVE!

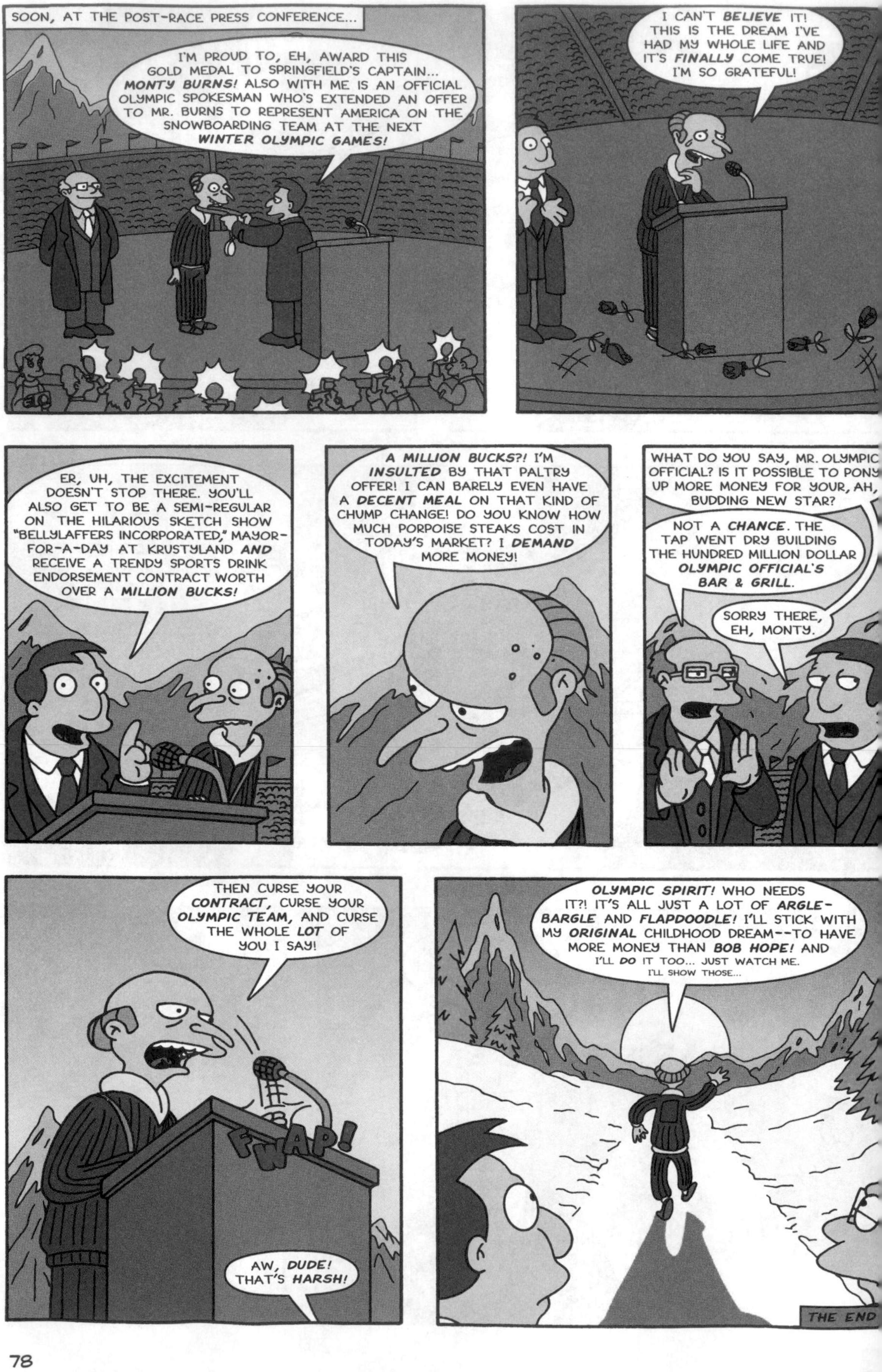
SOON, AT THE POST-RACE PRESS CONFERENCE...
I'M PROUD TO, EH, AWARD THIS GOLD MEDAL TO SPRINGFIELD'S CAPTAIN... MONTY BURNS! ALSO WITH ME IS AN OFFICIAL OLYMPIC SPOKESMAN WHO'S EXTENDED AN OFFER TO MR. BURNS TO REPRESENT AMERICA ON THE SNOWBOARDING TEAM AT THE NEXT WINTER OLYMPIC GAMES!
I CAN'T BELIEVE IT! THIS IS THE DREAM I'VE HAD MY WHOLE LIFE AND IT'S FINALLY COME TRUE! I'M SO GRATEFUL!
ER, UH, THE EXCITEMENT DOESN'T STOP THERE. YOU'LL ALSO GET TO BE A SEMI-REGULAR ON THE HILARIOUS SKETCH SHOW "BELLYLAFFERS INCORPORATED," MAYOR-FOR-A-DAY AT KRUSTYLAND AND RECEIVE A TRENDY SPORTS DRINK ENDORSEMENT CONTRACT WORTH OVER A MILLION BUCKS!
A MILLION BUCKS?! I'M INSULTED BY THAT PALTRY OFFER! I CAN BARELY EVEN HAVE A DECENT MEAL ON THAT KIND OF CHUMP CHANGE! DO YOU KNOW HOW MUCH PORPOISE STEAKS COST IN TODAY'S MARKET? I DEMAND MORE MONEY!
WHAT DO YOU SAY, MR. OLYMPIC OFFICIAL? IS IT POSSIBLE TO PONY UP MORE MONEY FOR YOUR, AH, BUDDING NEW STAR?
NOT A CHANCE. THE TAP WENT DRY BUILDING THE HUNDRED MILLION DOLLAR OLYMPIC OFFICIAL'S BAR & GRILL.
SORRY THERE, EH, MONTY.
THEN CURSE YOUR CONTRACT, CURSE YOUR OLYMPIC TEAM, AND CURSE THE WHOLE LOT OF YOU I SAY!
FWAP!
AW, DUDE! THAT'S HARSH!
OLYMPIC SPIRIT! WHO NEEDS IT?! IT'S ALL JUST A LOT OF ARGLE-BARGLE AND FLAPDOODLE! I'LL STICK WITH MY ORIGINAL CHILDHOOD DREAM--TO HAVE MORE MONEY THAN BOB HOPE! AND I'LL DO IT TOO... JUST WATCH ME. I'LL SHOW THOSE...
THE END

BELIEVE US, WE GET LETTERS! SO MANY, IN FACT, THAT WE HAVE LOST SIX INTERNS THIS YEAR ALONE TO MAIL-SLIDES AND OTHER BULK POSTAGE MISHAPS. DUE TO THIS INCREDIBLE (AND DANGEROUS) VOLUME OF MAIL, WE ARE UNABLE TO ANSWER YOUR LETTERS INDIVIDUALLY. BUT WE DO LISTEN TO YOUR IDEAS AND CRITICISMS, AS EVIDENCED IN THE FOLLOWING FEATURE! SEE YOUR DREAMS FOR BONGO COME TO LIFE IN THE NEXT FOUR PAGES AS WE TAKE A SIMPLE STORY AND PUT IT THROUGH...

THE SIMPSONS SUPPORTERS' SUGGESTION SPIN CYCLE!

FIRST, LET'S TAKE A LOOK AT WHAT OUR STORY WOULD LOOK LIKE WITHOUT YOUR VALUABLE INPUT. NEXT, SEE HOW YOUR LETTERS AFFECT BONGO'S UNIQUE BRAND OF STORYCRAFTING.

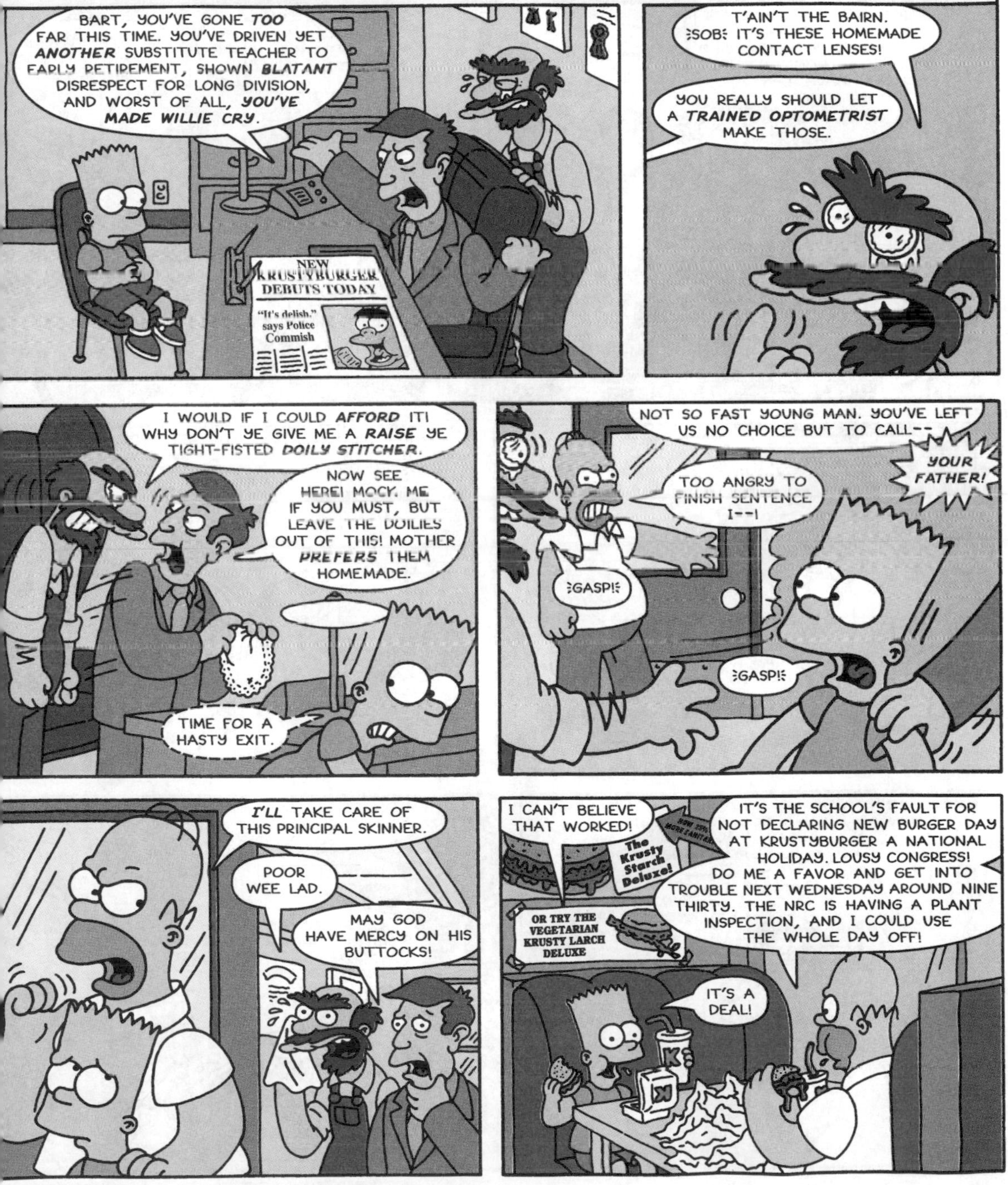

BART, YOU'VE GONE TOO FAR THIS TIME. YOU'VE DRIVEN YET ANOTHER SUBSTITUTE TEACHER TO EARLY RETIREMENT, SHOWN BLATANT DISRESPECT FOR LONG DIVISION, AND WORST OF ALL, YOU'VE MADE WILLIE CRY.
NEW KRUSTYBURGER DEBUTS TODAY
"It's delish." says Police Commish
T'AIN'T THE BAIRN. ;SOB; IT'S THESE HOMEMADE CONTACT LENSES!
YOU REALLY SHOULD LET A TRAINED OPTOMETRIST MAKE THOSE.
I WOULD IF I COULD AFFORD IT! WHY DON'T YE GIVE ME A RAISE YE TIGHT-FISTED DOILY STITCHER.
NOW SEE HERE! MOCK ME IF YOU MUST, BUT LEAVE THE DOILIES OUT OF THIS! MOTHER PREFERS THEM HOMEMADE.
TIME FOR A HASTY EXIT.
NOT SO FAST YOUNG MAN. YOU'VE LEFT US NO CHOICE BUT TO CALL--
YOUR FATHER!
TOO ANGRY TO FINISH SENTENCE I--!
;GASP!;
;GASP!;
I'LL TAKE CARE OF THIS PRINCIPAL SKINNER.
POOR WEE LAD.
MAY GOD HAVE MERCY ON HIS BUTTOCKS!
I CAN'T BELIEVE THAT WORKED!
The Krusty Starch Deluxe!
OR TRY THE VEGETARIAN KRUSTY LARCH DELUXE
IT'S THE SCHOOL'S FAULT FOR NOT DECLARING NEW BURGER DAY AT KRUSTYBURGER A NATIONAL HOLIDAY. LOUSY CONGRESS! DO ME A FAVOR AND GET INTO TROUBLE NEXT WEDNESDAY AROUND NINE THIRTY. THE NRC IS HAVING A PLANT INSPECTION, AND I COULD USE THE WHOLE DAY OFF!
IT'S A DEAL!

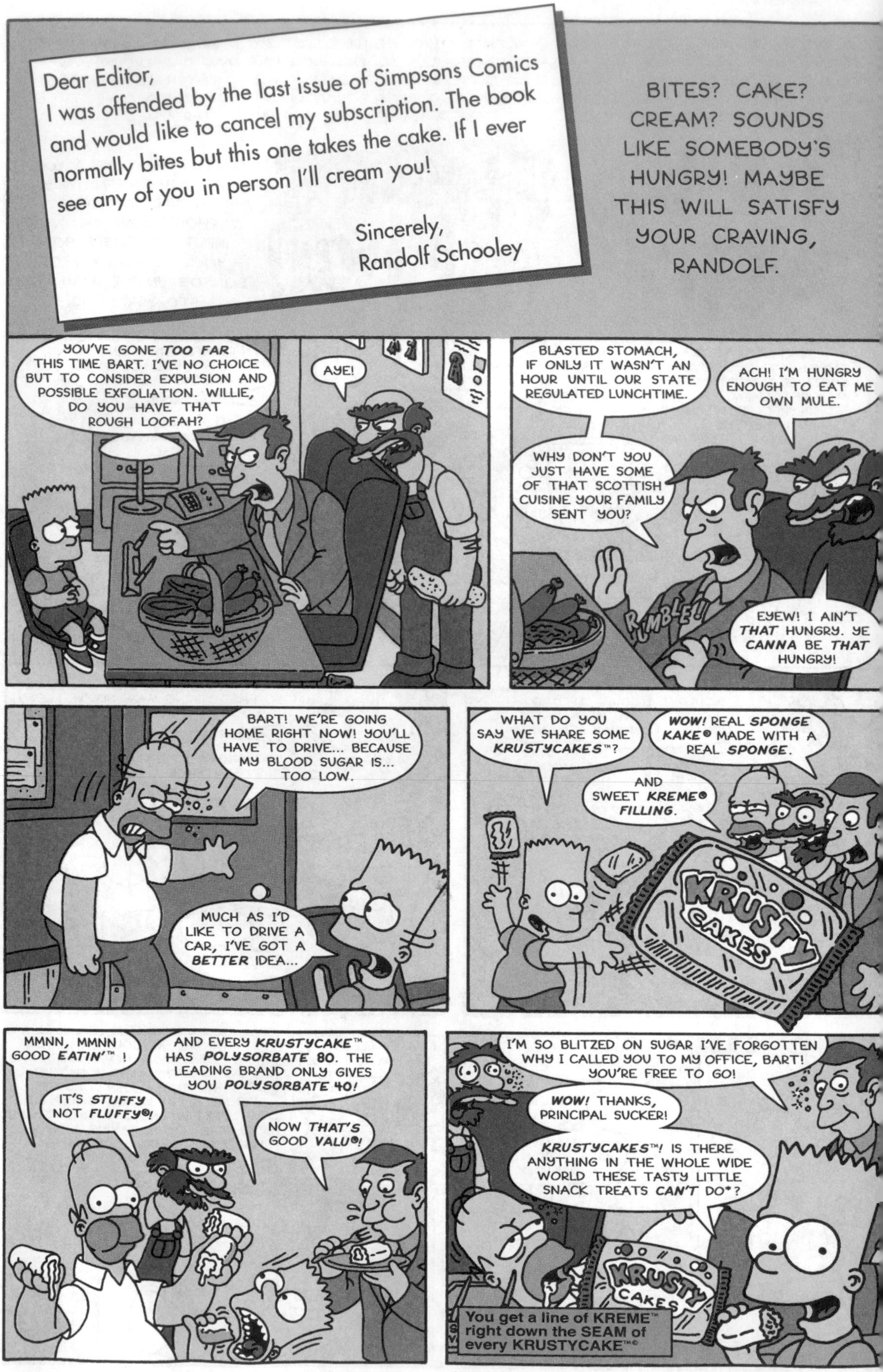

Dear Editor,
I was offended by the last issue of Simpsons Comics and would like to cancel my subscription. The book normally bites but this one takes the cake. If I ever see any of you in person I'll cream you!
Sincerely,
Randolf Schooley
BITES? CAKE? CREAM? SOUNDS LIKE SOMEBODY'S HUNGRY! MAYBE THIS WILL SATISFY YOUR CRAVING, RANDOLF.
YOU'VE GONE TOO FAR THIS TIME BART. I'VE NO CHOICE BUT TO CONSIDER EXPULSION AND POSSIBLE EXFOLIATION. WILLIE, DO YOU HAVE THAT ROUGH LOOFAH?
AYE!
BLASTED STOMACH, IF ONLY IT WASN'T AN HOUR UNTIL OUR STATE REGULATED LUNCHTIME.
ACH! I'M HUNGRY ENOUGH TO EAT ME OWN MULE.
WHY DON'T YOU JUST HAVE SOME OF THAT SCOTTISH CUISINE YOUR FAMILY SENT YOU?
RUMBLE!!
EYEW! I AIN'T THAT HUNGRY. YE CANNA BE THAT HUNGRY!
BART! WE'RE GOING HOME RIGHT NOW! YOU'LL HAVE TO DRIVE... BECAUSE MY BLOOD SUGAR IS... TOO LOW.
MUCH AS I'D LIKE TO DRIVE A CAR, I'VE GOT A BETTER IDEA...
WHAT DO YOU SAY WE SHARE SOME KRUSTYCAKES™?
WOW! REAL SPONGE KAKE® MADE WITH A REAL SPONGE.
AND SWEET KREME® FILLING.
KRUSTY CAKES
MMNN, MMNN GOOD EATIN'™ !
AND EVERY KRUSTYCAKE™ HAS POLYSORBATE 80. THE LEADING BRAND ONLY GIVES YOU POLYSORBATE 40!
IT'S STUFFY NOT FLUFFY®!
NOW THAT'S GOOD VALU®!
I'M SO BLITZED ON SUGAR I'VE FORGOTTEN WHY I CALLED YOU TO MY OFFICE, BART! YOU'RE FREE TO GO!
WOW! THANKS, PRINCIPAL SUCKER!
KRUSTYCAKES™! IS THERE ANYTHING IN THE WHOLE WIDE WORLD THESE TASTY LITTLE SNACK TREATS CAN'T DO*?
KRUSTY CAKES
You get a line of KREME™ right down the SEAM of every KRUSTYCAKE™©

*THIS IS A RHETORICAL QUESTION. PLEASE DO NOT SEND KRUSTY THE CLOWN OR HIS AGENTS ANY ANSWERS TO THIS QUESTION UNLESS ACCOMPANIED BY CHECKS OR MONEY ORDERS TO COVER LETTER DISPOSAL COSTS.

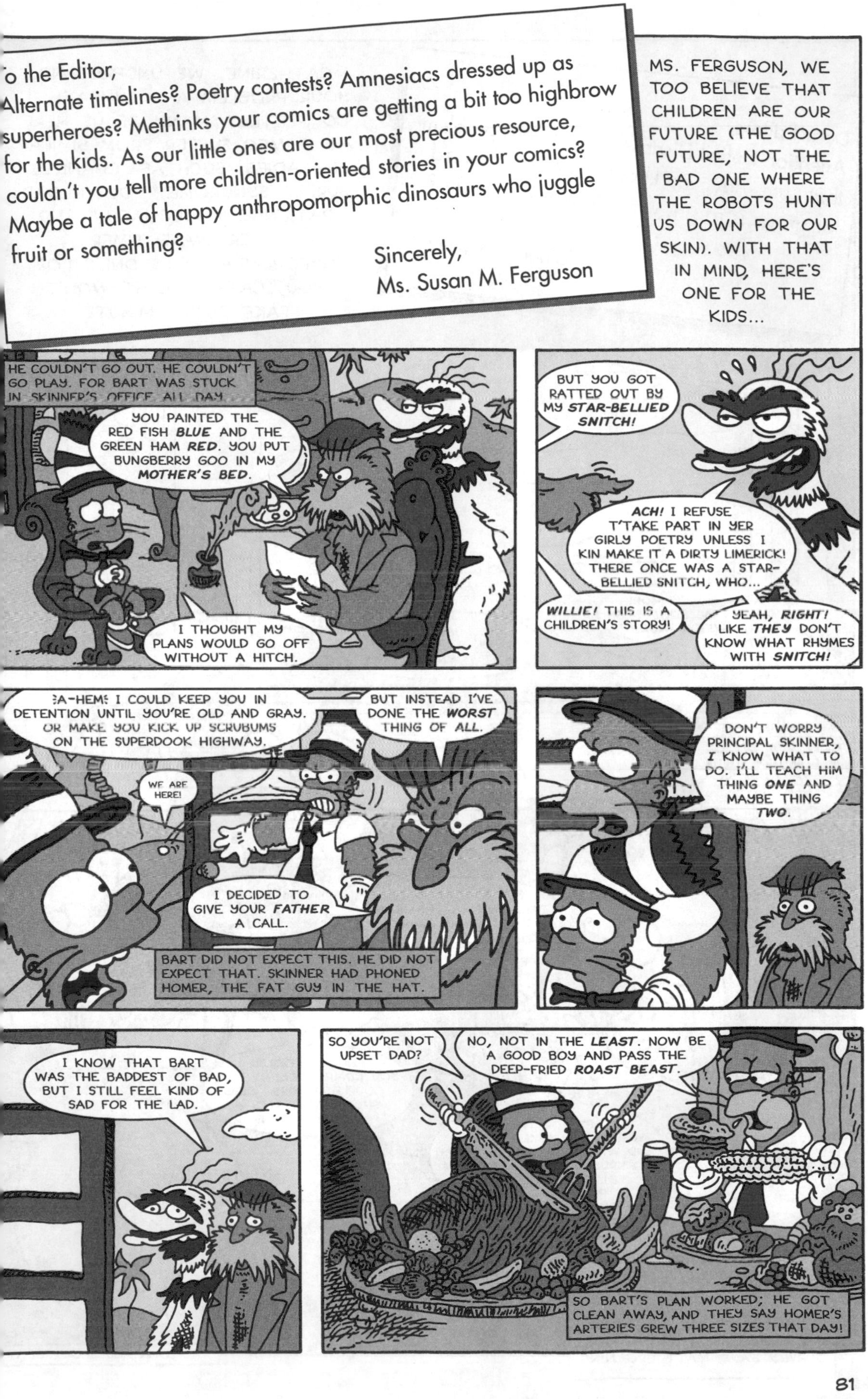

o the Editor,
Alternate timelines? Poetry contests? Amnesiacs dressed up as superheroes? Methinks your comics are getting a bit too highbrow for the kids. As our little ones are our most precious resource, couldn't you tell more children-oriented stories in your comics? Maybe a tale of happy anthropomorphic dinosaurs who juggle fruit or something?
Sincerely,
Ms. Susan M. Ferguson
MS. FERGUSON, WE TOO BELIEVE THAT CHILDREN ARE OUR FUTURE (THE GOOD FUTURE, NOT THE BAD ONE WHERE THE ROBOTS HUNT US DOWN FOR OUR SKIN). WITH THAT IN MIND, HERE'S ONE FOR THE KIDS...
HE COULDN'T GO OUT. HE COULDN'T GO PLAY. FOR BART WAS STUCK IN SKINNER'S OFFICE ALL DAY.
YOU PAINTED THE RED FISH BLUE AND THE GREEN HAM RED. YOU PUT BUNGBERRY GOO IN MY MOTHER'S BED.
I THOUGHT MY PLANS WOULD GO OFF WITHOUT A HITCH.
BUT YOU GOT RATTED OUT BY MY STAR-BELLIED SNITCH!
ACH! I REFUSE T'TAKE PART IN YER GIRLY POETRY UNLESS I KIN MAKE IT A DIRTY LIMERICK! THERE ONCE WAS A STAR-BELLIED SNITCH, WHO...
WILLIE! THIS IS A CHILDREN'S STORY!
YEAH, RIGHT! LIKE THEY DON'T KNOW WHAT RHYMES WITH SNITCH!
A-HEM! I COULD KEEP YOU IN DETENTION UNTIL YOU'RE OLD AND GRAY. OR MAKE YOU KICK UP SCRUBUMS ON THE SUPERDOOK HIGHWAY.
BUT INSTEAD I'VE DONE THE WORST THING OF ALL.
WE ARE HERE!
I DECIDED TO GIVE YOUR FATHER A CALL.
BART DID NOT EXPECT THIS. HE DID NOT EXPECT THAT. SKINNER HAD PHONED HOMER, THE FAT GUY IN THE HAT.
DON'T WORRY PRINCIPAL SKINNER, I KNOW WHAT TO DO. I'LL TEACH HIM THING ONE AND MAYBE THING TWO.
I KNOW THAT BART WAS THE BADDEST OF BAD, BUT I STILL FEEL KIND OF SAD FOR THE LAD.
SO YOU'RE NOT UPSET DAD?
NO, NOT IN THE LEAST. NOW BE A GOOD BOY AND PASS THE DEEP-FRIED ROAST BEAST.
SO BART'S PLAN WORKED; HE GOT CLEAN AWAY, AND THEY SAY HOMER'S ARTERIES GREW THREE SIZES THAT DAY!

Dear Editors,
Attention Deficit Disorder is a serious problem that...um...say, you know, if the French word for grape is raisin, what do they call raisins?

Catherine Kinsey

CATHERINE, WE UNDERSTAND YOUR PROBLEM AND SYMPATHIZE COMPLETELY. MANY OF US HERE AT ***BONGO*** SUFFER FROM SIMILAR MALADIES, SUCH AS "CHANNEL SURFER SYNDROME," "DOWNLOAD PATIENCE INADEQUACY," AND "MICROWAVE TIMER HYPOPLASIA." THIS ONE'S FOR YOU, CATHERINE. IT WON'T TAKE BUT A MINUTE.

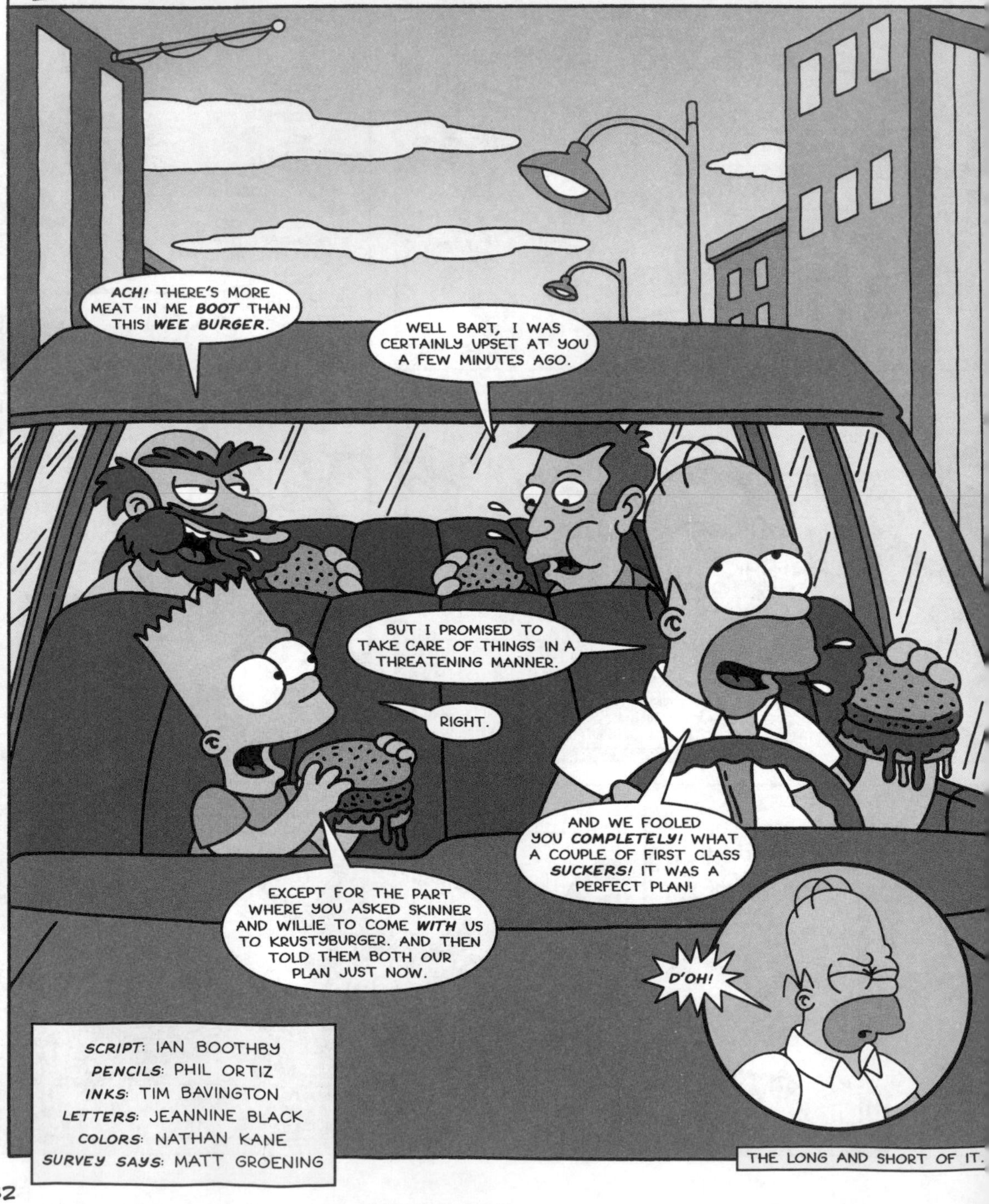
ACH! THERE'S MORE MEAT IN ME BOOT THAN THIS WEE BURGER.
WELL BART, I WAS CERTAINLY UPSET AT YOU A FEW MINUTES AGO.
BUT I PROMISED TO TAKE CARE OF THINGS IN A THREATENING MANNER.
RIGHT.
AND WE FOOLED YOU COMPLETELY! WHAT A COUPLE OF FIRST CLASS SUCKERS! IT WAS A PERFECT PLAN!
EXCEPT FOR THE PART WHERE YOU ASKED SKINNER AND WILLIE TO COME WITH US TO KRUSTYBURGER. AND THEN TOLD THEM BOTH OUR PLAN JUST NOW.
D'OH!
SCRIPT: IAN BOOTHBY
PENCILS: PHIL ORTIZ
INKS: TIM BAVINGTON
LETTERS: JEANNINE BLACK
COLORS: NATHAN KANE
SURVEY SAYS: MATT GROENING
THE LONG AND SHORT OF IT.

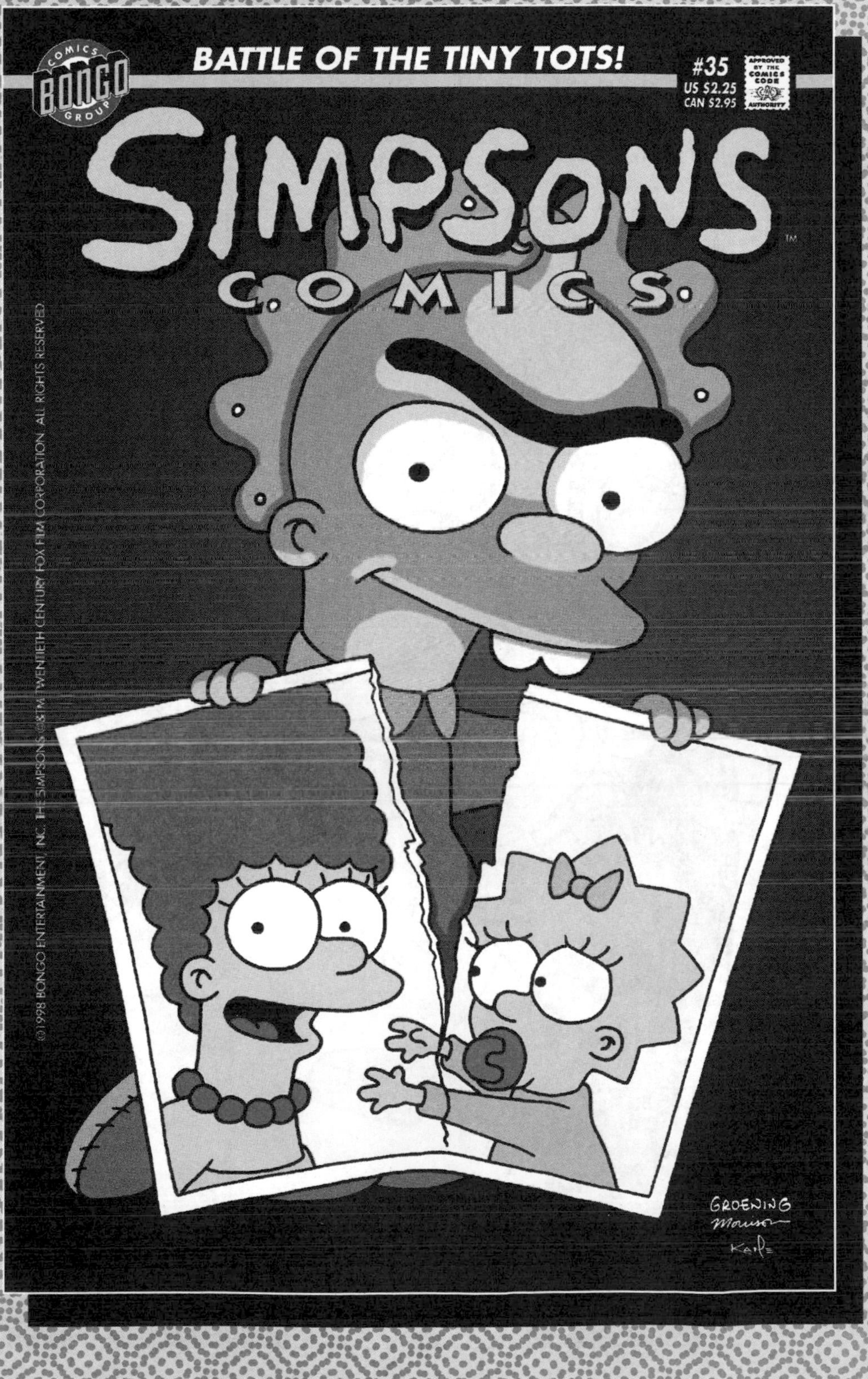
BONGO COMICS GROUP
BATTLE OF THE TINY TOTS!
#35
US $2.25
CAN $2.95
APPROVED BY THE COMICS CODE AUTHORITY
SIMPSONS COMICS
©1998 BONGO ENTERTAINMENT, INC. THE SIMPSONS ©&TM TWENTIETH CENTURY FOX FILM CORPORATION. ALL RIGHTS RESERVED
GROENING

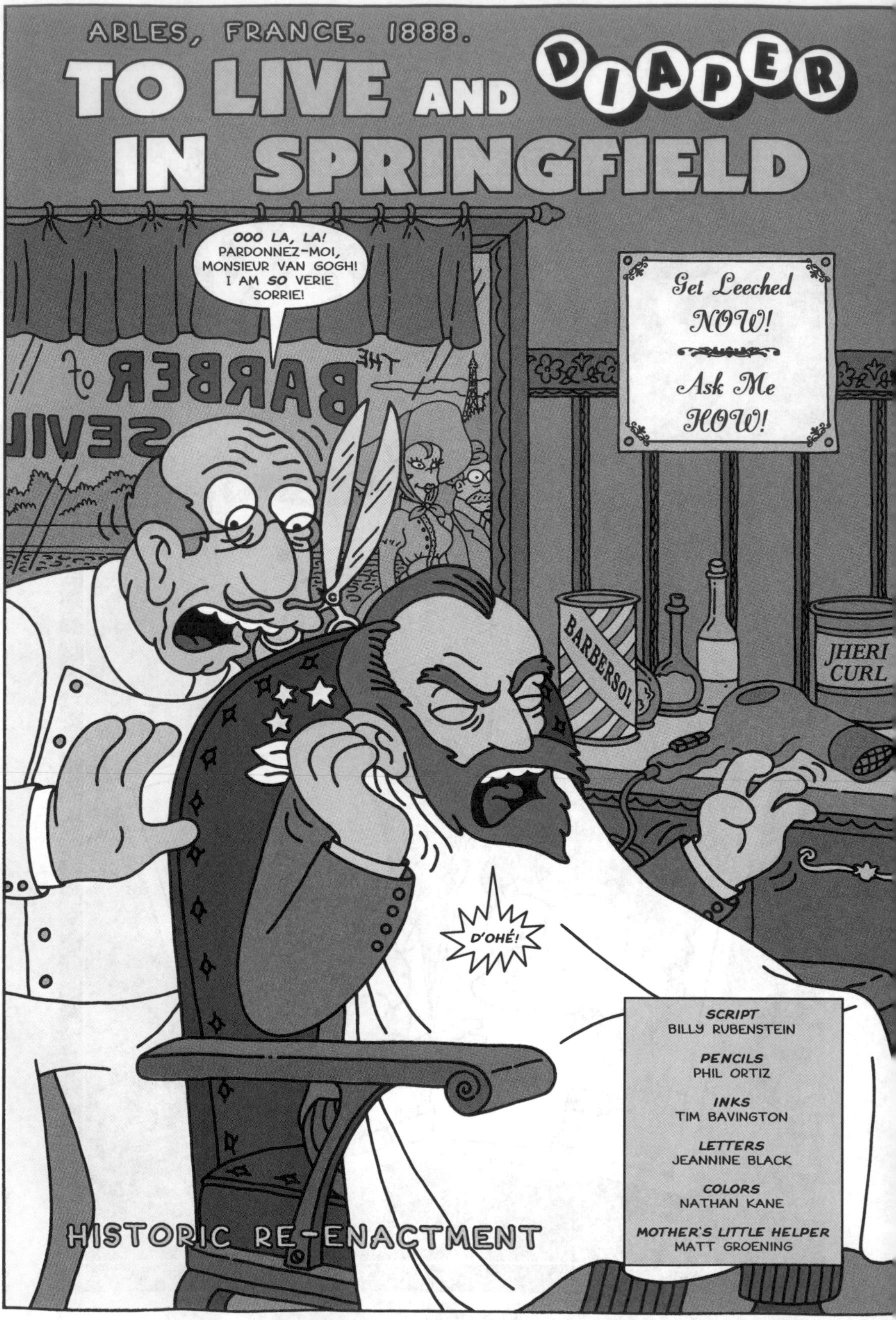
ARLES, FRANCE. 1888.
TO LIVE AND DIAPER IN SPRINGFIELD
OOO LA, LA! PARDONNEZ-MOI, MONSIEUR VAN GOGH! I AM *SO* VERIE SORRIE!
THE BARBER of SEVIL
Get Leeched NOW! Ask Me HOW!
BARBERSOL
JHERI CURL
D'OHÉ!
SCRIPT BILLY RUBENSTEIN
PENCILS PHIL ORTIZ
INKS TIM BAVINGTON
LETTERS JEANNINE BLACK
COLORS NATHAN KANE
MOTHER'S LITTLE HELPER MATT GROENING
HISTORIC RE-ENACTMENT

...*"UNSOLVED MISTAKEN AMPUTATIONS"* WILL BE RIGHT BACK! AND NOW THESE MESSAGES...

KRUSTY KHOLESTRA MAKADAMIA KHIPS

HI, I'M *TROY MCCLURE.* YOU MAY REMEMBER ME FROM OTHER HIGH-END, SPECIALTY GIFT COMMERCIALS SUCH AS *SPORTS AUTOGRAPH FORGERIES-- "YOUR KIDS WILL NEVER KNOW THE DIFFERENCE"* AND *"NON-SWISS ARMY KNIVES-'CAUSE NEUTRALITY MAKES FOR A DULL BLADE".* TONIGHT, I'M HERE ON BEHALF OF *CHIC AFFECTIONS* TO INFORM YOU ABOUT A LIMITED-TIME OFFER THAT WILL *CHANGE* YOUR LIFE.

ARE YOU TIRED OF EXERTING YOURSELF UNNECESSARILY?

DEFINITELY.

DO YOU HATE WASTING PRECIOUS PERSONAL ENERGY?

YOU BET.

ARE YOU ALWAYS TRYING TO FIND MORE EFFICIENT WAYS OF EXPENDING *LESS* ENERGY, NO MATTER HOW SMALL?

YEAH.

THEN YOU, MY FRIEND, OWE IT TO YOURSELF TO GET THE LUXURIOUS, FEATHERLIGHT, RUGGED, ELEGANT, THERMOSTATICALLY CONTROLLED, GLOW IN THE DARK, CHROME-PLATED, AUTOMATIC, HEATED, STEREO COMMODE *PAPER DISPENSER!*

DEVELOPED DURING DESERT STORM, THIS *MADE IN THE USA* WONDER USES THE SAME SHOCK RESISTANT POLYMER CASING TECHNOLOGY AS THE BULLET TRAIN, HAS A WHISPER-QUIET, HIGH TORQUE MOTOR, CONCERT HALL SOUND, MICROCIRCUITRY THAT'S WATER RESISTANT TO 300 FEET, AN L.E.D. COUNTER TO TELL YOU HOW MANY SHEETS ARE LEFT, A BUILT IN THERMODYNAMIC HEATER, FOUR QUADRAPHONIC SPEAKERS WITH DELUXE BASE AMPLIFICATION, *AND* AN ILLUMINATED FINGER-TOUCH ACTIVATION SENSOR SWITCH. *ALL* FOR ONLY $299.98!

THIS IS A LIMITED-EDITION OFFER, ONLY AVAILABLE IN OUR *CHIC AFFECTIONS* STORES OR THROUGH OUR CATALOGUE. *INDULGE* YOURSELF! YOU'RE WORTH IT!

sittin' on the dock of the bay...

"MADE IN THE USA" IS ONLY A FIGURE OF SPEECH. PRODUCT ACTUALLY MADE IN PAKISTAN.

MARGE, YOU CAN STOP LOOKING. I KNOW WHAT I WANT FOR MY BIRTHDAY! A COMMO... A COMMU... A COMMU... A TOILET THINGY FROM CHIC AFFECTATIONS!

HOMEY, I HAVEN'T EVEN STARTED LOOKING. YOUR BIRTHDAY ISN'T FOR ANOTHER MONTH. BESIDES, THAT STORE IS VERY EXPENSIVE.

ASHKENAZI AND SEPHARDIC DESSERTS
101 Lactose-free Treats
Oy, oh boy!

CHORES LIST

LISA	BART
✓dishes	take out garbage
✓homework	walk dog
✓feed pets	homework
	✓FLAMING TOILET EXPERIMENT

IT'S ONLY $299.98.

OH, COME ON MARGE. I'VE SEEN ALL THOSE CATALOGUES THAT COME IN THE MAIL. I KNOW YOU'RE LOOKING FOR A GIFT FOR ME.

$299.98?!

HOMER, I DON'T WANT TO DISAPPOINT YOU, BUT I DON'T ASK FOR ALL THOSE CATALOGUES. THE MAILMAN JUST BRINGS THEM.

OH, SURE MARGE. LIKE I'M SUPPOSED TO BELIEVE THAT ALL THOSE COMPANIES ARE JUST SENDING YOU ALL THOSE BIG, GLOSSY CATALOGUES, SPENDING ALL THAT MONEY ON POSTAGE, WITHOUT YOU EVEN ASKING THEM TO?

HRRMMMM. I DON'T KNOW. REMEMBER ALL THOSE OTHER EXPENSIVE GIFTS THAT YOU'VE BEGGED FOR IN THE PAST? WHERE ARE THEY NOW?

I THINK THERE'S A PEA UNDER MY MATTRESS.

LEATHER-BOUND COLLECTION

5 STEPS ON SUCCESSFUL HOBBITS

Make Your Own Barbed Wire Kit

ITCHY AND SCRATCHY BAG O' BALL BEARINGS

LEARN BRAILLE ON CASSETTE TAPE

$59.95

DALAI LAMA CHIA PET

EXTEND-A-LOOFAH

BUT MARGE, THIS IS DIFFERENT. IT'S BEEN MY LIFELONG DREAM TO OWN ONE OF THOSE THINGIES!

I THOUGHT YOUR LIFELONG DREAM WAS TO RIDE IN A TWO-HUMPED CAMEL RACE. YOU DID THAT LAST YEAR AT SPRINGFIELD'S TASTE OF THE PEOPLE'S REPUBLIC OF YEMEN FOOD FEST.

MMMMM.... BABA GANOUSH.

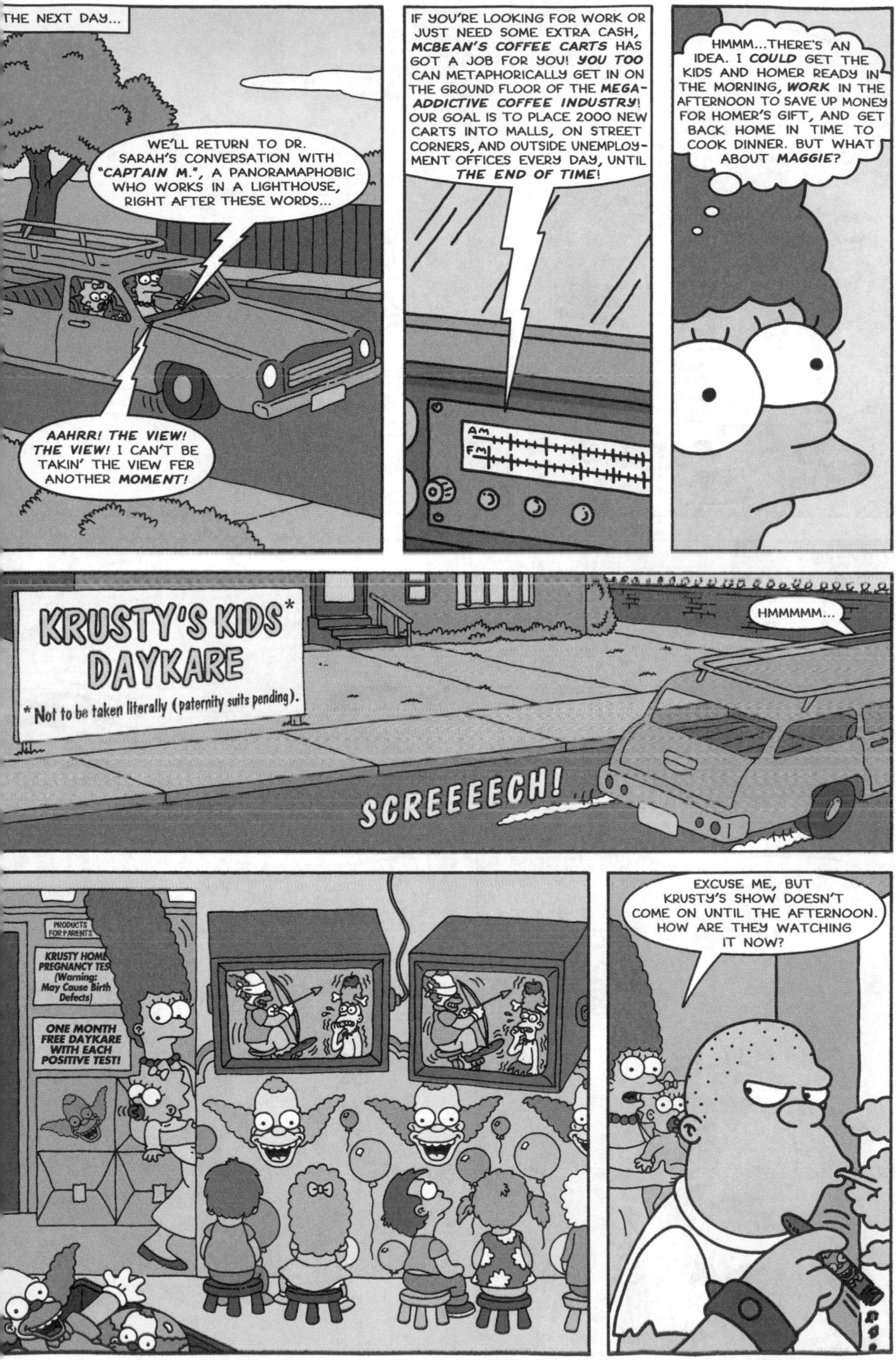
THE NEXT DAY...
WE'LL RETURN TO DR. SARAH'S CONVERSATION WITH "CAPTAIN M.", A PANORAMAPHOBIC WHO WORKS IN A LIGHTHOUSE, RIGHT AFTER THESE WORDS...
AAHRR! THE VIEW! THE VIEW! I CAN'T BE TAKIN' THE VIEW FER ANOTHER MOMENT!
IF YOU'RE LOOKING FOR WORK OR JUST NEED SOME EXTRA CASH, MCBEAN'S COFFEE CARTS HAS GOT A JOB FOR YOU! YOU TOO CAN METAPHORICALLY GET IN ON THE GROUND FLOOR OF THE MEGA-ADDICTIVE COFFEE INDUSTRY! OUR GOAL IS TO PLACE 2000 NEW CARTS INTO MALLS, ON STREET CORNERS, AND OUTSIDE UNEMPLOYMENT OFFICES EVERY DAY, UNTIL THE END OF TIME!
AM
FM
HMMM...THERE'S AN IDEA. I COULD GET THE KIDS AND HOMER READY IN THE MORNING, WORK IN THE AFTERNOON TO SAVE UP MONEY FOR HOMER'S GIFT, AND GET BACK HOME IN TIME TO COOK DINNER. BUT WHAT ABOUT MAGGIE?
KRUSTY'S KIDS* DAYKARE
* Not to be taken literally (paternity suits pending).
HMMMMM...
SCREEEEECH!
PRODUCTS FOR PARENTS
KRUSTY HOME PREGNANCY TEST (Warning: May Cause Birth Defects)
ONE MONTH FREE DAYKARE WITH EACH POSITIVE TEST!
EXCUSE ME, BUT KRUSTY'S SHOW DOESN'T COME ON UNTIL THE AFTERNOON. HOW ARE THEY WATCHING IT NOW?

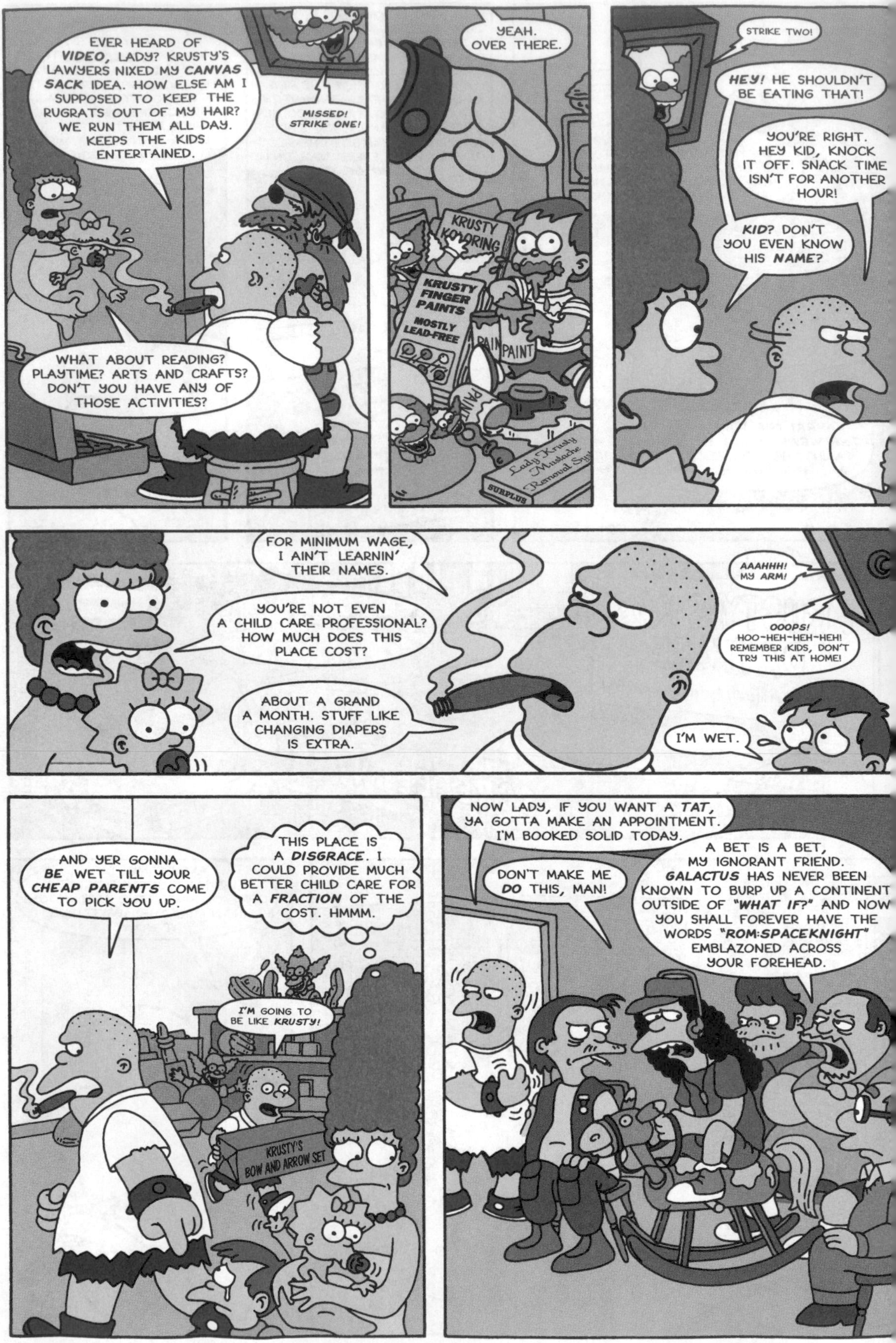
EVER HEARD OF VIDEO, LADY? KRUSTY'S LAWYERS NIXED MY CANVAS SACK IDEA. HOW ELSE AM I SUPPOSED TO KEEP THE RUGRATS OUT OF MY HAIR? WE RUN THEM ALL DAY. KEEPS THE KIDS ENTERTAINED.
MISSED! STRIKE ONE!
WHAT ABOUT READING? PLAYTIME? ARTS AND CRAFTS? DON'T YOU HAVE ANY OF THOSE ACTIVITIES?
YEAH. OVER THERE.
KRUSTY KOLORING
KRUSTY FINGER PAINTS MOSTLY LEAD-FREE
PAINT
Lady Krusty Mustache Removal System
SURPLUS
STRIKE TWO!
HEY! HE SHOULDN'T BE EATING THAT!
YOU'RE RIGHT. HEY KID, KNOCK IT OFF. SNACK TIME ISN'T FOR ANOTHER HOUR!
KID? DON'T YOU EVEN KNOW HIS NAME?
FOR MINIMUM WAGE, I AIN'T LEARNIN' THEIR NAMES.
YOU'RE NOT EVEN A CHILD CARE PROFESSIONAL? HOW MUCH DOES THIS PLACE COST?
ABOUT A GRAND A MONTH. STUFF LIKE CHANGING DIAPERS IS EXTRA.
AAAHHH! MY ARM!
OOOPS! HOO-HEH-HEH-HEH! REMEMBER KIDS, DON'T TRY THIS AT HOME!
I'M WET.
AND YER GONNA BE WET TILL YOUR CHEAP PARENTS COME TO PICK YOU UP.
THIS PLACE IS A DISGRACE. I COULD PROVIDE MUCH BETTER CHILD CARE FOR A FRACTION OF THE COST. HMMM.
I'M GOING TO BE LIKE KRUSTY!
KRUSTY'S BOW AND ARROW SET
NOW LADY, IF YOU WANT A TAT, YA GOTTA MAKE AN APPOINTMENT. I'M BOOKED SOLID TODAY.
DON'T MAKE ME DO THIS, MAN!
A BET IS A BET, MY IGNORANT FRIEND. GALACTUS HAS NEVER BEEN KNOWN TO BURP UP A CONTINENT OUTSIDE OF "WHAT IF?" AND NOW YOU SHALL FOREVER HAVE THE WORDS "ROM:SPACEKNIGHT" EMBLAZONED ACROSS YOUR FOREHEAD.

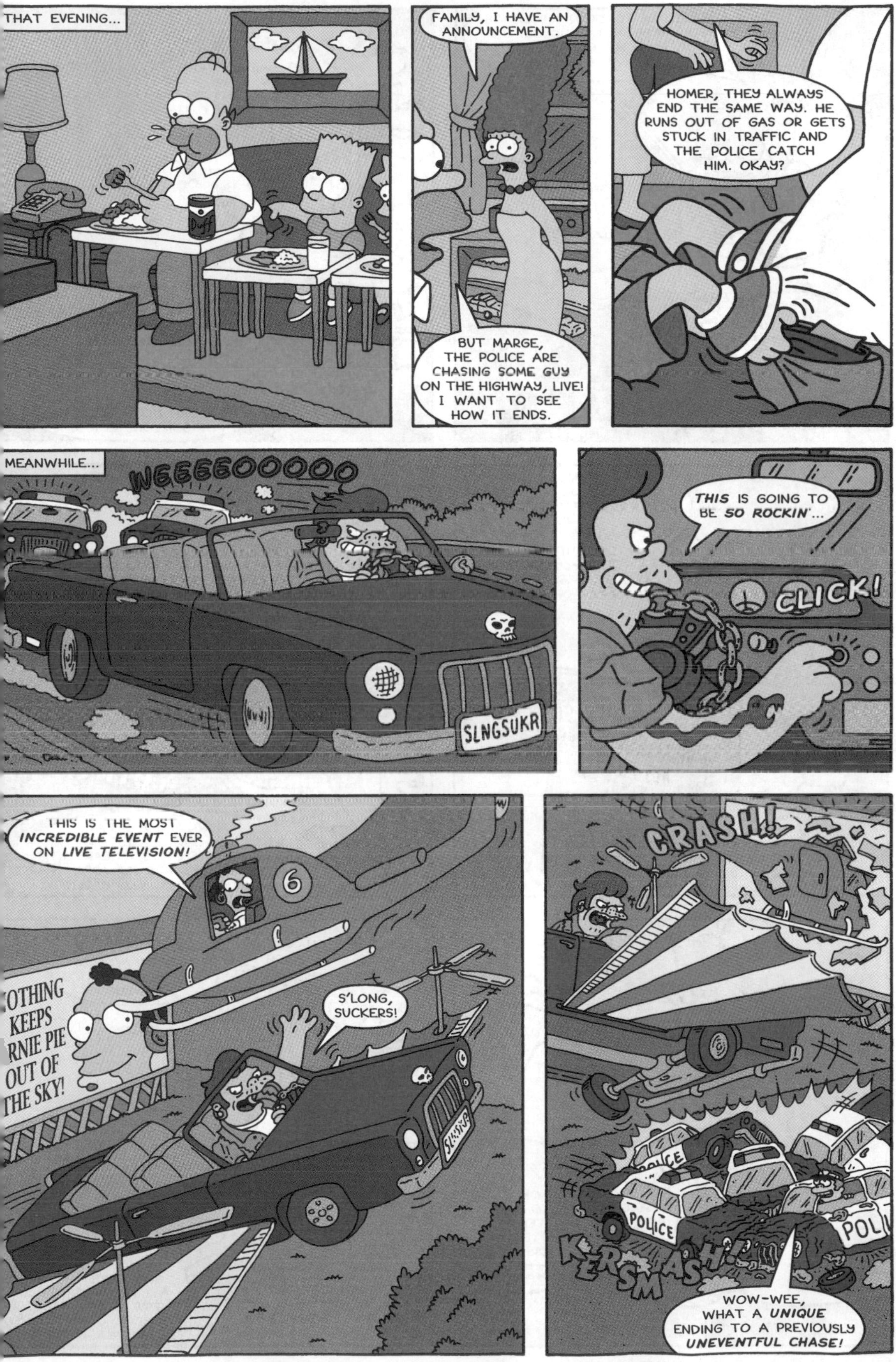
THAT EVENING...
FAMILY, I HAVE AN ANNOUNCEMENT.
BUT MARGE, THE POLICE ARE CHASING SOME GUY ON THE HIGHWAY, LIVE! I WANT TO SEE HOW IT ENDS.
HOMER, THEY ALWAYS END THE SAME WAY. HE RUNS OUT OF GAS OR GETS STUCK IN TRAFFIC AND THE POLICE CATCH HIM. OKAY?
MEANWHILE...
WEEEEOOOOOO
SLNGSUKR
THIS IS GOING TO BE SO ROCKIN'...
CLICK!
THIS IS THE MOST INCREDIBLE EVENT EVER ON LIVE TELEVISION!
6
OTHING KEEPS RNIE PIE OUT OF THE SKY!
S'LONG, SUCKERS!
CRASH!!
POLICE
POLICE
POLI
KERSMASH!
WOW-WEE, WHAT A UNIQUE ENDING TO A PREVIOUSLY UNEVENTFUL CHASE!

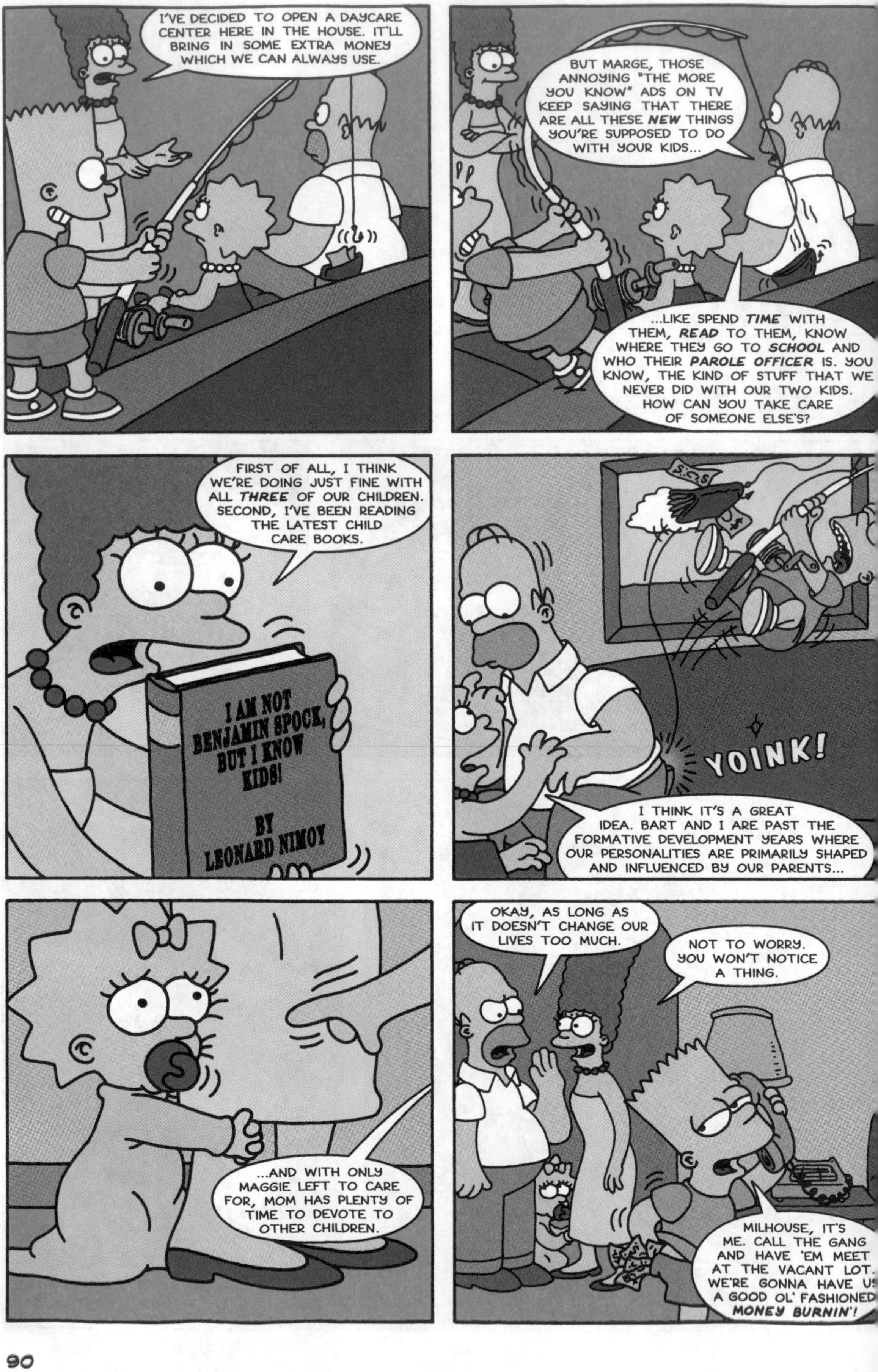
I'VE DECIDED TO OPEN A DAYCARE CENTER HERE IN THE HOUSE. IT'LL BRING IN SOME EXTRA MONEY WHICH WE CAN ALWAYS USE.
BUT MARGE, THOSE ANNOYING "THE MORE YOU KNOW" ADS ON TV KEEP SAYING THAT THERE ARE ALL THESE *NEW* THINGS YOU'RE SUPPOSED TO DO WITH YOUR KIDS...
...LIKE SPEND *TIME* WITH THEM, *READ* TO THEM, KNOW WHERE THEY GO TO *SCHOOL* AND WHO THEIR *PAROLE OFFICER* IS. YOU KNOW, THE KIND OF STUFF THAT WE NEVER DID WITH OUR TWO KIDS. HOW CAN YOU TAKE CARE OF SOMEONE ELSE'S?
FIRST OF ALL, I THINK WE'RE DOING JUST FINE WITH ALL *THREE* OF OUR CHILDREN. SECOND, I'VE BEEN READING THE LATEST CHILD CARE BOOKS.
I AM NOT BENJAMIN SPOCK, BUT I KNOW KIDS! BY LEONARD NIMOY
YOINK!
I THINK IT'S A GREAT IDEA. BART AND I ARE PAST THE FORMATIVE DEVELOPMENT YEARS WHERE OUR PERSONALITIES ARE PRIMARILY SHAPED AND INFLUENCED BY OUR PARENTS...
...AND WITH ONLY MAGGIE LEFT TO CARE FOR, MOM HAS PLENTY OF TIME TO DEVOTE TO OTHER CHILDREN.
OKAY, AS LONG AS IT DOESN'T CHANGE OUR LIVES TOO MUCH.
NOT TO WORRY. YOU WON'T NOTICE A THING.
MILHOUSE, IT'S ME. CALL THE GANG AND HAVE 'EM MEET AT THE VACANT LOT. WE'RE GONNA HAVE U A GOOD OL' FASHIONED *MONEY BURNIN'*!

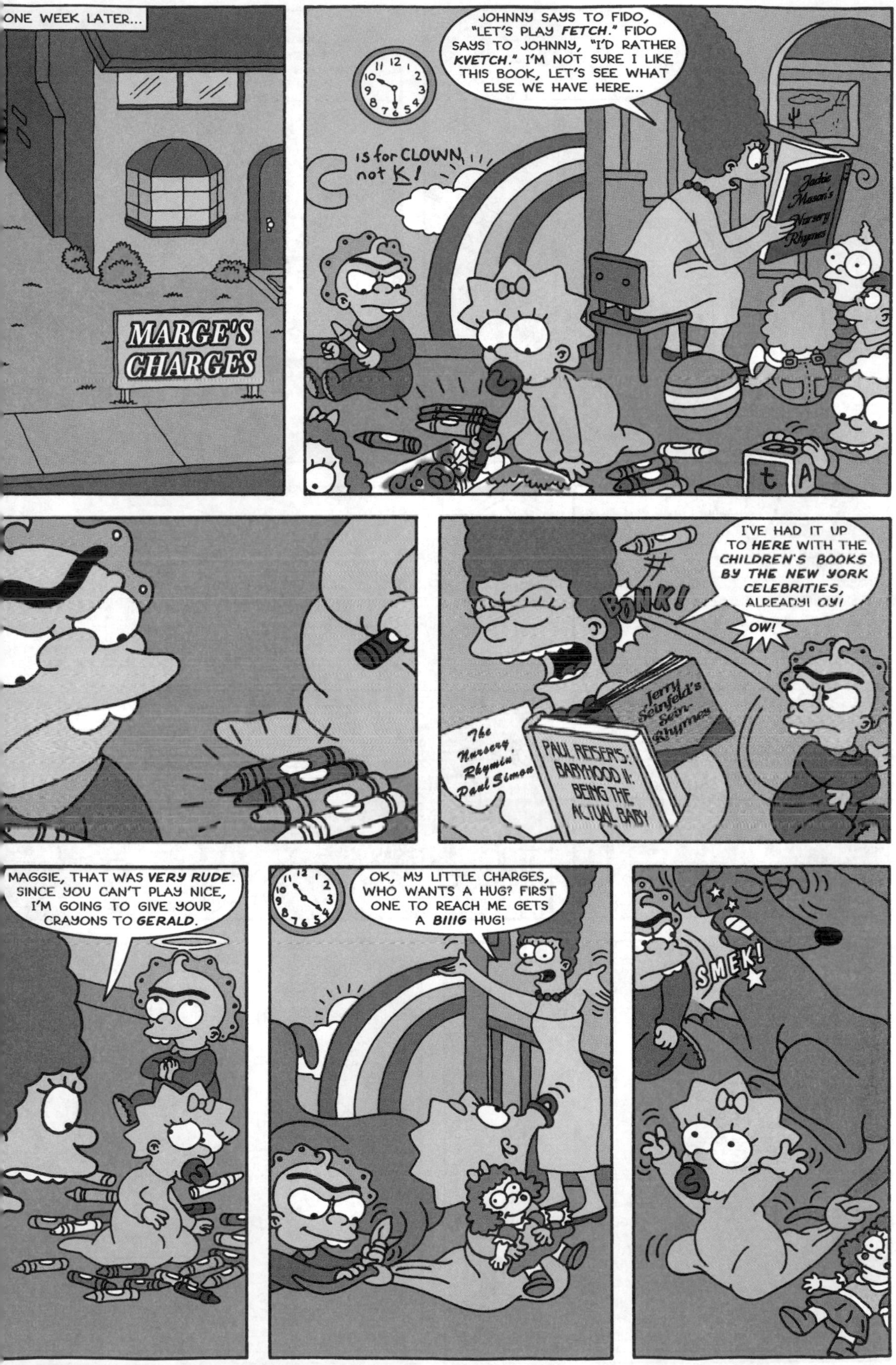
ONE WEEK LATER...
MARGE'S CHARGES
JOHNNY SAYS TO FIDO, "LET'S PLAY FETCH." FIDO SAYS TO JOHNNY, "I'D RATHER KVETCH." I'M NOT SURE I LIKE THIS BOOK, LET'S SEE WHAT ELSE WE HAVE HERE...
C is for CLOWN, not K!
Jackie Mason's Nursery Rhymes
I'VE HAD IT UP TO HERE WITH THE CHILDREN'S BOOKS BY THE NEW YORK CELEBRITIES, ALREADY! OY!
BONK!
OW!
Jerry Seinfeld's Sein-Rhymes
The Nursery Rhymin' Paul Simon
PAUL REISER'S: BABYHOOD II: BEING THE ACTUAL BABY
MAGGIE, THAT WAS VERY RUDE. SINCE YOU CAN'T PLAY NICE, I'M GOING TO GIVE YOUR CRAYONS TO GERALD.
OK, MY LITTLE CHARGES, WHO WANTS A HUG? FIRST ONE TO REACH ME GETS A BIIIG HUG!
SMEK!

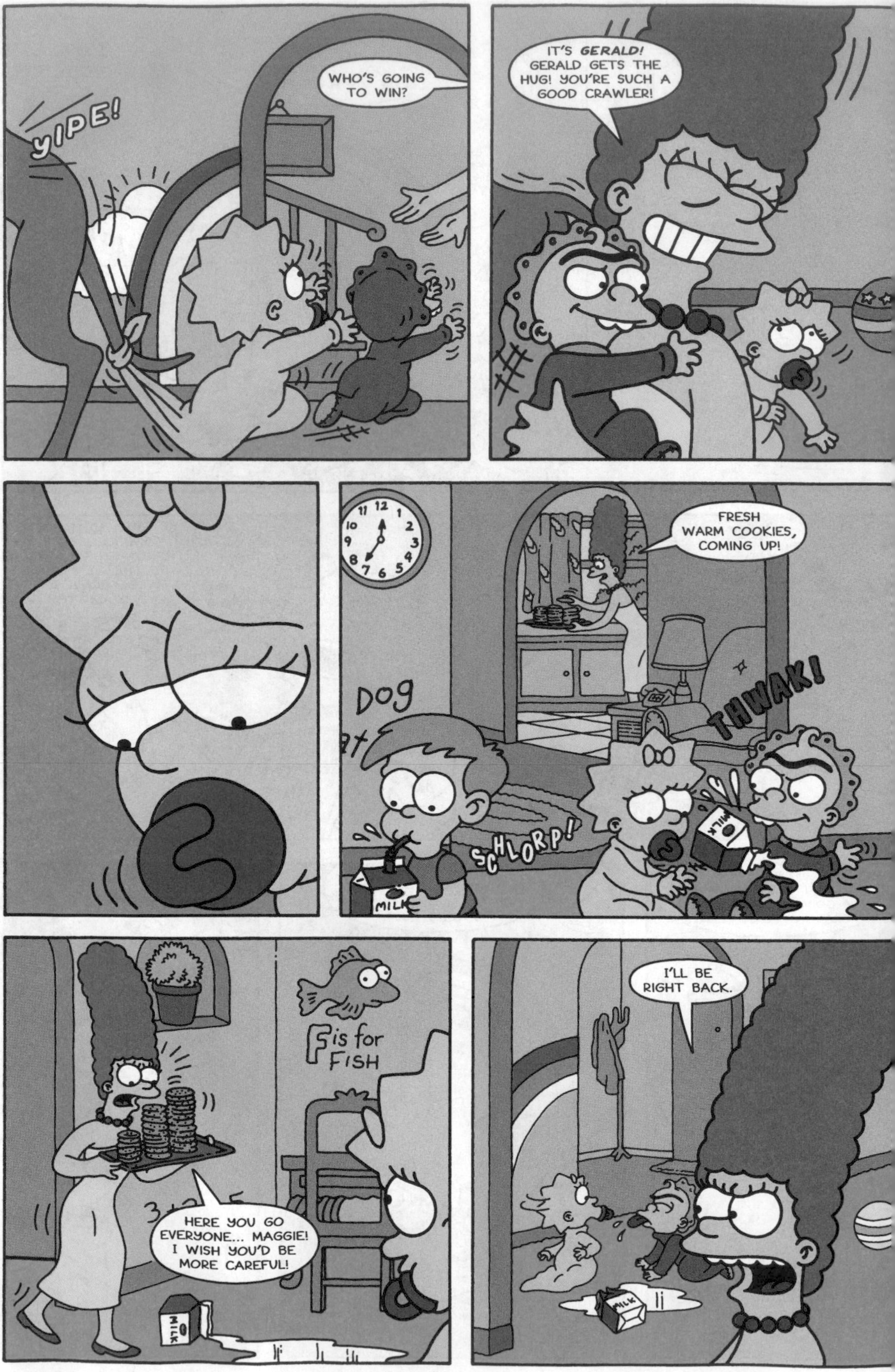
YIPE!
WHO'S GOING TO WIN?
IT'S GERALD! GERALD GETS THE HUG! YOU'RE SUCH A GOOD CRAWLER!
FRESH WARM COOKIES, COMING UP!
DOG
THWAK!
SCHLORP!
MILK
MILK
F is for FISH
HERE YOU GO EVERYONE... MAGGIE! I WISH YOU'D BE MORE CAREFUL!
MILK
I'LL BE RIGHT BACK.
MILK

COW
tree
2
+2
4
3
-1
S
is for Sun
5
POP!
3+3=6
Boat
CRASH!
WHAT WAS *THAT*?

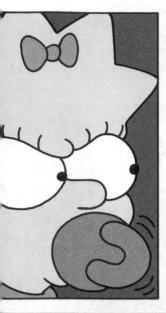

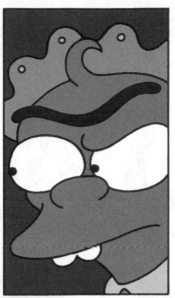

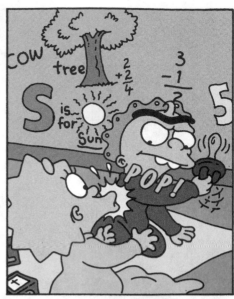

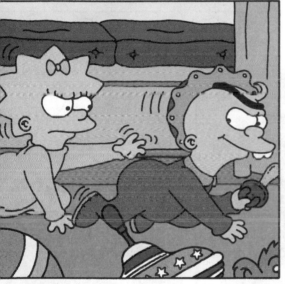

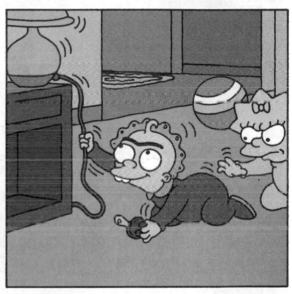

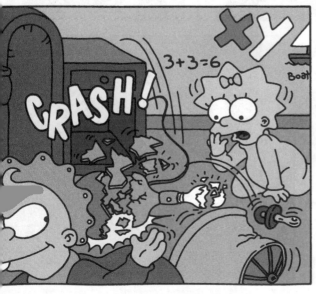

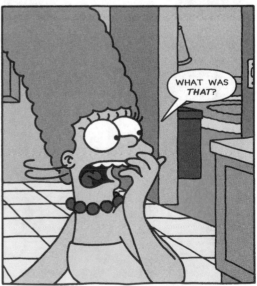

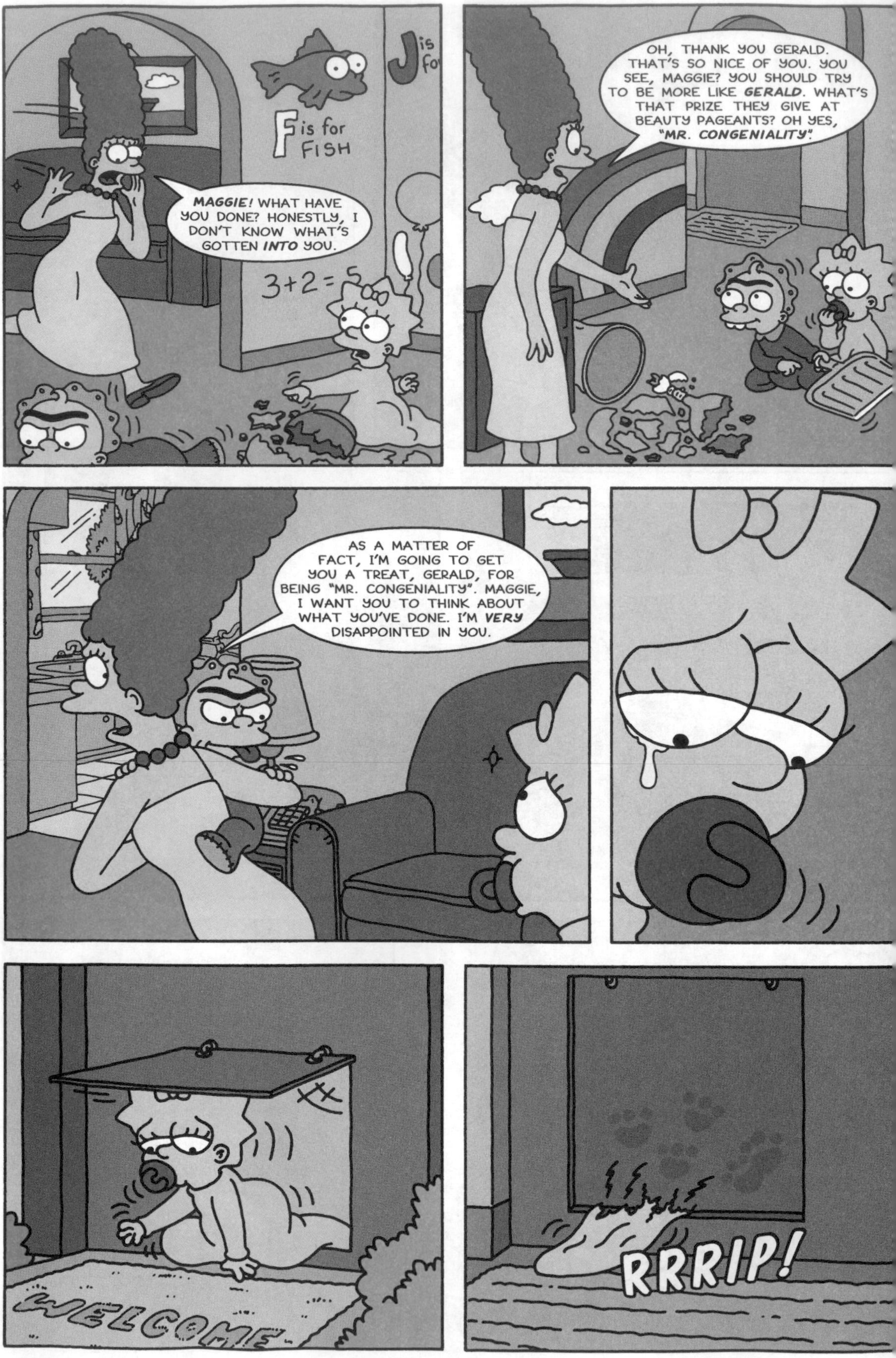
J is for
F is for FISH
MAGGIE! WHAT HAVE YOU DONE? HONESTLY, I DON'T KNOW WHAT'S GOTTEN INTO YOU.
3+2=5
OH, THANK YOU GERALD. THAT'S SO NICE OF YOU. YOU SEE, MAGGIE? YOU SHOULD TRY TO BE MORE LIKE GERALD. WHAT'S THAT PRIZE THEY GIVE AT BEAUTY PAGEANTS? OH YES, "MR. CONGENIALITY".
AS A MATTER OF FACT, I'M GOING TO GET YOU A TREAT, GERALD, FOR BEING "MR. CONGENIALITY". MAGGIE, I WANT YOU TO THINK ABOUT WHAT YOU'VE DONE. I'M VERY DISAPPOINTED IN YOU.
WELCOME
RRRIP!

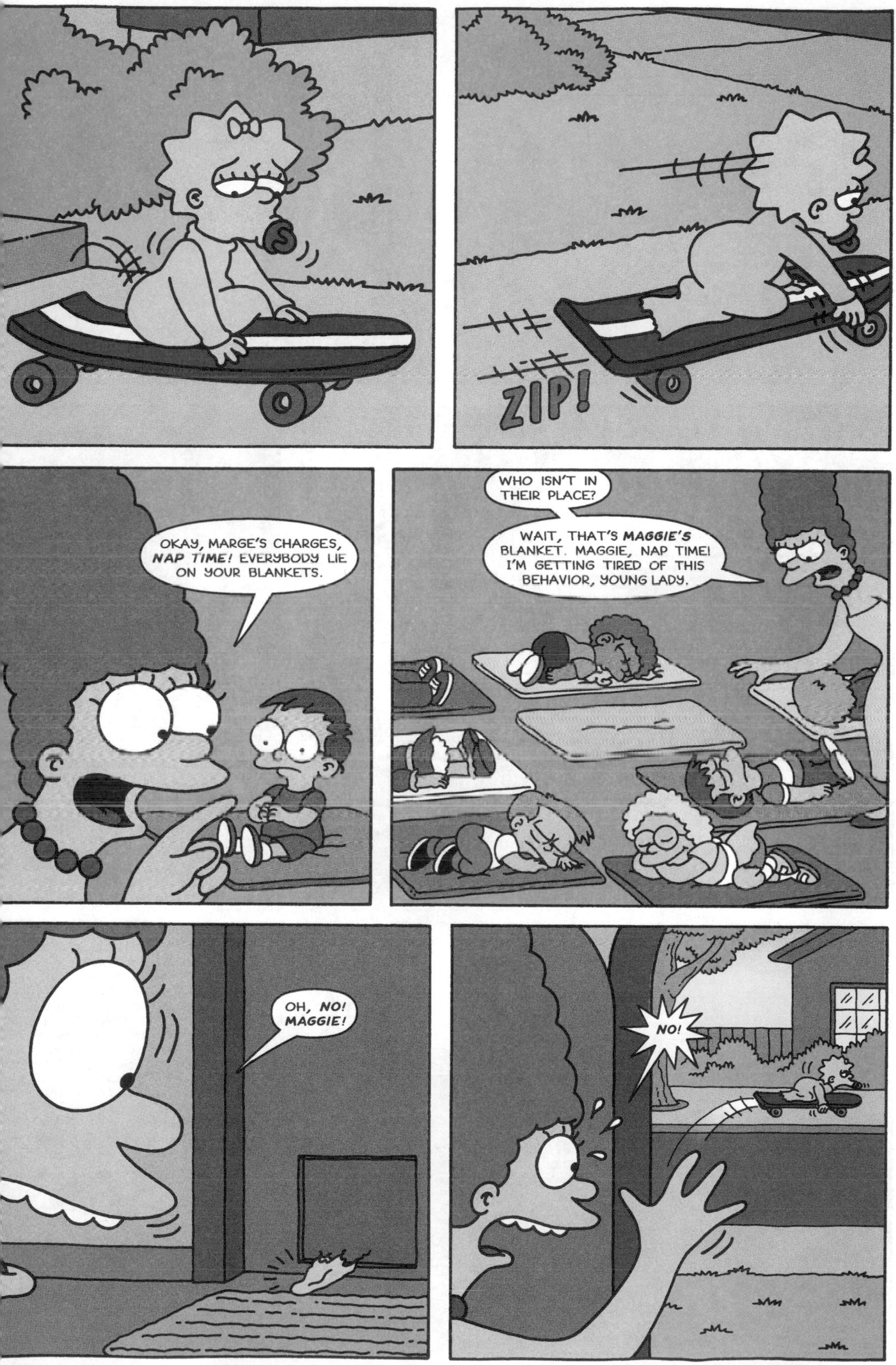
ZIP!
OKAY, MARGE'S CHARGES, NAP TIME! EVERYBODY LIE ON YOUR BLANKETS.
WHO ISN'T IN THEIR PLACE?
WAIT, THAT'S MAGGIE'S BLANKET. MAGGIE, NAP TIME! I'M GETTING TIRED OF THIS BEHAVIOR, YOUNG LADY.
OH, NO! MAGGIE!
NO!

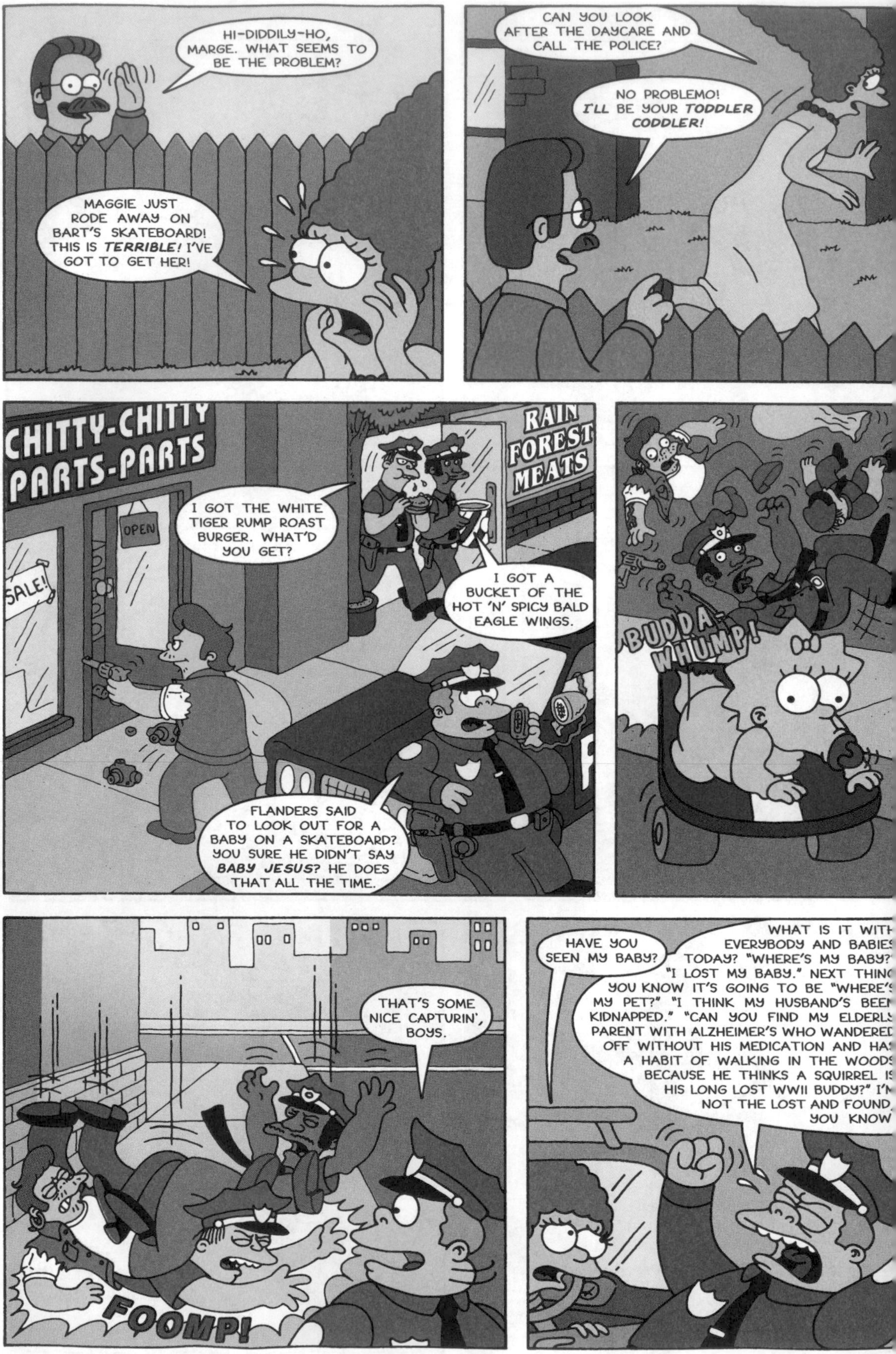
HI-DIDDILY-HO, MARGE. WHAT SEEMS TO BE THE PROBLEM?
MAGGIE JUST RODE AWAY ON BART'S SKATEBOARD! THIS IS TERRIBLE! I'VE GOT TO GET HER!
CAN YOU LOOK AFTER THE DAYCARE AND CALL THE POLICE?
NO PROBLEMO! I'LL BE YOUR TODDLER CODDLER!
CHITTY-CHITTY PARTS-PARTS
OPEN
SALE!
RAIN FOREST MEATS
I GOT THE WHITE TIGER RUMP ROAST BURGER. WHAT'D YOU GET?
I GOT A BUCKET OF THE HOT 'N' SPICY BALD EAGLE WINGS.
FLANDERS SAID TO LOOK OUT FOR A BABY ON A SKATEBOARD? YOU SURE HE DIDN'T SAY BABY JESUS? HE DOES THAT ALL THE TIME.
BUDDA-WHUMP!
THAT'S SOME NICE CAPTURIN', BOYS.
FOOMP!
HAVE YOU SEEN MY BABY?
WHAT IS IT WITH EVERYBODY AND BABIES TODAY? "WHERE'S MY BABY?" "I LOST MY BABY." NEXT THING YOU KNOW IT'S GOING TO BE "WHERE'S MY PET?" "I THINK MY HUSBAND'S BEEN KIDNAPPED." "CAN YOU FIND MY ELDERLY PARENT WITH ALZHEIMER'S WHO WANDERED OFF WITHOUT HIS MEDICATION AND HAS A HABIT OF WALKING IN THE WOODS BECAUSE HE THINKS A SQUIRREL IS HIS LONG LOST WWII BUDDY?" I'M NOT THE LOST AND FOUND, YOU KNOW

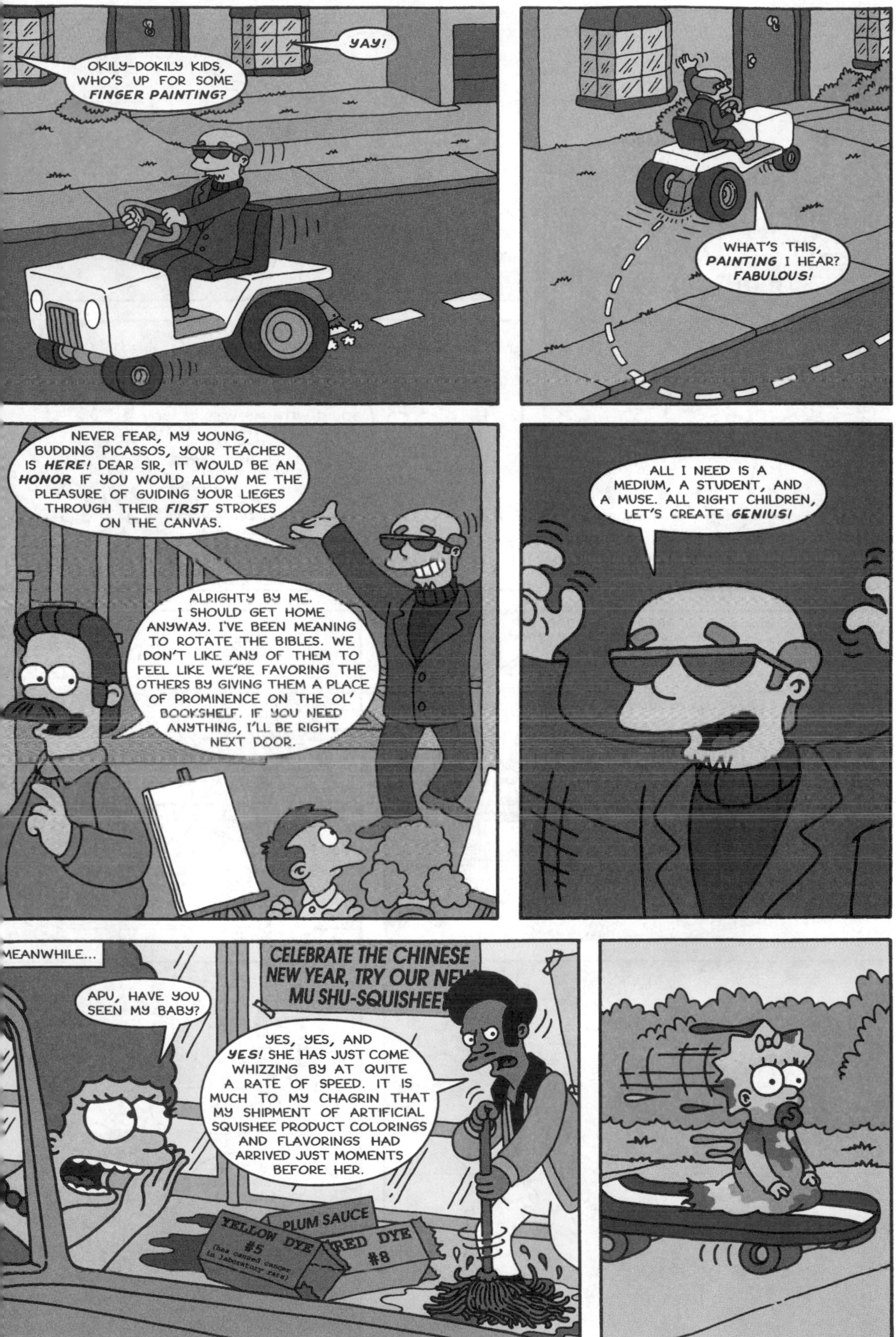
OKILY-DOKILY KIDS, WHO'S UP FOR SOME FINGER PAINTING?
YAY!
WHAT'S THIS, PAINTING I HEAR? FABULOUS!
NEVER FEAR, MY YOUNG, BUDDING PICASSOS, YOUR TEACHER IS HERE! DEAR SIR, IT WOULD BE AN HONOR IF YOU WOULD ALLOW ME THE PLEASURE OF GUIDING YOUR LIEGES THROUGH THEIR FIRST STROKES ON THE CANVAS.
ALRIGHTY BY ME. I SHOULD GET HOME ANYWAY. I'VE BEEN MEANING TO ROTATE THE BIBLES. WE DON'T LIKE ANY OF THEM TO FEEL LIKE WE'RE FAVORING THE OTHERS BY GIVING THEM A PLACE OF PROMINENCE ON THE OL' BOOKSHELF. IF YOU NEED ANYTHING, I'LL BE RIGHT NEXT DOOR.
ALL I NEED IS A MEDIUM, A STUDENT, AND A MUSE. ALL RIGHT CHILDREN, LET'S CREATE GENIUS!
MEANWHILE...
CELEBRATE THE CHINESE NEW YEAR, TRY OUR NEW MU SHU-SQUISHEE!
APU, HAVE YOU SEEN MY BABY?
YES, YES, AND YES! SHE HAS JUST COME WHIZZING BY AT QUITE A RATE OF SPEED. IT IS MUCH TO MY CHAGRIN THAT MY SHIPMENT OF ARTIFICIAL SQUISHEE PRODUCT COLORINGS AND FLAVORINGS HAD ARRIVED JUST MOMENTS BEFORE HER.
PLUM SAUCE
YELLOW DYE #5
RED DYE #8

BEAUTIFUL! THAT'S *PERFECT!* CRAWL AWAY!

OH *NO!* MUCH AS I'M A FAN OF EXPRESSIONISM, I FEAR THAT *YOU* DOTH EXPRESS *TOO MUCH!* WHAT AM I TO DO?

DR. NICK'S SPIT 'N' ARSENIC CLEANING SOLUTION—MADE WITH REAL BUFFALO SALIVA AND ORGANIC ARSENIC!

JINGLE! JINGLE!

BRILLIANT!

HI, EVERYBODY! I'M *DR. NICK.*

MY WORK HERE IS DONE. I'M OFF TO ENLIGHTEN OTHER FORTUNATE SOULS WITH MY WISDOM. YOU THERE, THE THUG WITH THE SPRAY CAN--WAIT FOR ME! I SEE *BRILLIANCE* IN YOUR FUTURE!

HI, DR. NICK!

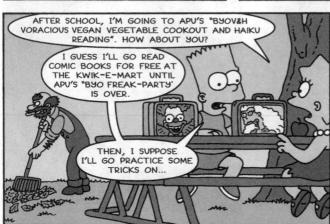

AFTER SCHOOL, I'M GOING TO APU'S "BYOV&H VORACIOUS VEGAN VEGETABLE COOKOUT AND HAIKU READING". HOW ABOUT YOU?

I GUESS I'LL GO READ COMIC BOOKS FOR FREE AT THE KWIK-E-MART UNTIL APU'S "BYO FREAK-PARTY" IS OVER.

THEN, I SUPPOSE I'LL GO PRACTICE SOME TRICKS ON...

...MY SKATEBOARD!!

MAGGIE!

SHE WENT THAT WAY, MOM!

KIDS, HAVE YOU SEEN MAGGIE?

4TH GRADE COMPOST HEAP

COME ON, KIDS, LET'S GO!

OH, MY. THAT STINKS SO BADLY, I'VE LOST MY ACCENT!

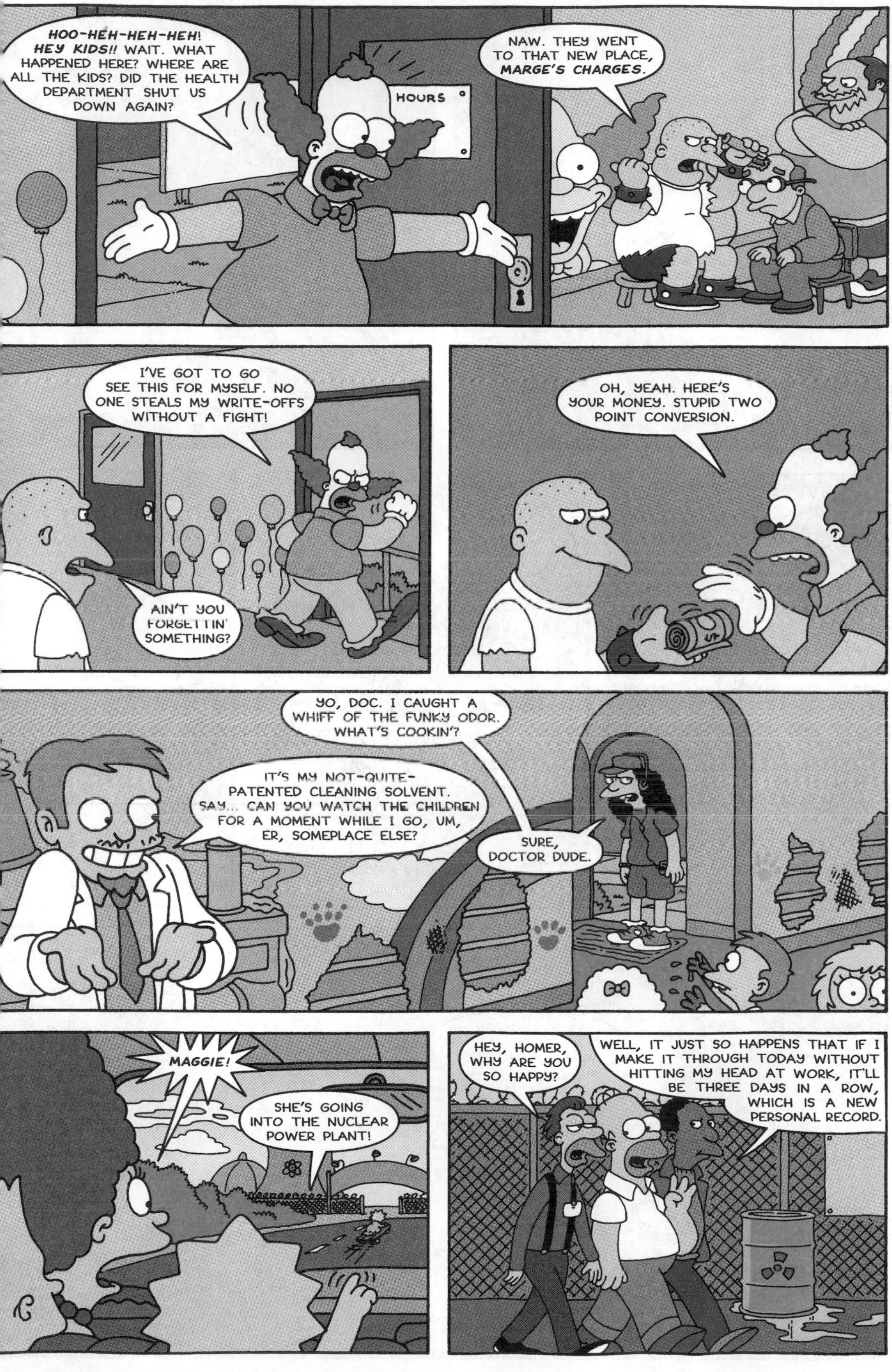
HOO-HEH-HEH-HEH! HEY KIDS!! WAIT. WHAT HAPPENED HERE? WHERE ARE ALL THE KIDS? DID THE HEALTH DEPARTMENT SHUT US DOWN AGAIN?
HOURS
NAW. THEY WENT TO THAT NEW PLACE, MARGE'S CHARGES.
I'VE GOT TO GO SEE THIS FOR MYSELF. NO ONE STEALS MY WRITE-OFFS WITHOUT A FIGHT!
AIN'T YOU FORGETTIN' SOMETHING?
OH, YEAH. HERE'S YOUR MONEY. STUPID TWO POINT CONVERSION.
IT'S MY NOT-QUITE-PATENTED CLEANING SOLVENT. SAY... CAN YOU WATCH THE CHILDREN FOR A MOMENT WHILE I GO, UM, ER, SOMEPLACE ELSE?
YO, DOC. I CAUGHT A WHIFF OF THE FUNKY ODOR. WHAT'S COOKIN'?
SURE, DOCTOR DUDE.
MAGGIE!
SHE'S GOING INTO THE NUCLEAR POWER PLANT!
HEY, HOMER, WHY ARE YOU SO HAPPY?
WELL, IT JUST SO HAPPENS THAT IF I MAKE IT THROUGH TODAY WITHOUT HITTING MY HEAD AT WORK, IT'LL BE THREE DAYS IN A ROW, WHICH IS A NEW PERSONAL RECORD.

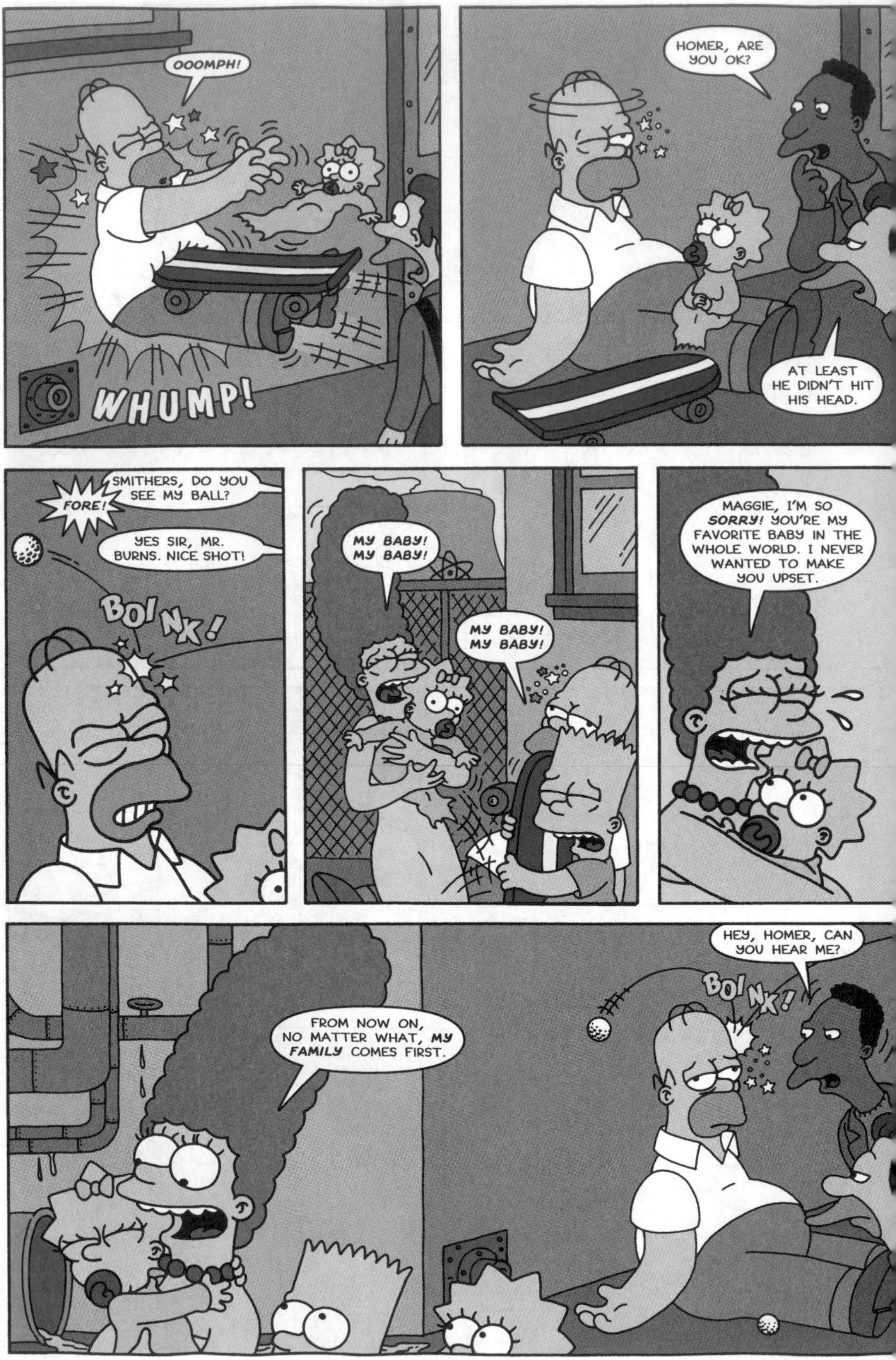
OOOMPH!
WHUMP!
HOMER, ARE YOU OK?
AT LEAST HE DIDN'T HIT HIS HEAD.
FORE!
SMITHERS, DO YOU SEE MY BALL?
YES SIR, MR. BURNS. NICE SHOT!
BOINK!
MY BABY! MY BABY!
MY BABY! MY BABY!
MAGGIE, I'M SO SORRY! YOU'RE MY FAVORITE BABY IN THE WHOLE WORLD. I NEVER WANTED TO MAKE YOU UPSET.
FROM NOW ON, NO MATTER WHAT, MY FAMILY COMES FIRST.
HEY, HOMER, CAN YOU HEAR ME?
BOINK!

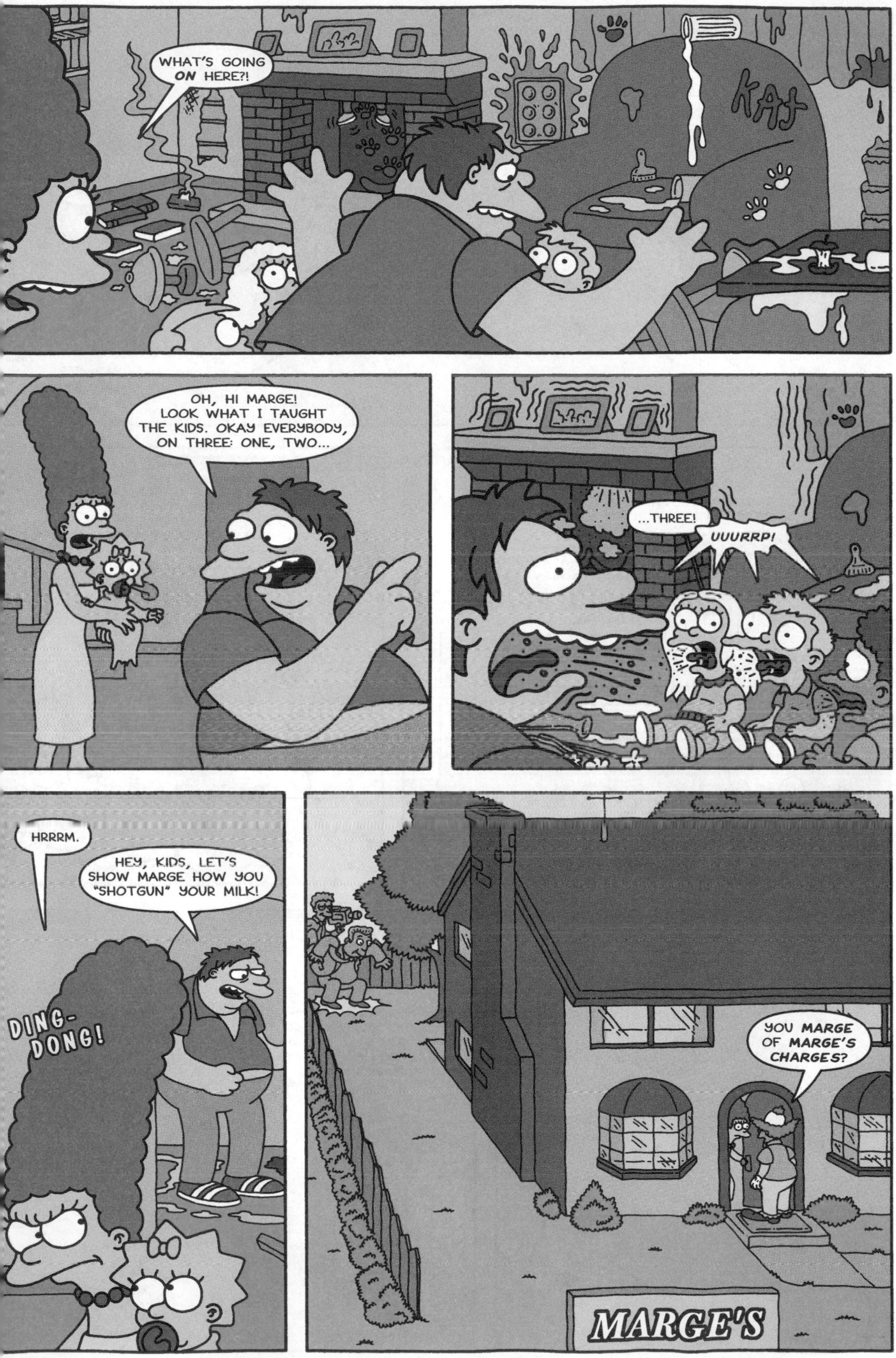
WHAT'S GOING ON HERE?!
OH, HI MARGE! LOOK WHAT I TAUGHT THE KIDS. OKAY EVERYBODY, ON THREE: ONE, TWO...
...THREE!
UUURRP!
HRRRM.
HEY, KIDS, LET'S SHOW MARGE HOW YOU "SHOTGUN" YOUR MILK!
DING-DONG!
YOU MARGE OF MARGE'S CHARGES?
MARGE'S

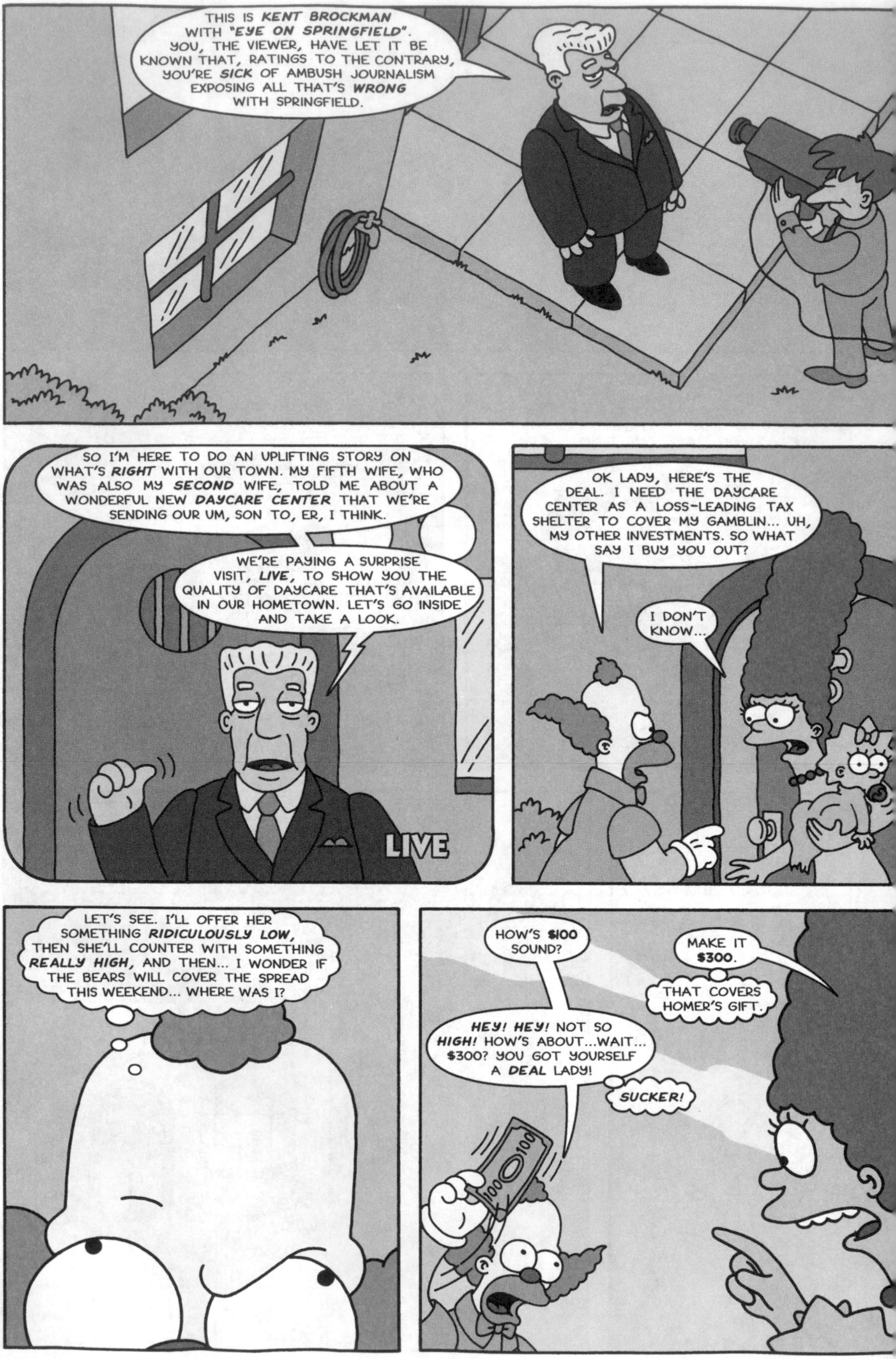
THIS IS KENT BROCKMAN WITH "EYE ON SPRINGFIELD". YOU, THE VIEWER, HAVE LET IT BE KNOWN THAT, RATINGS TO THE CONTRARY, YOU'RE SICK OF AMBUSH JOURNALISM EXPOSING ALL THAT'S WRONG WITH SPRINGFIELD.
SO I'M HERE TO DO AN UPLIFTING STORY ON WHAT'S RIGHT WITH OUR TOWN. MY FIFTH WIFE, WHO WAS ALSO MY SECOND WIFE, TOLD ME ABOUT A WONDERFUL NEW DAYCARE CENTER THAT WE'RE SENDING OUR UM, SON TO, ER, I THINK.
WE'RE PAYING A SURPRISE VISIT, LIVE, TO SHOW YOU THE QUALITY OF DAYCARE THAT'S AVAILABLE IN OUR HOMETOWN. LET'S GO INSIDE AND TAKE A LOOK.
LIVE
OK LADY, HERE'S THE DEAL. I NEED THE DAYCARE CENTER AS A LOSS-LEADING TAX SHELTER TO COVER MY GAMBLIN... UH, MY OTHER INVESTMENTS. SO WHAT SAY I BUY YOU OUT?
I DON'T KNOW...
LET'S SEE. I'LL OFFER HER SOMETHING RIDICULOUSLY LOW, THEN SHE'LL COUNTER WITH SOMETHING REALLY HIGH, AND THEN... I WONDER IF THE BEARS WILL COVER THE SPREAD THIS WEEKEND... WHERE WAS I?
HOW'S $100 SOUND?
MAKE IT $300.
THAT COVERS HOMER'S GIFT.
HEY! HEY! NOT SO HIGH! HOW'S ABOUT...WAIT... $300? YOU GOT YOURSELF A DEAL LADY!
SUCKER!
100

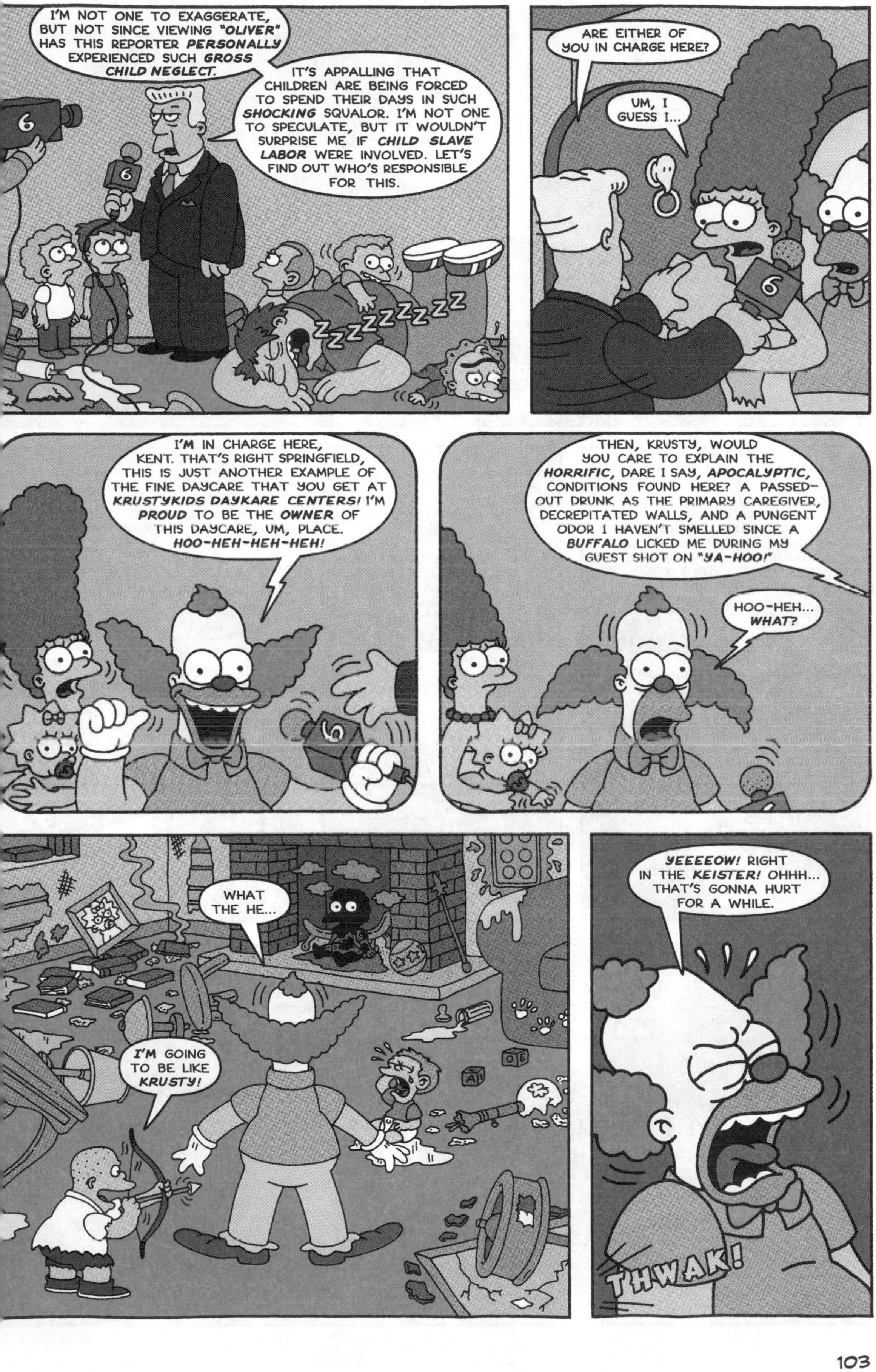
I'M NOT ONE TO EXAGGERATE, BUT NOT SINCE VIEWING "OLIVER" HAS THIS REPORTER PERSONALLY EXPERIENCED SUCH GROSS CHILD NEGLECT.
IT'S APPALLING THAT CHILDREN ARE BEING FORCED TO SPEND THEIR DAYS IN SUCH SHOCKING SQUALOR. I'M NOT ONE TO SPECULATE, BUT IT WOULDN'T SURPRISE ME IF CHILD SLAVE LABOR WERE INVOLVED. LET'S FIND OUT WHO'S RESPONSIBLE FOR THIS.
ZZZZZZZZZZ
ARE EITHER OF YOU IN CHARGE HERE?
UM, I GUESS I...
I'M IN CHARGE HERE, KENT. THAT'S RIGHT SPRINGFIELD, THIS IS JUST ANOTHER EXAMPLE OF THE FINE DAYCARE THAT YOU GET AT KRUSTYKIDS DAYKARE CENTERS! I'M PROUD TO BE THE OWNER OF THIS DAYCARE, UM, PLACE. HOO-HEH-HEH-HEH!
THEN, KRUSTY, WOULD YOU CARE TO EXPLAIN THE HORRIFIC, DARE I SAY, APOCALYPTIC, CONDITIONS FOUND HERE? A PASSED-OUT DRUNK AS THE PRIMARY CAREGIVER, DECREPITATED WALLS, AND A PUNGENT ODOR I HAVEN'T SMELLED SINCE A BUFFALO LICKED ME DURING MY GUEST SHOT ON "YA-HOO!"
HOO-HEH... WHAT?
WHAT THE HE...
I'M GOING TO BE LIKE KRUSTY!
YEEEEOW! RIGHT IN THE KEISTER! OHHH... THAT'S GONNA HURT FOR A WHILE.
THWAK!

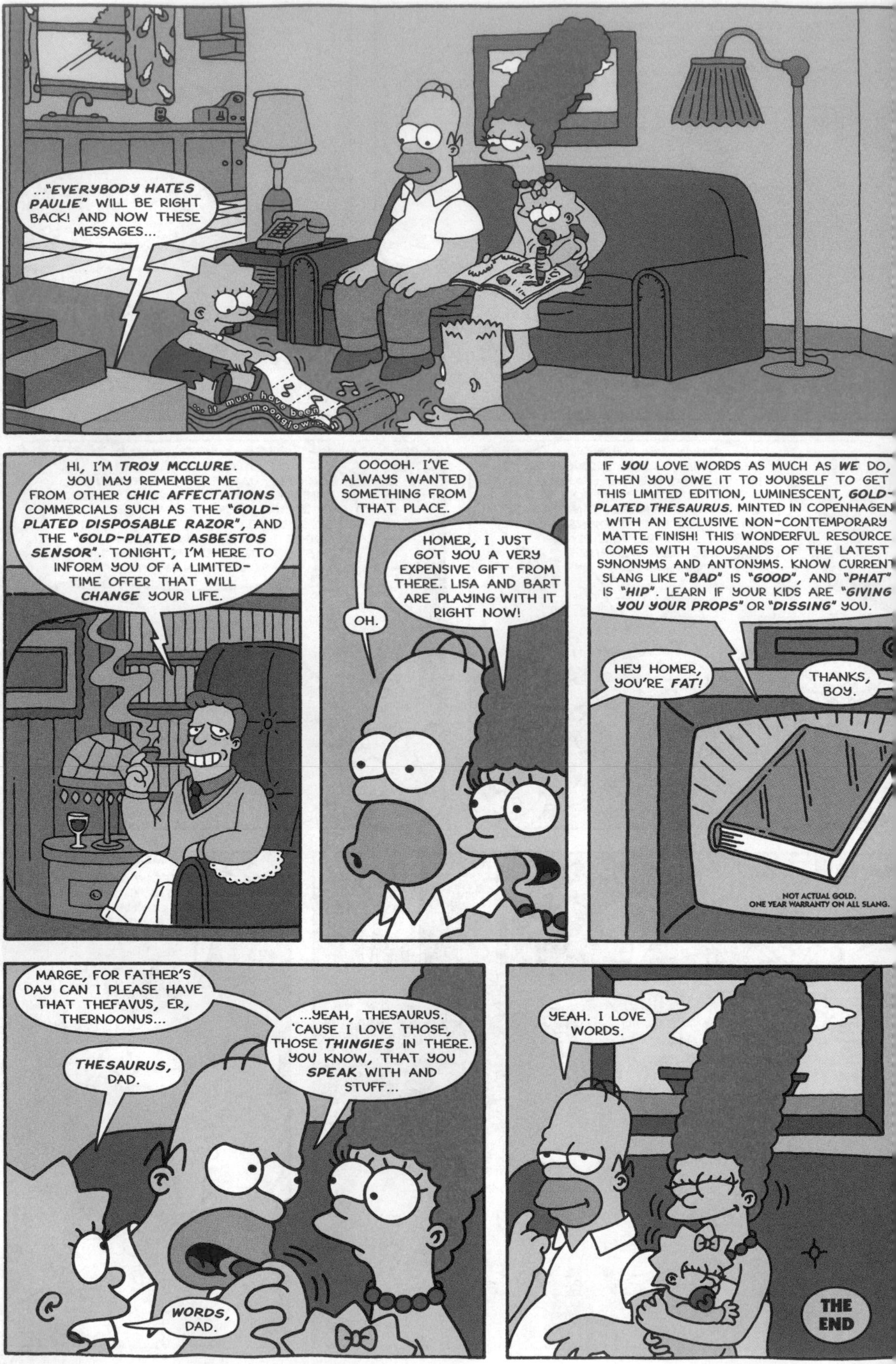
..."EVERYBODY HATES PAULIE" WILL BE RIGHT BACK! AND NOW THESE MESSAGES...
...it must have been moonglow...
HI, I'M TROY MCCLURE. YOU MAY REMEMBER ME FROM OTHER CHIC AFFECTATIONS COMMERCIALS SUCH AS THE "GOLD-PLATED DISPOSABLE RAZOR", AND THE "GOLD-PLATED ASBESTOS SENSOR". TONIGHT, I'M HERE TO INFORM YOU OF A LIMITED-TIME OFFER THAT WILL CHANGE YOUR LIFE.
OOOOH. I'VE ALWAYS WANTED SOMETHING FROM THAT PLACE.
HOMER, I JUST GOT YOU A VERY EXPENSIVE GIFT FROM THERE. LISA AND BART ARE PLAYING WITH IT RIGHT NOW!
OH.
IF YOU LOVE WORDS AS MUCH AS WE DO, THEN YOU OWE IT TO YOURSELF TO GET THIS LIMITED EDITION, LUMINESCENT, GOLD-PLATED THESAURUS. MINTED IN COPENHAGEN WITH AN EXCLUSIVE NON-CONTEMPORARY MATTE FINISH! THIS WONDERFUL RESOURCE COMES WITH THOUSANDS OF THE LATEST SYNONYMS AND ANTONYMS. KNOW CURRENT SLANG LIKE "BAD" IS "GOOD", AND "PHAT" IS "HIP". LEARN IF YOUR KIDS ARE "GIVING YOU YOUR PROPS" OR "DISSING" YOU.
HEY HOMER, YOU'RE FAT!
THANKS, BOY.
NOT ACTUAL GOLD.
ONE YEAR WARRANTY ON ALL SLANG.
MARGE, FOR FATHER'S DAY CAN I PLEASE HAVE THAT THEFAVUS, ER, THERNOONUS...
THESAURUS, DAD.
...YEAH, THESAURUS. 'CAUSE I LOVE THOSE, THOSE THINGIES IN THERE. YOU KNOW, THAT YOU SPEAK WITH AND STUFF...
WORDS, DAD.
YEAH. I LOVE WORDS.
THE END

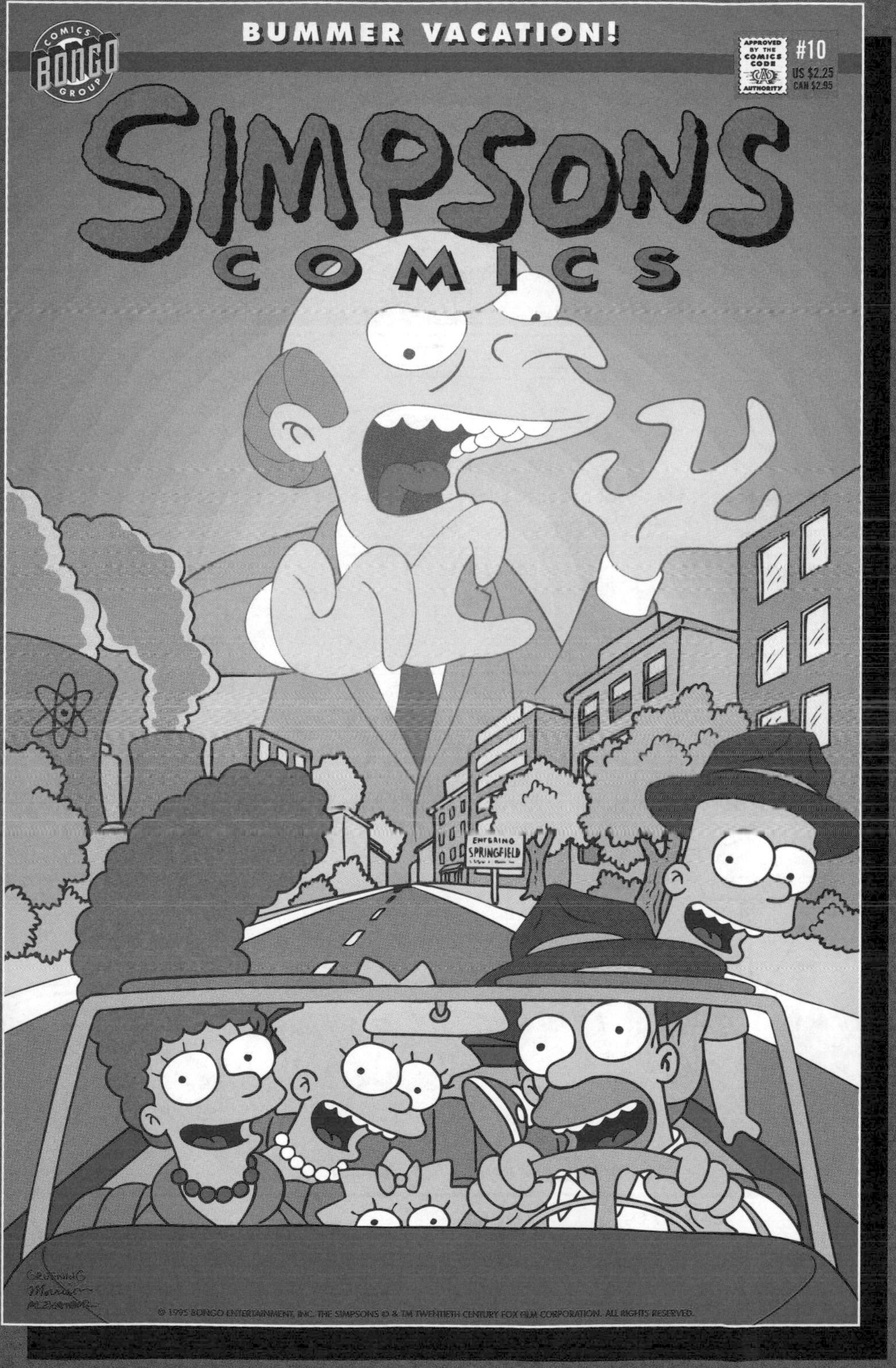
BUMMER VACATION!
COMICS BONGO GROUP
APPROVED BY THE COMICS CODE AUTHORITY
#10
US $2.25
CAN $2.95
SIMPSONS
COMICS
ENTERING SPRINGFIELD
© 1995 BONGO ENTERTAINMENT, INC. THE SIMPSONS © & TM TWENTIETH CENTURY FOX FILM CORPORATION. ALL RIGHTS RESERVED.

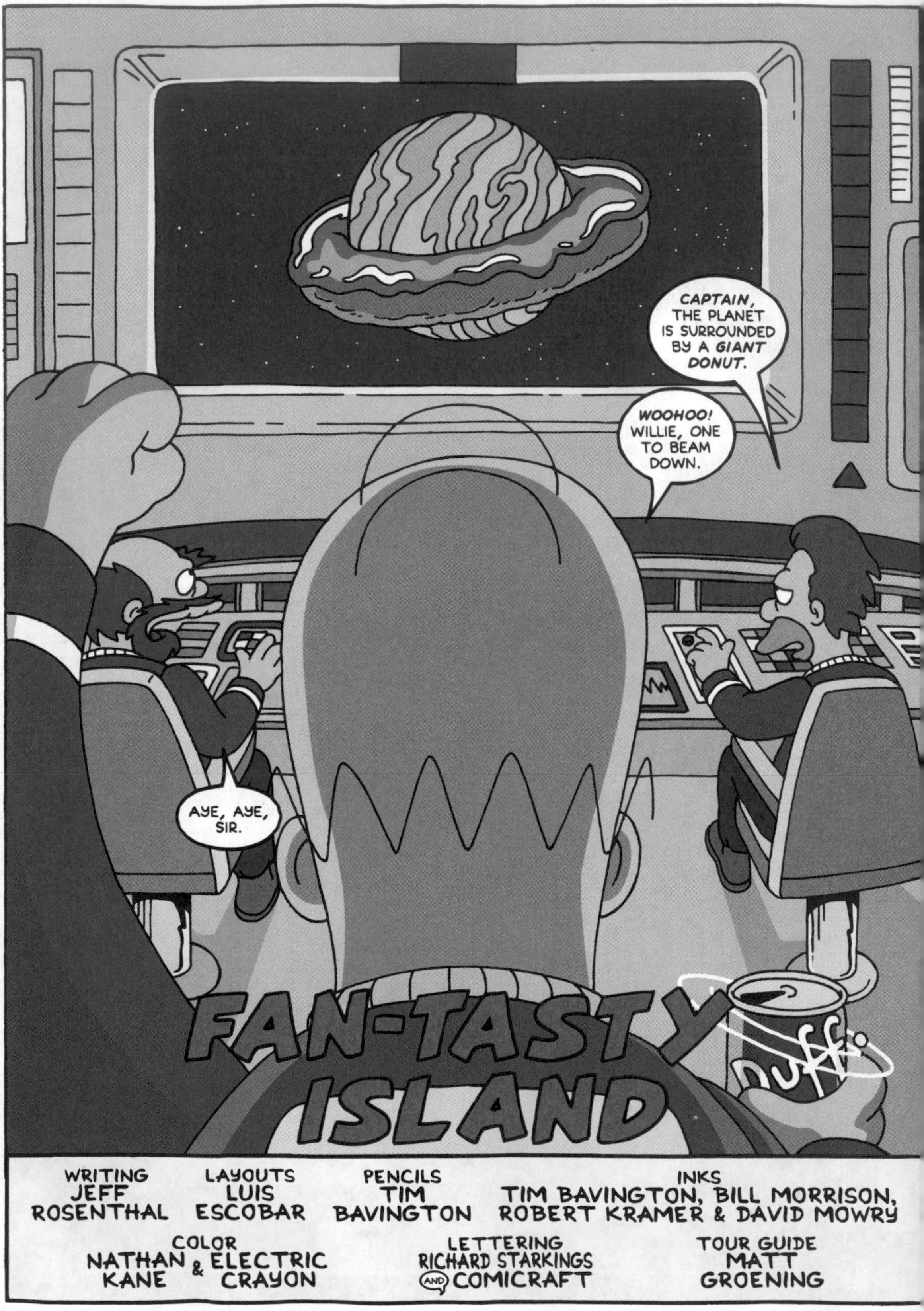
CAPTAIN, THE PLANET IS SURROUNDED BY A GIANT DONUT.
WOOHOO! WILLIE, ONE TO BEAM DOWN.
AYE, AYE, SIR.
FAN-TASTY ISLAND
Duff

WRITING JEFF ROSENTHAL · LAYOUTS LUIS ESCOBAR · PENCILS TIM BAVINGTON · INKS TIM BAVINGTON, BILL MORRISON, ROBERT KRAMER & DAVID MOWRY

COLOR NATHAN KANE & ELECTRIC CRAYON · LETTERING RICHARD STARKINGS AND COMICRAFT · TOUR GUIDE MATT GROENING

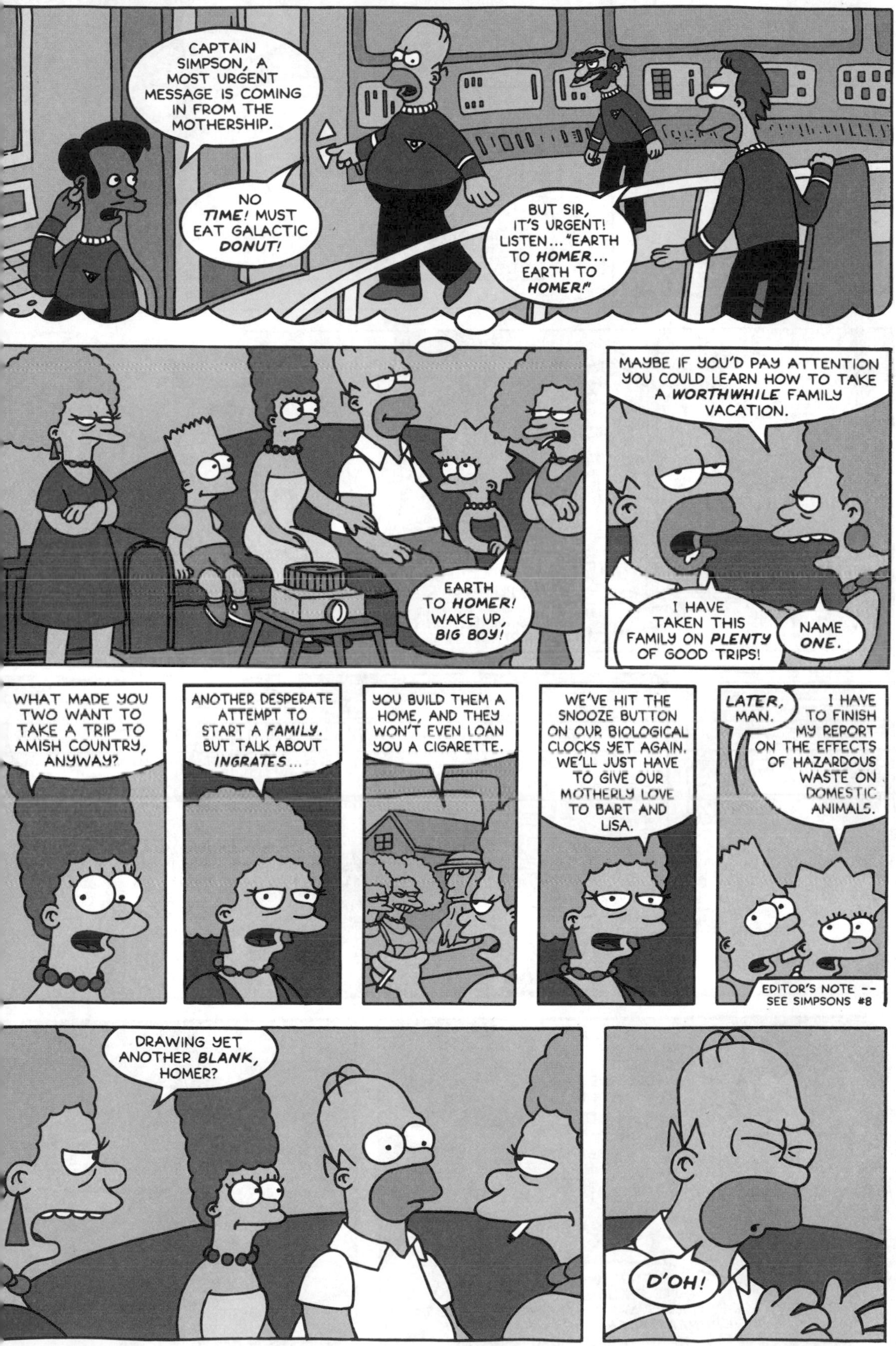
CAPTAIN SIMPSON, A MOST URGENT MESSAGE IS COMING IN FROM THE MOTHERSHIP.
NO *TIME!* MUST EAT GALACTIC *DONUT!*
BUT SIR, IT'S URGENT! LISTEN... "EARTH TO *HOMER*... EARTH TO *HOMER!*"
EARTH TO *HOMER!* WAKE UP, *BIG BOY!*
MAYBE IF YOU'D PAY ATTENTION YOU COULD LEARN HOW TO TAKE A *WORTHWHILE* FAMILY VACATION.
I HAVE TAKEN THIS FAMILY ON *PLENTY* OF GOOD TRIPS!
NAME *ONE.*
WHAT MADE YOU TWO WANT TO TAKE A TRIP TO AMISH COUNTRY, ANYWAY?
ANOTHER DESPERATE ATTEMPT TO START A *FAMILY.* BUT TALK ABOUT *INGRATES*...
YOU BUILD THEM A HOME, AND THEY WON'T EVEN LOAN YOU A CIGARETTE.
WE'VE HIT THE SNOOZE BUTTON ON OUR BIOLOGICAL CLOCKS YET AGAIN. WE'LL JUST HAVE TO GIVE OUR MOTHERLY LOVE TO BART AND LISA.
LATER, MAN.
I HAVE TO FINISH MY REPORT ON THE EFFECTS OF HAZARDOUS WASTE ON DOMESTIC ANIMALS.
EDITOR'S NOTE -- SEE SIMPSONS #8
DRAWING YET ANOTHER *BLANK,* HOMER?
D'OH!

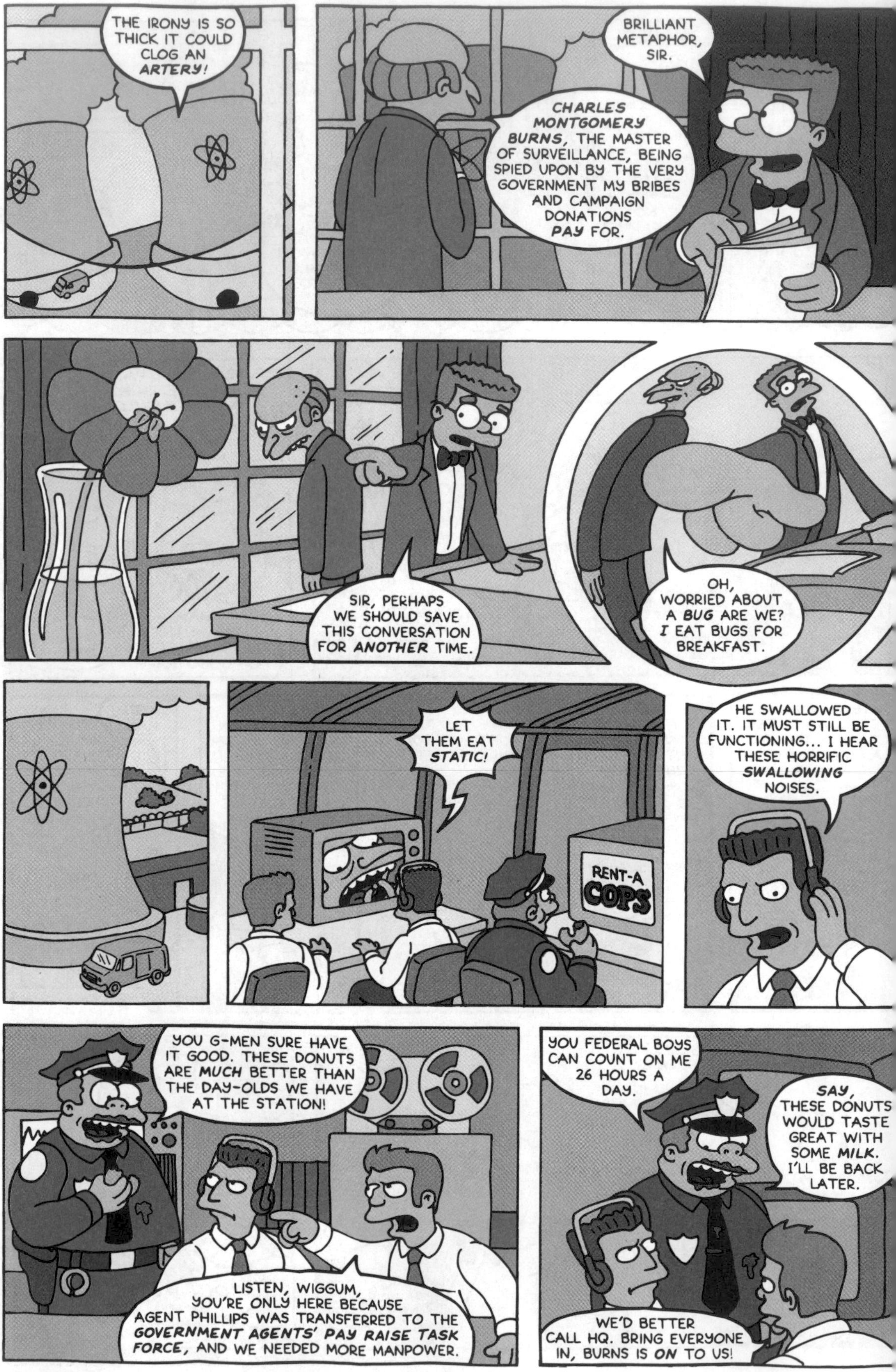
THE IRONY IS SO THICK IT COULD CLOG AN ARTERY!
BRILLIANT METAPHOR, SIR.
CHARLES MONTGOMERY BURNS, THE MASTER OF SURVEILLANCE, BEING SPIED UPON BY THE VERY GOVERNMENT MY BRIBES AND CAMPAIGN DONATIONS PAY FOR.
SIR, PERHAPS WE SHOULD SAVE THIS CONVERSATION FOR ANOTHER TIME.
OH, WORRIED ABOUT A BUG ARE WE? I EAT BUGS FOR BREAKFAST.
LET THEM EAT STATIC!
RENT-A COPS
HE SWALLOWED IT. IT MUST STILL BE FUNCTIONING... I HEAR THESE HORRIFIC SWALLOWING NOISES.
YOU G-MEN SURE HAVE IT GOOD. THESE DONUTS ARE MUCH BETTER THAN THE DAY-OLDS WE HAVE AT THE STATION!
LISTEN, WIGGUM, YOU'RE ONLY HERE BECAUSE AGENT PHILLIPS WAS TRANSFERRED TO THE GOVERNMENT AGENTS' PAY RAISE TASK FORCE, AND WE NEEDED MORE MANPOWER.
YOU FEDERAL BOYS CAN COUNT ON ME 26 HOURS A DAY.
SAY, THESE DONUTS WOULD TASTE GREAT WITH SOME MILK. I'LL BE BACK LATER.
WE'D BETTER CALL HQ. BRING EVERYONE IN, BURNS IS ON TO US!

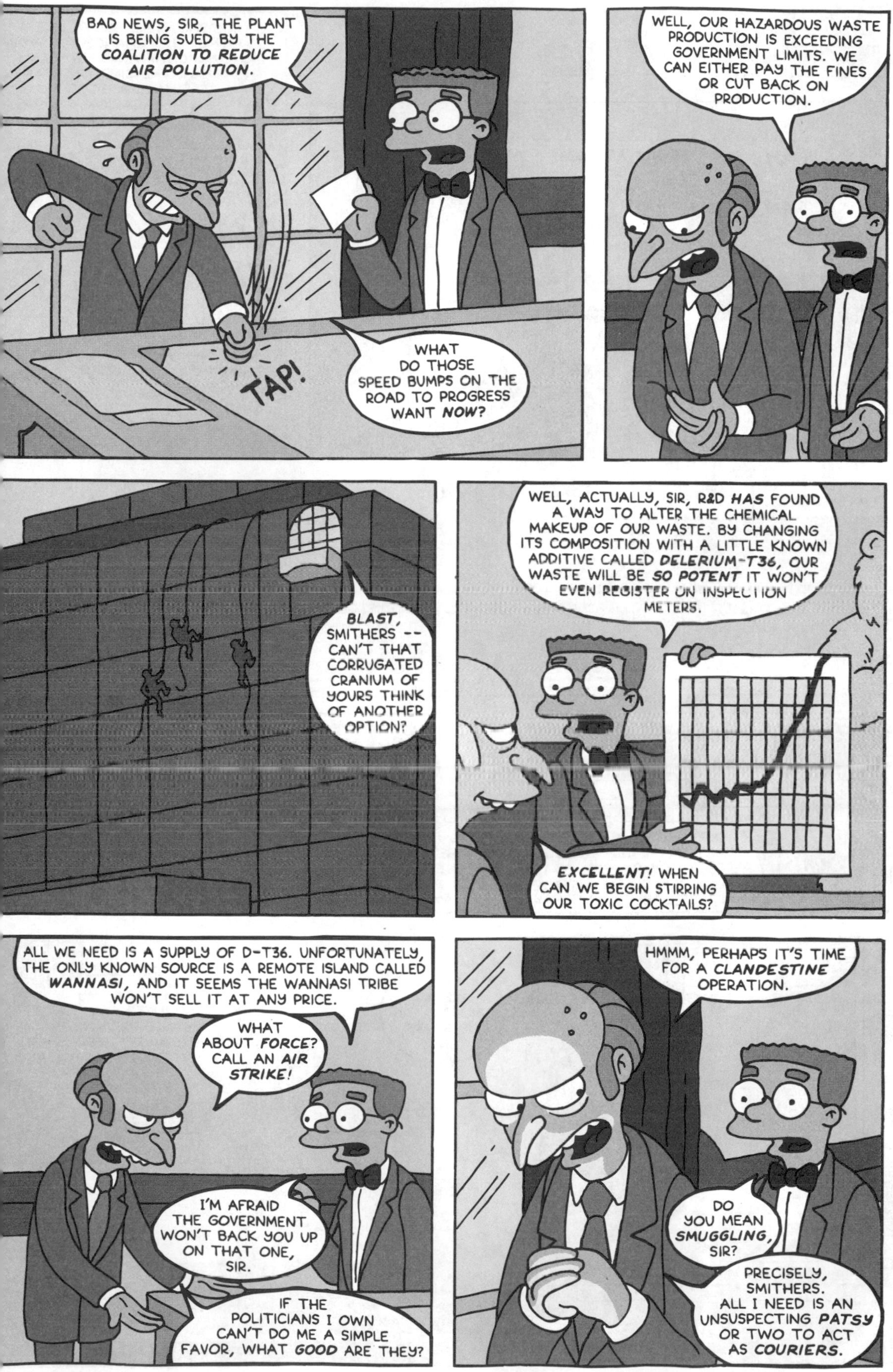
BAD NEWS, SIR, THE PLANT IS BEING SUED BY THE COALITION TO REDUCE AIR POLLUTION.
TAP!
WHAT DO THOSE SPEED BUMPS ON THE ROAD TO PROGRESS WANT NOW?
WELL, OUR HAZARDOUS WASTE PRODUCTION IS EXCEEDING GOVERNMENT LIMITS. WE CAN EITHER PAY THE FINES OR CUT BACK ON PRODUCTION.
BLAST, SMITHERS -- CAN'T THAT CORRUGATED CRANIUM OF YOURS THINK OF ANOTHER OPTION?
WELL, ACTUALLY, SIR, R&D HAS FOUND A WAY TO ALTER THE CHEMICAL MAKEUP OF OUR WASTE. BY CHANGING ITS COMPOSITION WITH A LITTLE KNOWN ADDITIVE CALLED DELERIUM-T36, OUR WASTE WILL BE SO POTENT IT WON'T EVEN REGISTER ON INSPECTION METERS.
EXCELLENT! WHEN CAN WE BEGIN STIRRING OUR TOXIC COCKTAILS?
ALL WE NEED IS A SUPPLY OF D-T36. UNFORTUNATELY, THE ONLY KNOWN SOURCE IS A REMOTE ISLAND CALLED WANNASI, AND IT SEEMS THE WANNASI TRIBE WON'T SELL IT AT ANY PRICE.
WHAT ABOUT FORCE? CALL AN AIR STRIKE!
I'M AFRAID THE GOVERNMENT WON'T BACK YOU UP ON THAT ONE, SIR.
IF THE POLITICIANS I OWN CAN'T DO ME A SIMPLE FAVOR, WHAT GOOD ARE THEY?
HMMM, PERHAPS IT'S TIME FOR A CLANDESTINE OPERATION.
DO YOU MEAN SMUGGLING, SIR?
PRECISELY, SMITHERS. ALL I NEED IS AN UNSUSPECTING PATSY OR TWO TO ACT AS COURIERS.

LATER...

EMPLOYEE APPRECIATION CONTEST

SIGN UP TO WIN A **FREE** *TROPICAL VACATION!*

ATTE

SAY, THIS LOOKS LIKE HOMER J.'S CHANCE TO SHOW MY *CHIMNEYS-IN-LAW* THAT THE SIMPSONS *CAN* HAVE A GOOD VACATION.

SIGN UP NOW!

RRY SMITH
AM DONALDSON
UGH WALPO
ARY GOTLEIB
INDY SIMMONS
BE VIGODA
ERT STANLEY
MER SIMPSON
SA SIMPSON
ART SIMPSO
GE SIMPSO
IE SIMPSO

LATER STILL...

LOOK, SMITHERS -- THE FISH HAVE TAKEN THE *BAIT!*

SIR, THE LAST FOUR NAMES ON THE LIST ARE NOT REALLY EMPLOYEES.

WHAT DO *I* CARE. I'M ONLY INTERESTED IN THEIR *BAGGAGE.* IN FACT, A *FAMILY* WOULD PROVIDE THE PERFECT COVER. AND, AS LONG AS *THEY* BRING THE D-T36 INTO SPRINGFIELD, *I* WON'T BE LIABLE FOR BREAKING ANY LAWS!

YOU ARE AS BRILLIANT AS THE STARS, SIR.

RISE, MY ADULATING ADJUNCT, AND PREPARE MY *LUGGAGE!* NOTIFY *MR. WHOZITS* THAT HE AND HIS FAMILY LEAVE *TOMORROW!*

BURNS

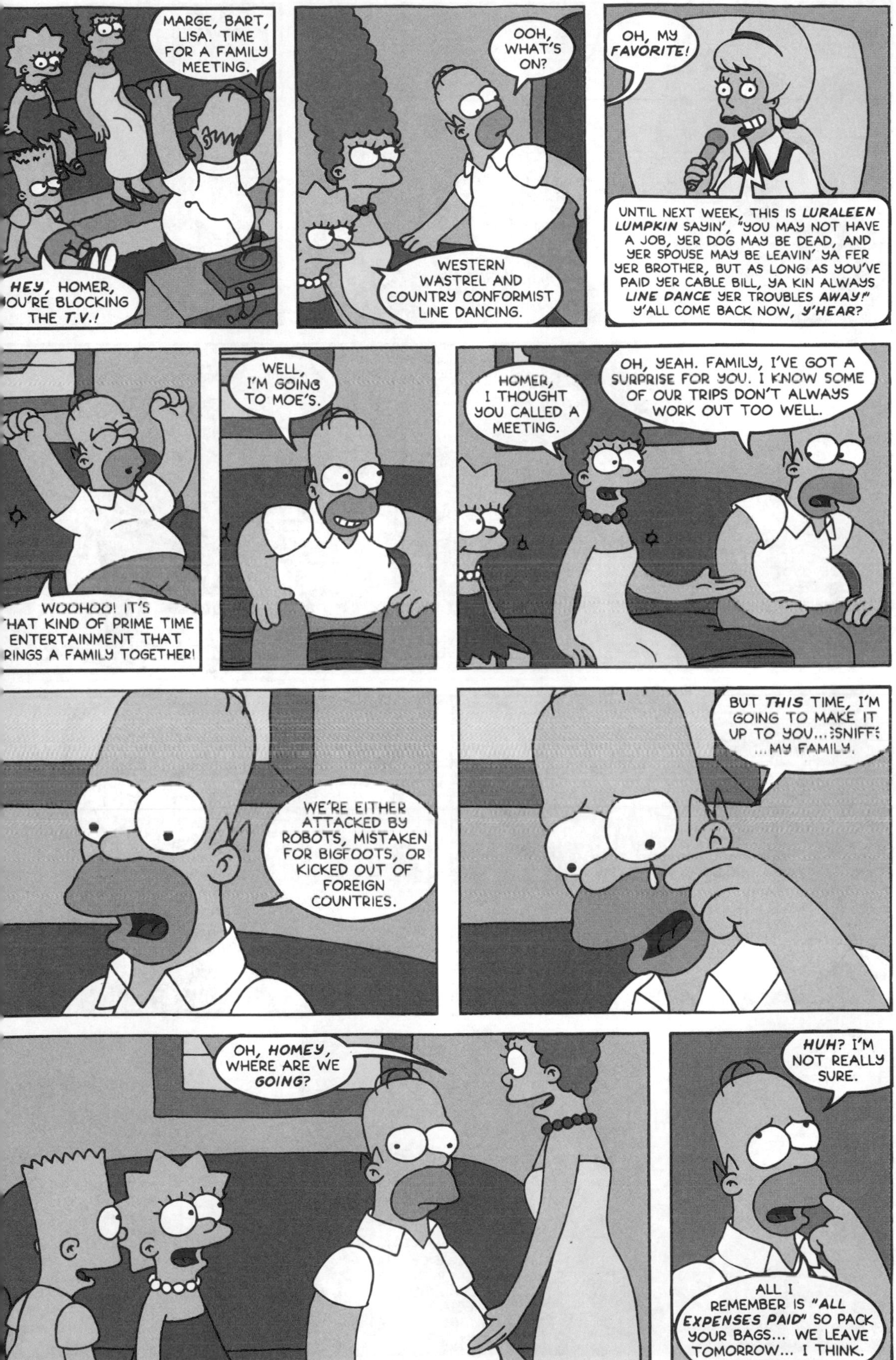
MARGE, BART, LISA. TIME FOR A FAMILY MEETING.
HEY, HOMER, YOU'RE BLOCKING THE T.V.!
OOH, WHAT'S ON?
WESTERN WASTREL AND COUNTRY CONFORMIST LINE DANCING.
OH, MY FAVORITE!
UNTIL NEXT WEEK, THIS IS LURALEEN LUMPKIN SAYIN', "YOU MAY NOT HAVE A JOB, YER DOG MAY BE DEAD, AND YER SPOUSE MAY BE LEAVIN' YA FER YER BROTHER, BUT AS LONG AS YOU'VE PAID YER CABLE BILL, YA KIN ALWAYS LINE DANCE YER TROUBLES AWAY!" Y'ALL COME BACK NOW, Y'HEAR?
WOOHOO! IT'S THAT KIND OF PRIME TIME ENTERTAINMENT THAT BRINGS A FAMILY TOGETHER!
WELL, I'M GOING TO MOE'S.
HOMER, I THOUGHT YOU CALLED A MEETING.
OH, YEAH. FAMILY, I'VE GOT A SURPRISE FOR YOU. I KNOW SOME OF OUR TRIPS DON'T ALWAYS WORK OUT TOO WELL.
WE'RE EITHER ATTACKED BY ROBOTS, MISTAKEN FOR BIGFOOTS, OR KICKED OUT OF FOREIGN COUNTRIES.
BUT THIS TIME, I'M GOING TO MAKE IT UP TO YOU...:SNIFF: ...MY FAMILY.
OH, HOMEY, WHERE ARE WE GOING?
HUH? I'M NOT REALLY SURE.
ALL I REMEMBER IS "ALL EXPENSES PAID" SO PACK YOUR BAGS... WE LEAVE TOMORROW... I THINK.

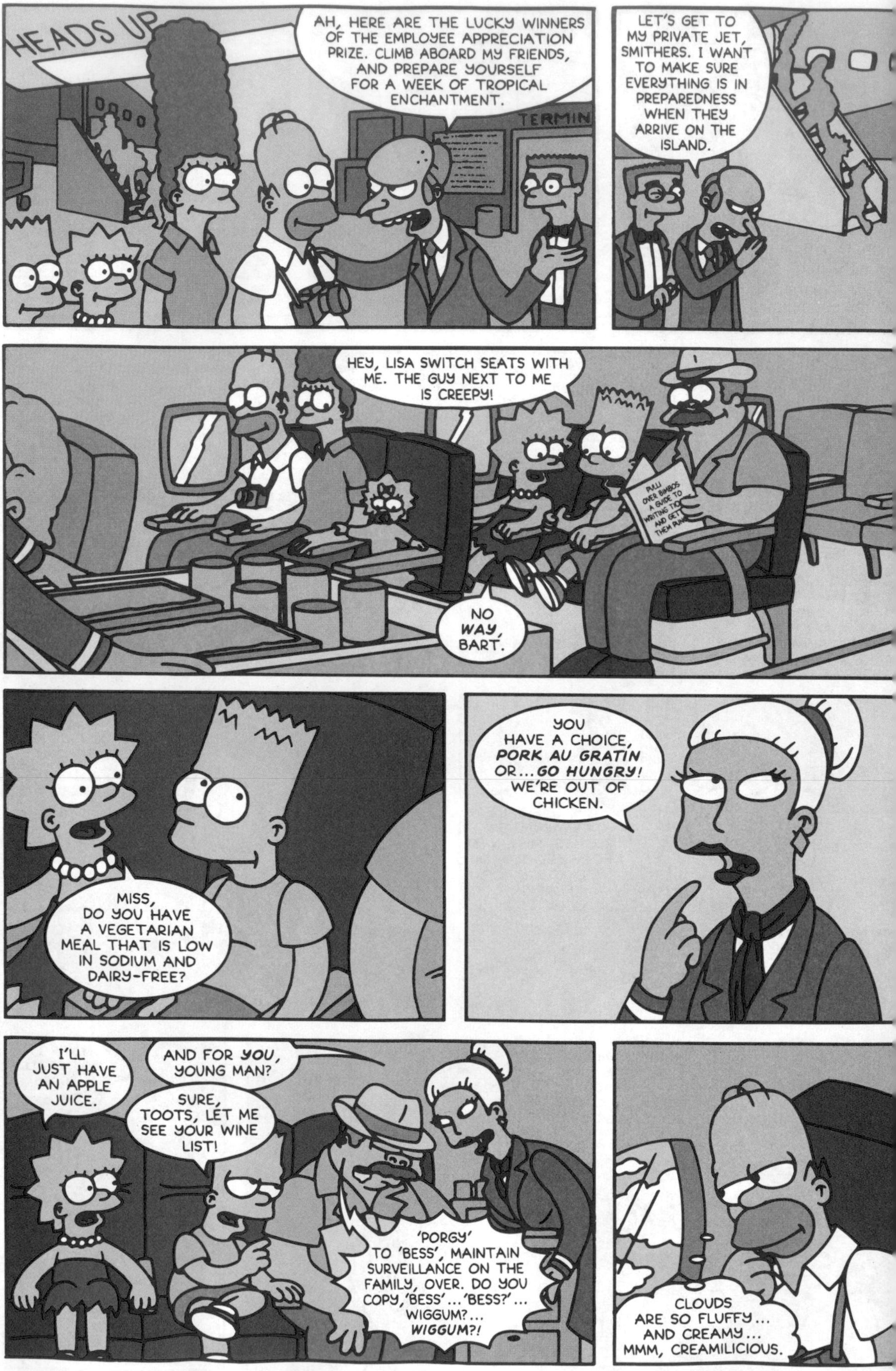
HEADS UP
AH, HERE ARE THE LUCKY WINNERS OF THE EMPLOYEE APPRECIATION PRIZE. CLIMB ABOARD MY FRIENDS, AND PREPARE YOURSELF FOR A WEEK OF TROPICAL ENCHANTMENT.
LET'S GET TO MY PRIVATE JET, SMITHERS. I WANT TO MAKE SURE EVERYTHING IS IN PREPAREDNESS WHEN THEY ARRIVE ON THE ISLAND.
HEY, LISA SWITCH SEATS WITH ME. THE GUY NEXT TO ME IS CREEPY!
NO *WAY*, BART.
MISS, DO YOU HAVE A VEGETARIAN MEAL THAT IS LOW IN SODIUM AND DAIRY-FREE?
YOU HAVE A CHOICE, ***PORK AU GRATIN*** OR... ***GO HUNGRY***! WE'RE OUT OF CHICKEN.
I'LL JUST HAVE AN APPLE JUICE.
AND FOR *YOU*, YOUNG MAN?
SURE, TOOTS, LET ME SEE YOUR WINE LIST!
'PORGY' TO 'BESS', MAINTAIN SURVEILLANCE ON THE FAMILY, OVER. DO YOU COPY, 'BESS'... 'BESS?'... WIGGUM?... ***WIGGUM?!***
CLOUDS ARE SO FLUFFY... AND CREAMY... MMM, CREAMILICIOUS.

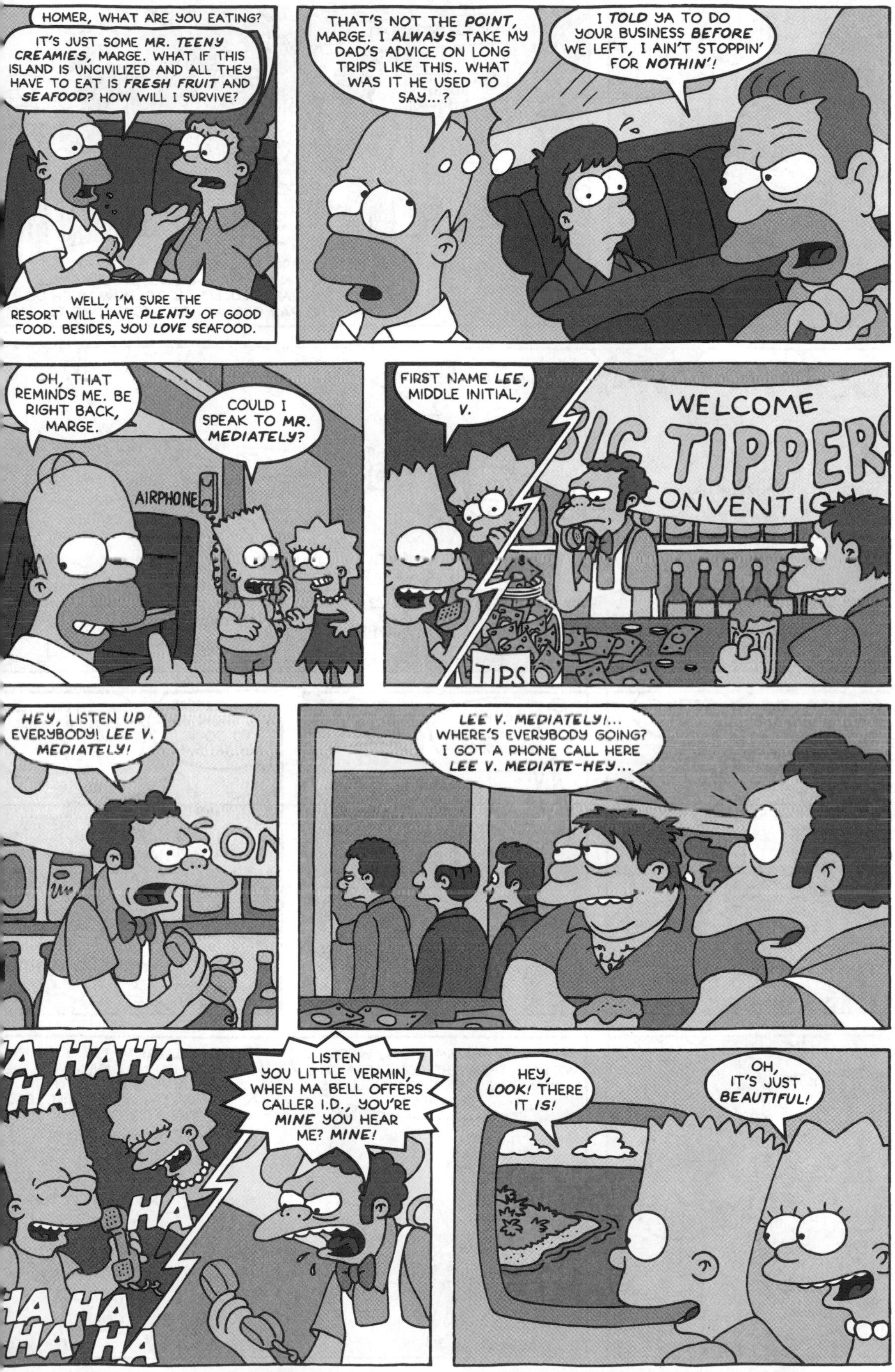
HOMER, WHAT ARE YOU EATING?
IT'S JUST SOME MR. TEENY CREAMIES, MARGE. WHAT IF THIS ISLAND IS UNCIVILIZED AND ALL THEY HAVE TO EAT IS FRESH FRUIT AND SEAFOOD? HOW WILL I SURVIVE?
WELL, I'M SURE THE RESORT WILL HAVE PLENTY OF GOOD FOOD. BESIDES, YOU LOVE SEAFOOD.
THAT'S NOT THE POINT, MARGE. I ALWAYS TAKE MY DAD'S ADVICE ON LONG TRIPS LIKE THIS. WHAT WAS IT HE USED TO SAY...?
I TOLD YA TO DO YOUR BUSINESS BEFORE WE LEFT, I AIN'T STOPPIN' FOR NOTHIN'!
OH, THAT REMINDS ME. BE RIGHT BACK, MARGE.
COULD I SPEAK TO MR. MEDIATELY?
AIRPHONE
FIRST NAME LEE, MIDDLE INITIAL, V.
WELCOME BIG TIPPERS CONVENTION
TIPS
HEY, LISTEN UP EVERYBODY! LEE V. MEDIATELY!
LEE V. MEDIATELY!... WHERE'S EVERYBODY GOING? I GOT A PHONE CALL HERE LEE V. MEDIATE-HEY...
HA HAHA HA
HA
HA HA HA HA
LISTEN YOU LITTLE VERMIN, WHEN MA BELL OFFERS CALLER I.D., YOU'RE MINE YOU HEAR ME? MINE!
HEY, LOOK! THERE IT IS!
OH, IT'S JUST BEAUTIFUL!

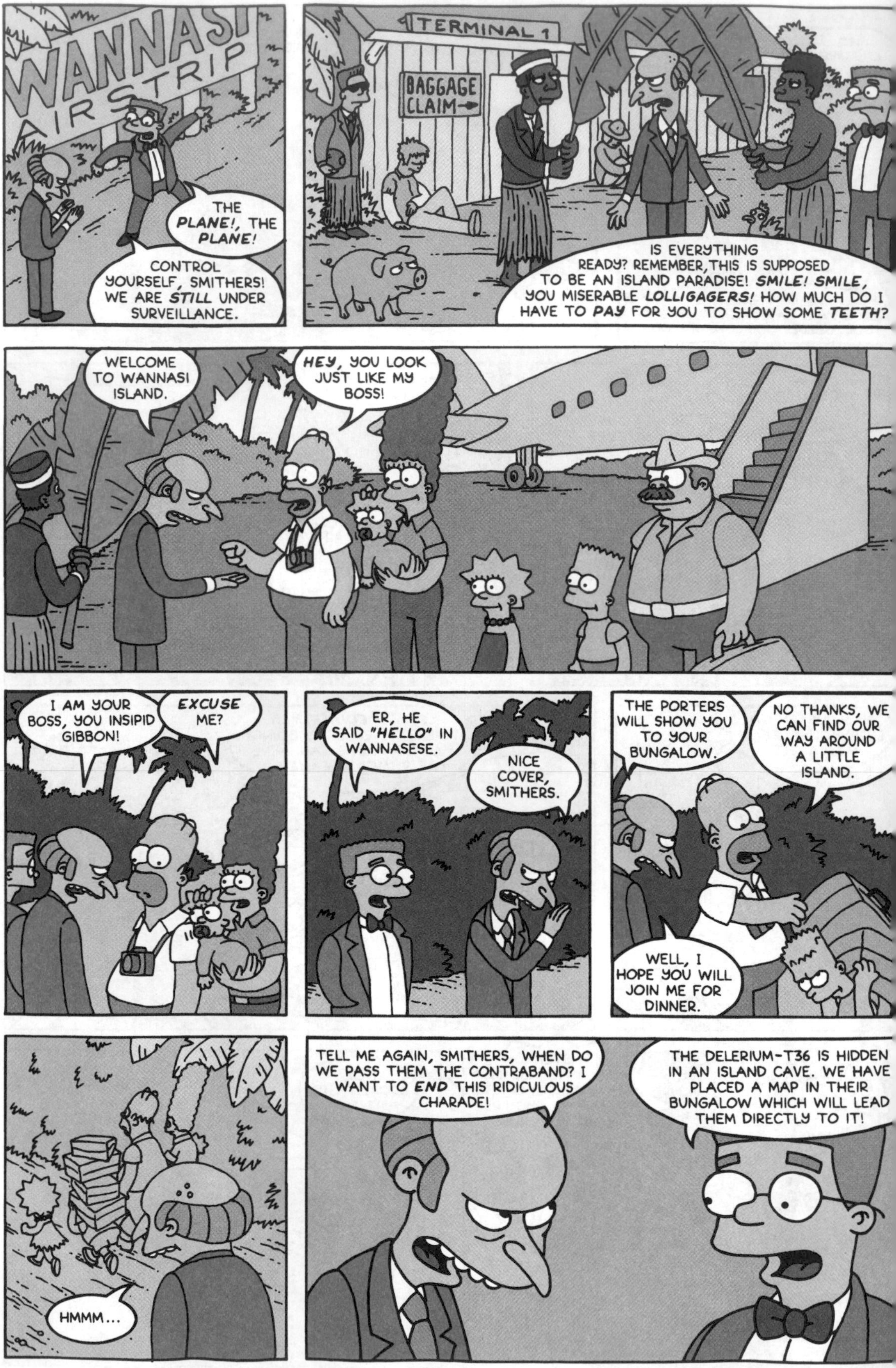

WANNASI AIRSTRIP
THE PLANE!, THE PLANE!
CONTROL YOURSELF, SMITHERS! WE ARE STILL UNDER SURVEILLANCE.
TERMINAL 1
BAGGAGE CLAIM
IS EVERYTHING READY? REMEMBER, THIS IS SUPPOSED TO BE AN ISLAND PARADISE! SMILE! SMILE, YOU MISERABLE LOLLIGAGERS! HOW MUCH DO I HAVE TO PAY FOR YOU TO SHOW SOME TEETH?
WELCOME TO WANNASI ISLAND.
HEY, YOU LOOK JUST LIKE MY BOSS!
I AM YOUR BOSS, YOU INSIPID GIBBON!
EXCUSE ME?
ER, HE SAID "HELLO" IN WANNASESE.
NICE COVER, SMITHERS.
THE PORTERS WILL SHOW YOU TO YOUR BUNGALOW.
NO THANKS, WE CAN FIND OUR WAY AROUND A LITTLE ISLAND.
WELL, I HOPE YOU WILL JOIN ME FOR DINNER.
HMMM...
TELL ME AGAIN, SMITHERS, WHEN DO WE PASS THEM THE CONTRABAND? I WANT TO END THIS RIDICULOUS CHARADE!
THE DELERIUM-T36 IS HIDDEN IN AN ISLAND CAVE. WE HAVE PLACED A MAP IN THEIR BUNGALOW WHICH WILL LEAD THEM DIRECTLY TO IT!

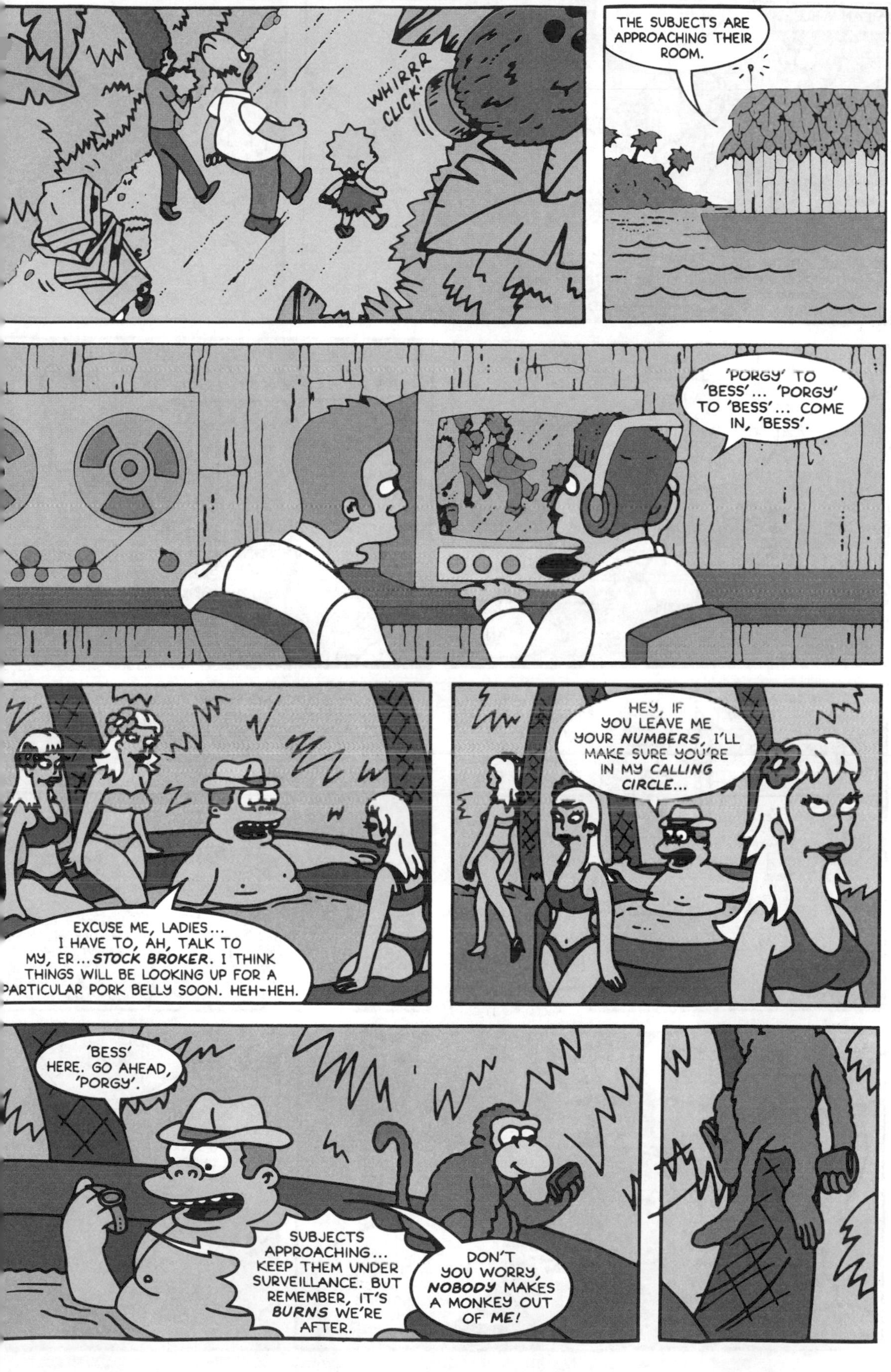
WHIRRR CLICK!
THE SUBJECTS ARE APPROACHING THEIR ROOM.
'PORGY' TO 'BESS'... 'PORGY' TO 'BESS'... COME IN, 'BESS'.
EXCUSE ME, LADIES... I HAVE TO, AH, TALK TO MY, ER...STOCK BROKER. I THINK THINGS WILL BE LOOKING UP FOR A PARTICULAR PORK BELLY SOON. HEH-HEH.
HEY, IF YOU LEAVE ME YOUR NUMBERS, I'LL MAKE SURE YOU'RE IN MY CALLING CIRCLE...
'BESS' HERE. GO AHEAD, 'PORGY'.
SUBJECTS APPROACHING... KEEP THEM UNDER SURVEILLANCE. BUT REMEMBER, IT'S BURNS WE'RE AFTER.
DON'T YOU WORRY, NOBODY MAKES A MONKEY OUT OF ME!

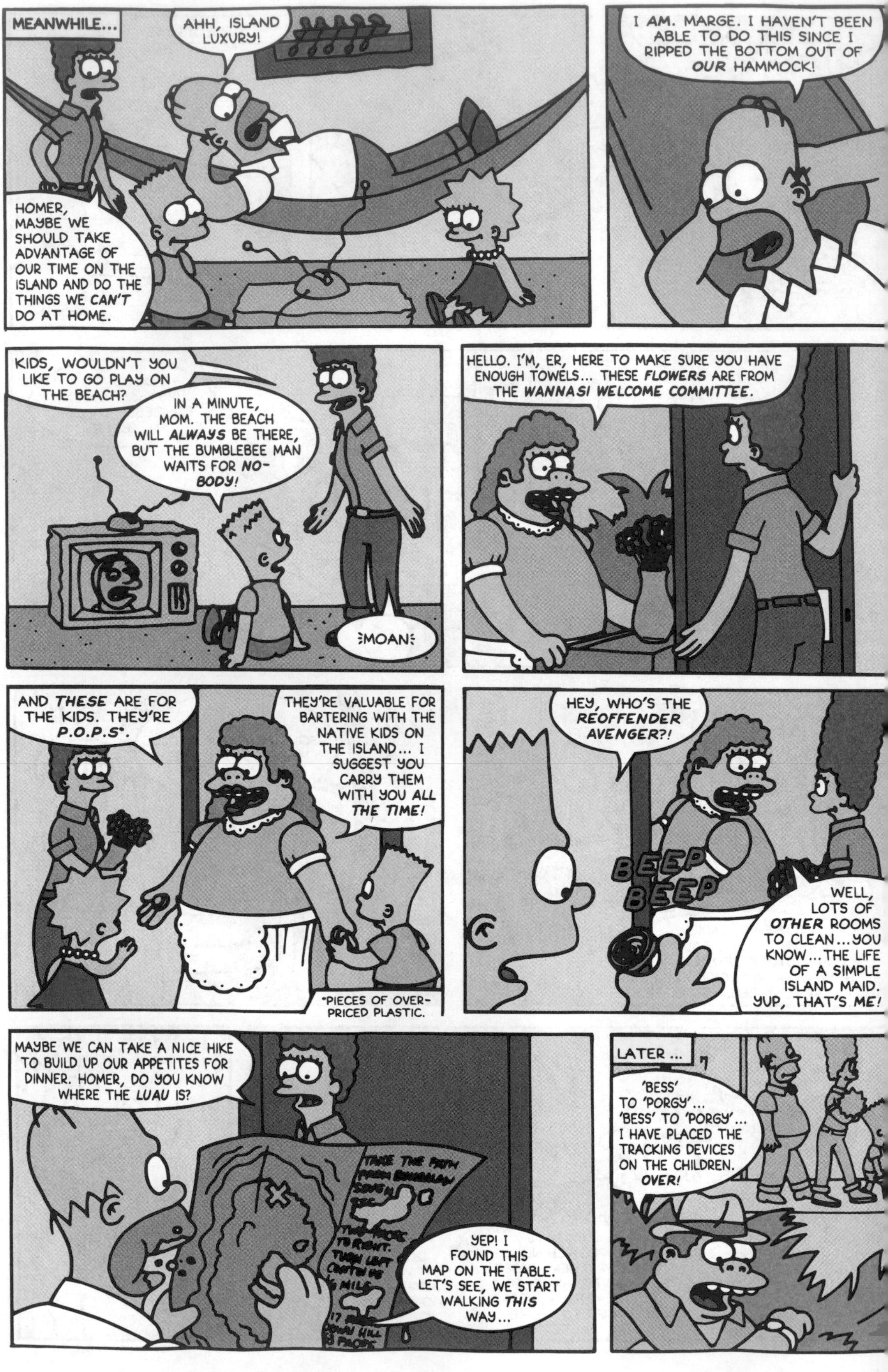
MEANWHILE...
AHH, ISLAND LUXURY!
HOMER, MAYBE WE SHOULD TAKE ADVANTAGE OF OUR TIME ON THE ISLAND AND DO THE THINGS WE CAN'T DO AT HOME.
I AM. MARGE. I HAVEN'T BEEN ABLE TO DO THIS SINCE I RIPPED THE BOTTOM OUT OF OUR HAMMOCK!
KIDS, WOULDN'T YOU LIKE TO GO PLAY ON THE BEACH?
IN A MINUTE, MOM. THE BEACH WILL ALWAYS BE THERE, BUT THE BUMBLEBEE MAN WAITS FOR NO-BODY!
MOAN
HELLO. I'M, ER, HERE TO MAKE SURE YOU HAVE ENOUGH TOWELS... THESE FLOWERS ARE FROM THE WANNASI WELCOME COMMITTEE.
AND THESE ARE FOR THE KIDS. THEY'RE P.O.P.S*.
THEY'RE VALUABLE FOR BARTERING WITH THE NATIVE KIDS ON THE ISLAND... I SUGGEST YOU CARRY THEM WITH YOU ALL THE TIME!
*PIECES OF OVER-PRICED PLASTIC.
HEY, WHO'S THE REOFFENDER AVENGER?!
BEEP BEEP
WELL, LOTS OF OTHER ROOMS TO CLEAN...YOU KNOW...THE LIFE OF A SIMPLE ISLAND MAID. YUP, THAT'S ME!
MAYBE WE CAN TAKE A NICE HIKE TO BUILD UP OUR APPETITES FOR DINNER. HOMER, DO YOU KNOW WHERE THE LUAU IS?
YEP! I FOUND THIS MAP ON THE TABLE. LET'S SEE, WE START WALKING THIS WAY...
LATER ...
'BESS' TO 'PORGY'... 'BESS' TO 'PORGY'... I HAVE PLACED THE TRACKING DEVICES ON THE CHILDREN. OVER!

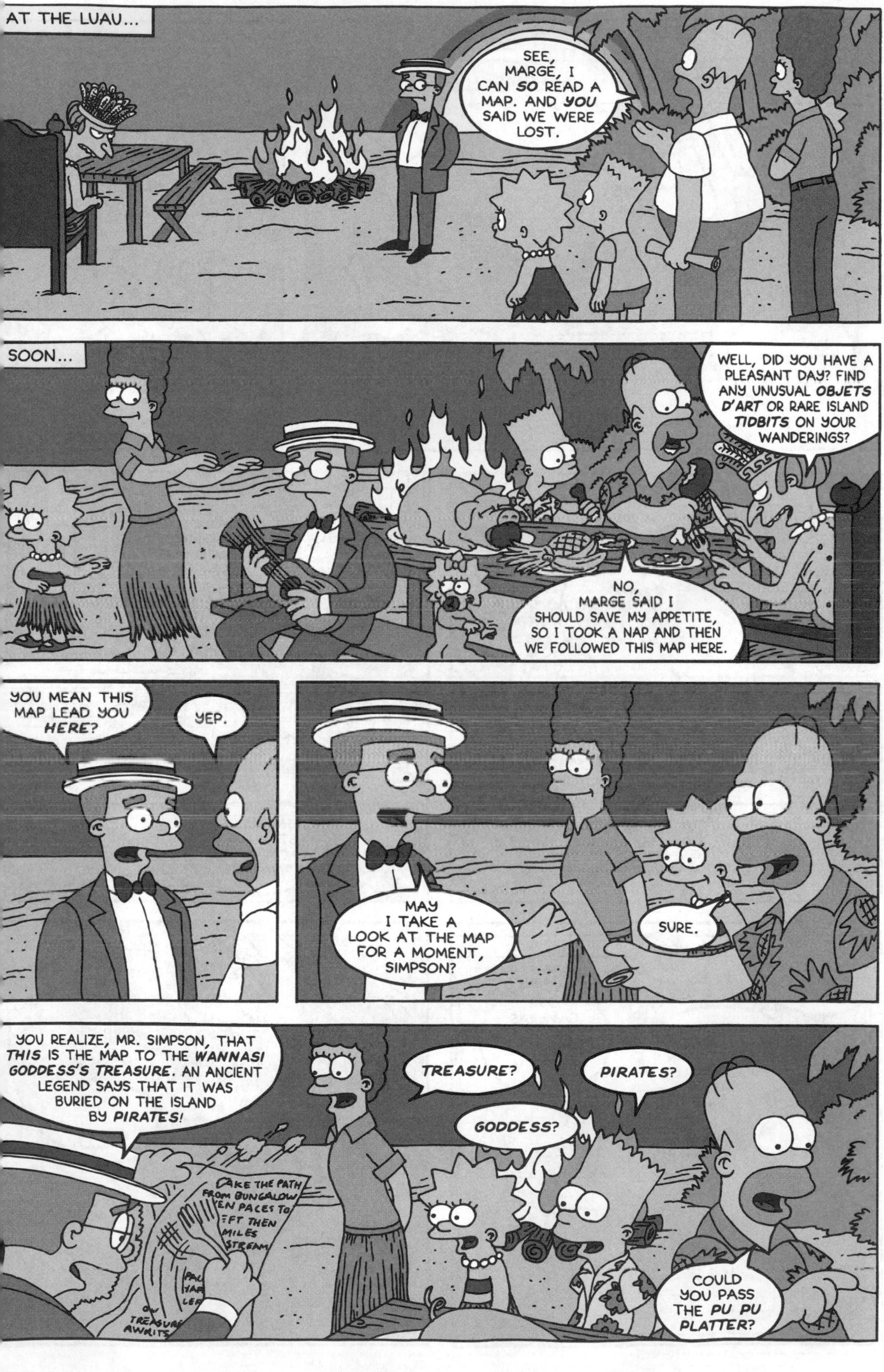
AT THE LUAU...
SEE, MARGE, I CAN SO READ A MAP. AND YOU SAID WE WERE LOST.
SOON...
WELL, DID YOU HAVE A PLEASANT DAY? FIND ANY UNUSUAL OBJETS D'ART OR RARE ISLAND TIDBITS ON YOUR WANDERINGS?
NO, MARGE SAID I SHOULD SAVE MY APPETITE, SO I TOOK A NAP AND THEN WE FOLLOWED THIS MAP HERE.
YOU MEAN THIS MAP LEAD YOU HERE?
YEP.
MAY I TAKE A LOOK AT THE MAP FOR A MOMENT, SIMPSON?
SURE.
YOU REALIZE, MR. SIMPSON, THAT THIS IS THE MAP TO THE WANNASI GODDESS'S TREASURE. AN ANCIENT LEGEND SAYS THAT IT WAS BURIED ON THE ISLAND BY PIRATES!
TREASURE?
GODDESS?
PIRATES?
COULD YOU PASS THE PU PU PLATTER?

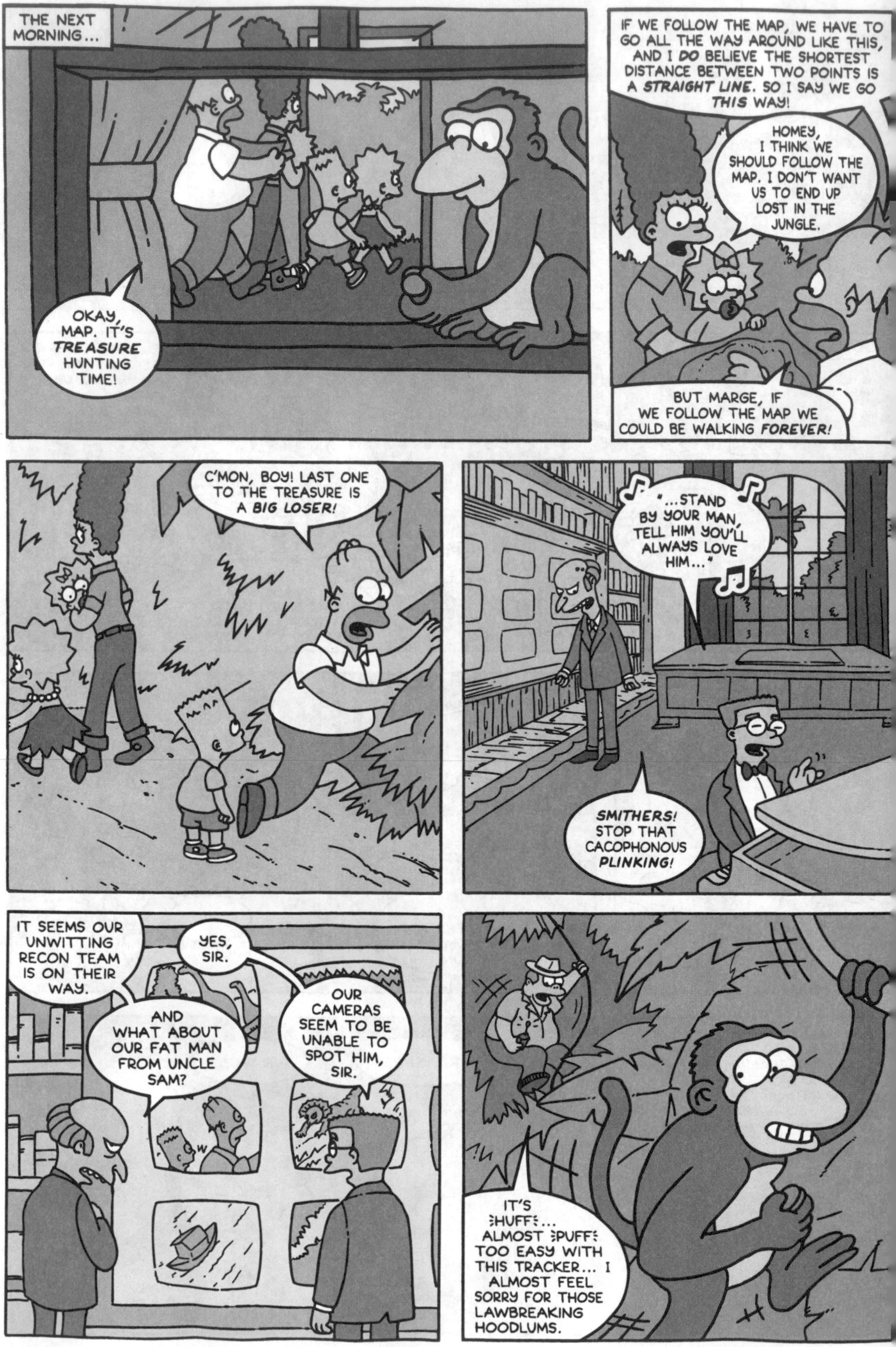
THE NEXT MORNING...
OKAY, MAP. IT'S TREASURE HUNTING TIME!
IF WE FOLLOW THE MAP, WE HAVE TO GO ALL THE WAY AROUND LIKE THIS, AND I DO BELIEVE THE SHORTEST DISTANCE BETWEEN TWO POINTS IS A STRAIGHT LINE. SO I SAY WE GO THIS WAY!
HOMEY, I THINK WE SHOULD FOLLOW THE MAP. I DON'T WANT US TO END UP LOST IN THE JUNGLE.
BUT MARGE, IF WE FOLLOW THE MAP WE COULD BE WALKING FOREVER!
C'MON, BOY! LAST ONE TO THE TREASURE IS A BIG LOSER!
"...STAND BY YOUR MAN, TELL HIM YOU'LL ALWAYS LOVE HIM..."
SMITHERS! STOP THAT CACOPHONOUS PLINKING!
IT SEEMS OUR UNWITTING RECON TEAM IS ON THEIR WAY.
YES, SIR.
AND WHAT ABOUT OUR FAT MAN FROM UNCLE SAM?
OUR CAMERAS SEEM TO BE UNABLE TO SPOT HIM, SIR.
IT'S ⋮HUFF⋮... ALMOST ⋮PUFF⋮ TOO EASY WITH THIS TRACKER... I ALMOST FEEL SORRY FOR THOSE LAWBREAKING HOODLUMS.

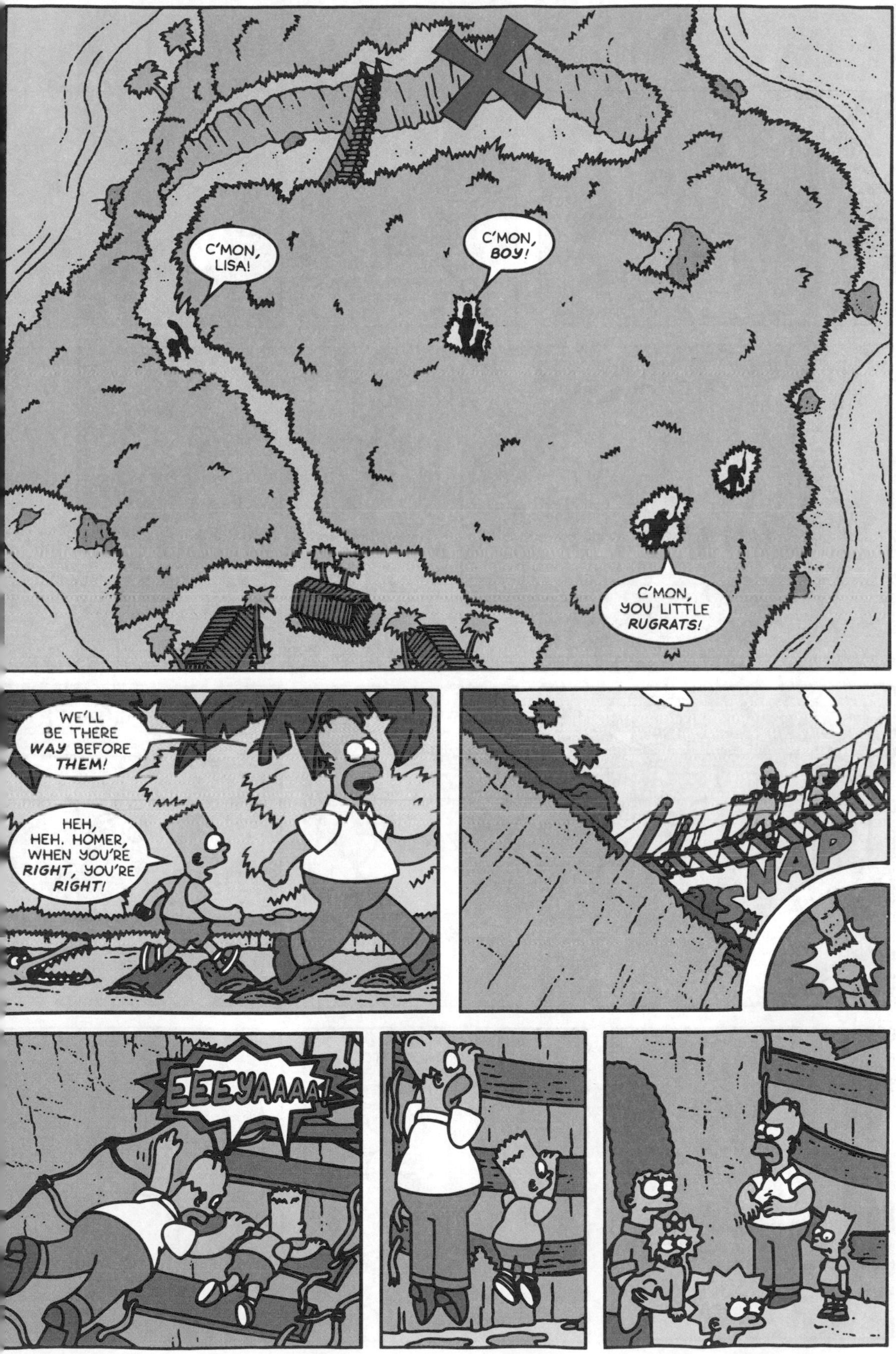
C'MON, LISA!
C'MON, BOY!
C'MON, YOU LITTLE RUGRATS!
WE'LL BE THERE WAY BEFORE THEM!
HEH, HEH. HOMER, WHEN YOU'RE RIGHT, YOU'RE RIGHT!
SNAP
EEEYAAAA!

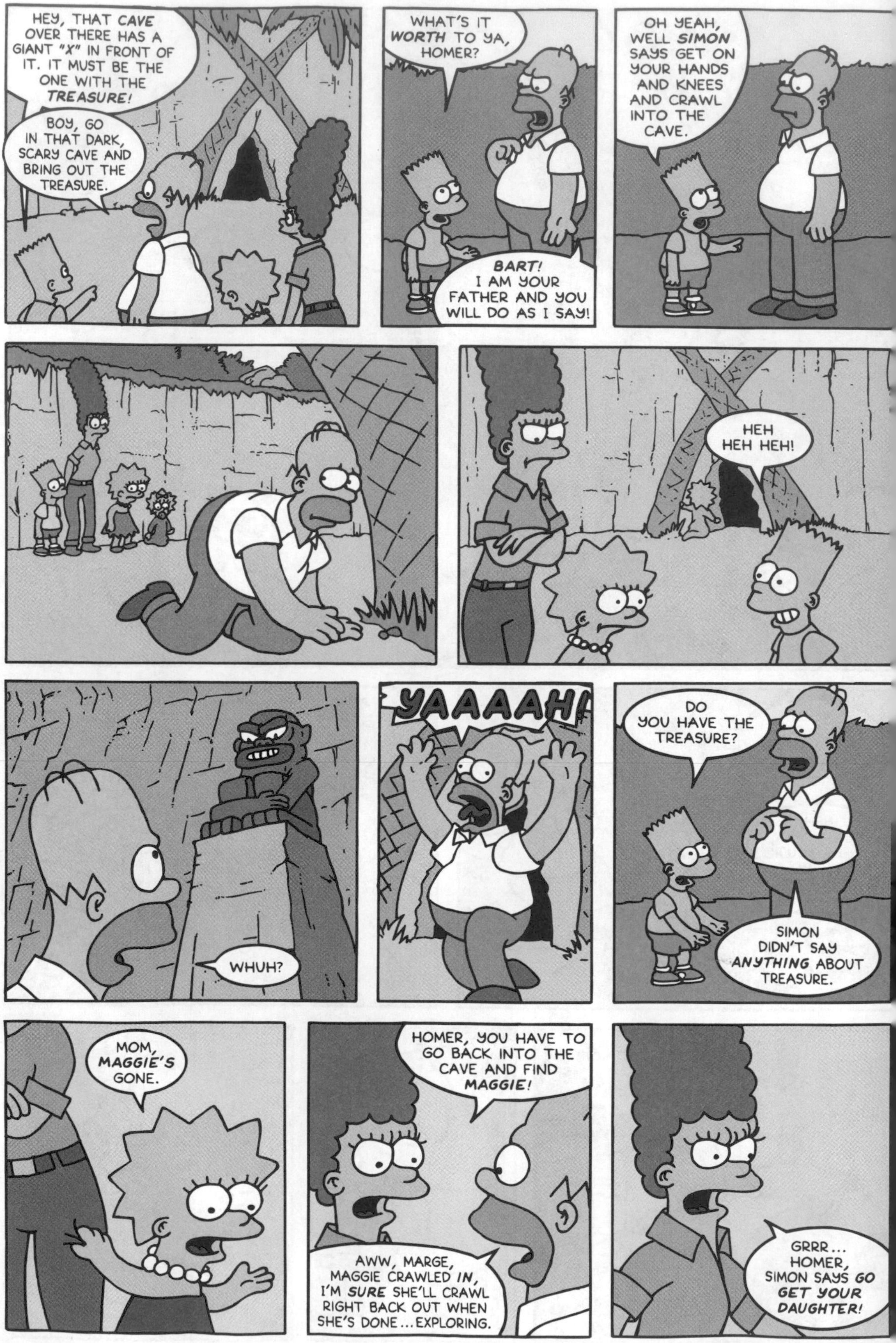
HEY, THAT CAVE OVER THERE HAS A GIANT "X" IN FRONT OF IT. IT MUST BE THE ONE WITH THE TREASURE!
BOY, GO IN THAT DARK, SCARY CAVE AND BRING OUT THE TREASURE.
WHAT'S IT WORTH TO YA, HOMER?
BART! I AM YOUR FATHER AND YOU WILL DO AS I SAY!
OH YEAH, WELL SIMON SAYS GET ON YOUR HANDS AND KNEES AND CRAWL INTO THE CAVE.
HEH HEH HEH!
WHUH?
YAAAAH!
DO YOU HAVE THE TREASURE?
SIMON DIDN'T SAY ANYTHING ABOUT TREASURE.
MOM, MAGGIE'S GONE.
HOMER, YOU HAVE TO GO BACK INTO THE CAVE AND FIND MAGGIE!
AWW, MARGE, MAGGIE CRAWLED IN, I'M SURE SHE'LL CRAWL RIGHT BACK OUT WHEN SHE'S DONE...EXPLORING.
GRRR... HOMER, SIMON SAYS GO GET YOUR DAUGHTER!

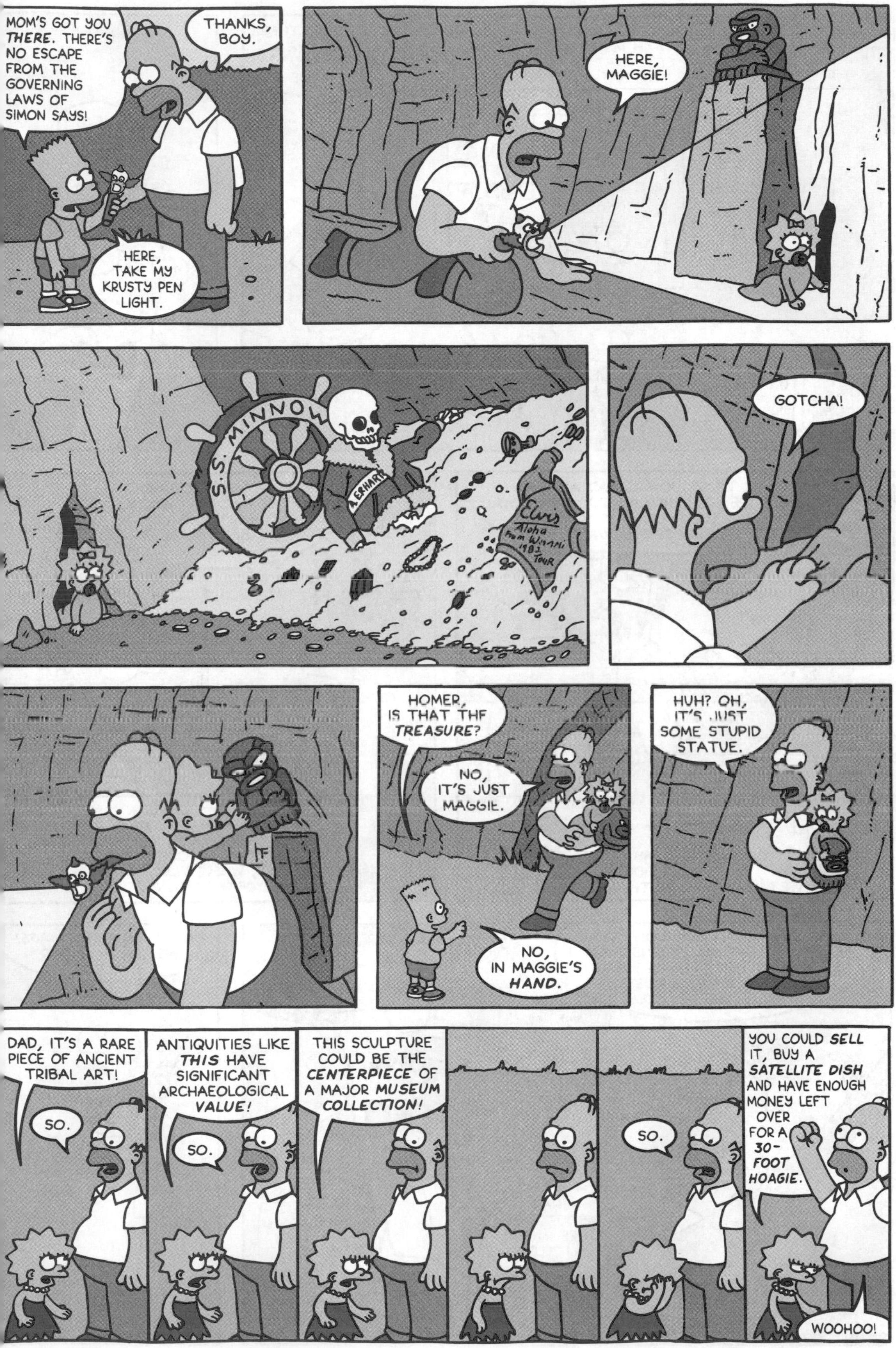

MOM'S GOT YOU THERE. THERE'S NO ESCAPE FROM THE GOVERNING LAWS OF SIMON SAYS!
THANKS, BOY.
HERE, TAKE MY KRUSTY PEN LIGHT.
HERE, MAGGIE!
S.S. MINNOW
Elvis
GOTCHA!
HOMER, IS THAT THE TREASURE?
NO, IT'S JUST MAGGIE.
NO, IN MAGGIE'S HAND.
HUH? OH, IT'S JUST SOME STUPID STATUE.
DAD, IT'S A RARE PIECE OF ANCIENT TRIBAL ART!
SO.
ANTIQUITIES LIKE THIS HAVE SIGNIFICANT ARCHAEOLOGICAL VALUE!
SO.
THIS SCULPTURE COULD BE THE CENTERPIECE OF A MAJOR MUSEUM COLLECTION!
SO.
YOU COULD SELL IT, BUY A SATELLITE DISH AND HAVE ENOUGH MONEY LEFT OVER FOR A 30-FOOT HOAGIE.
WOOHOO!

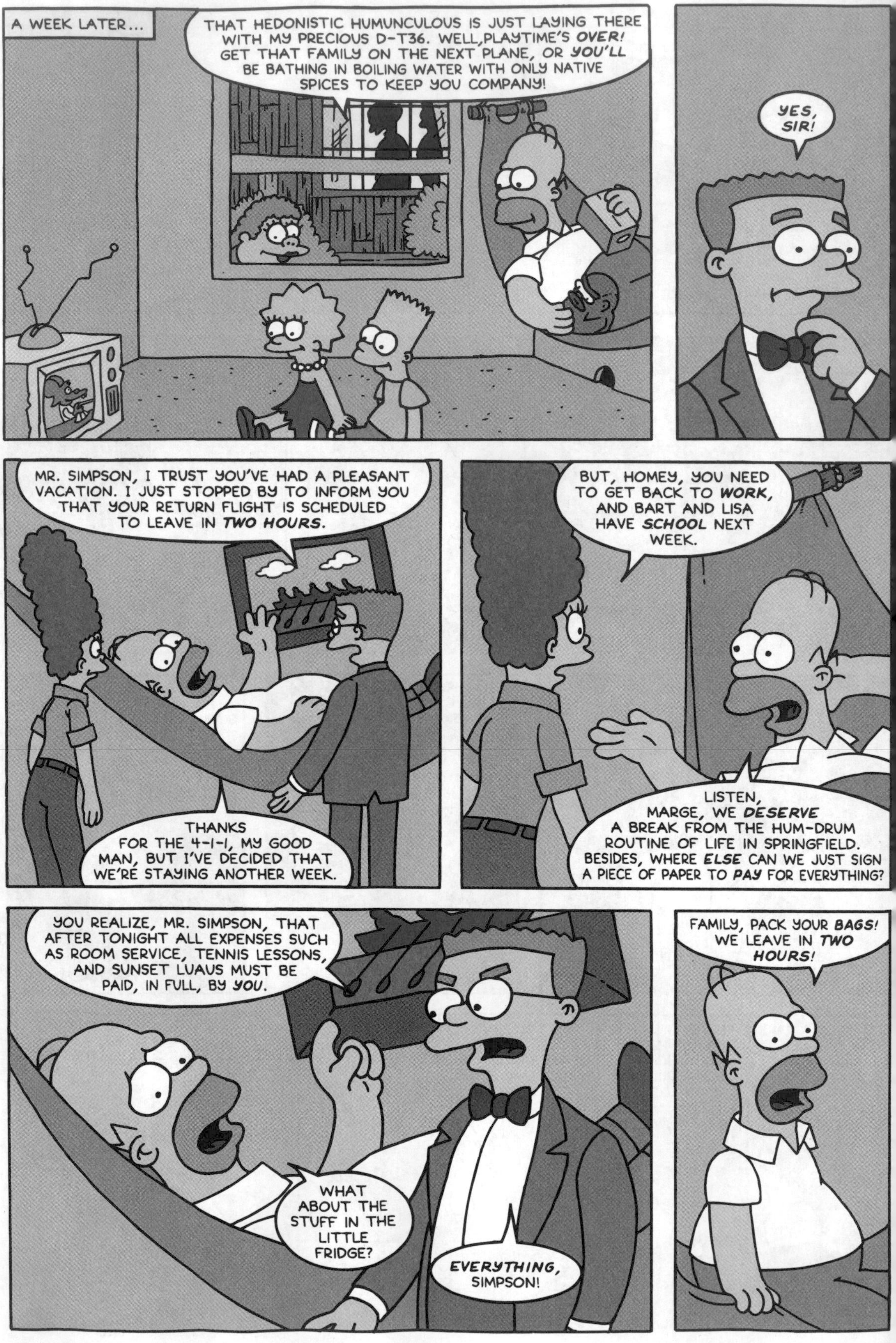
A WEEK LATER...
THAT HEDONISTIC HUMUNCULOUS IS JUST LAYING THERE WITH MY PRECIOUS D-T36. WELL, PLAYTIME'S OVER! GET THAT FAMILY ON THE NEXT PLANE, OR YOU'LL BE BATHING IN BOILING WATER WITH ONLY NATIVE SPICES TO KEEP YOU COMPANY!
YES, SIR!
MR. SIMPSON, I TRUST YOU'VE HAD A PLEASANT VACATION. I JUST STOPPED BY TO INFORM YOU THAT YOUR RETURN FLIGHT IS SCHEDULED TO LEAVE IN TWO HOURS.
THANKS FOR THE 4-1-1, MY GOOD MAN, BUT I'VE DECIDED THAT WE'RE STAYING ANOTHER WEEK.
BUT, HOMEY, YOU NEED TO GET BACK TO WORK, AND BART AND LISA HAVE SCHOOL NEXT WEEK.
LISTEN, MARGE, WE DESERVE A BREAK FROM THE HUM-DRUM ROUTINE OF LIFE IN SPRINGFIELD. BESIDES, WHERE ELSE CAN WE JUST SIGN A PIECE OF PAPER TO PAY FOR EVERYTHING?
YOU REALIZE, MR. SIMPSON, THAT AFTER TONIGHT ALL EXPENSES SUCH AS ROOM SERVICE, TENNIS LESSONS, AND SUNSET LUAUS MUST BE PAID, IN FULL, BY YOU.
WHAT ABOUT THE STUFF IN THE LITTLE FRIDGE?
EVERYTHING, SIMPSON!
FAMILY, PACK YOUR BAGS! WE LEAVE IN TWO HOURS!

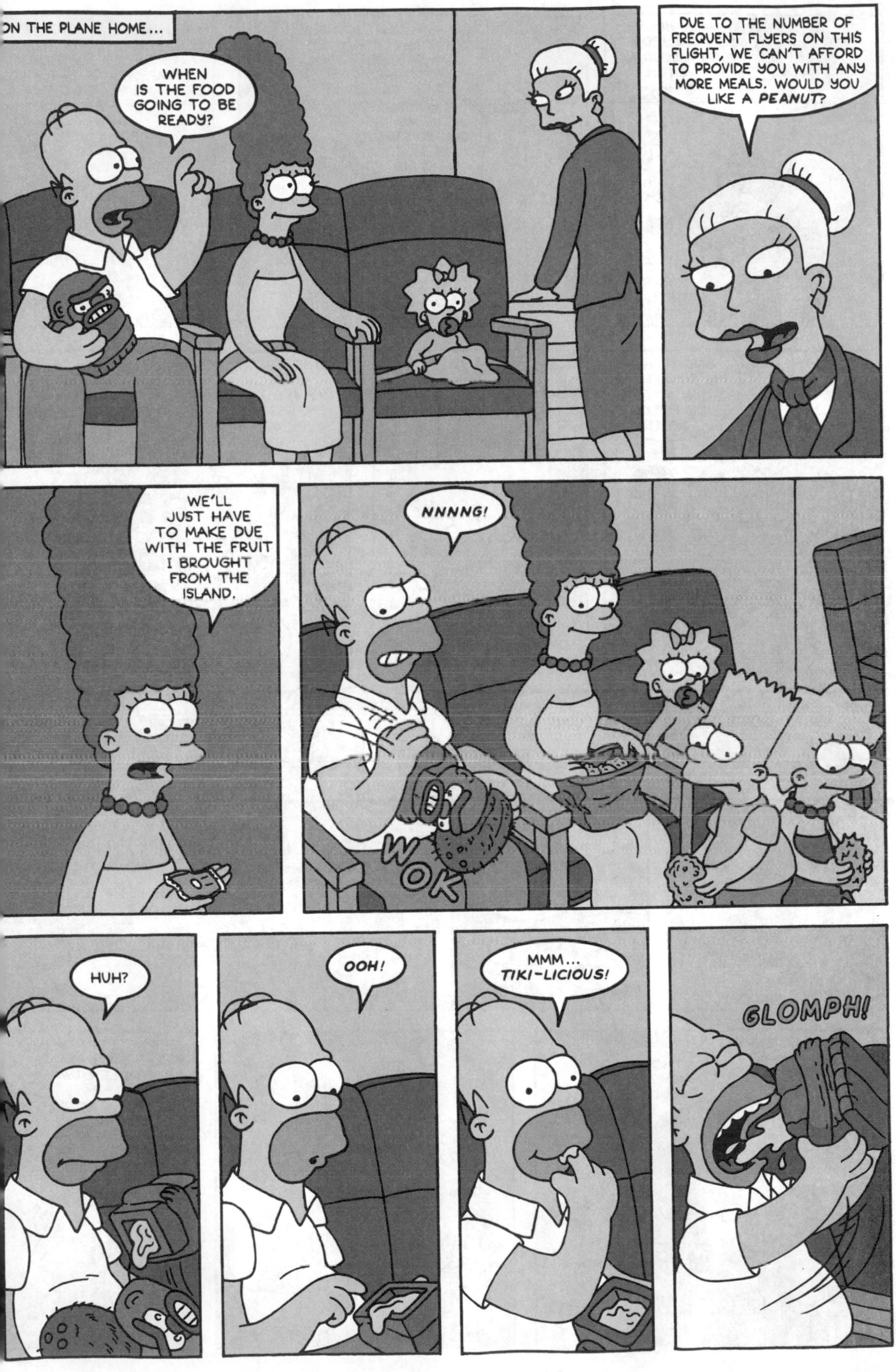

ON THE PLANE HOME...
WHEN IS THE FOOD GOING TO BE READY?
DUE TO THE NUMBER OF FREQUENT FLYERS ON THIS FLIGHT, WE CAN'T AFFORD TO PROVIDE YOU WITH ANY MORE MEALS. WOULD YOU LIKE A PEANUT?
WE'LL JUST HAVE TO MAKE DUE WITH THE FRUIT I BROUGHT FROM THE ISLAND.
NNNNG!
WOK
HUH?
OOH!
MMM... TIKI-LICIOUS!
GLOMPH!

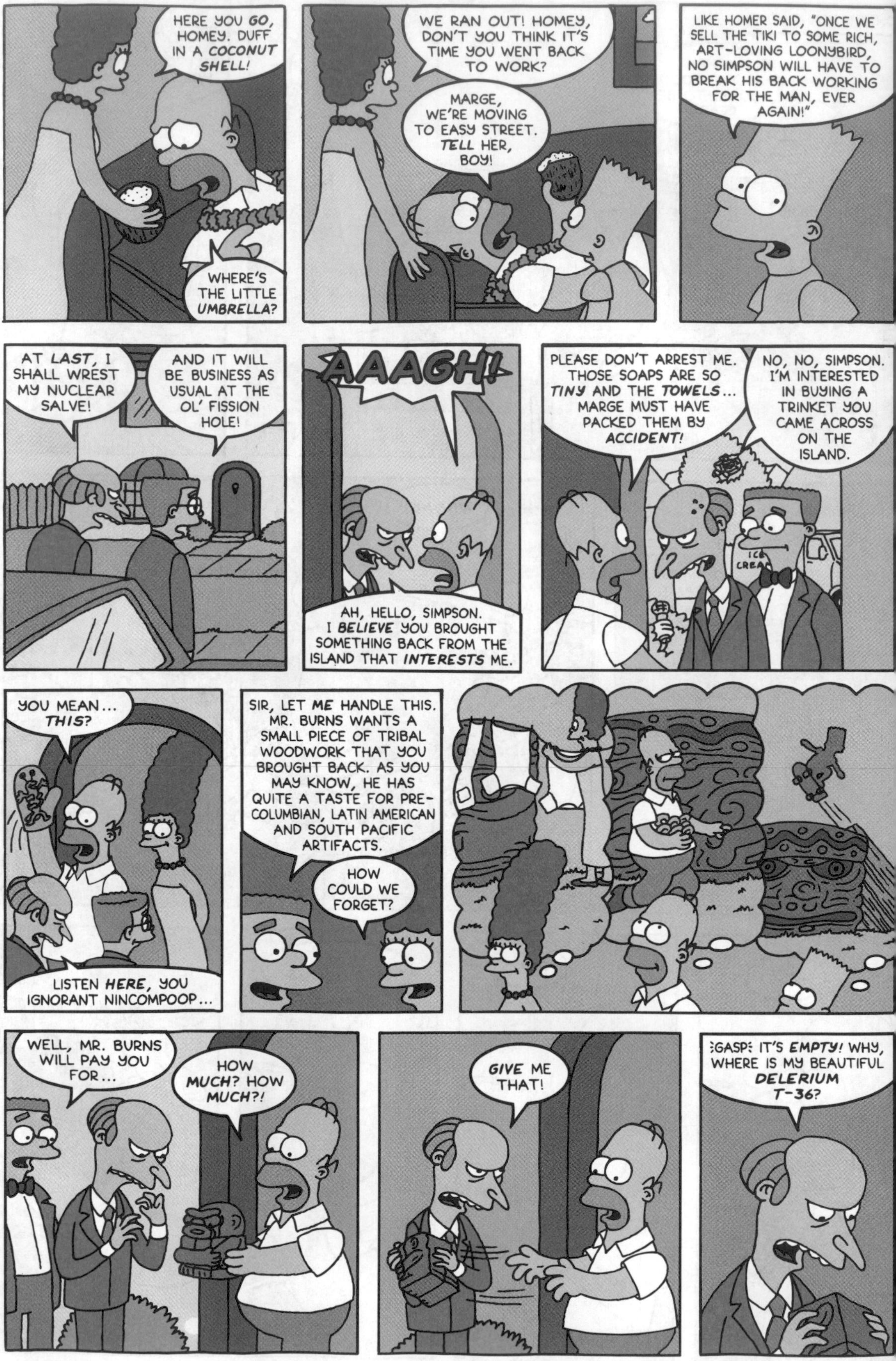
HERE YOU GO, HOMEY. DUFF IN A COCONUT SHELL!
WHERE'S THE LITTLE UMBRELLA?
WE RAN OUT! HOMEY, DON'T YOU THINK IT'S TIME YOU WENT BACK TO WORK?
MARGE, WE'RE MOVING TO EASY STREET. TELL HER, BOY!
LIKE HOMER SAID, "ONCE WE SELL THE TIKI TO SOME RICH, ART-LOVING LOONYBIRD, NO SIMPSON WILL HAVE TO BREAK HIS BACK WORKING FOR THE MAN, EVER AGAIN!"
AT LAST, I SHALL WREST MY NUCLEAR SALVE!
AND IT WILL BE BUSINESS AS USUAL AT THE OL' FISSION HOLE!
AAAGH!
AH, HELLO, SIMPSON. I BELIEVE YOU BROUGHT SOMETHING BACK FROM THE ISLAND THAT INTERESTS ME.
PLEASE DON'T ARREST ME. THOSE SOAPS ARE SO TINY AND THE TOWELS... MARGE MUST HAVE PACKED THEM BY ACCIDENT!
NO, NO, SIMPSON. I'M INTERESTED IN BUYING A TRINKET YOU CAME ACROSS ON THE ISLAND.
YOU MEAN... THIS?
LISTEN HERE, YOU IGNORANT NINCOMPOOP...
SIR, LET ME HANDLE THIS. MR. BURNS WANTS A SMALL PIECE OF TRIBAL WOODWORK THAT YOU BROUGHT BACK. AS YOU MAY KNOW, HE HAS QUITE A TASTE FOR PRE-COLUMBIAN, LATIN AMERICAN AND SOUTH PACIFIC ARTIFACTS.
HOW COULD WE FORGET?
WELL, MR. BURNS WILL PAY YOU FOR...
HOW MUCH? HOW MUCH?!
GIVE ME THAT!
:GASP: IT'S EMPTY! WHY, WHERE IS MY BEAUTIFUL DELERIUM T-36?

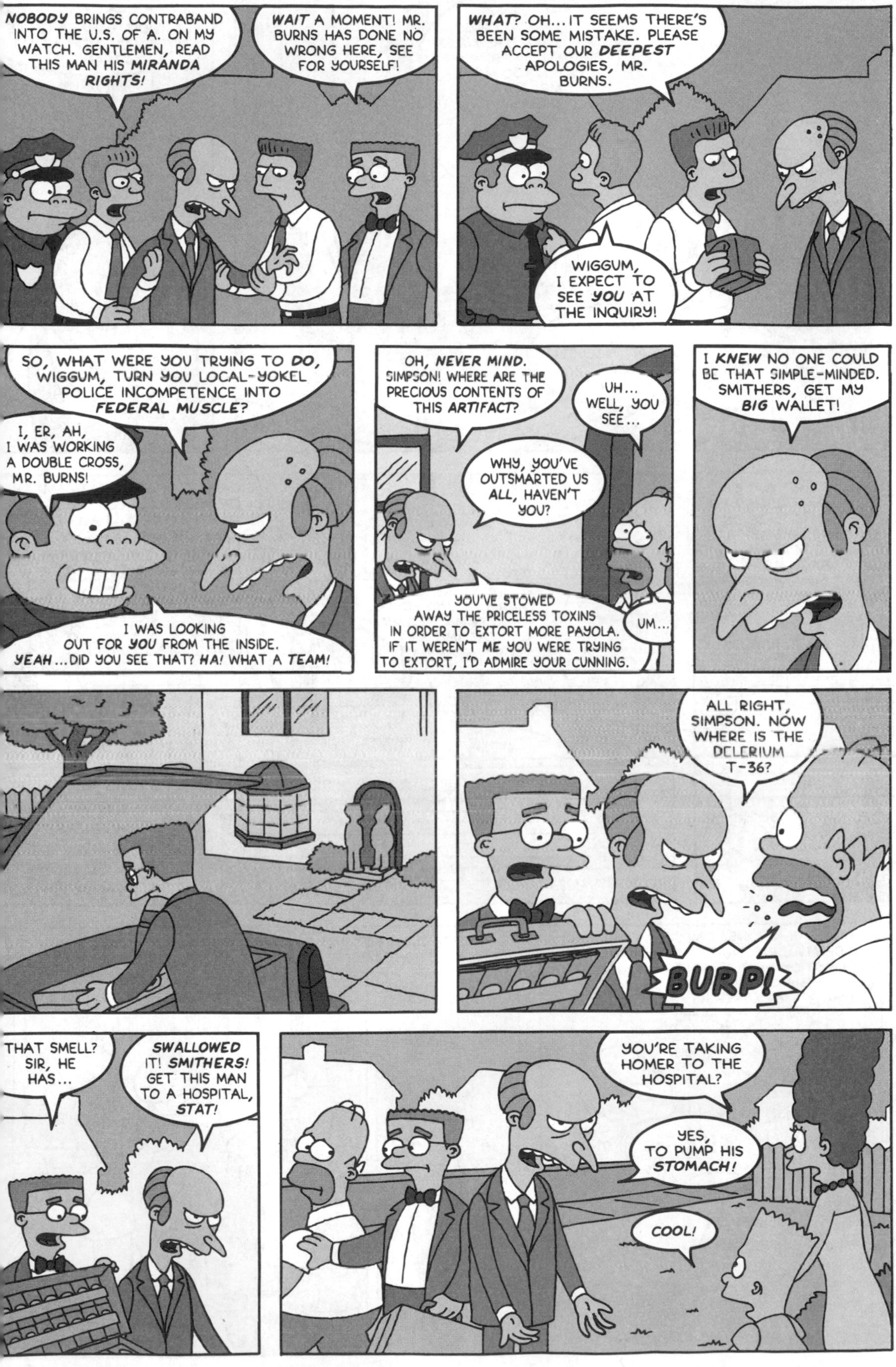
NOBODY BRINGS CONTRABAND INTO THE U.S. OF A. ON MY WATCH. GENTLEMEN, READ THIS MAN HIS MIRANDA RIGHTS!
WAIT A MOMENT! MR. BURNS HAS DONE NO WRONG HERE, SEE FOR YOURSELF!
WHAT? OH... IT SEEMS THERE'S BEEN SOME MISTAKE. PLEASE ACCEPT OUR DEEPEST APOLOGIES, MR. BURNS.
WIGGUM, I EXPECT TO SEE YOU AT THE INQUIRY!
SO, WHAT WERE YOU TRYING TO DO, WIGGUM, TURN YOU LOCAL-YOKEL POLICE INCOMPETENCE INTO FEDERAL MUSCLE?
I, ER, AH, I WAS WORKING A DOUBLE CROSS, MR. BURNS!
I WAS LOOKING OUT FOR YOU FROM THE INSIDE. YEAH... DID YOU SEE THAT? HA! WHAT A TEAM!
OH, NEVER MIND. SIMPSON! WHERE ARE THE PRECIOUS CONTENTS OF THIS ARTIFACT?
UH... WELL, YOU SEE...
WHY, YOU'VE OUTSMARTED US ALL, HAVEN'T YOU?
YOU'VE STOWED AWAY THE PRICELESS TOXINS IN ORDER TO EXTORT MORE PAYOLA. IF IT WEREN'T ME YOU WERE TRYING TO EXTORT, I'D ADMIRE YOUR CUNNING.
UM...
I KNEW NO ONE COULD BE THAT SIMPLE-MINDED. SMITHERS, GET MY BIG WALLET!
ALL RIGHT, SIMPSON. NOW WHERE IS THE DELERIUM T-36?
BURP!
THAT SMELL? SIR, HE HAS...
SWALLOWED IT! SMITHERS! GET THIS MAN TO A HOSPITAL, STAT!
YOU'RE TAKING HOMER TO THE HOSPITAL?
YES, TO PUMP HIS STOMACH!
COOL!

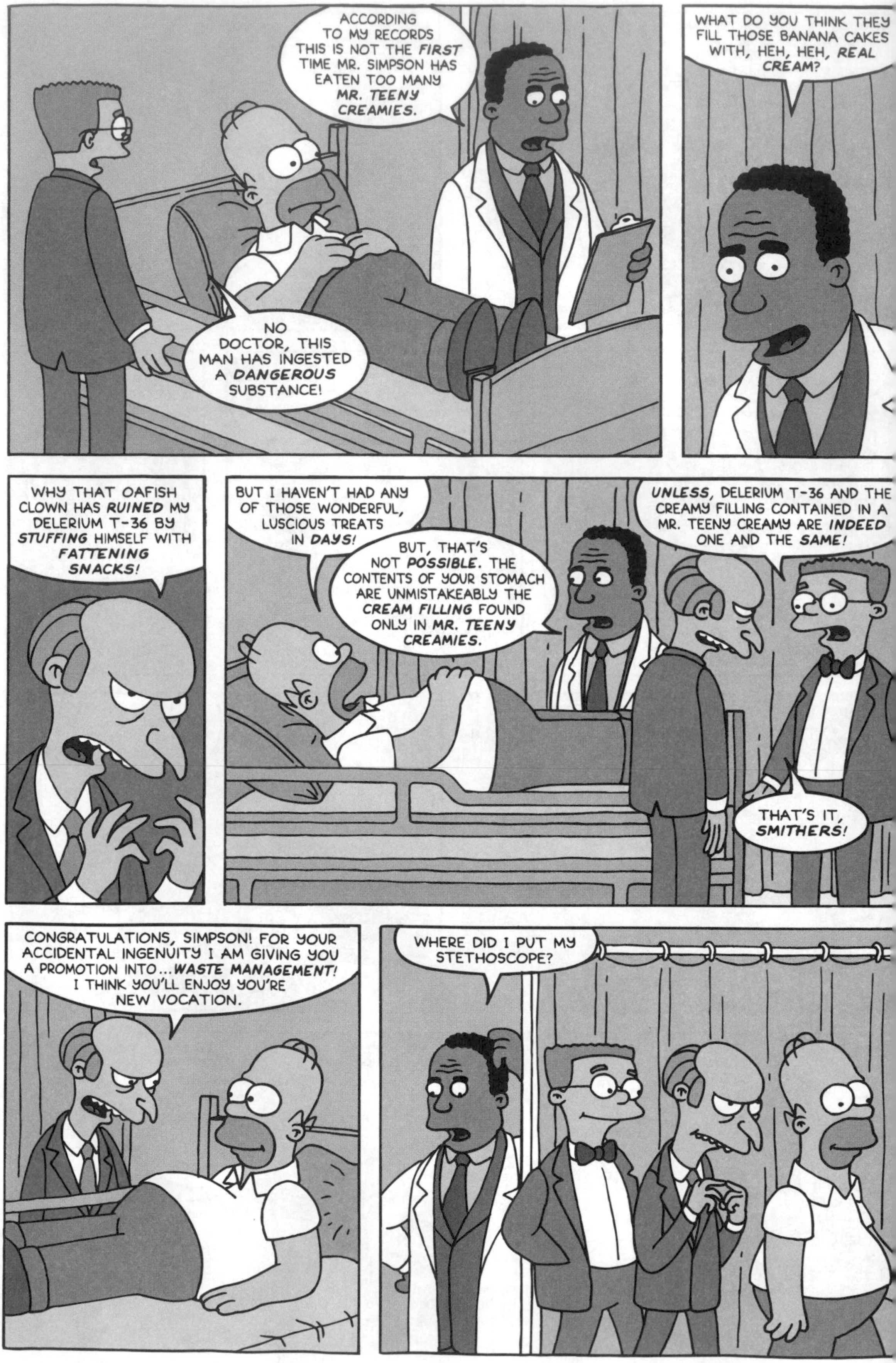
ACCORDING TO MY RECORDS THIS IS NOT THE FIRST TIME MR. SIMPSON HAS EATEN TOO MANY MR. TEENY CREAMIES.
NO DOCTOR, THIS MAN HAS INGESTED A DANGEROUS SUBSTANCE!
WHAT DO YOU THINK THEY FILL THOSE BANANA CAKES WITH, HEH, HEH, REAL CREAM?
WHY THAT OAFISH CLOWN HAS RUINED MY DELERIUM T-36 BY STUFFING HIMSELF WITH FATTENING SNACKS!
BUT I HAVEN'T HAD ANY OF THOSE WONDERFUL, LUSCIOUS TREATS IN DAYS!
BUT, THAT'S NOT POSSIBLE. THE CONTENTS OF YOUR STOMACH ARE UNMISTAKEABLY THE CREAM FILLING FOUND ONLY IN MR. TEENY CREAMIES.
UNLESS, DELERIUM T-36 AND THE CREAMY FILLING CONTAINED IN A MR. TEENY CREAMY ARE INDEED ONE AND THE SAME!
THAT'S IT, SMITHERS!
CONGRATULATIONS, SIMPSON! FOR YOUR ACCIDENTAL INGENUITY I AM GIVING YOU A PROMOTION INTO...WASTE MANAGEMENT! I THINK YOU'LL ENJOY YOU'RE NEW VOCATION.
WHERE DID I PUT MY STETHOSCOPE?

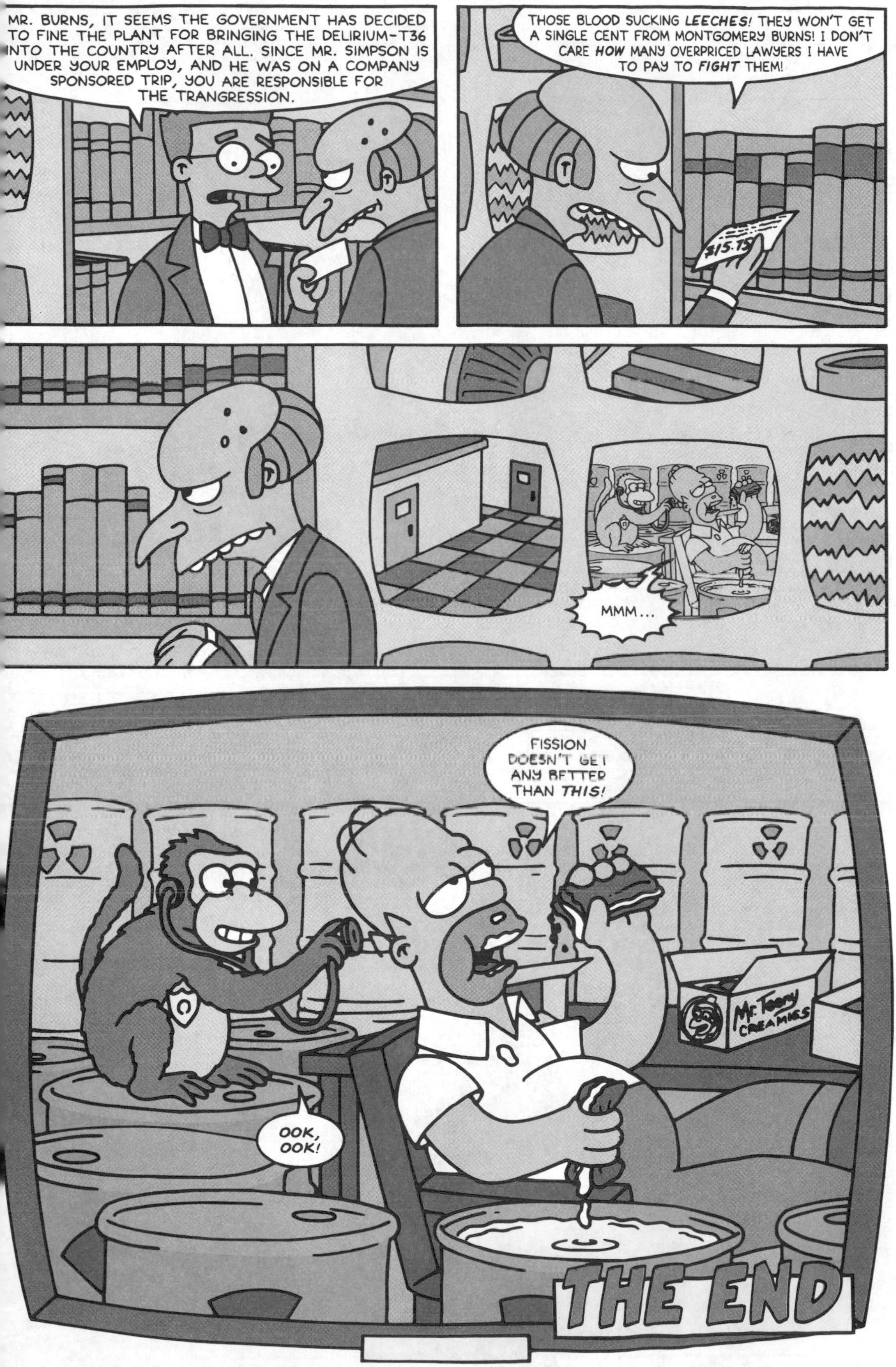
MR. BURNS, IT SEEMS THE GOVERNMENT HAS DECIDED TO FINE THE PLANT FOR BRINGING THE DELIRIUM-T36 INTO THE COUNTRY AFTER ALL. SINCE MR. SIMPSON IS UNDER YOUR EMPLOY, AND HE WAS ON A COMPANY SPONSORED TRIP, YOU ARE RESPONSIBLE FOR THE TRANGRESSION.
THOSE BLOOD SUCKING *LEECHES!* THEY WON'T GET A SINGLE CENT FROM MONTGOMERY BURNS! I DON'T CARE *HOW* MANY OVERPRICED LAWYERS I HAVE TO PAY TO *FIGHT* THEM!
$15.75
MMM...
FISSION DOESN'T GET ANY BETTER THAN *THIS!*
OOK, OOK!
Mr. Teeny CREAMIES
THE END